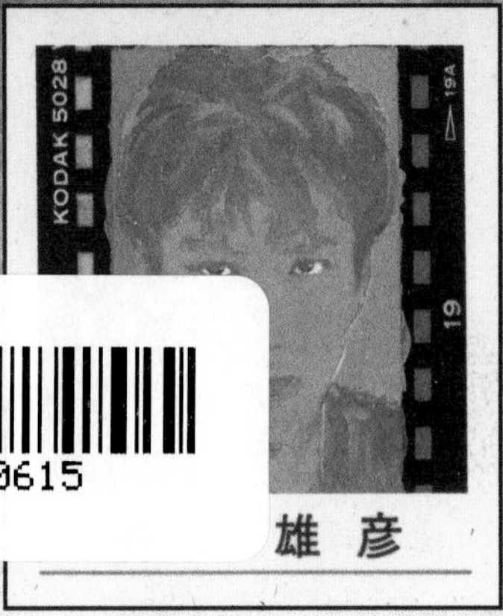
KODAK 5028
19A
19
雄 彦

Takehiko Inoue

SLAM DUNK HAS MADE IT TO VOLUME 10! WE COULD NOT HAVE DONE THAT WITHOUT YOUR SUPPORT. THANK YOU!

IT'S BEEN MORE THAN TWO YEARS SINCE WE BEGAN SERIALIZATION, BUT ONLY TWO MONTHS HAVE PASSED IN THE STORY. LET'S SEE... IF TWO YEARS EQUALS TWO MONTHS, THAT MEANS IT'LL TAKE SAKURAGI 36 YEARS TO GRADUATE FROM HIGH SCHOOL!

NAH...

Takehiko Inoue's *Slam Dunk* is one of the most popular manga of all time, having sold over 100 million copies worldwide. He followed that series up with two titles lauded by critics and fans alike—*Vagabond*, a fictional account of the life of Miyamoto Musashi, and *Real*, a manga about wheelchair basketball.

SLAM DUNK
Vol. 10: Rebound King Sakuragi

SHONEN JUMP Manga Edition

STORY AND ART BY TAKEHIKO INOUE

English Adaptation/Kelly Sue DeConnick
Translation/Joe Yamazaki
Touch-up Art & Lettering/James Gaubatz
Cover & Graphic Design/Sean Lee
Editor/Kit Fox

VP, Production/Alvin Lu
VP, Sales & Product Marketing/Gonzalo Ferreyra
VP, Creative/Linda Espinosa
Publisher/Hyoe Narita

Printed in the U.S.A.

Published by VIZ Media, LLC
P.O. Box 77010
San Francisco, CA 94107

10 9 8 7 6 5 4 3 2 1
First printing, June 2010

PARENTAL ADVISORY
SLAM DUNK is rated T for Teen and is recommended
for ages 13 and up. This volume contains realistic
violence and crude humor.
ratings.viz.com

THE WORLD'S
MOST POPULAR MANGA

www.shonenjump.com

STORY AND ART BY
TAKEHIKO INOUE

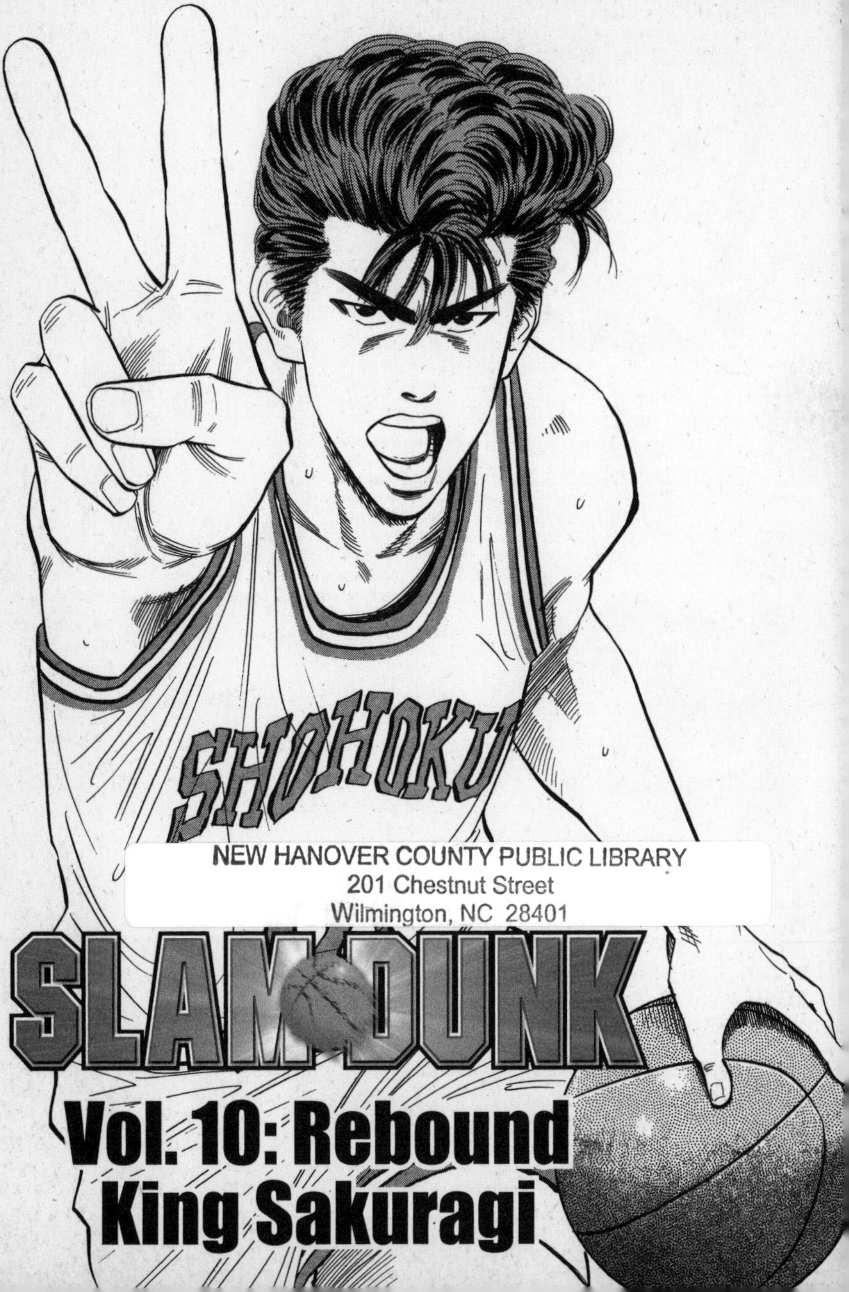
SHOHOKU

SLAM DUNK

Vol. 10: Rebound King Sakuragi

Character Introduction

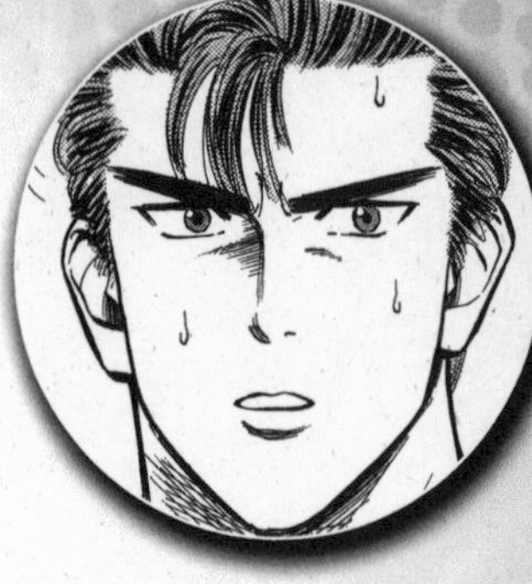

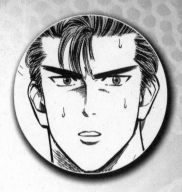

Hanamichi Sakuragi
A first-year at Shohoku High School, Sakuragi is in love with Haruko Akagi.

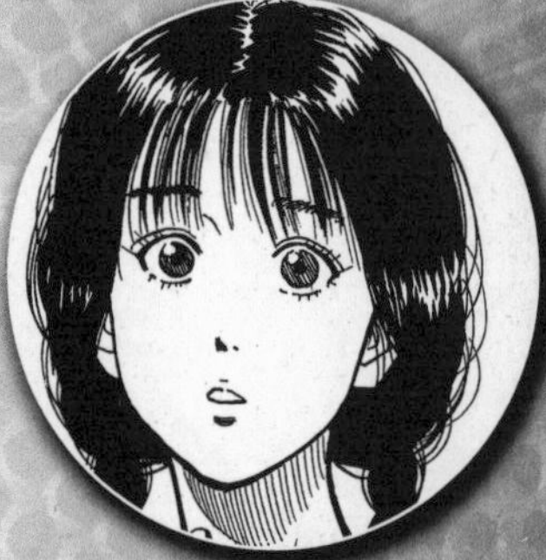

Haruko Akagi
Also a first-year at Shohoku, Takenori Akagi's little sister has a crush on Kaede Rukawa.

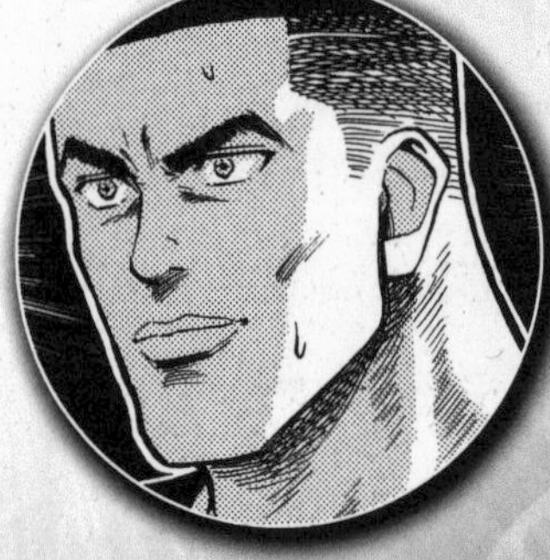

Takenori Akagi
A third-year and the basketball team's captain, Akagi has an intense passion for his sport.

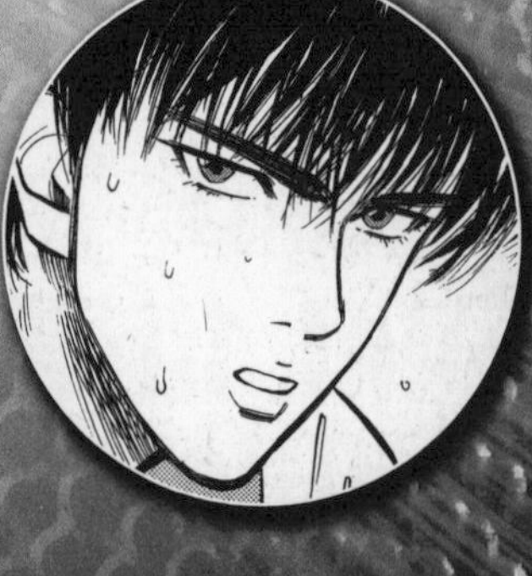

Kaede Rukawa
The object of Haruko's affection (and that of many of Shohoku's female students!), this first-year has been a star player since junior high.

Sakuragi's Friends

BRING IT ON.

Ohkusu   Mito   Takamiya   Noma

Ryota Miyagi
A problem child with
a thing for Ayako.

Ayako
Basketball Team
Manager

Hisashi Mitsui
An MVP during
junior high.

Our Story Thus Far

Hanamichi Sakuragi is rejected by close to 50 girls during his three years in junior high. In high school, he joins the basketball team in order to get closer to his beloved Haruko, whose brother is the team captain. However, the endless fundamental drills do not suit his personality, and he and Captain Akagi frequently butt heads.

After a good showing in their first exhibition game, the team already has its sights set on Nationals when Ryota Miyagi reclaims his position as Point Guard.

Not yet over his feud with Miyagi, former-player Hisashi Mitsui and his gang invade the gym and try to start a brawl, but Coach Anzai gets through to Mitsui and convinces him to rejoin the team. With Mitsui on board Shohoku advances through the early rounds of the tournament... despite Hanamichi's repeated foul outs.

Vol. 10:
Rebound King Sakuragi

Table of Contents

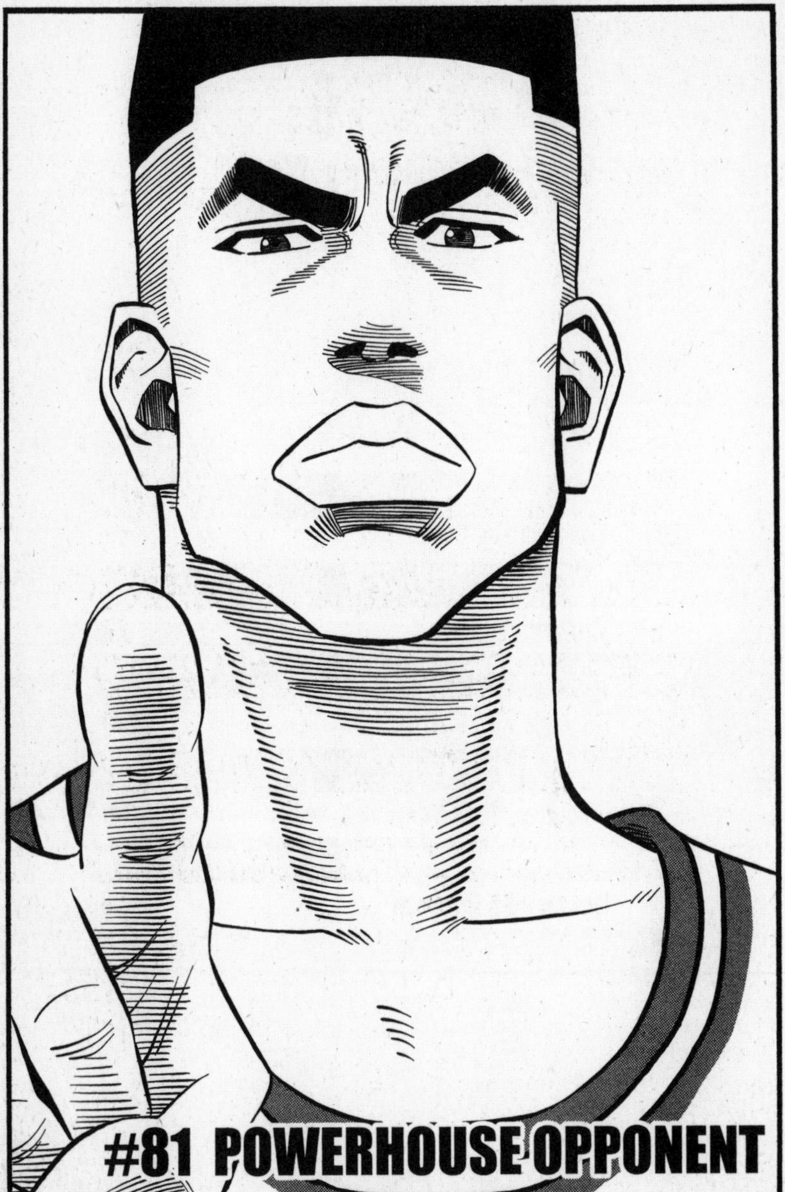
#81 POWERHOUSE OPPONENT

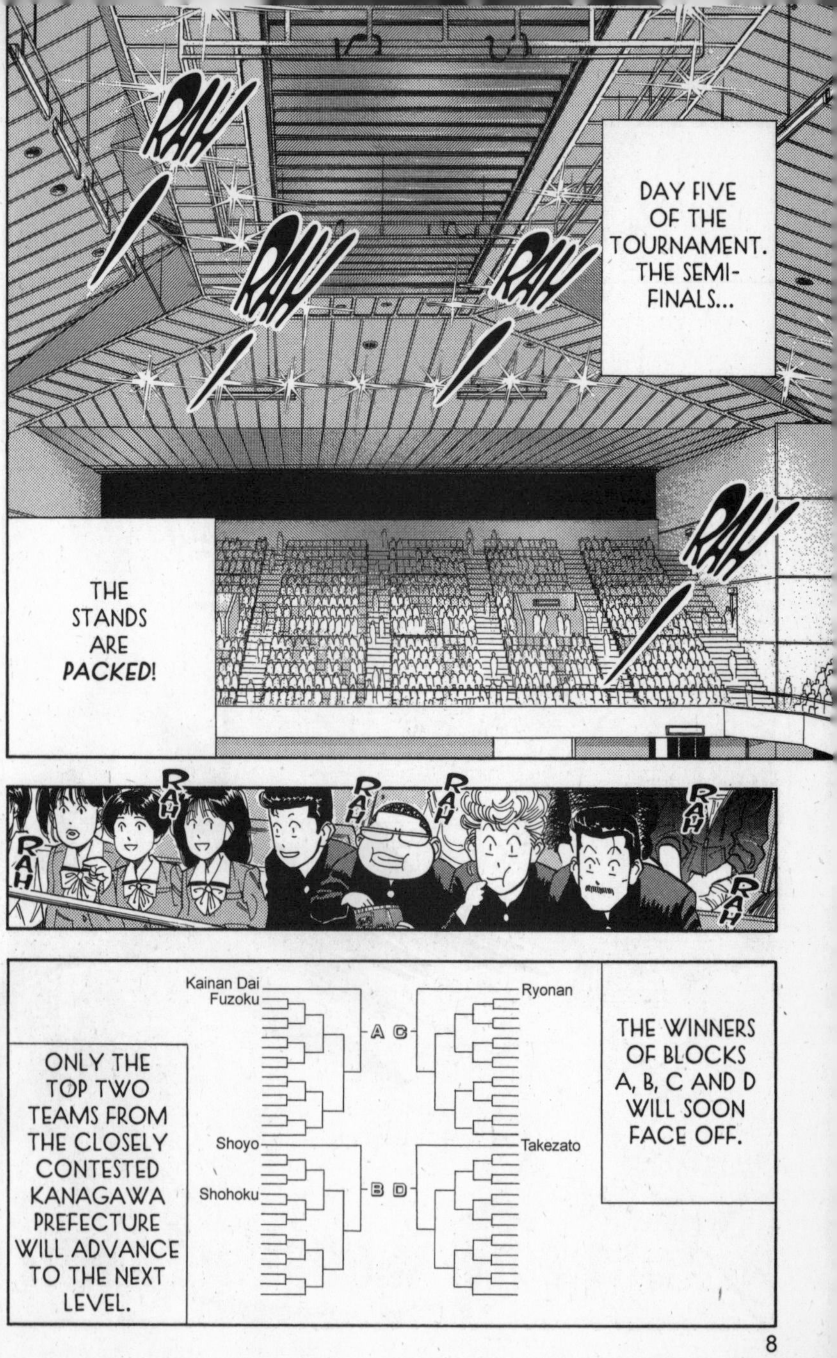
DAY FIVE OF THE TOURNAMENT. THE SEMI-FINALS...
RAH!
RAH!
RAH!
RAH!
THE STANDS ARE *PACKED*!
RAH
RAH
RAH
RAH
RAH
RAH
THE WINNERS OF BLOCKS A, B, C AND D WILL SOON FACE OFF.
Ryonan
Takezato
A C
B D
Kainan Dai Fuzoku
Shoyo
Shohoku
ONLY THE TOP TWO TEAMS FROM THE CLOSELY CONTESTED KANAGAWA PREFECTURE WILL ADVANCE TO THE NEXT LEVEL.

READ THIS WAY

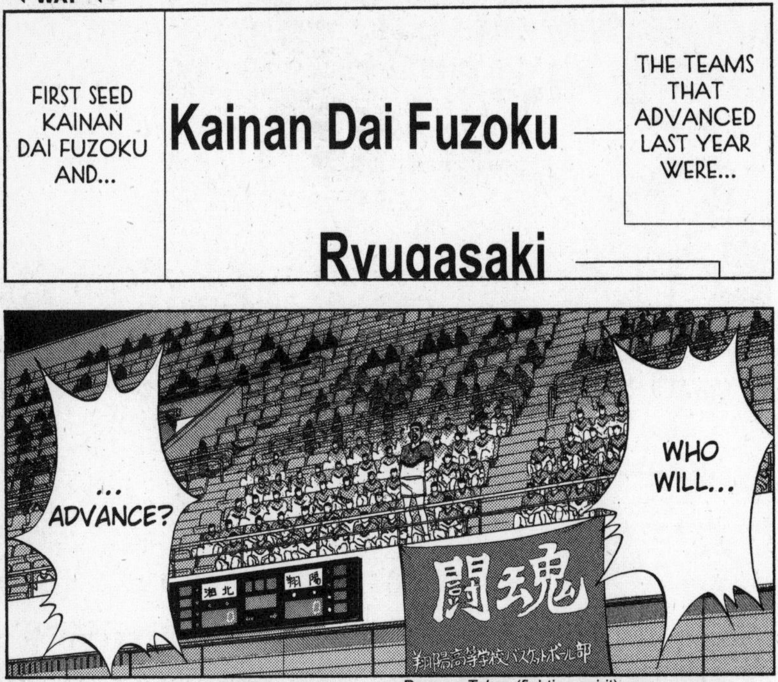
THE TEAMS THAT ADVANCED LAST YEAR WERE...
Kainan Dai Fuzoku
Ryugasaki
FIRST SEED KAINAN DAI FUZOKU AND...
WHO WILL...
...ADVANCE?
Banner: *Tokon* (fighting spirit)

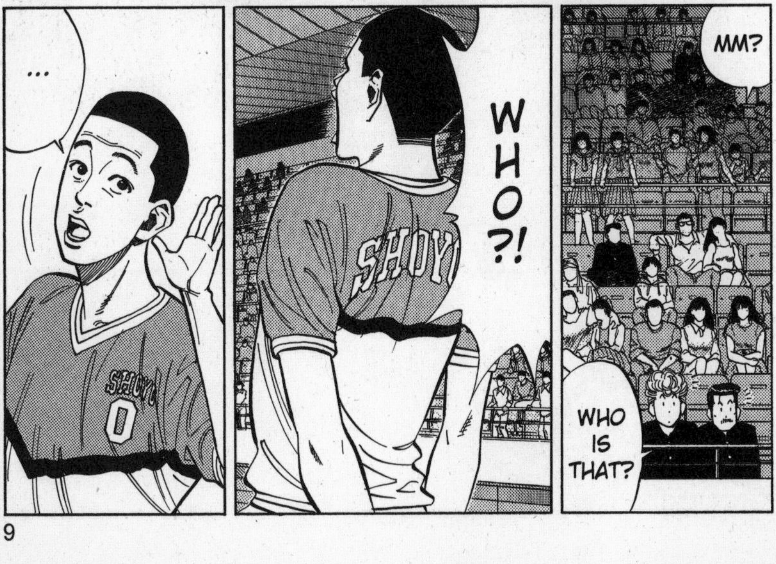
MM?
WHO IS THAT?
WHO?!
...

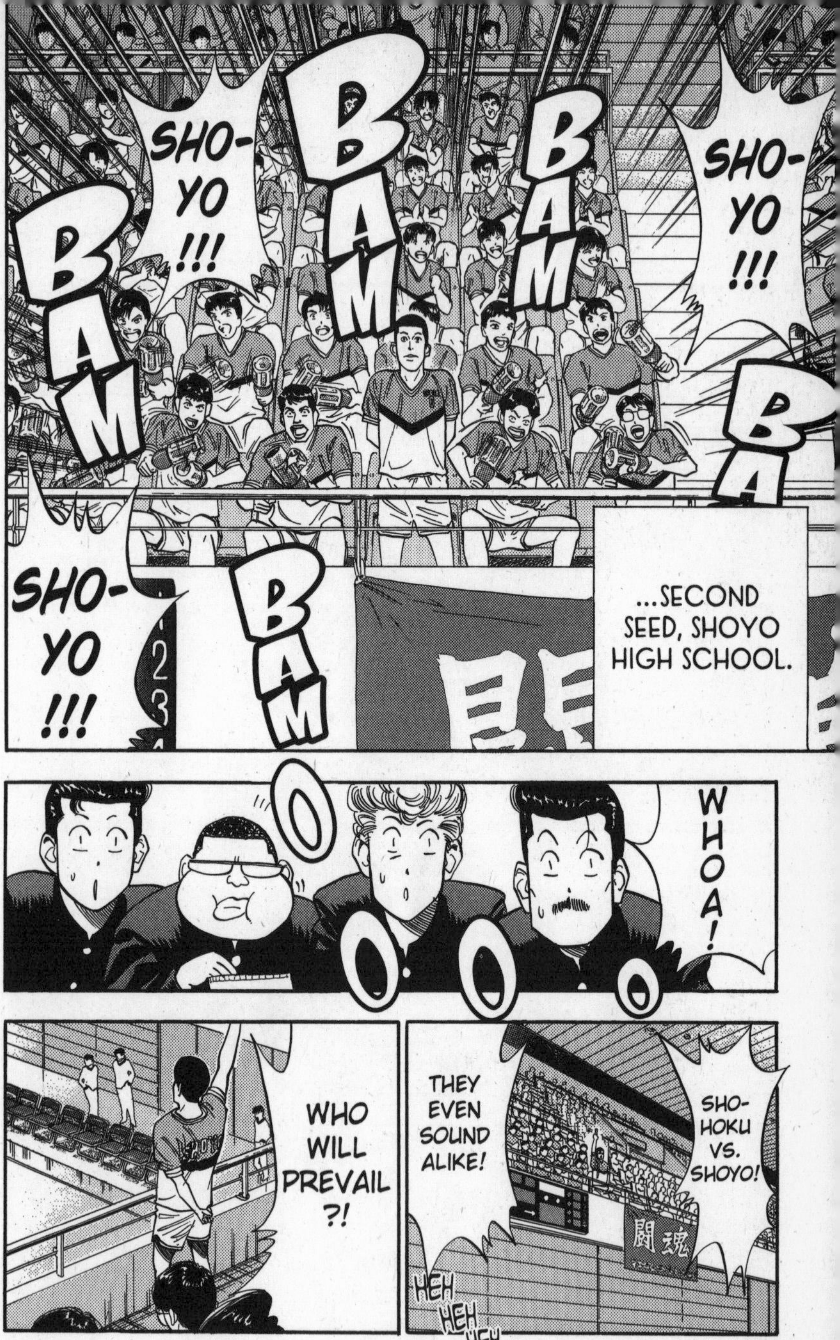
SHO-YO!!!
BAM
BAM
SHO-YO!!!
BAM
BA
...SECOND SEED, SHOYO HIGH SCHOOL.
BAM
SHO-YO!!!
WHOA!
OOOOO
SHO-HOKU VS. SHOYO!
THEY EVEN SOUND ALIKE!
HEH HEH HEH
WHO WILL PREVAIL?!

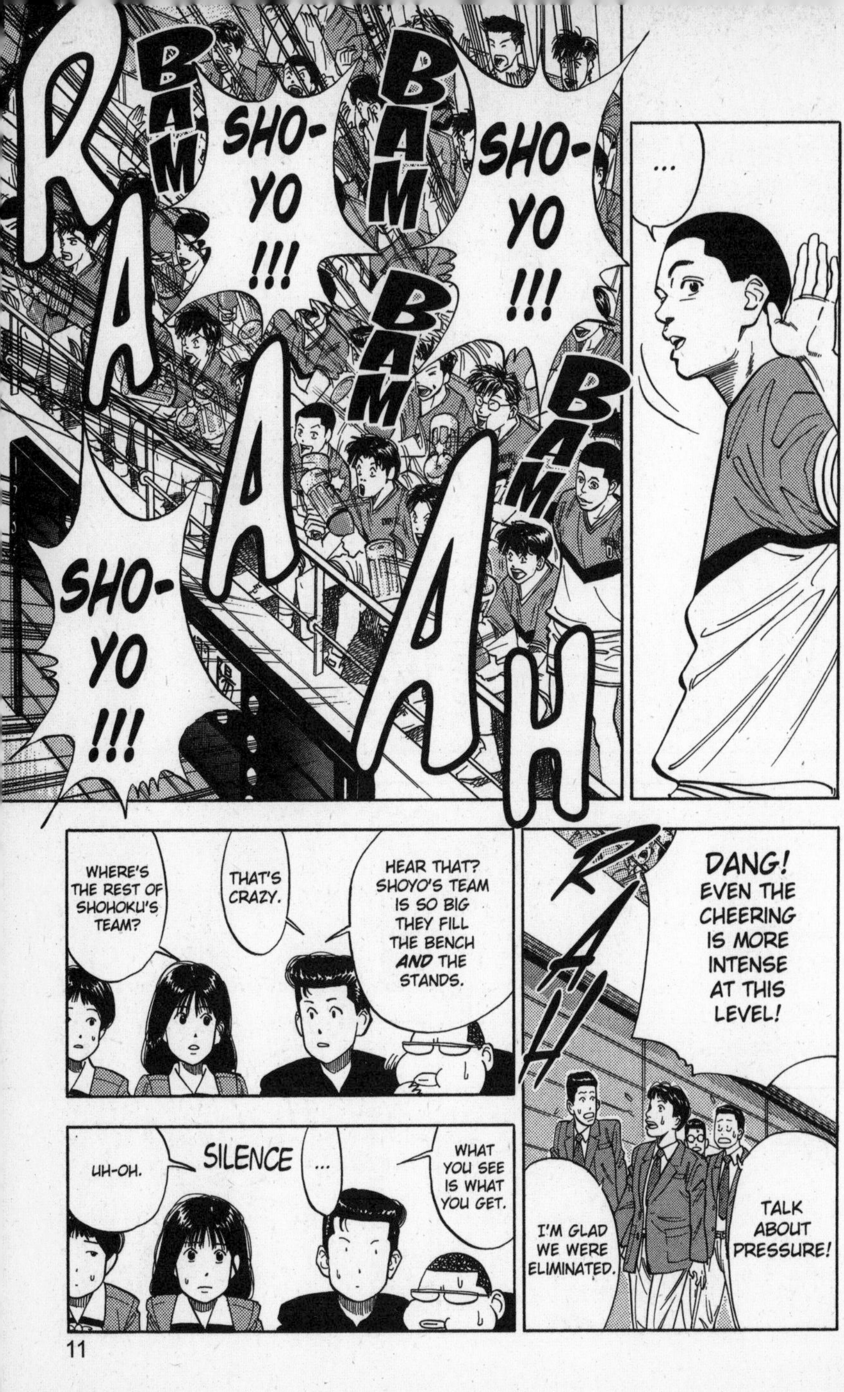
...
SHO-YO!!!
BAM BAM BAM
SHO-YO!!!
BAM
SHO-YO!!!
RAAAAH
DANG! EVEN THE CHEERING IS MORE INTENSE AT THIS LEVEL!
TALK ABOUT PRESSURE!
I'M GLAD WE WERE ELIMINATED.
HEAR THAT? SHOYO'S TEAM IS SO BIG THEY FILL THE BENCH *AND* THE STANDS.
THAT'S CRAZY.
WHERE'S THE REST OF SHOHOKU'S TEAM?
WHAT YOU SEE IS WHAT YOU GET.
...
SILENCE
UH-OH.

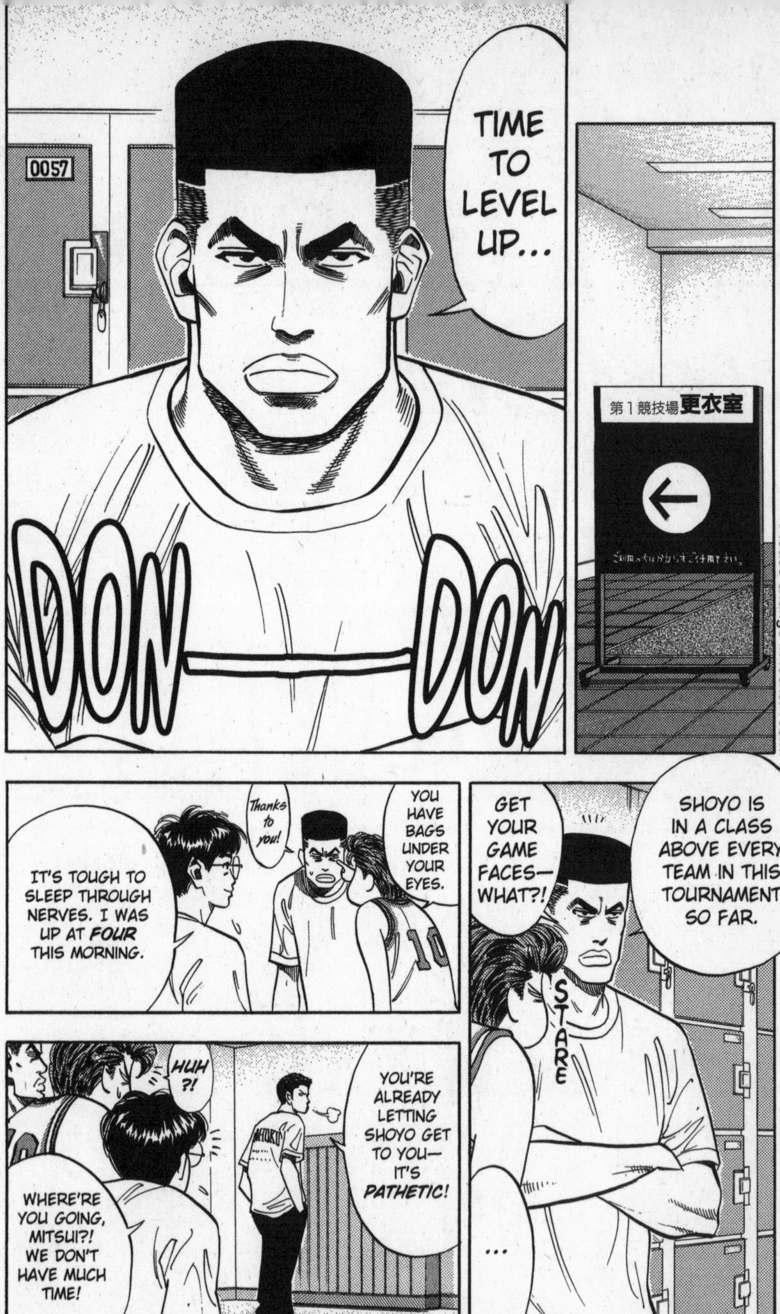

第1競技場更衣室
TIME TO LEVEL UP...
DON—DON
SHOYO IS IN A CLASS ABOVE EVERY TEAM IN THIS TOURNAMENT SO FAR.
GET YOUR GAME FACES— WHAT?!
STARE
...
YOU HAVE BAGS UNDER YOUR EYES.
Thanks to you!
IT'S TOUGH TO SLEEP THROUGH NERVES. I WAS UP AT ***FOUR*** THIS MORNING.
YOU'RE ALREADY LETTING SHOYO GET TO YOU— IT'S ***PATHETIC!***
HUH ?!
WHERE'RE YOU GOING, MITSUI?! WE DON'T HAVE MUCH TIME!

Sign: Arena 1 Locker Room
Please change in locker room.

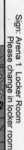

READ THIS WAY

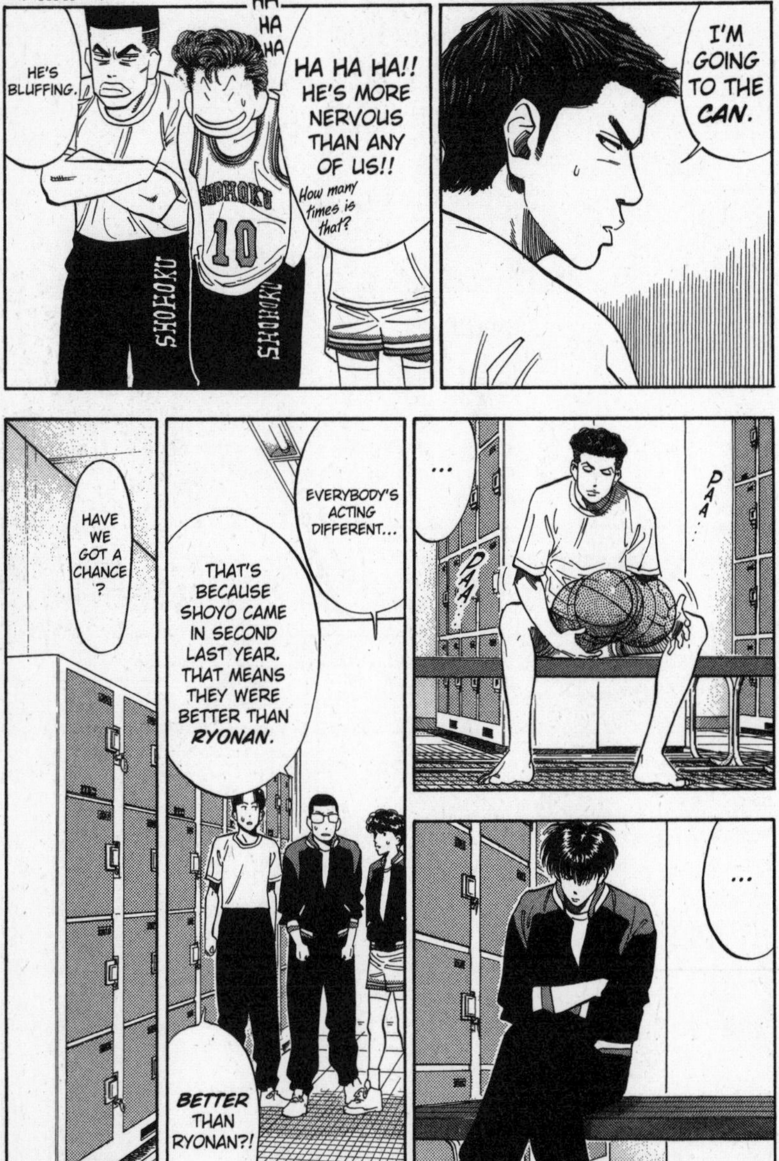
I'M GOING TO THE CAN.
HA HA HA!! HE'S MORE NERVOUS THAN ANY OF US!!
HA HA HA
How many times is that?
HE'S BLUFFING.
PAA...
...
PAA...
...
EVERYBODY'S ACTING DIFFERENT...
THAT'S BECAUSE SHOYO CAME IN SECOND LAST YEAR. THAT MEANS THEY WERE BETTER THAN RYONAN.
BETTER THAN RYONAN?!
HAVE WE GOT A CHANCE?

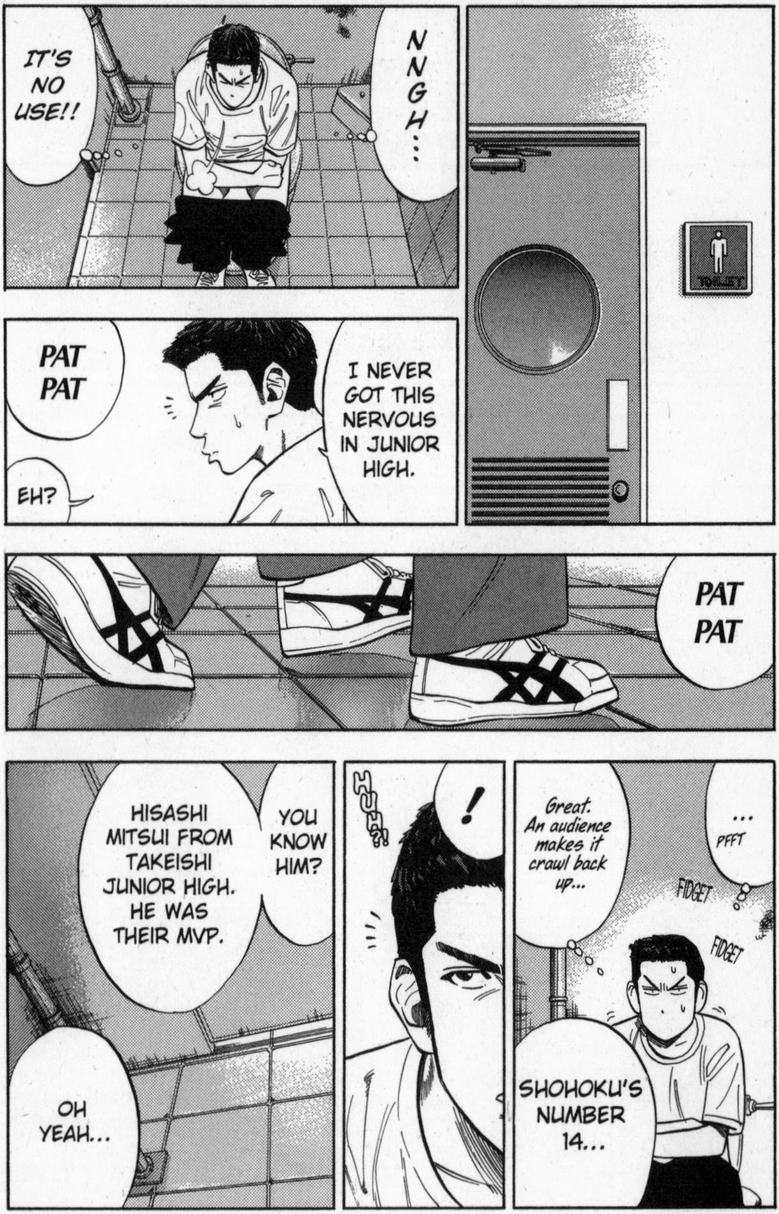
TOILET
NNGH...
IT'S NO USE!!
I NEVER GOT THIS NERVOUS IN JUNIOR HIGH.
PAT PAT
EH?
PAT PAT
...
PFFT
Great. An audience makes it crawl back up...
FIDGET
FIDGET
SHOHOKU'S NUMBER 14...
!
HUH?!
YOU KNOW HIM?
HISASHI MITSUI FROM TAKEISHI JUNIOR HIGH. HE WAS THEIR MVP.
OH YEAH...

READ THIS WAY

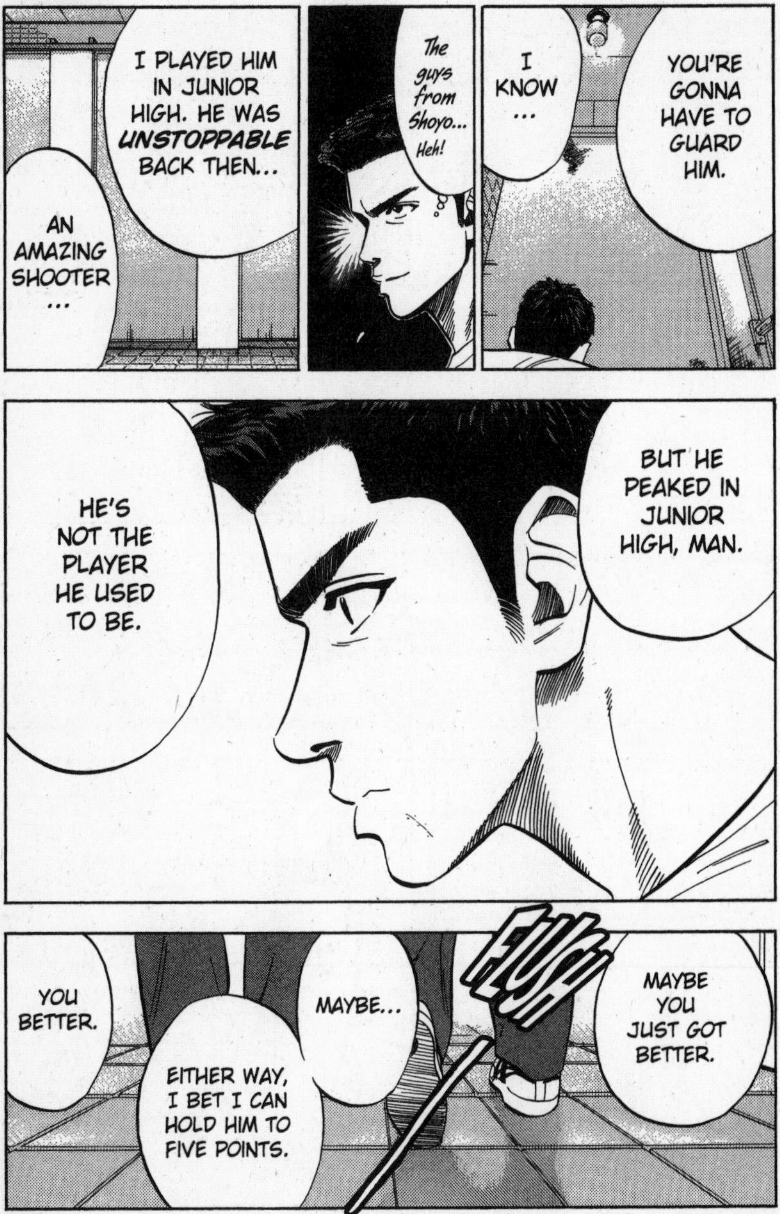
YOU'RE GONNA HAVE TO GUARD HIM.
I KNOW ...
The guys from Shoyo... Heh!
I PLAYED HIM IN JUNIOR HIGH. HE WAS UNSTOPPABLE BACK THEN...
AN AMAZING SHOOTER ...
BUT HE PEAKED IN JUNIOR HIGH, MAN.
HE'S NOT THE PLAYER HE USED TO BE.
MAYBE YOU JUST GOT BETTER.
FLUSH
MAYBE...
EITHER WAY, I BET I CAN HOLD HIM TO FIVE POINTS.
YOU BETTER.

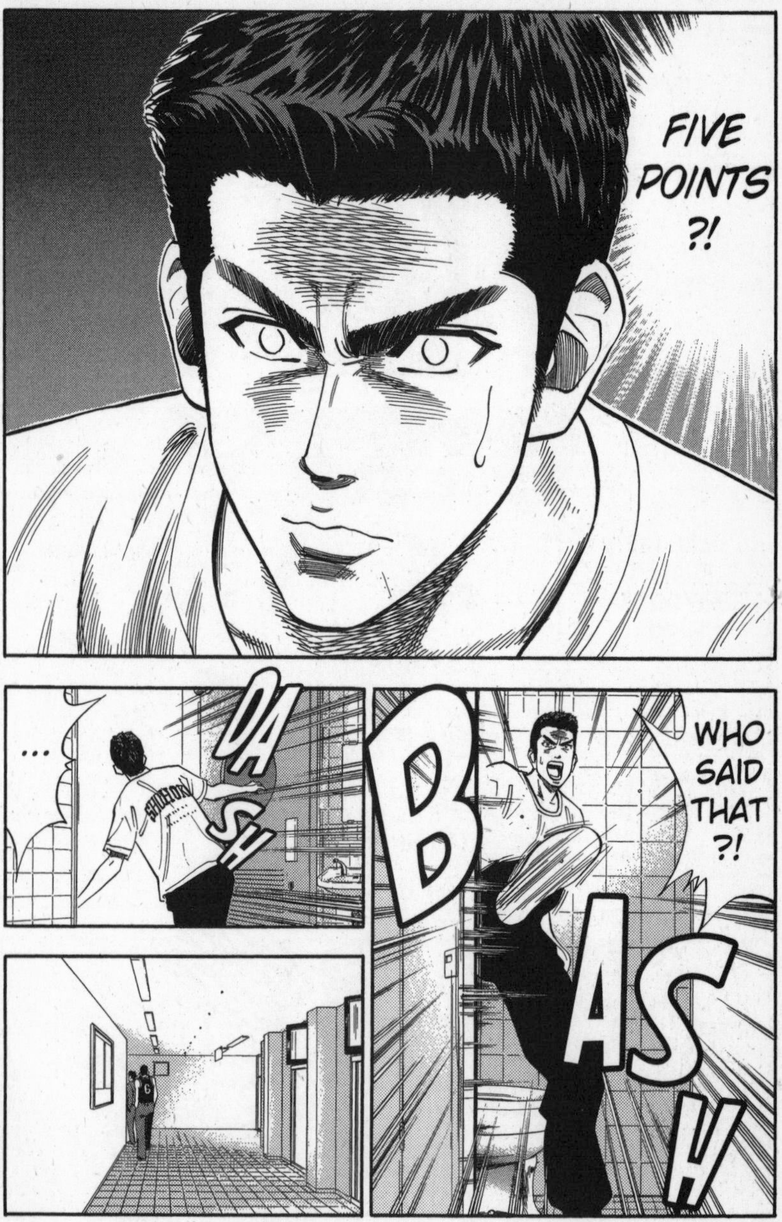
FIVE POINTS ?!
WHO SAID THAT ?!
BASH
DASH
...

READ THIS WAY

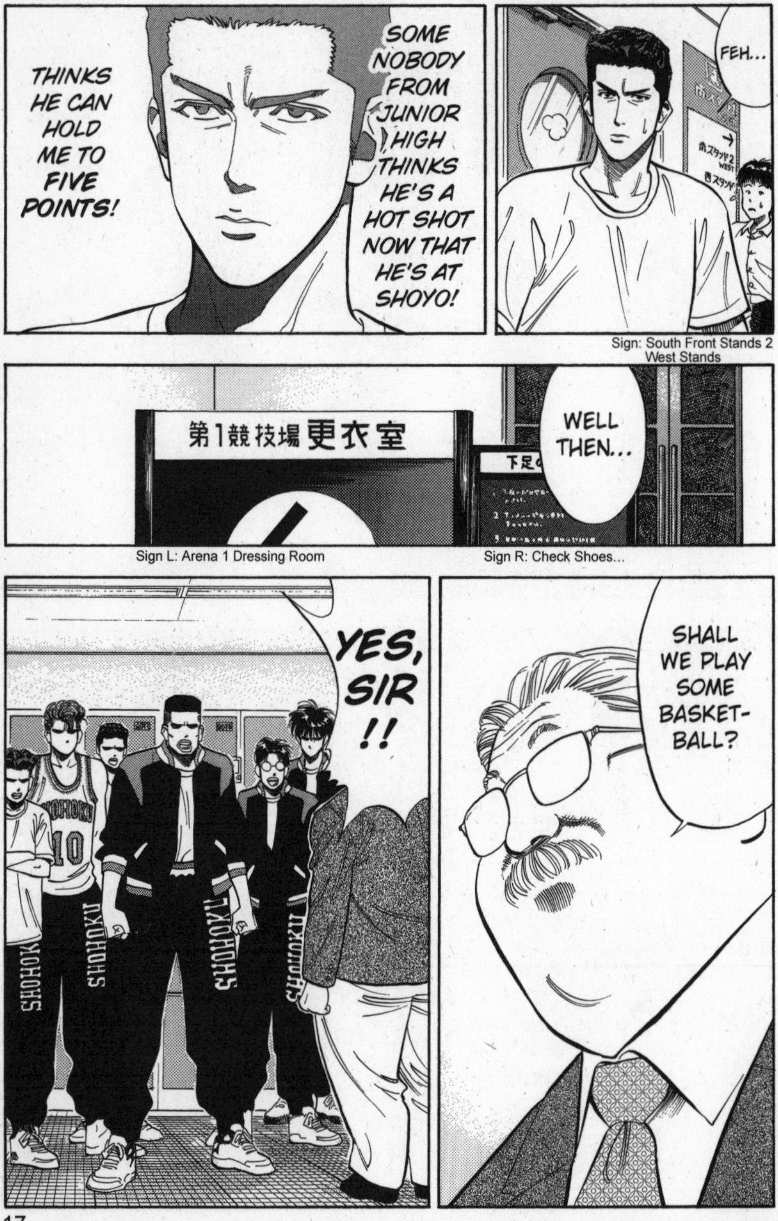
FEH...
SOME NOBODY FROM JUNIOR HIGH THINKS HE'S A HOT SHOT NOW THAT HE'S AT SHOYO!
THINKS HE CAN HOLD ME TO FIVE POINTS!
Sign: South Front Stands 2
West Stands
WELL THEN...
第1競技場更衣室
Sign L: Arena 1 Dressing Room
Sign R: Check Shoes...
SHALL WE PLAY SOME BASKET-BALL?
YES, SIR!!

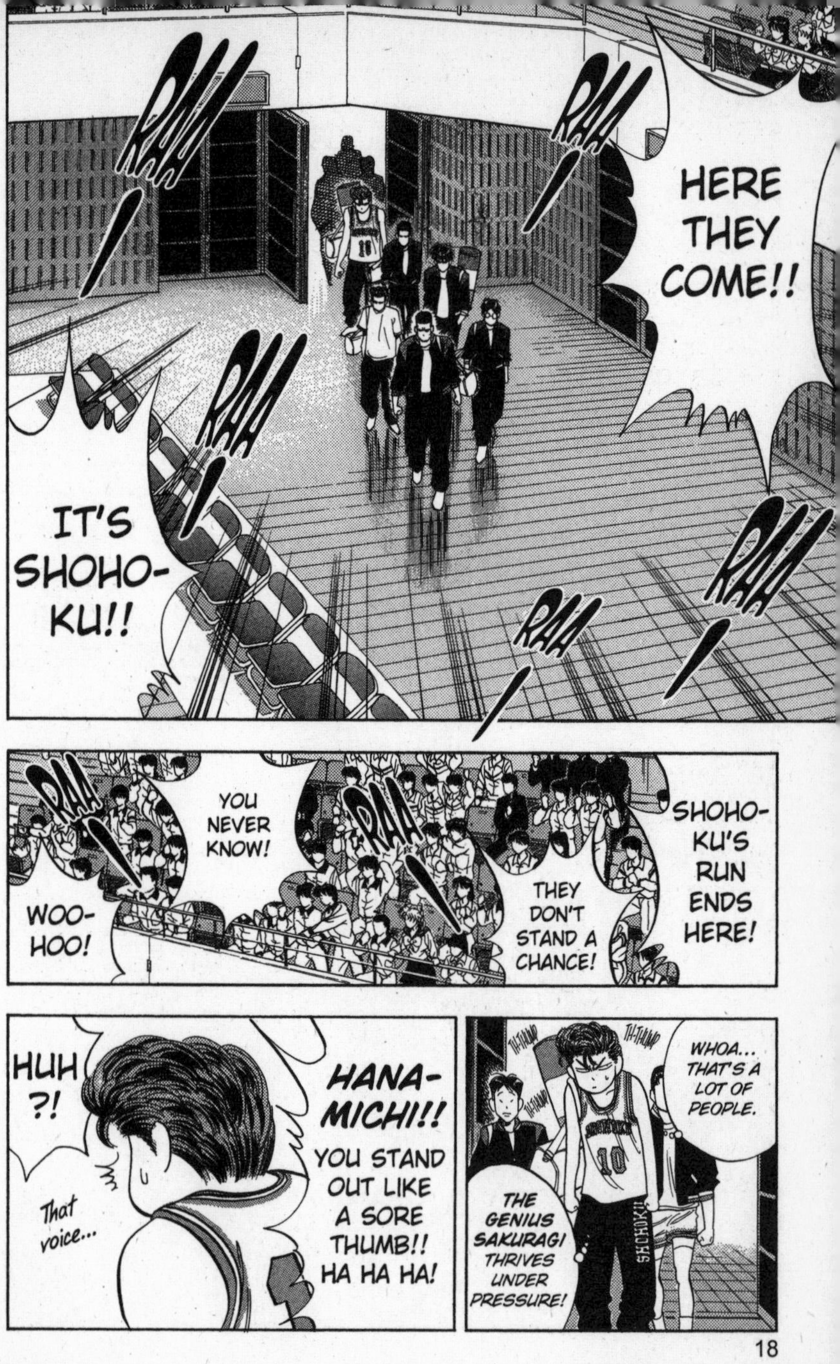
RAAA!
HERE THEY COME!!
RAAA!
RAAA!
IT'S SHOHO-KU!!
RAAA!
RAA!
SHOHO-KU'S RUN ENDS HERE!
THEY DON'T STAND A CHANCE!
RAAA!
YOU NEVER KNOW!
RAA!
WOO-HOO!
WHOA... THAT'S A LOT OF PEOPLE.
TH-THUMP
TH-THUMP
TH-THUMP
THE GENIUS SAKURAGI THRIVES UNDER PRESSURE!
HANA-MICHI!!
YOU STAND OUT LIKE A SORE THUMB!! HA HA HA!
HUH ?!
That voice...

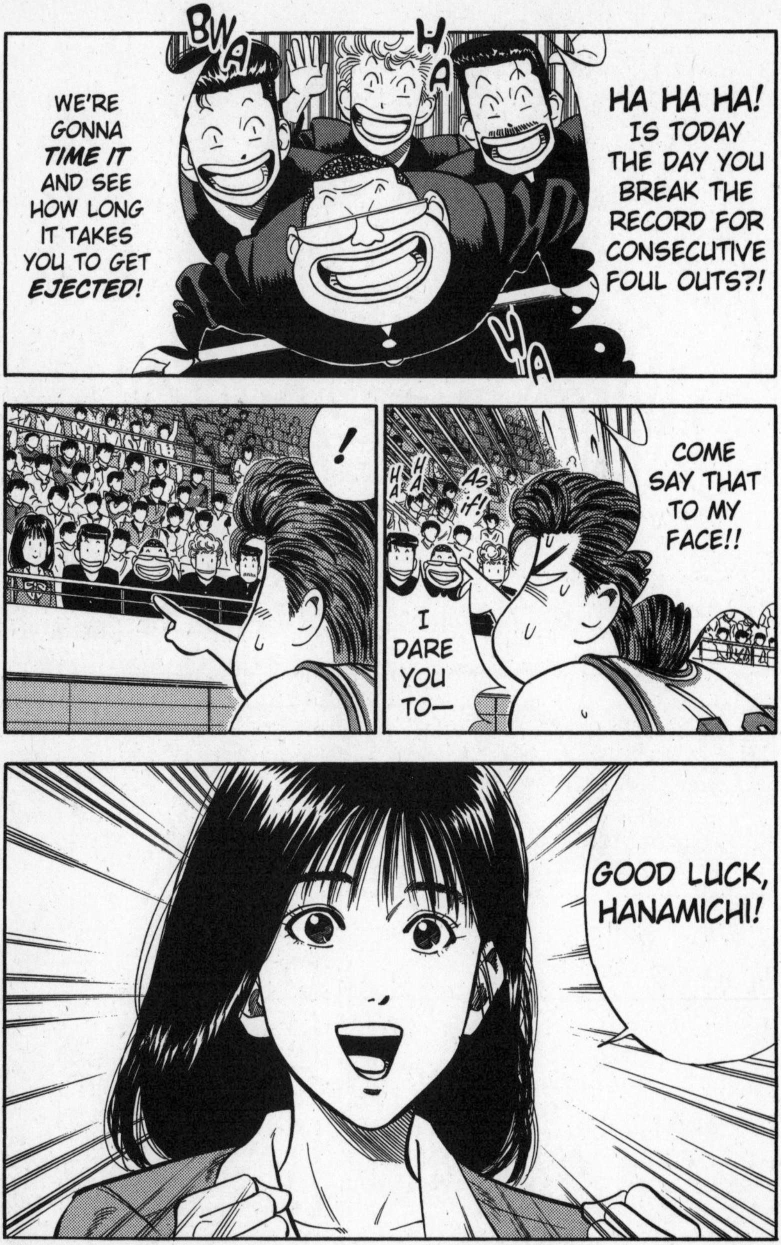
HA HA HA! IS TODAY THE DAY YOU BREAK THE RECORD FOR CONSECUTIVE FOUL OUTS?!
HA
HA
BWA
WE'RE GONNA TIME IT AND SEE HOW LONG IT TAKES YOU TO GET EJECTED!
HA
COME SAY THAT TO MY FACE!!
I DARE YOU TO—
As if!
HA HA
HA HA
!
GOOD LUCK, HANAMICHI!

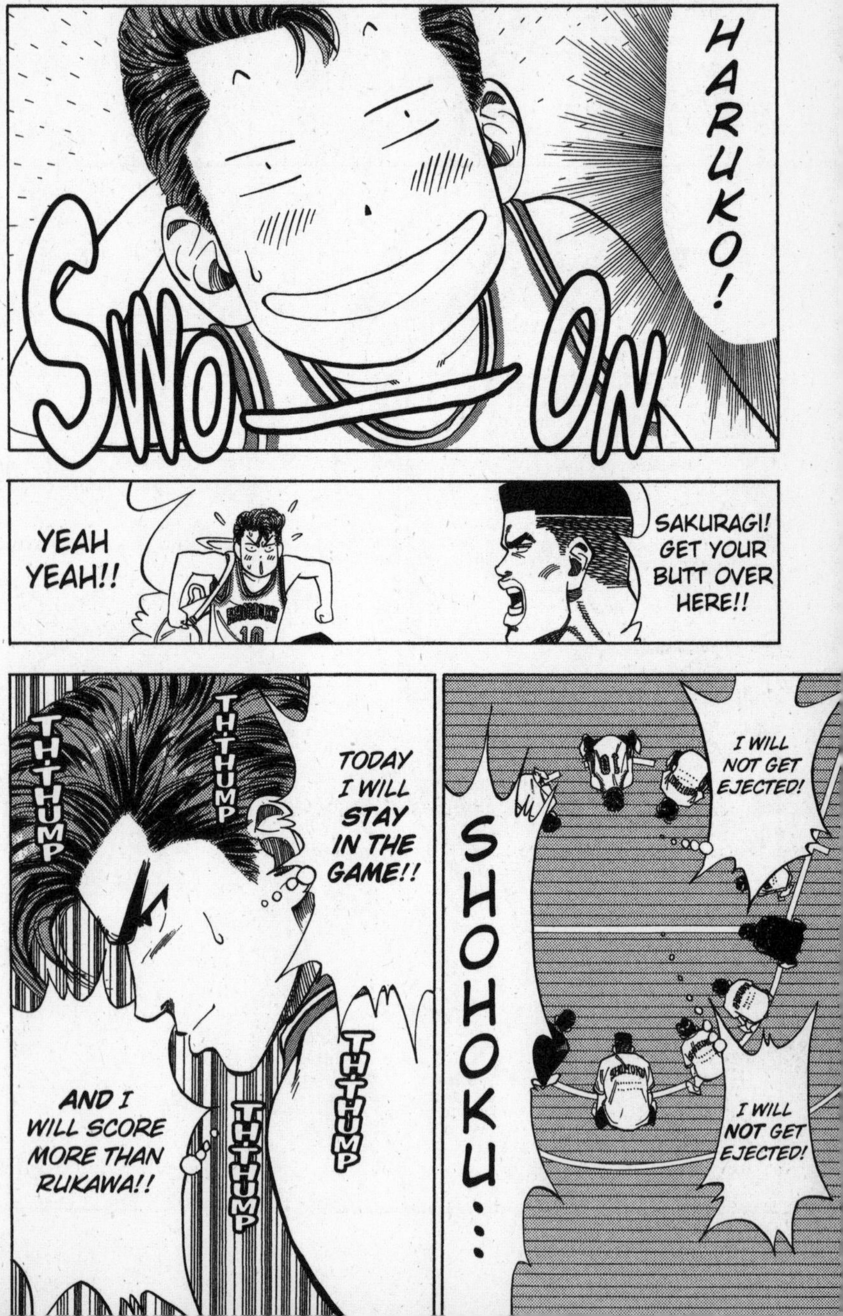
HARUKO!
SWO—ON
SAKURAGI! GET YOUR BUTT OVER HERE!!
YEAH YEAH!!
I WILL NOT GET EJECTED!
SHOHOKU...
I WILL NOT GET EJECTED!
TH-THUMP
TODAY I WILL STAY IN THE GAME!!
TH-THUMP
TH-THUMP
AND I WILL SCORE MORE THAN RUKAWA!!
TH-THUMP

READ THIS WAY

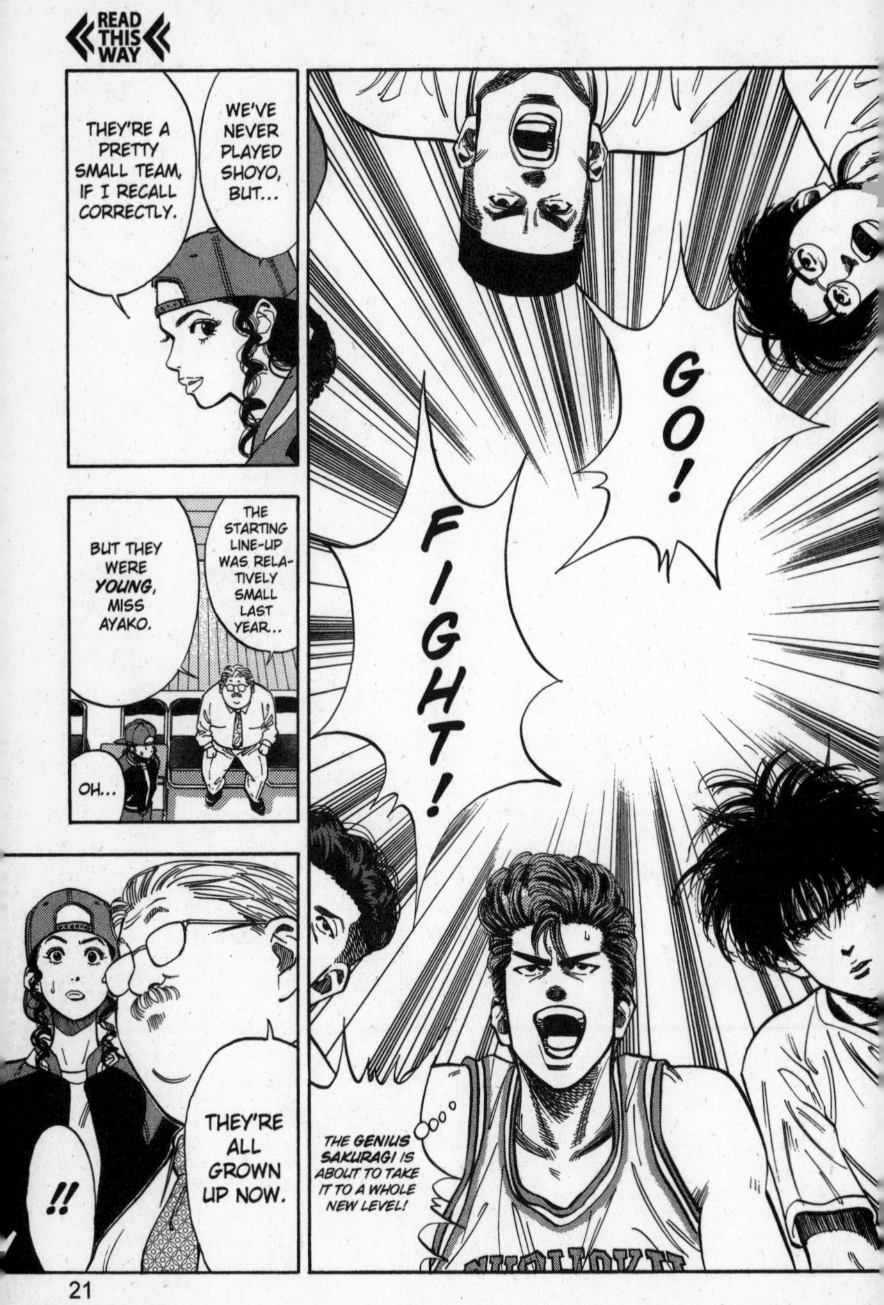
GO!
FIGHT!
THE GENIUS SAKURAGI IS ABOUT TO TAKE IT TO A WHOLE NEW LEVEL!
WE'VE NEVER PLAYED SHOYO, BUT...
THEY'RE A PRETTY SMALL TEAM, IF I RECALL CORRECTLY.
THE STARTING LINE-UP WAS RELA-TIVELY SMALL LAST YEAR...
BUT THEY WERE YOUNG, MISS AYAKO.
OH...
THEY'RE ALL GROWN UP NOW.
!!

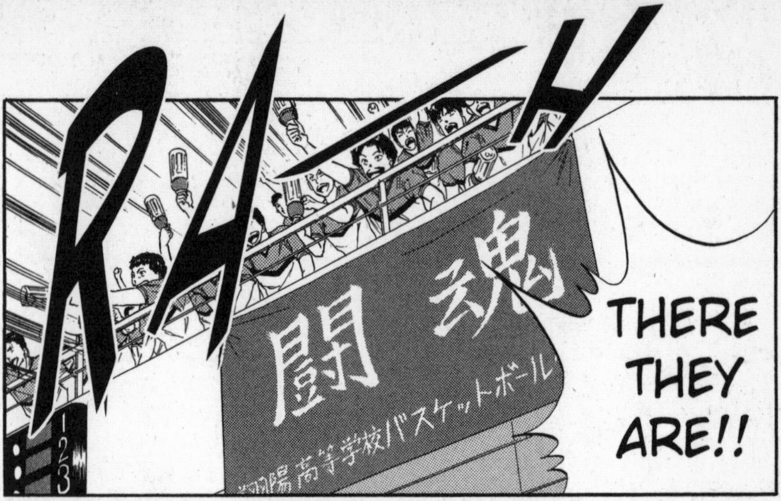
RA—H
THERE THEY ARE!!
闘魂
翔陽高等学校バスケットボール
Banner: *Tokon* (fighting spirit), Shoyo High School Basketball Team

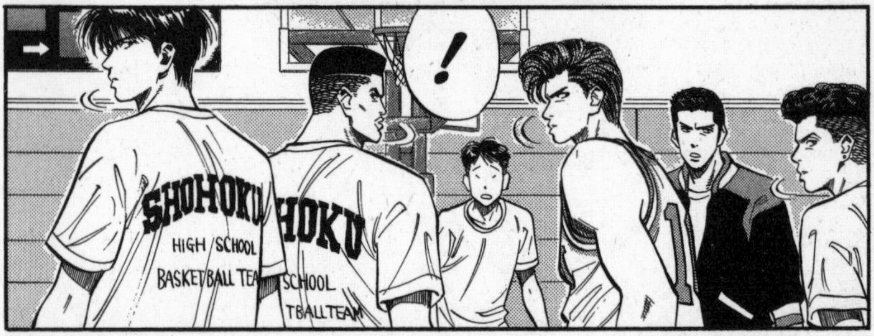
!
SHOHOKU HIGH SCHOOL BASKETBALL TEAM

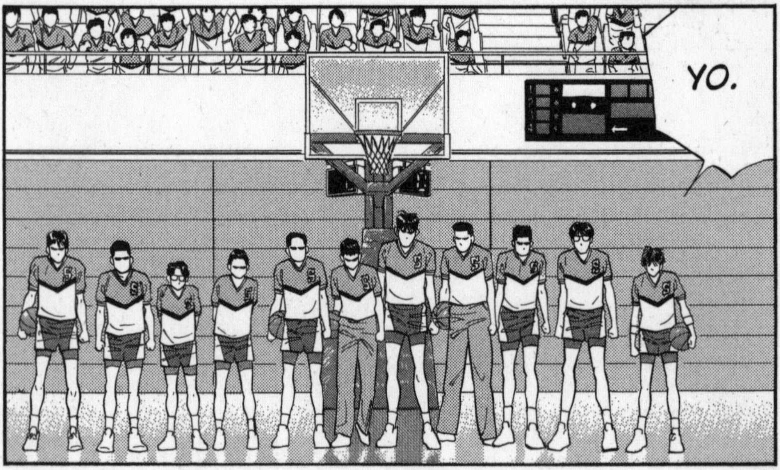
YO.

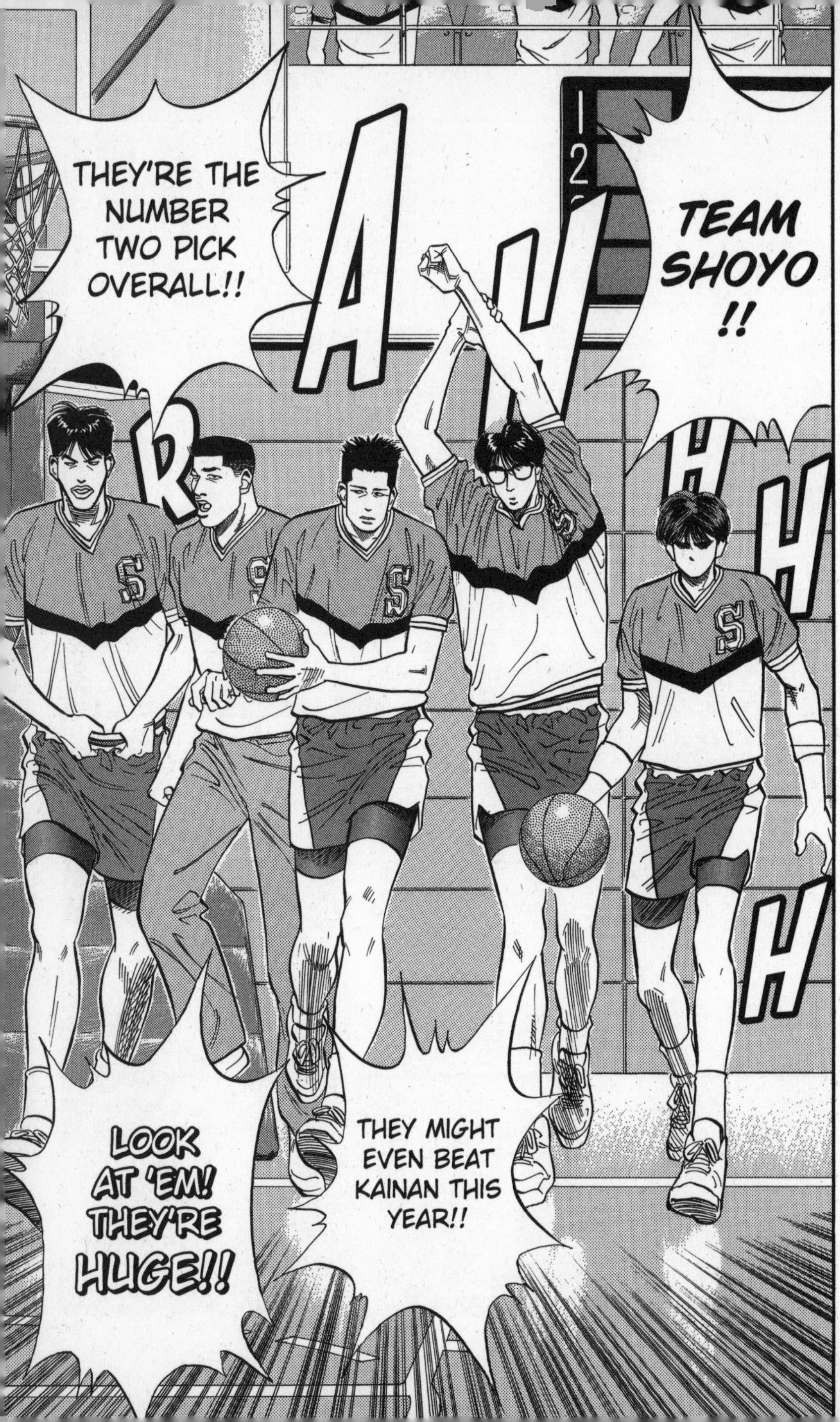
TEAM SHOYO!!
THEY'RE THE NUMBER TWO PICK OVERALL!!
RAAHHH
THEY MIGHT EVEN BEAT KAINAN THIS YEAR!!
LOOK AT 'EM! THEY'RE HUGE!!

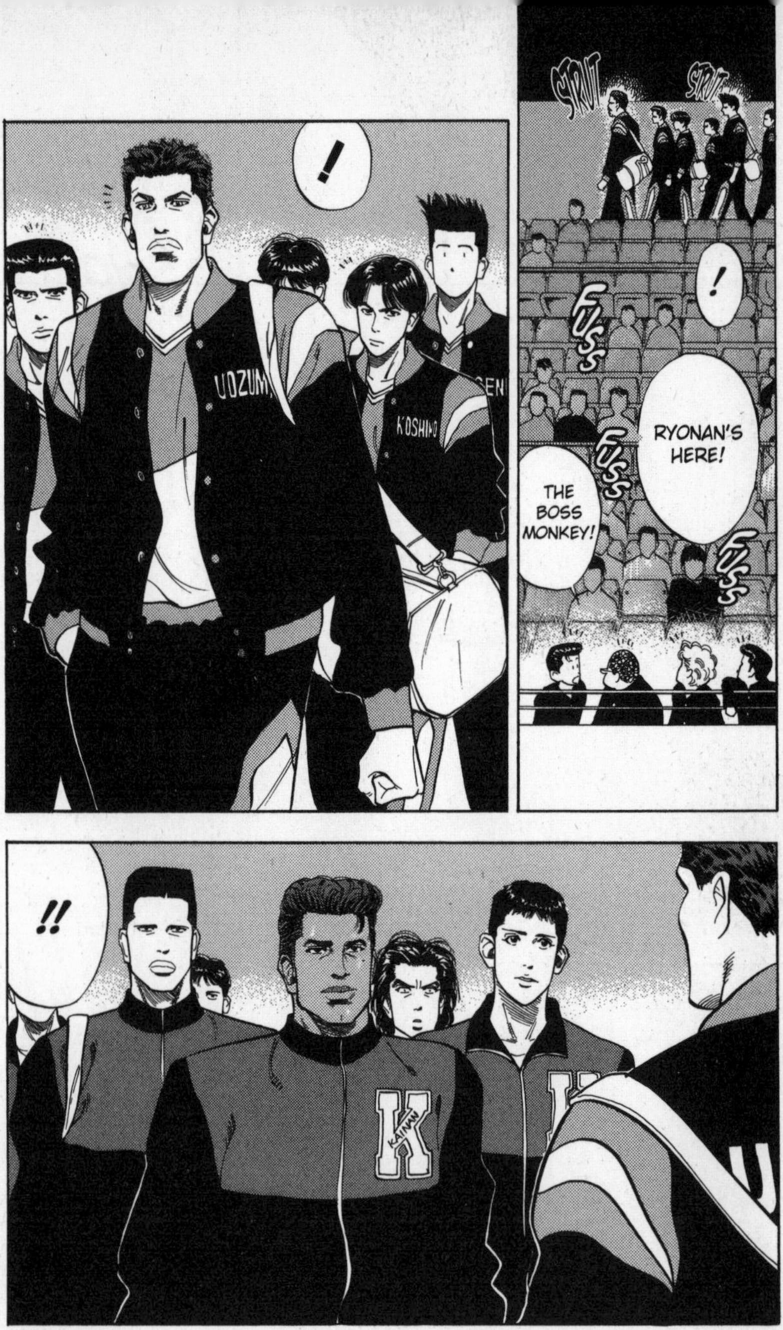
STRUT
STRUT
!
FUSS
RYONAN'S HERE!
FUSS
THE BOSS MONKEY!
FUSS
!
!!

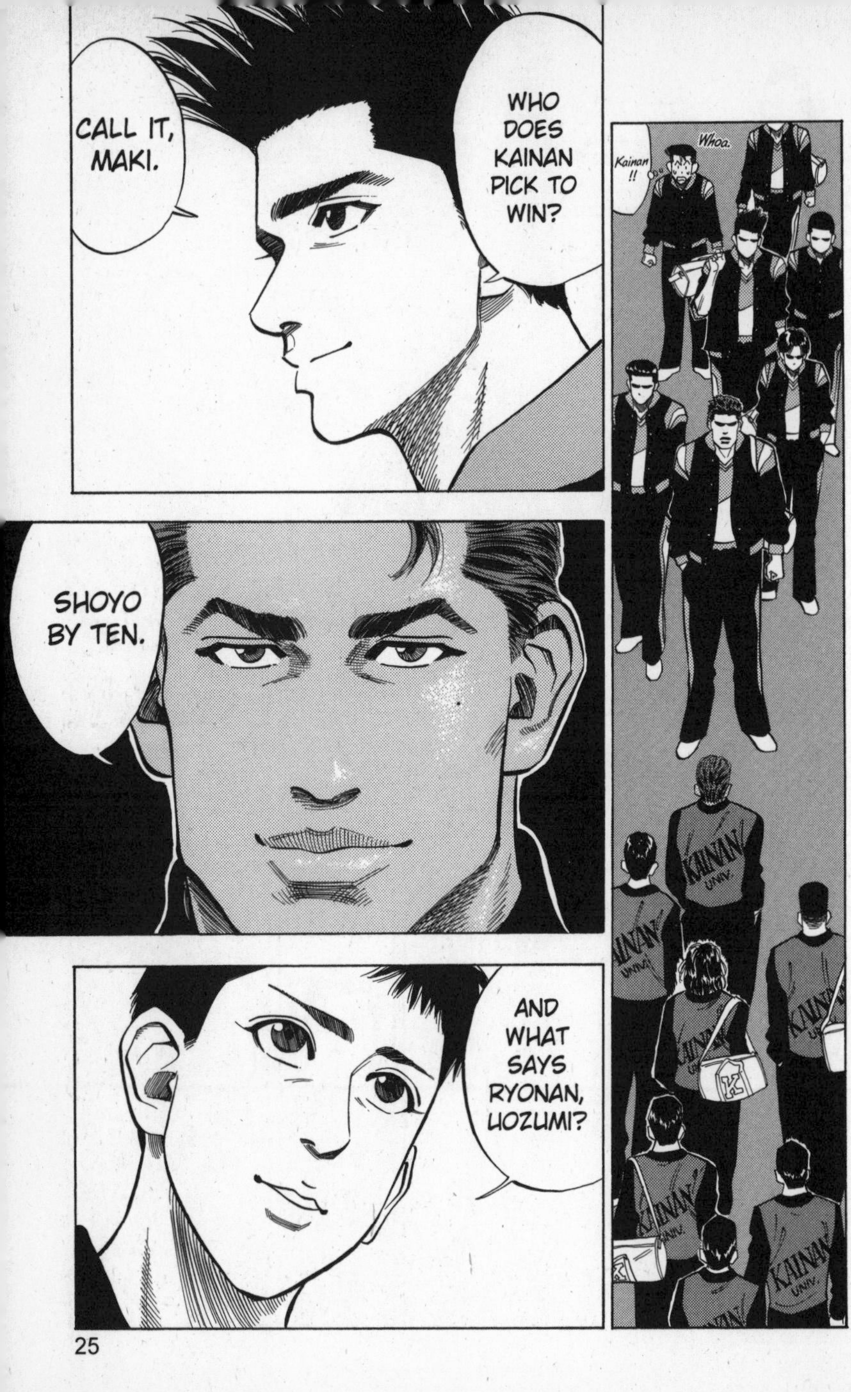
Whoa.
Kainan !!
WHO DOES KAINAN PICK TO WIN?
CALL IT, MAKI.
SHOYO BY TEN.
AND WHAT SAYS RYONAN, UOZUMI?

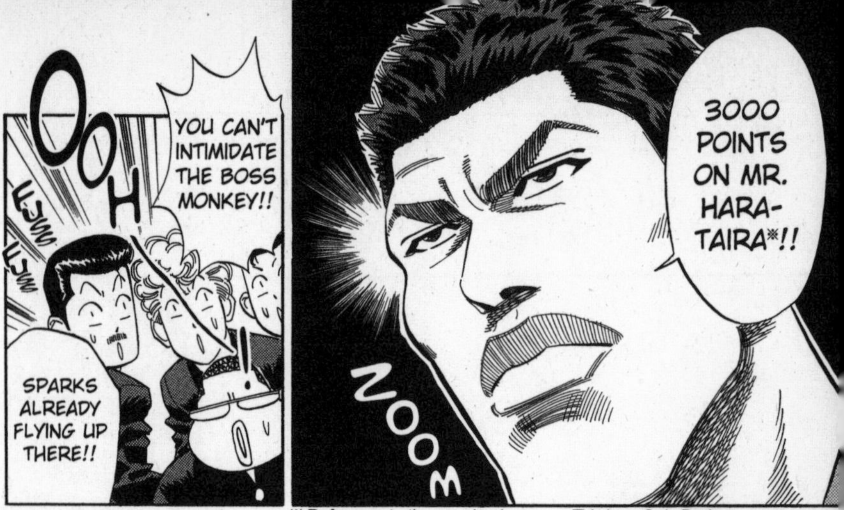

3000 POINTS ON MR. HARA-TAIRA※!!
ZOOM
OOH
YOU CAN'T INTIMIDATE THE BOSS MONKEY!!
SPARKS ALREADY FLYING UP THERE!!

※ Reference to the popular Japanese TV show *Quiz Derby*.

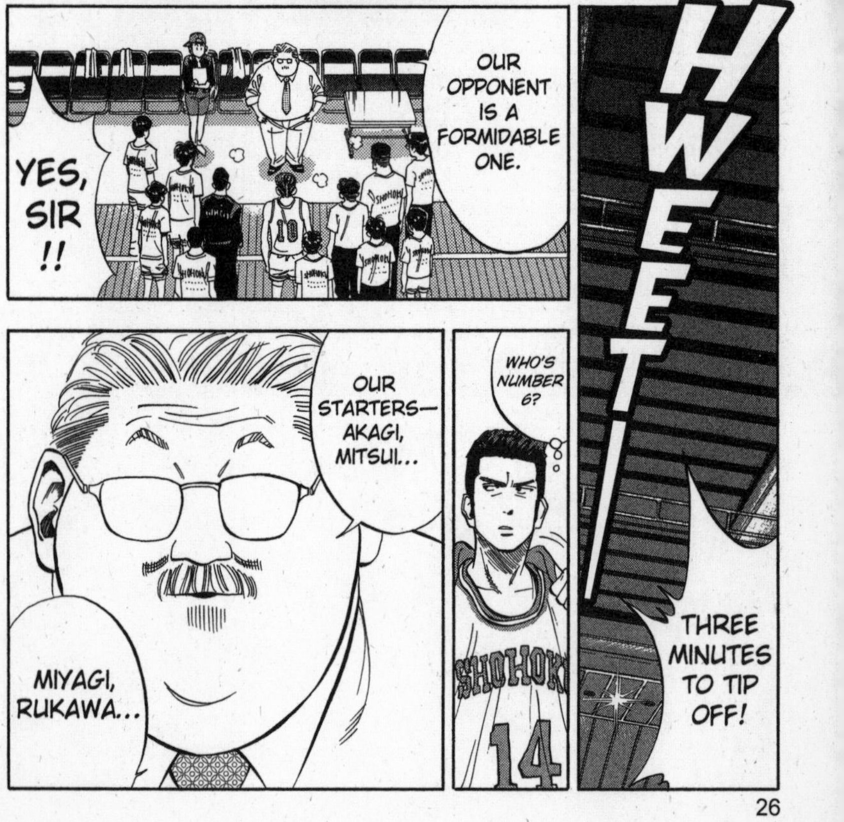

HWEET
THREE MINUTES TO TIP OFF!
OUR OPPONENT IS A FORMIDABLE ONE.
YES, SIR!!
WHO'S NUMBER 6?
OUR STARTERS— AKAGI, MITSUI...
MIYAGI, RUKAWA...

READ THIS WAY

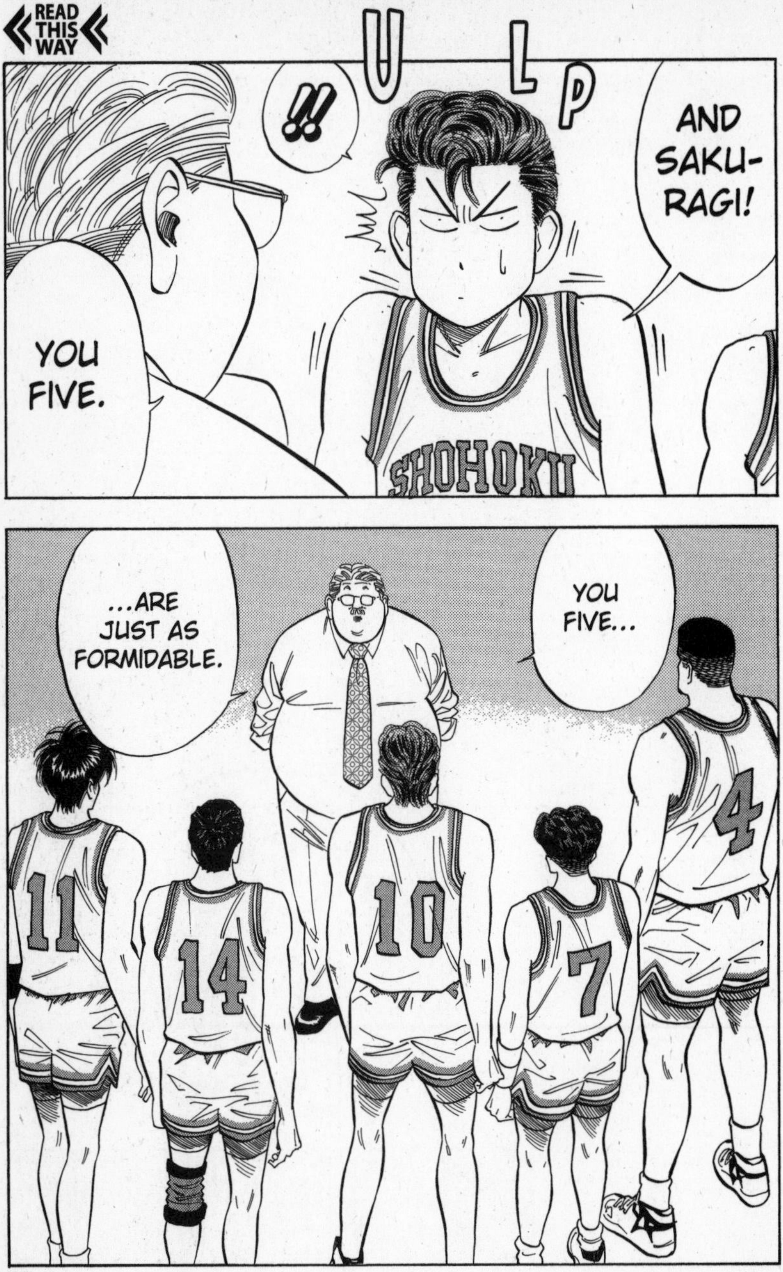
AND SAKURAGI!
ULP
!!
YOU FIVE.
YOU FIVE...
...ARE JUST AS FORMIDABLE.

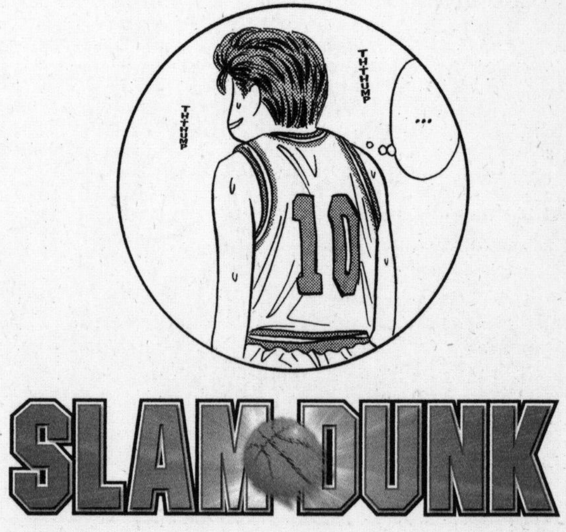
THTHUMP
...
THTHUMP

SLAM DUNK

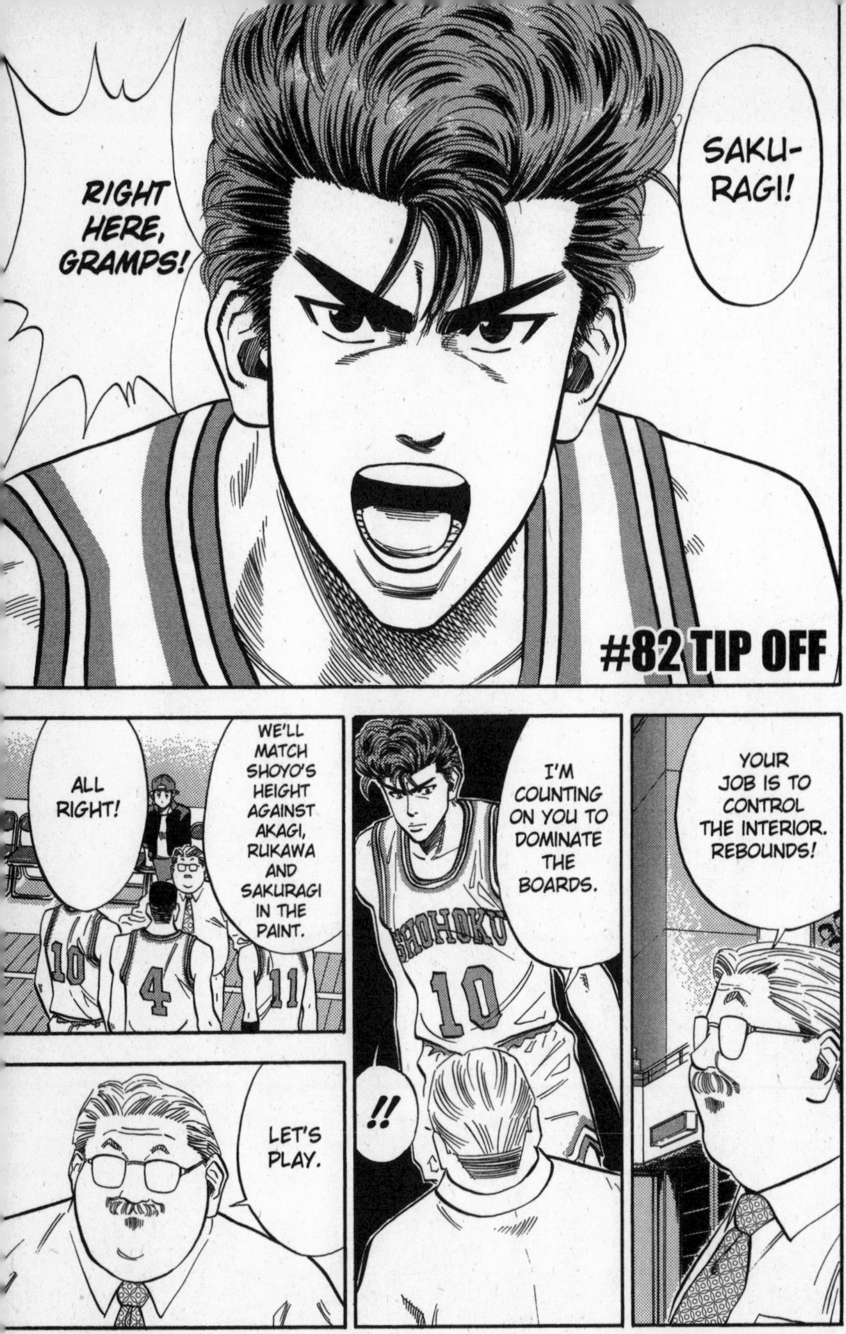
SAKU-RAGI!
RIGHT HERE, GRAMPS!
#82 TIP OFF
YOUR JOB IS TO CONTROL THE INTERIOR. REBOUNDS!
I'M COUNTING ON YOU TO DOMINATE THE BOARDS.
!!
WE'LL MATCH SHOYO'S HEIGHT AGAINST AKAGI, RUKAWA AND SAKURAGI IN THE PAINT.
ALL RIGHT!
LET'S PLAY.

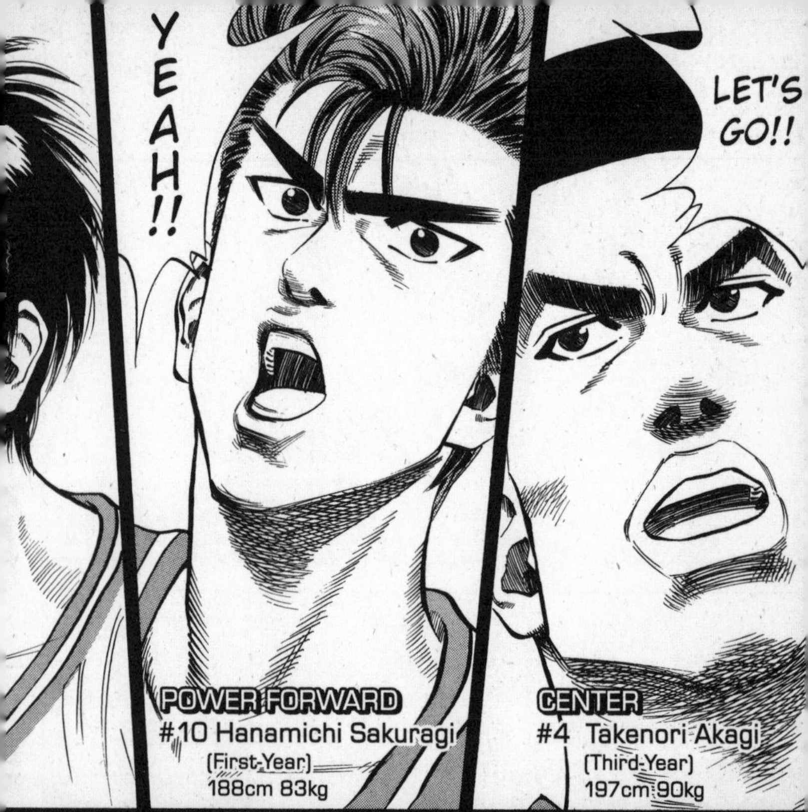
LET'S GO!!
CENTER
#4 Takenori Akagi
(Third-Year)
197cm 90kg
YEAH!!
POWER FORWARD
#10 Hanamichi Sakuragi
(First-Year)
188cm 83kg

6'6" 198 lbs.

6'2" 183 lbs.

#82 TIP OFF

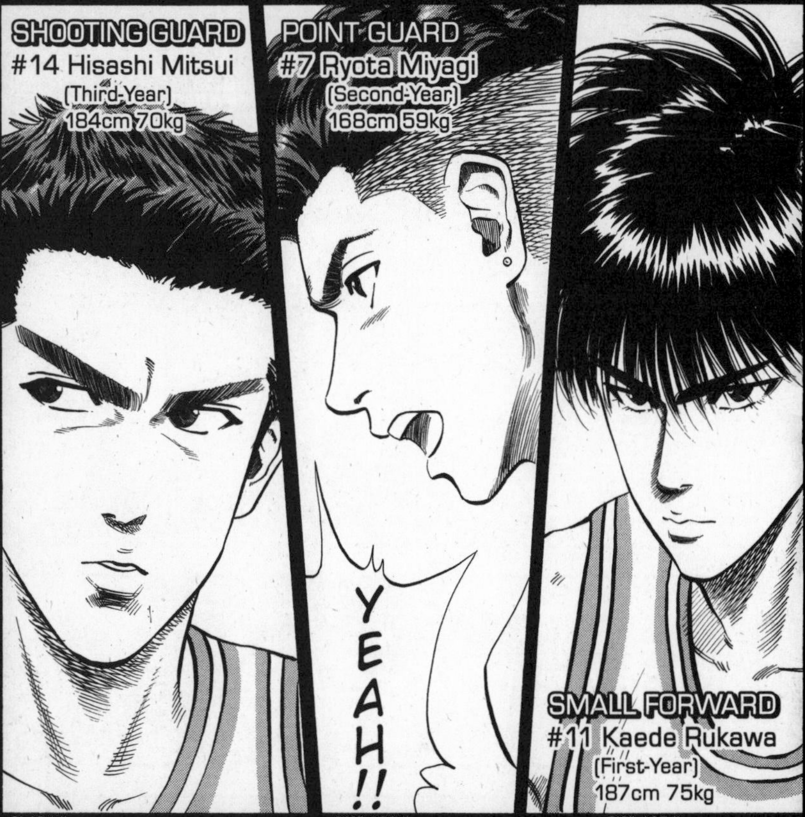
SMALL FORWARD
#11 Kaede Rukawa
(First-Year)
187cm 75kg
POINT GUARD
#7 Ryota Miyagi
(Second-Year)
168cm 59kg
YEAH!!
SHOOTING GUARD
#14 Hisashi Mitsui
(Third-Year)
184cm 70kg
6'2" 165 lbs.

5'6" 130 lbs.

6' 154 lbs.

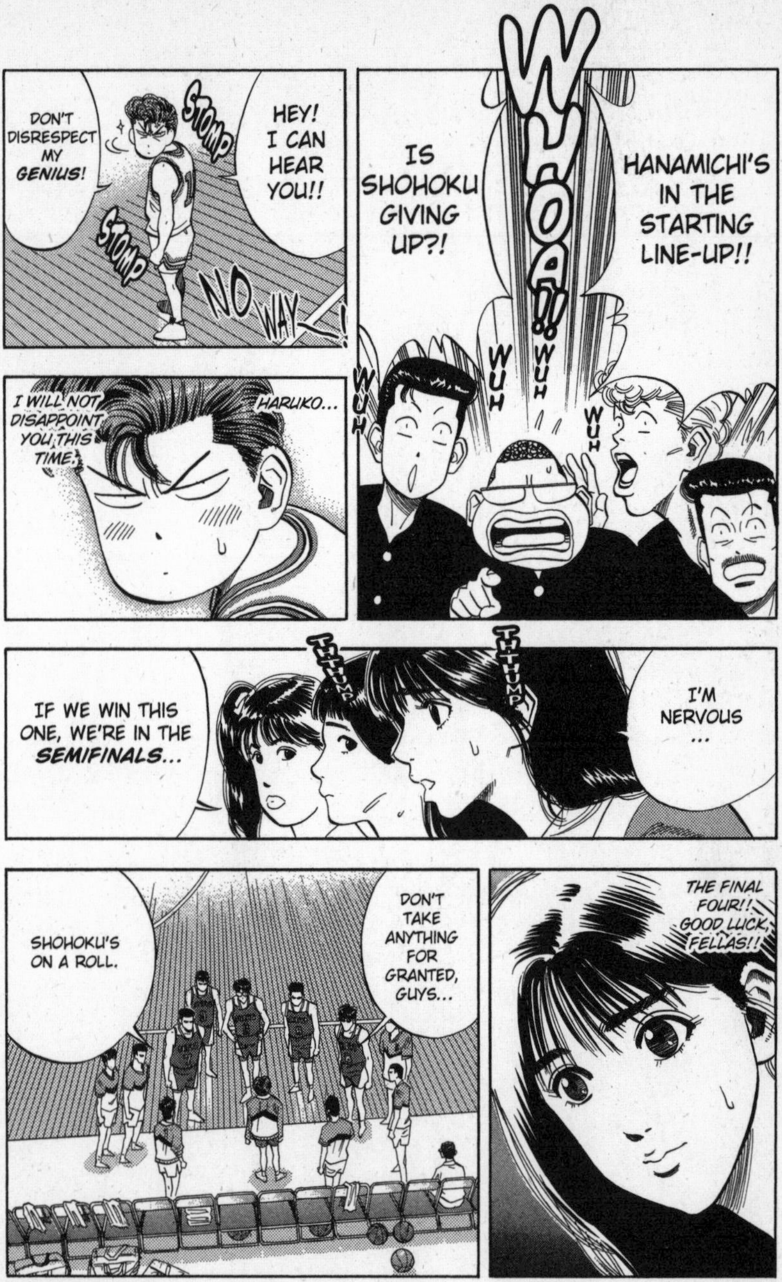
HANAMICHI'S IN THE STARTING LINE-UP!!
WHOA!!
IS SHOHOKU GIVING UP?!
WUH
WUH
WUH
WUH
HEY! I CAN HEAR YOU!!
STOMP
DON'T DISRESPECT MY GENIUS!
STOMP
NO WAY!
HARUKO...
I WILL NOT DISAPPOINT YOU THIS TIME.
I'M NERVOUS ...
THTHUMP
THTHUMP
IF WE WIN THIS ONE, WE'RE IN THE SEMIFINALS...
THE FINAL FOUR!! GOOD LUCK, FELLAS!!
DON'T TAKE ANYTHING FOR GRANTED, GUYS...
SHOHOKU'S ON A ROLL.

READ THIS WAY

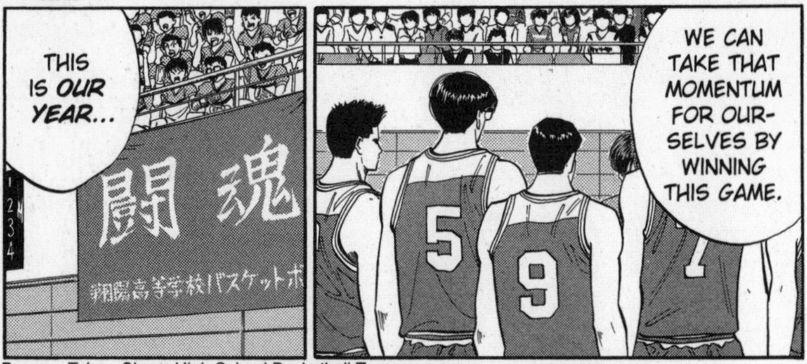
WE CAN TAKE THAT MOMENTUM FOR OUR-SELVES BY WINNING THIS GAME.
THIS IS *OUR YEAR...*
闘魂
翔陽高等学校バスケットボ

Banner: *Tokon,* Shoyo High School Basketball Team

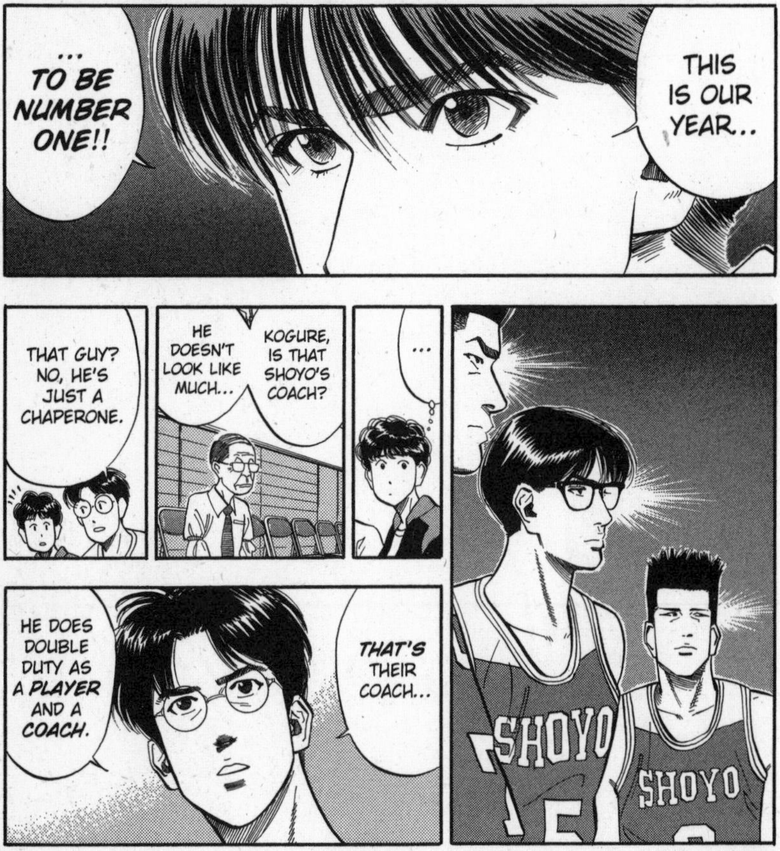
THIS IS OUR YEAR...
... *TO BE NUMBER ONE!!*
...
KOGURE, IS THAT SHOYO'S COACH?
HE DOESN'T LOOK LIKE MUCH...
THAT GUY? NO, HE'S JUST A CHAPERONE.
THAT'S THEIR COACH...
HE DOES DOUBLE DUTY AS A *PLAYER* AND A *COACH.*
SHOYO
SHOYO

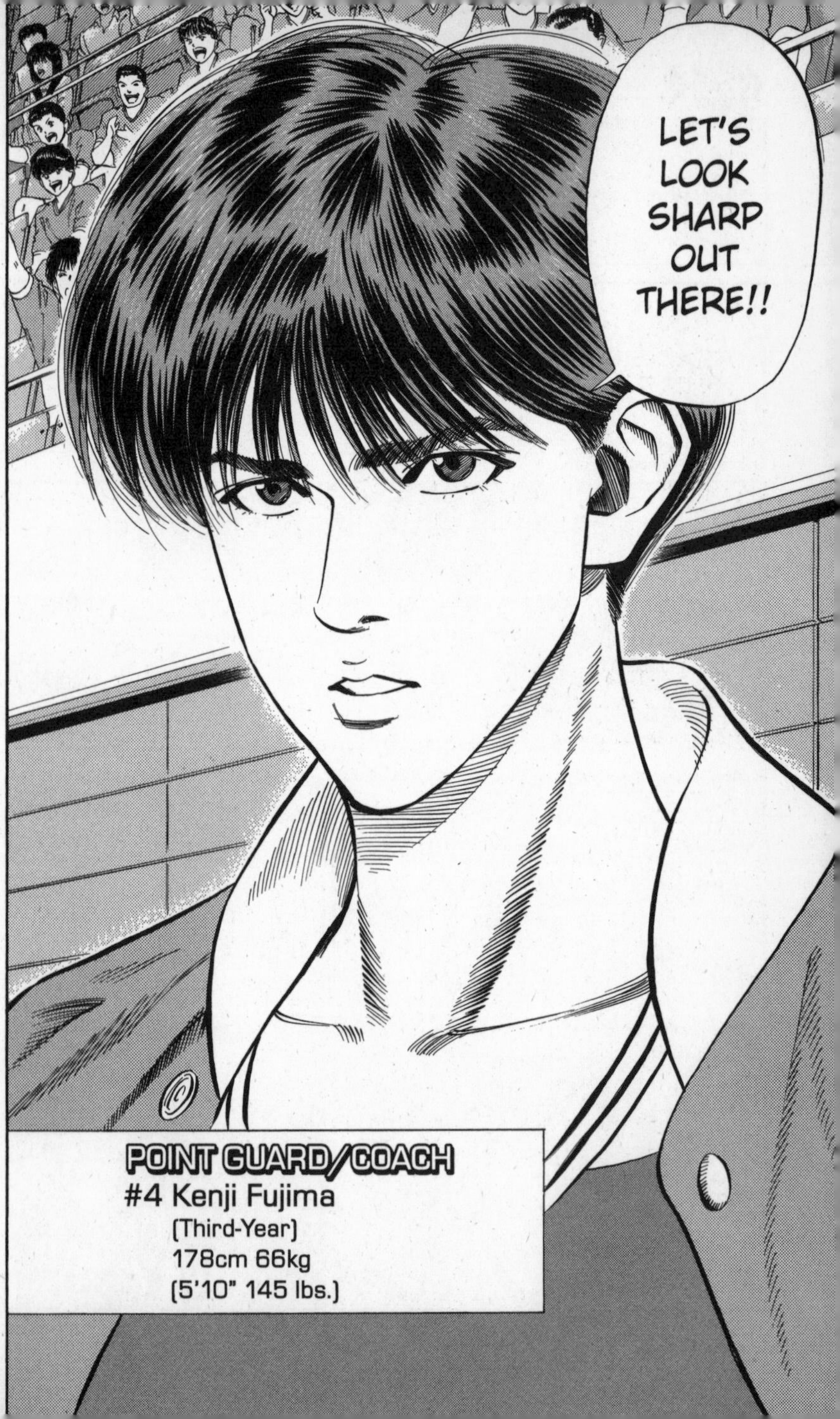
LET'S LOOK SHARP OUT THERE!!
POINT GUARD/COACH
#4 Kenji Fujima
(Third-Year)
178cm 66kg
(5'10" 145 lbs.)

READ THIS WAY

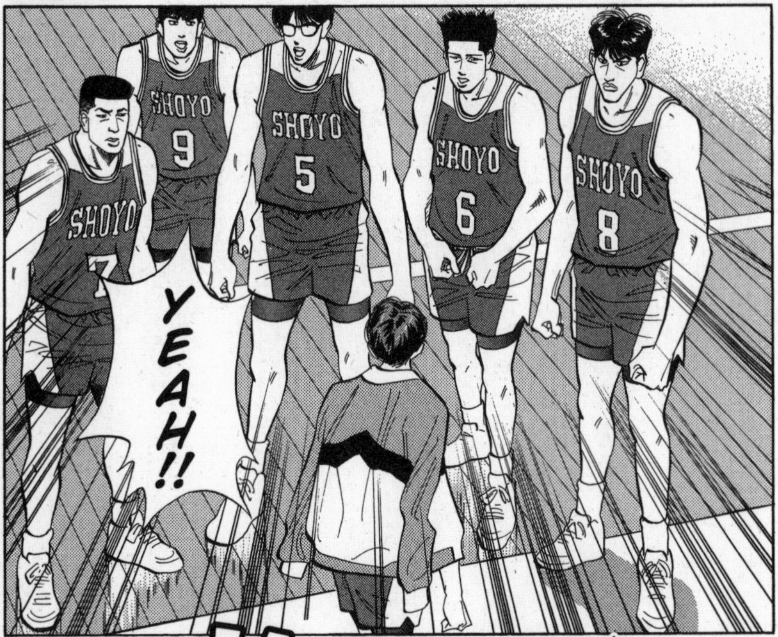
YEAH!!

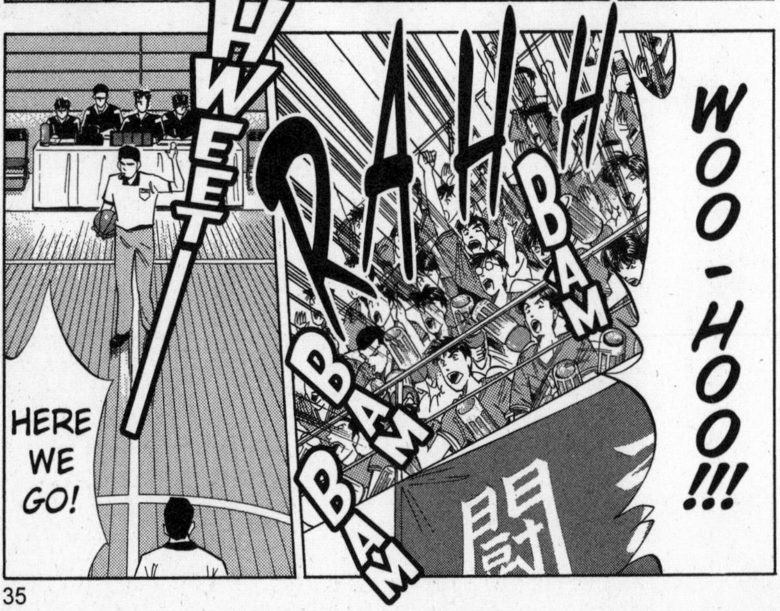
WOO-HOOO!!!
RAHH
BAM
BAM
BAM
闘
HWEET
HERE WE GO!

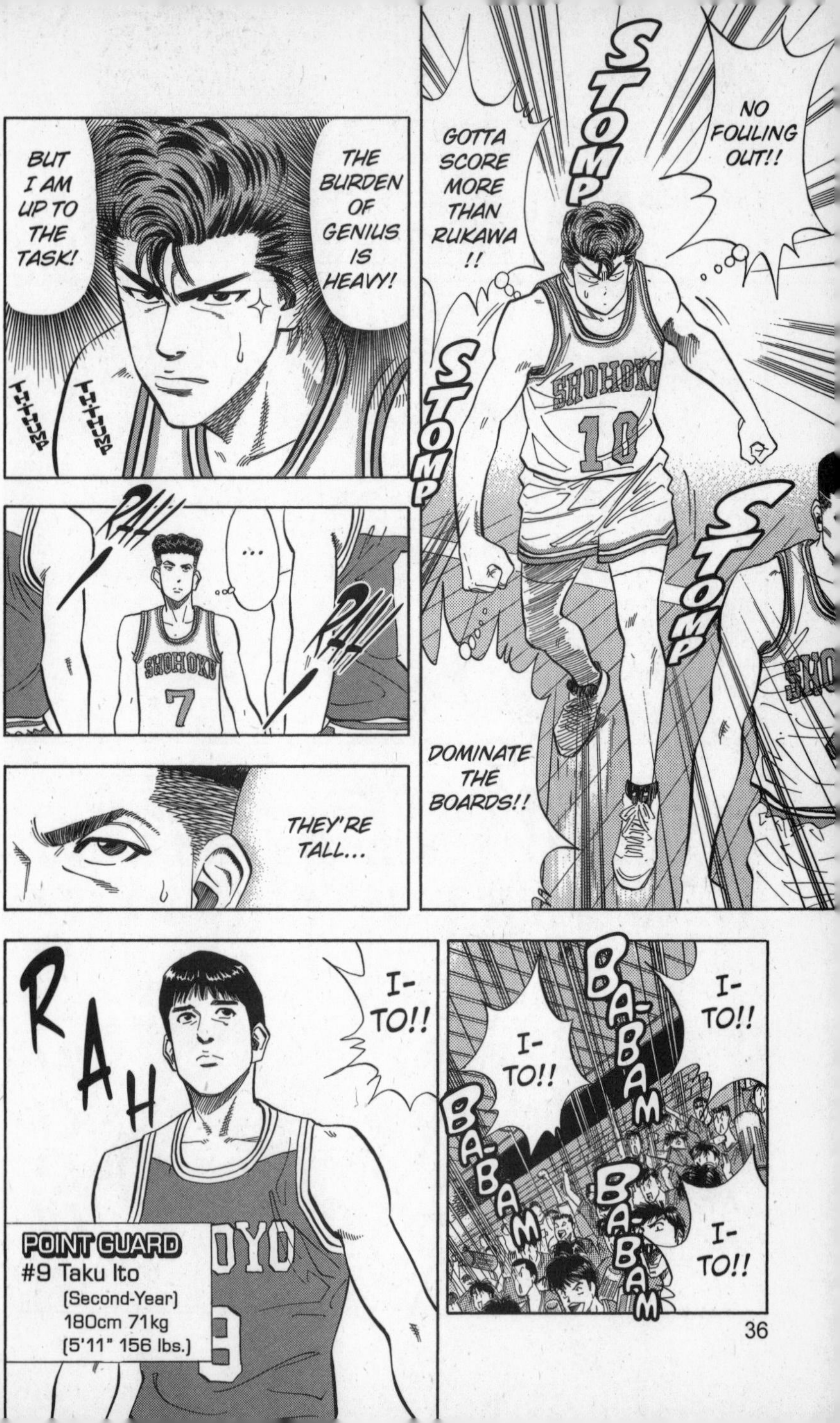
NO FOULING OUT!!
STOMP
GOTTA SCORE MORE THAN RUKAWA !!
STOMP
STOMP
DOMINATE THE BOARDS!!
THE BURDEN OF GENIUS IS HEAVY!
BUT I AM UP TO THE TASK!
THTHUMP
THTHUMP
RAH
...
RAH
THEY'RE TALL...
I-TO!!
BA-BAM
I-TO!!
BA-BAM
I-TO!!
BA-BAM
BA-BAM
I-TO!!
RAH
POINT GUARD
#9 Taku Ito
(Second-Year)
180cm 71kg
(5'11" 156 lbs.)

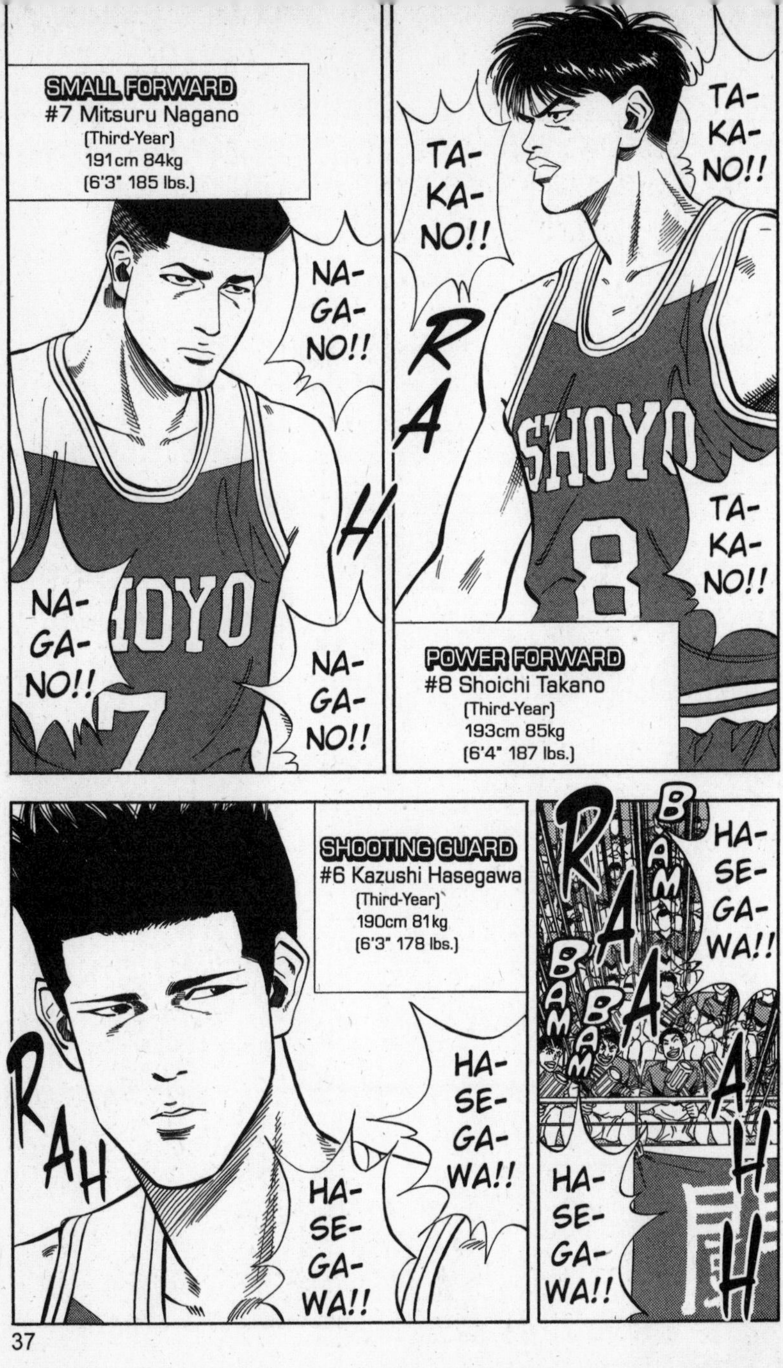

TA-KA-NO!!
TA-KA-NO!!
RAH
TA-KA-NO!!
POWER FORWARD
#8 Shoichi Takano
(Third-Year)
193cm 85kg
(6'4" 187 lbs.)
SMALL FORWARD
#7 Mitsuru Nagano
(Third-Year)
191cm 84kg
(6'3" 185 lbs.)
NA-GA-NO!!
NA-GA-NO!!
NA-GA-NO!!
HA-SE-GA-WA!!
BAM
RAAAH
BAM BAM BAM
HA-SE-GA-WA!!
AHH
SHOOTING GUARD
#6 Kazushi Hasegawa
(Third-Year)
190cm 81kg
(6'3" 178 lbs.)
HA-SE-GA-WA!!
RAH
HA-SE-GA-WA!!

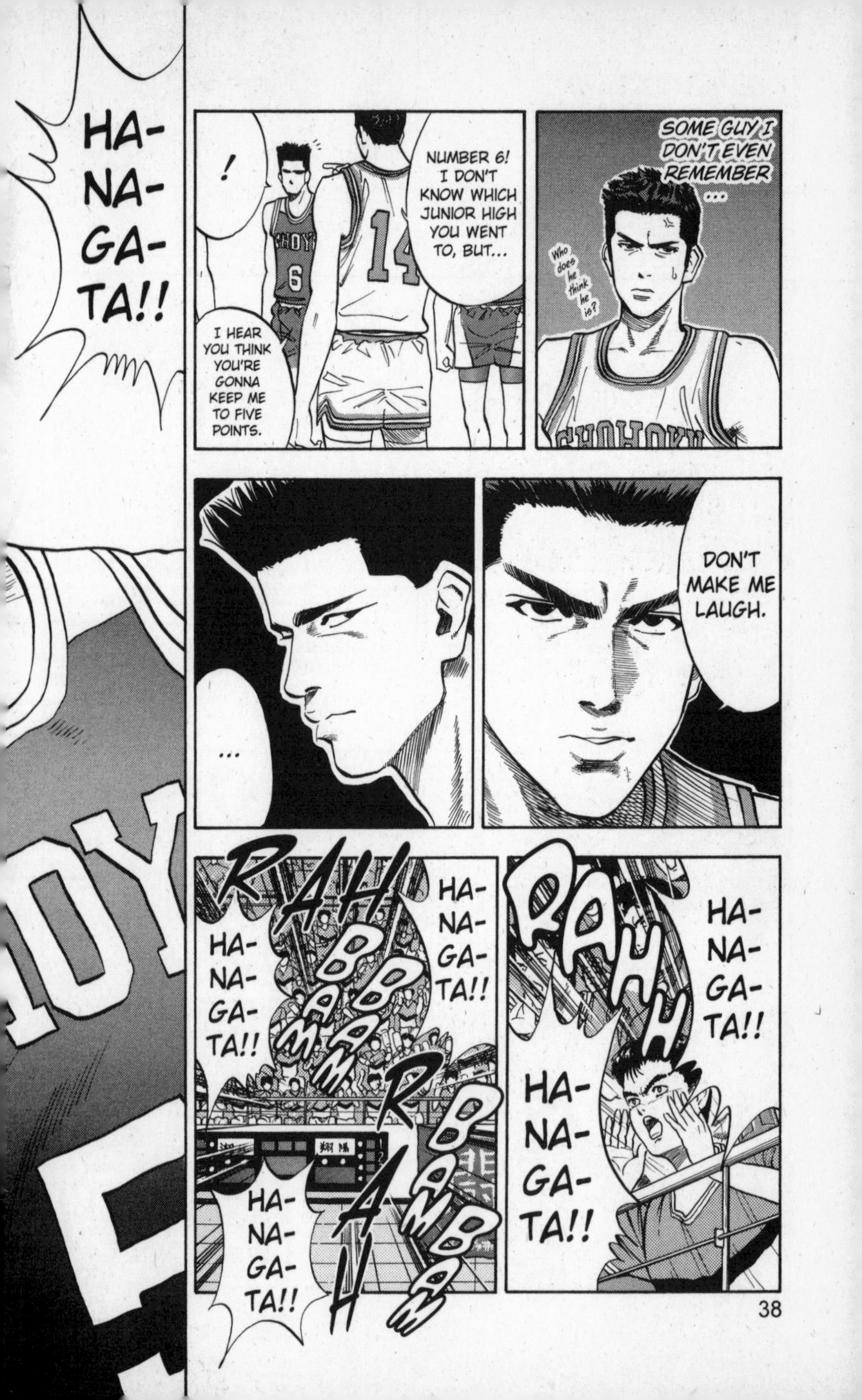
SOME GUY I DON'T EVEN REMEMBER...
Who does he think he is?
NUMBER 6! I DON'T KNOW WHICH JUNIOR HIGH YOU WENT TO, BUT...
I HEAR YOU THINK YOU'RE GONNA KEEP ME TO FIVE POINTS.
!
DON'T MAKE ME LAUGH.
...
RAAHH
HA-NA-GA-TA!!
HA-NA-GA-TA!!
RAHBBAAMM
RBBAMBAAMM
HA-NA-GA-TA!!
HA-NA-GA-TA!!
HA-NA-GA-TA!!
HA-NA-GA-TA!!

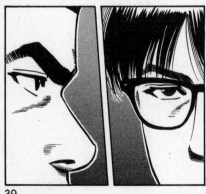

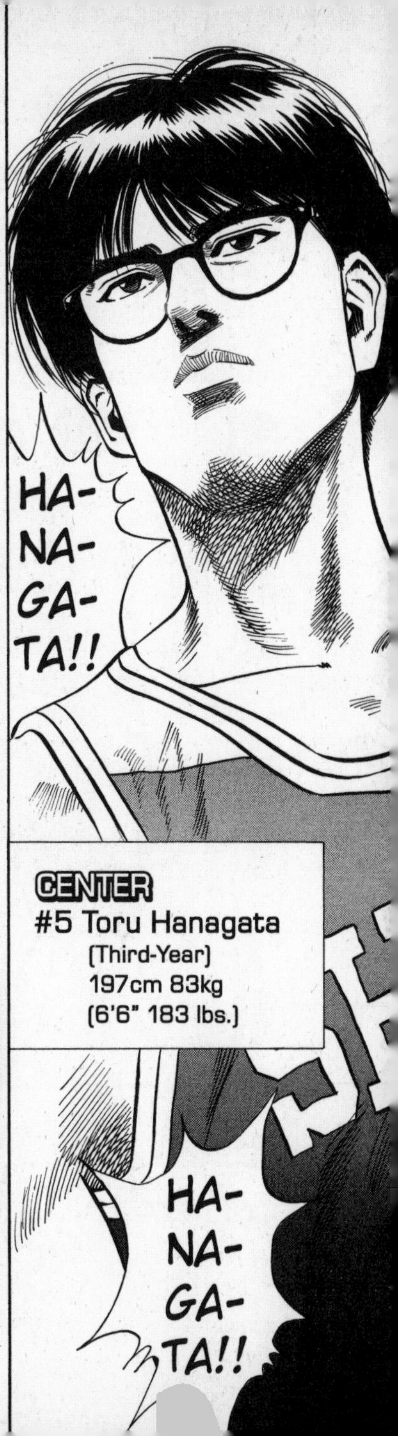
HA-NA-GA-TA!!
CENTER
#5 Toru Hanagata
(Third-Year)
197cm 83kg
(6'6" 183 lbs.)
HA-NA-GA-TA!!

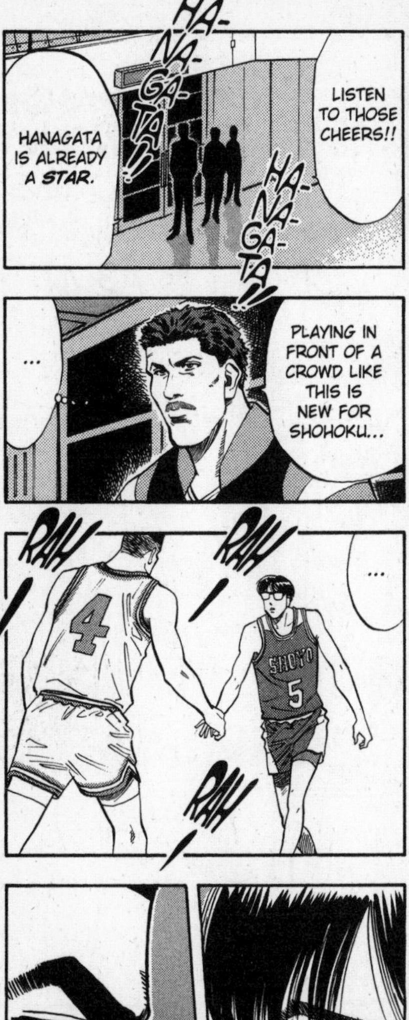
LISTEN TO THOSE CHEERS!!
HA-NA-GA-TA!!
HA-NA-GA-TA!!
HANAGATA IS ALREADY A STAR.
PLAYING IN FRONT OF A CROWD LIKE THIS IS NEW FOR SHOHOKU...
...
...
RAH
RAH
SHOYO
5
4
RAH

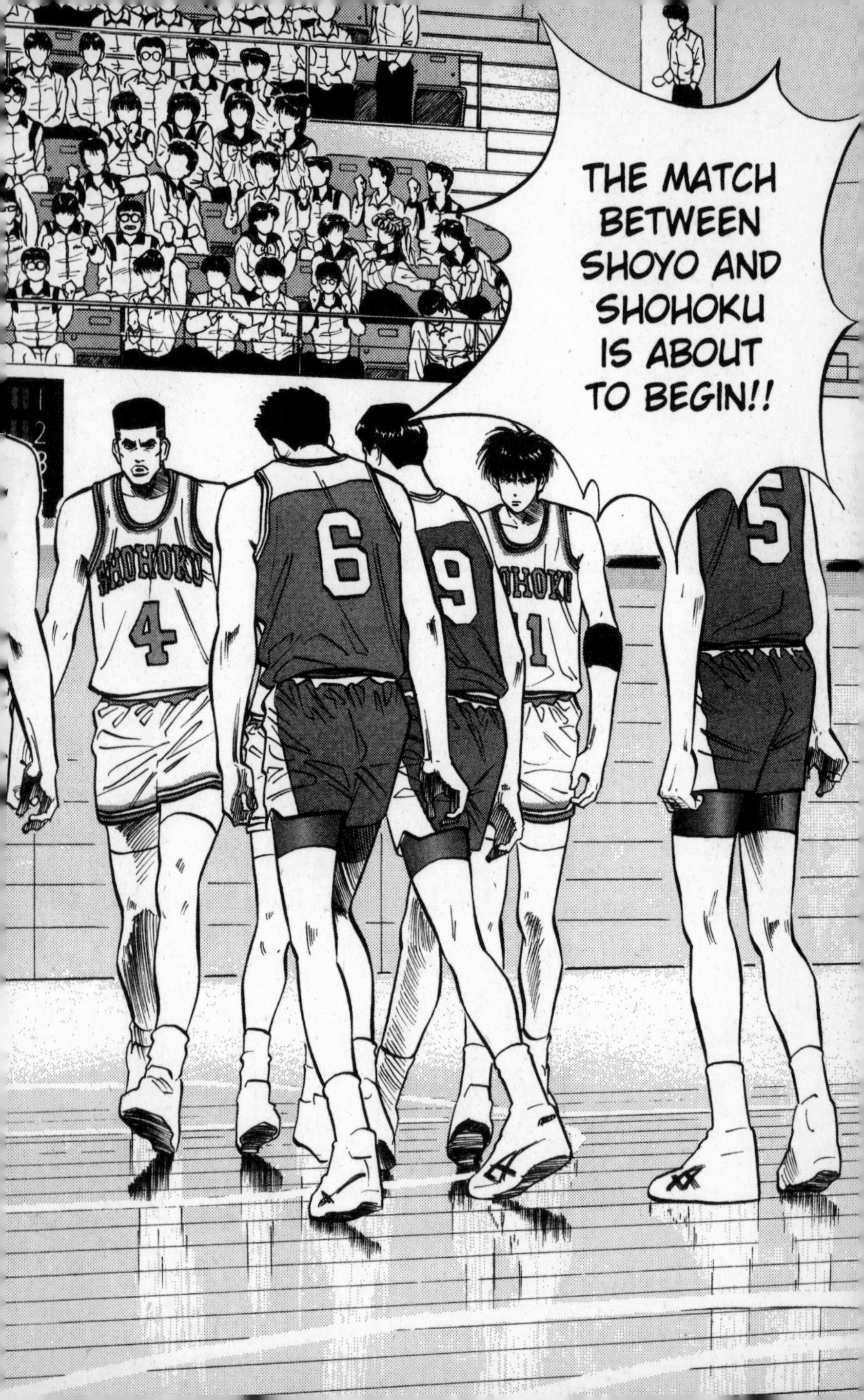
THE MATCH BETWEEN SHOYO AND SHOHOKU IS ABOUT TO BEGIN!!

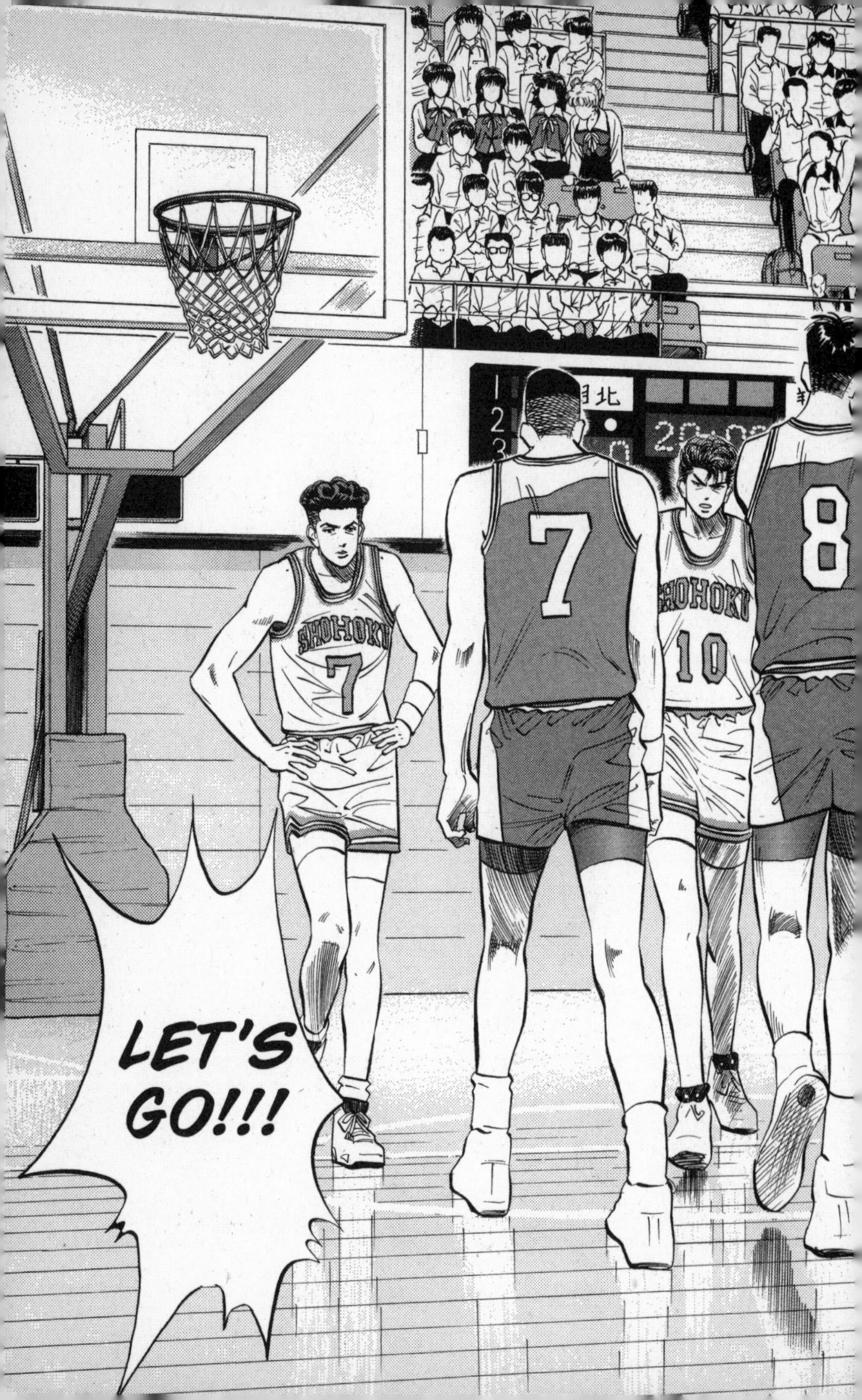
LET'S GO!!!

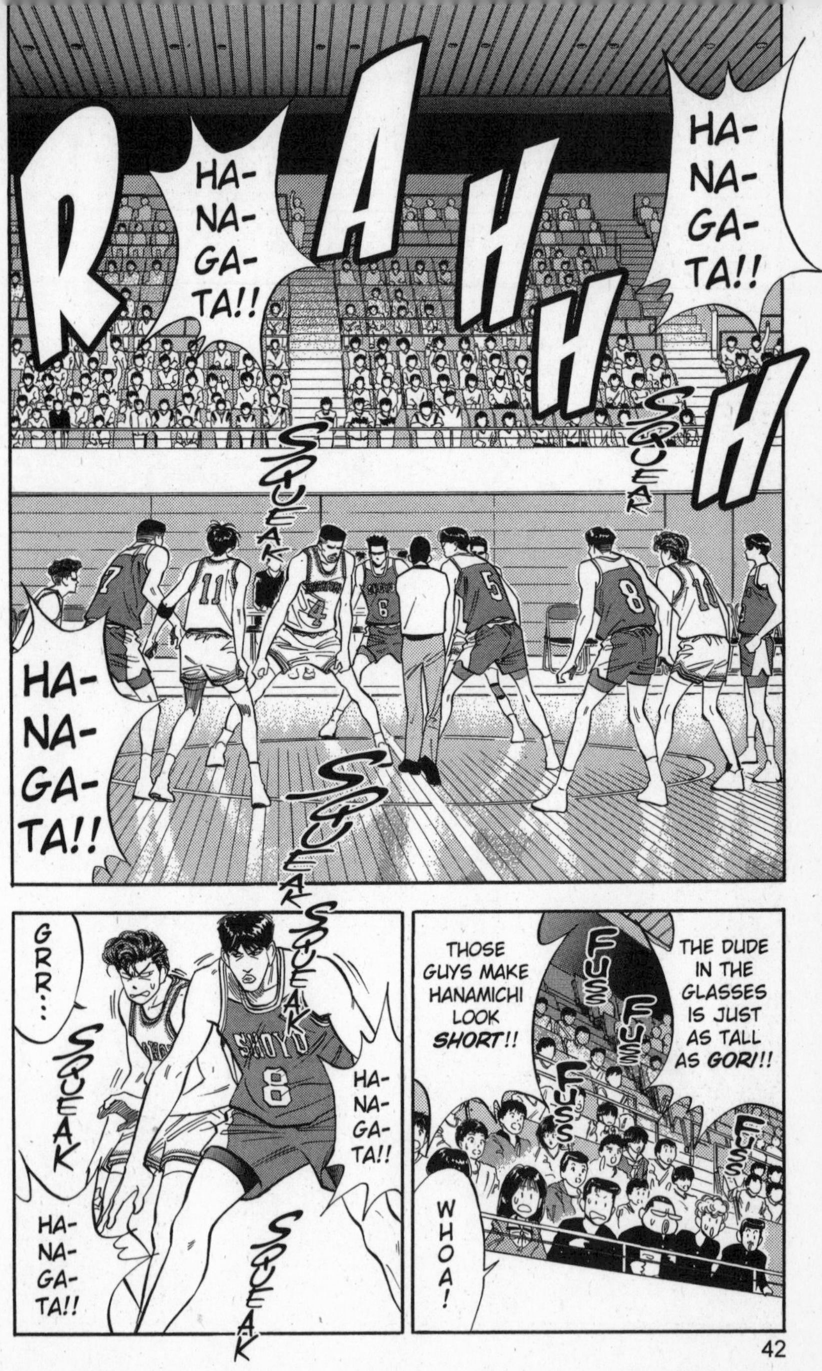
HA-NA-GA-TA!!
RAHHH
HA-NA-GA-TA!!
SQUEAK
SQUEAK
HA-NA-GA-TA!!
SQUEAK
THE DUDE IN THE GLASSES IS JUST AS TALL AS **GORI**!!
THOSE GUYS MAKE HANAMICHI LOOK **SHORT**!!
FUSS
FUSS
FUSS
FUSS
WHOA!
SQUEAK
HA-NA-GA-TA!!
GRR...
SQUEAK
SQUEAK
HA-NA-GA-TA!!

READ THIS WAY

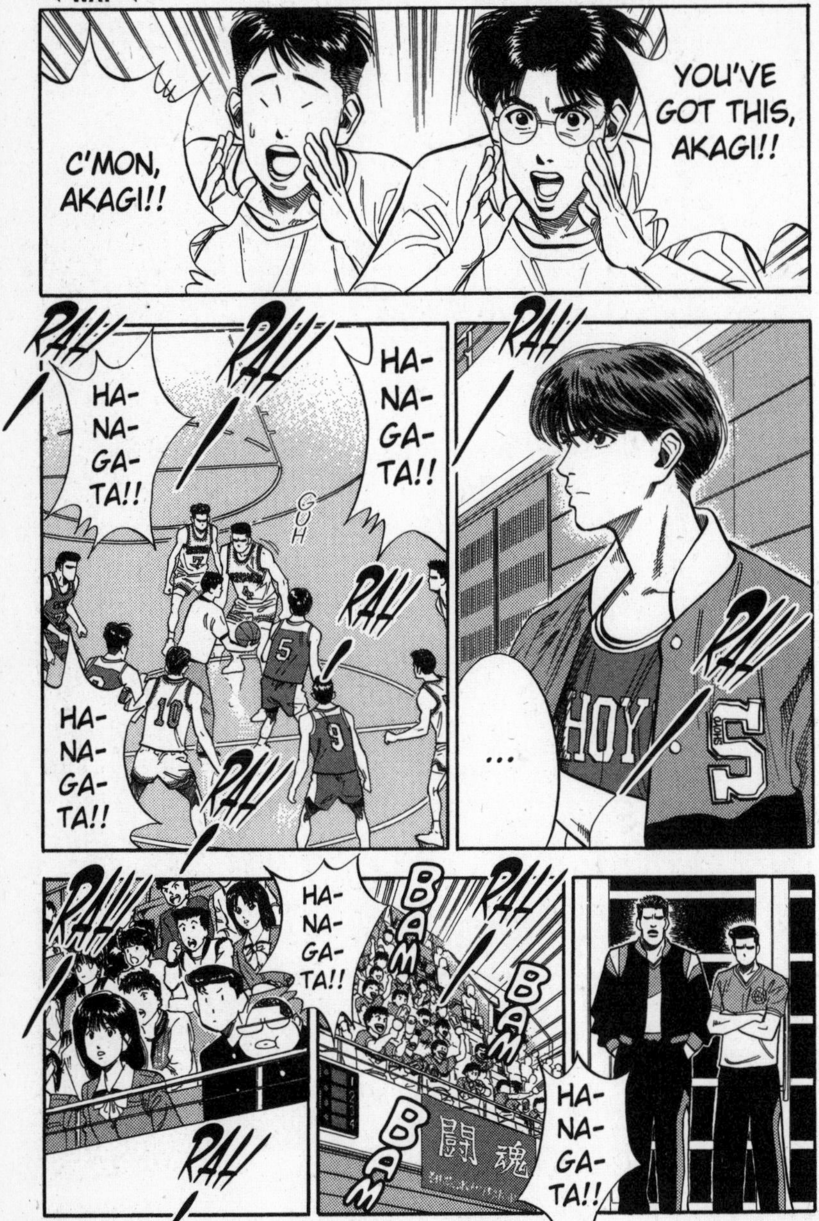
YOU'VE GOT THIS, AKAGI!!
C'MON, AKAGI!!
RAH!
RAH!
...
RAH!
HA-NA-GA-TA!!
RAH!
HA-NA-GA-TA!!
GUH
RAH!
HA-NA-GA-TA!!
RAH!
HA-NA-GA-TA!!
RAH!
BAM BAM
HA-NA-GA-TA!!
BAM BAM
RAH!
RAH!
闘 魂

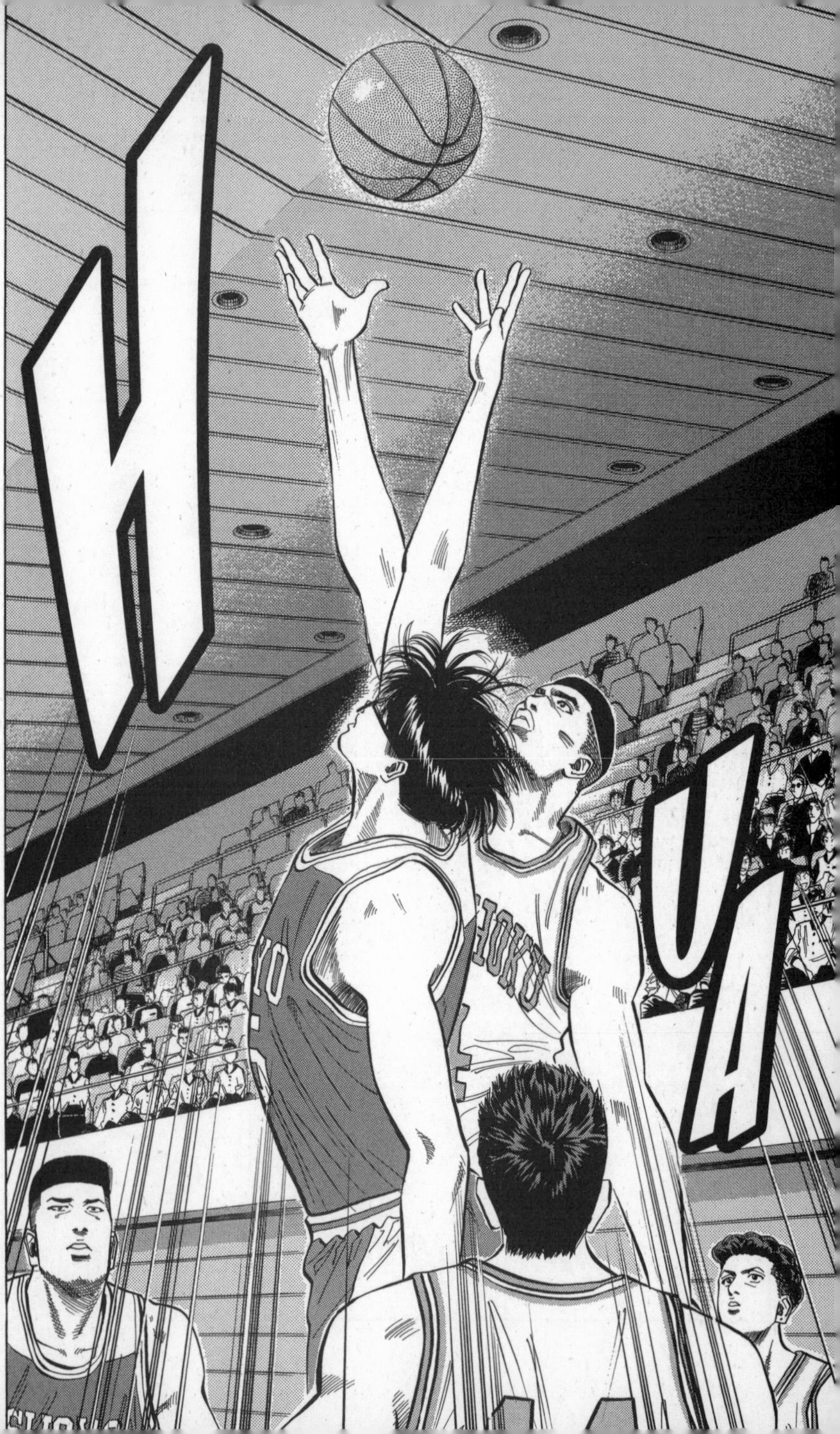
H
YA

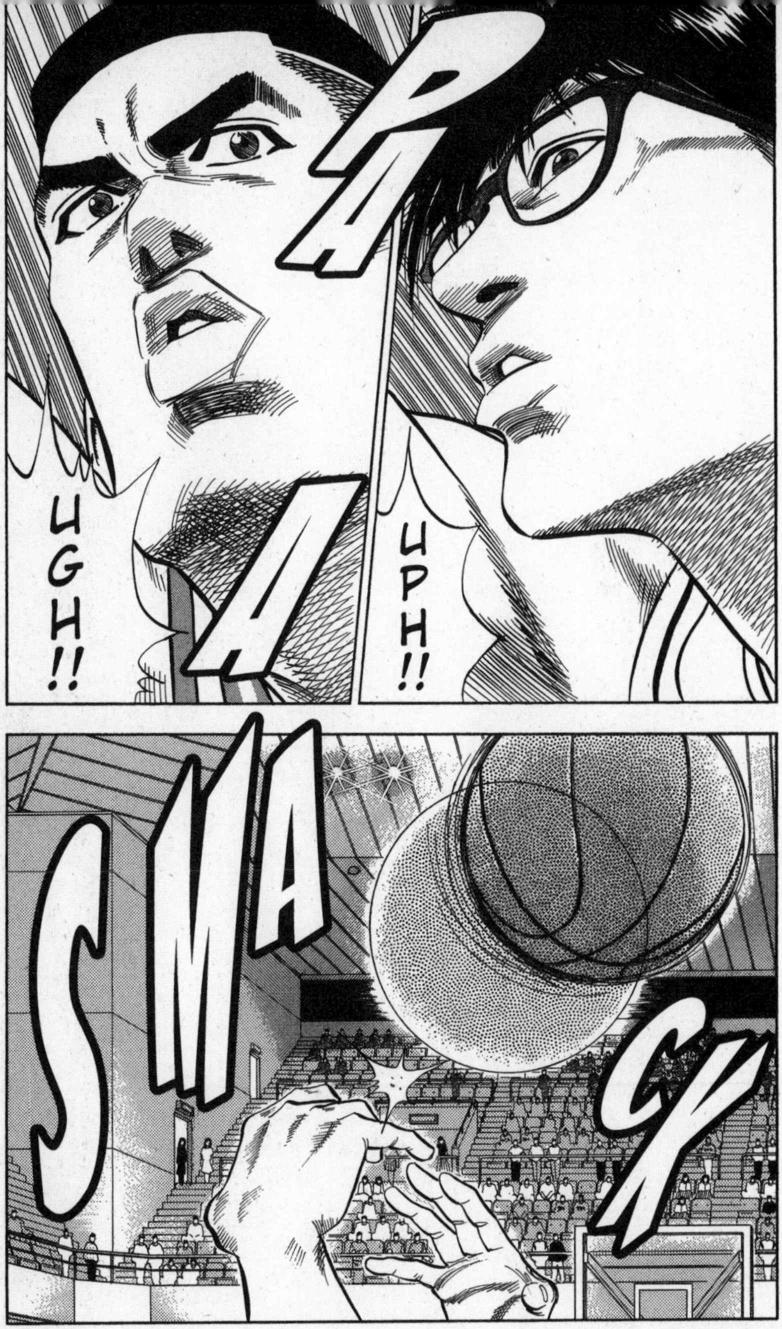
PAA
UPH!!
UGH!!
SMACK

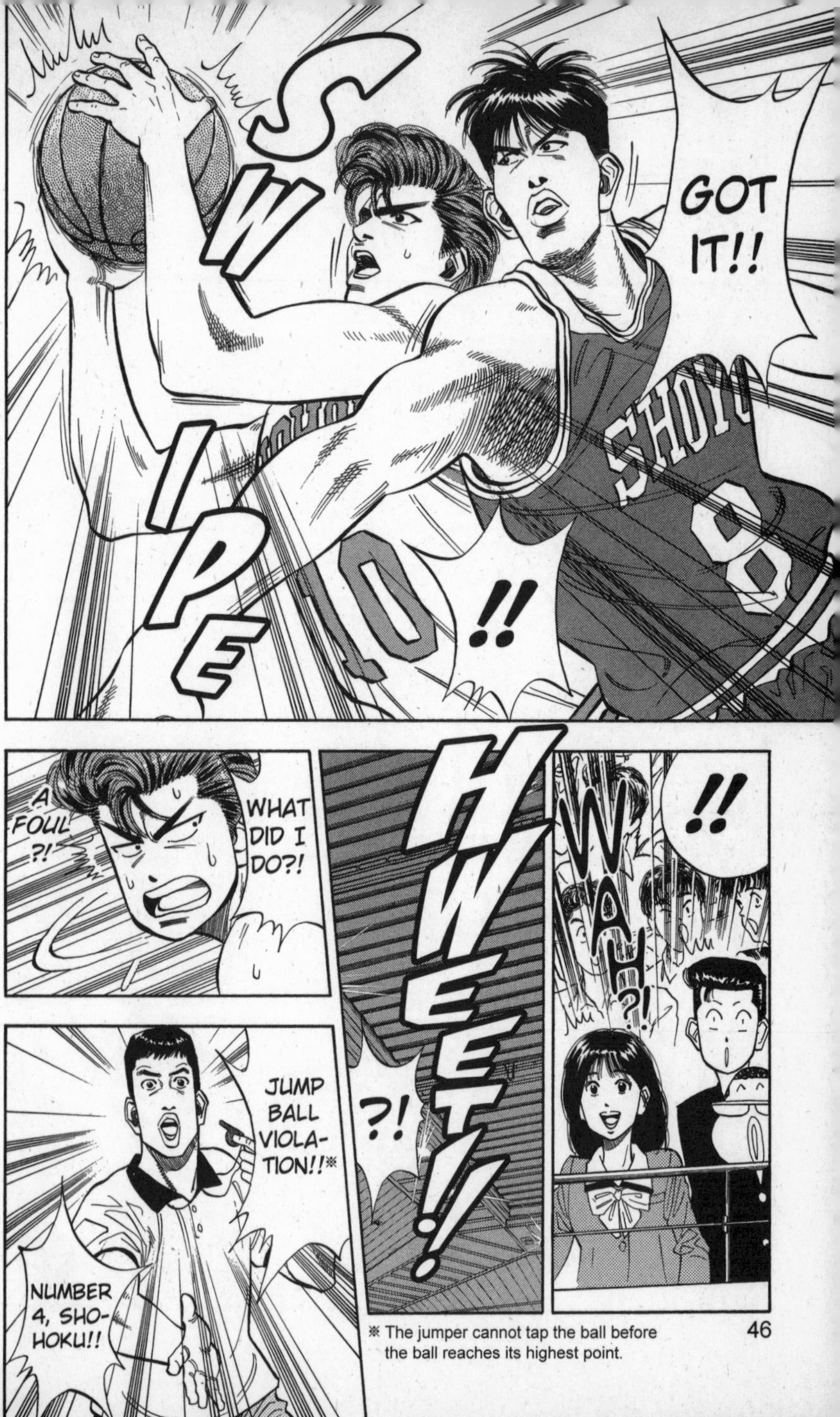
GOT IT!!
SWIPE
!!
!!
WAH?!
HWWEEET!!
?!
WHAT DID I DO?!
A FOUL ?!
JUMP BALL VIOLATION!!※
NUMBER 4, SHOHOKU!!

※ The jumper cannot tap the ball before the ball reaches its highest point.

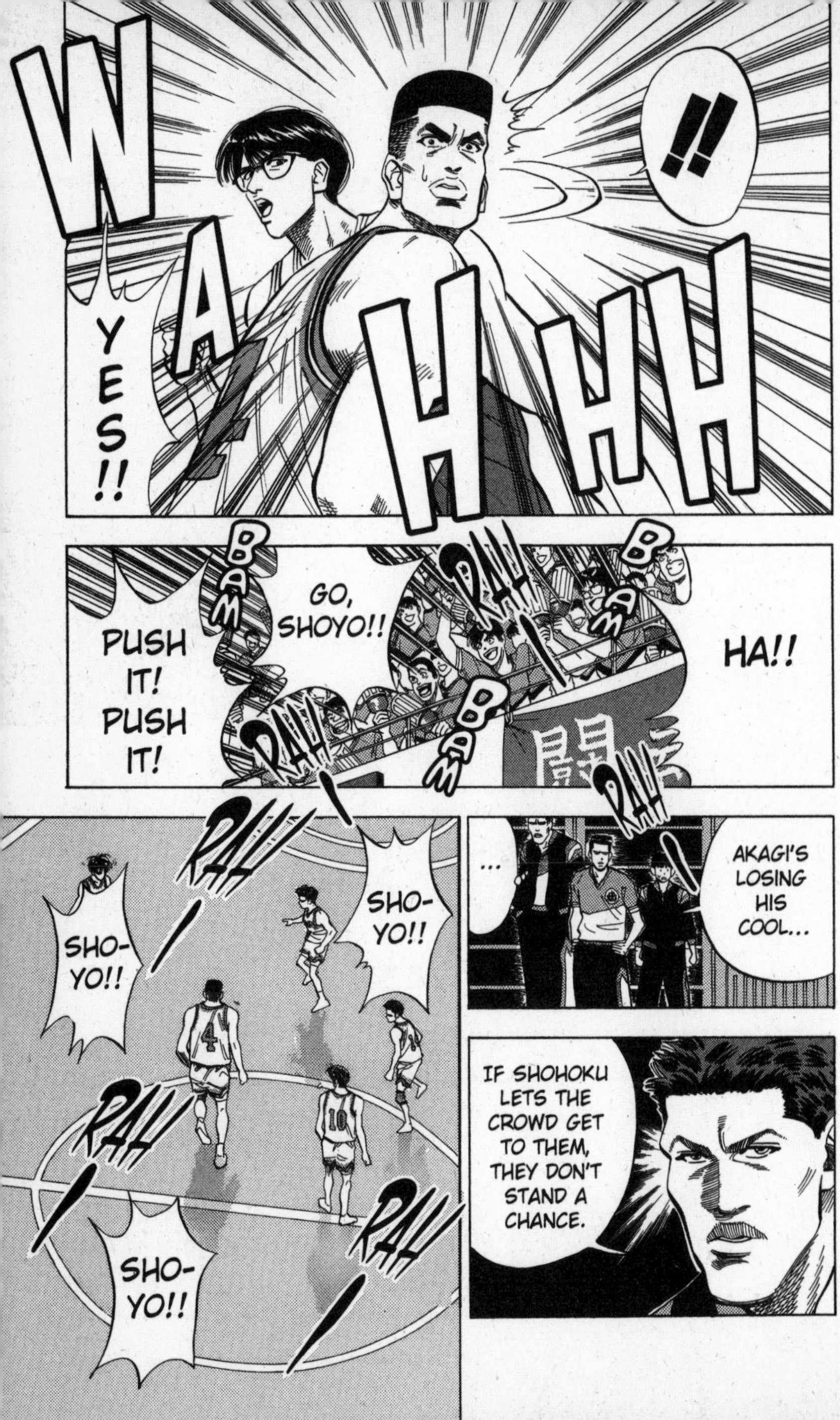
!!
WAHHH
YES!!
HA!!
BAM
RAH
GO, SHOYO!!
BAM
RAH
PUSH IT! PUSH IT!
RAH!
AKAGI'S LOSING HIS COOL...
...
IF SHOHOKU LETS THE CROWD GET TO THEM, THEY DON'T STAND A CHANCE.
SHO-YO!!
RAH!
SHO-YO!!
RAH!
RAH!
SHO-YO!!

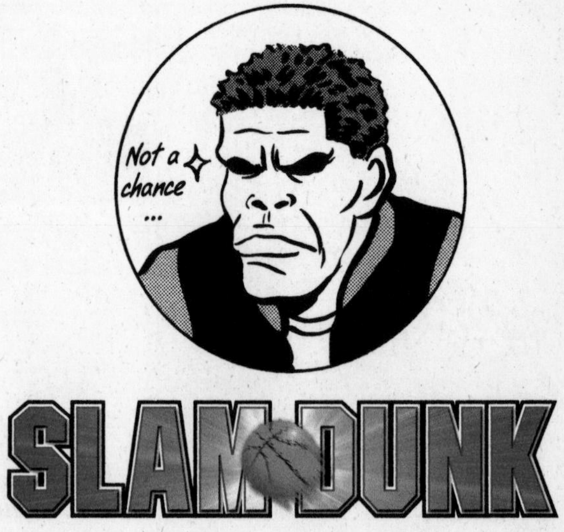
Not a chance ...

SLAM DUNK

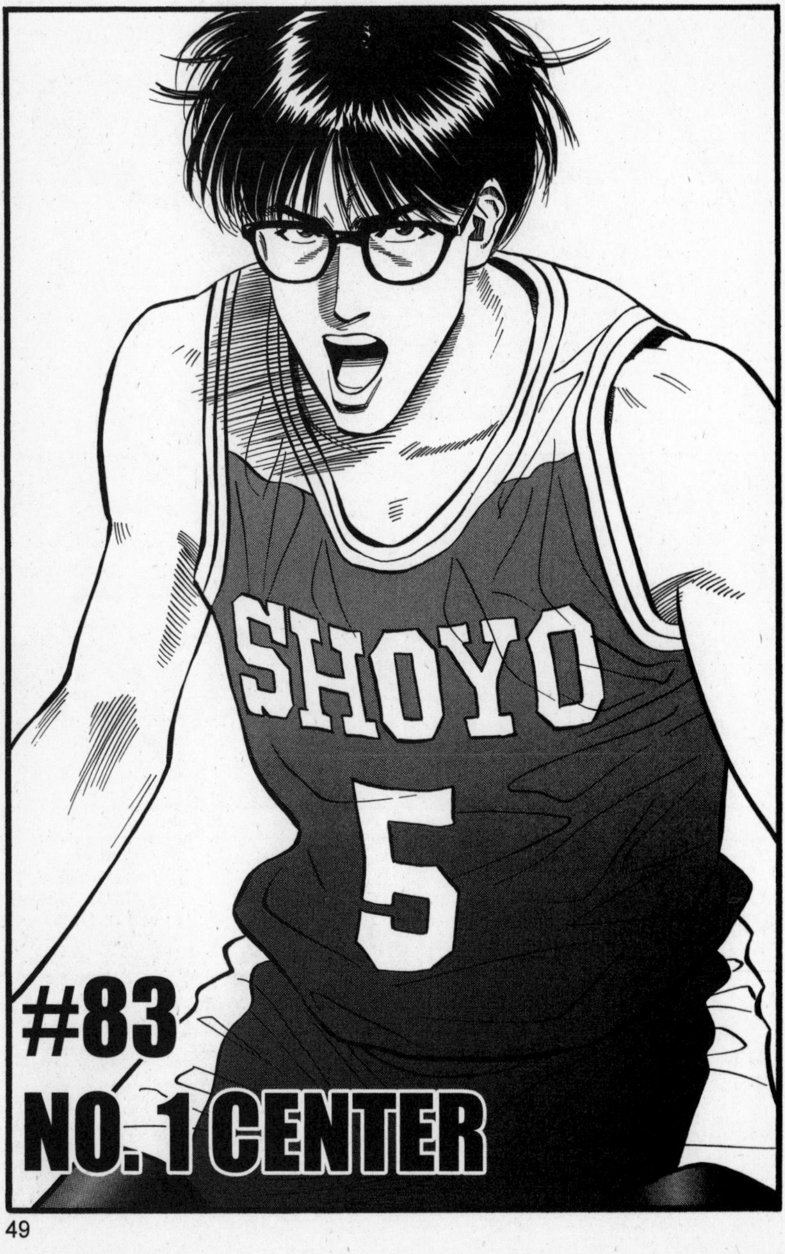
SHOYO
5
#83
NO. 1 CENTER

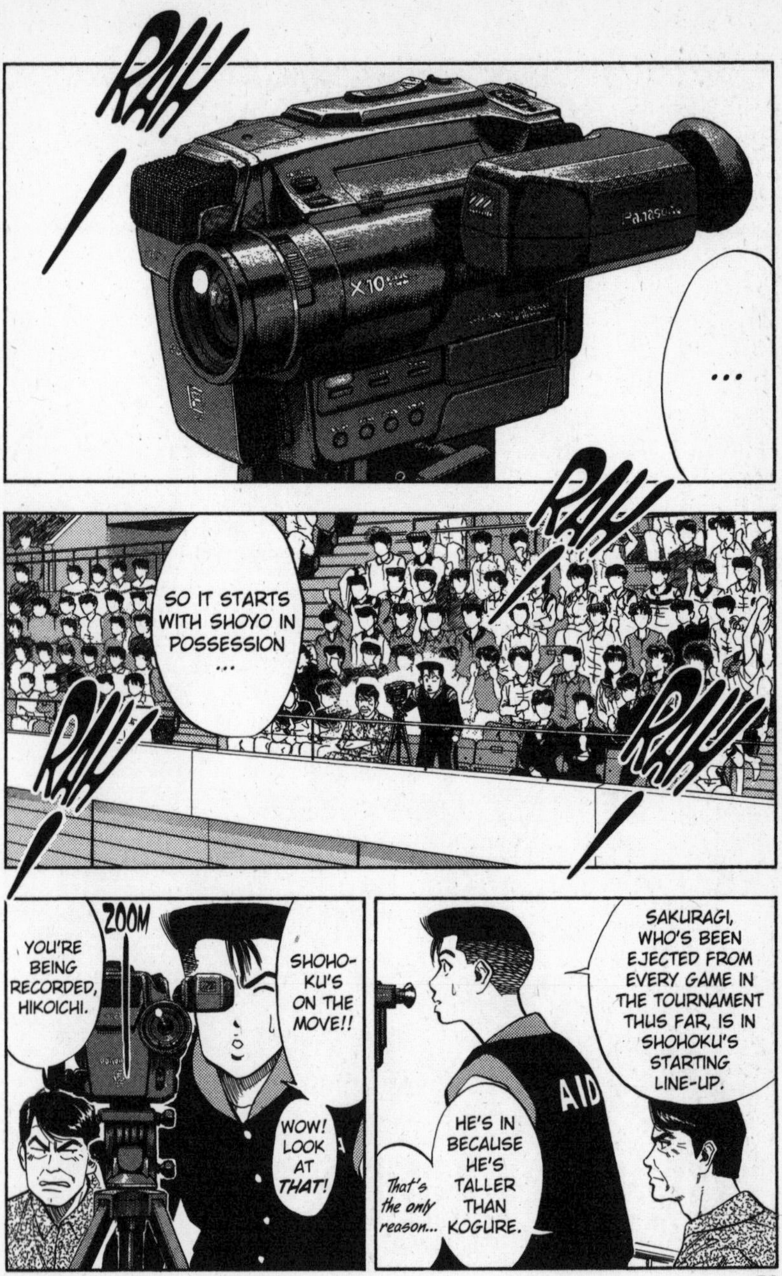
RAH!
...
RAH!
RAH!
SO IT STARTS WITH SHOYO IN POSSESSION ...
RAH!
SAKURAGI, WHO'S BEEN EJECTED FROM EVERY GAME IN THE TOURNAMENT THUS FAR, IS IN SHOHOKU'S STARTING LINE-UP.
HE'S IN BECAUSE HE'S TALLER THAN KOGURE.
That's the only reason...
SHOHOKU'S ON THE MOVE!!
ZOOM
YOU'RE BEING RECORDED, HIKOICHI.
WOW! LOOK AT THAT!

READ THIS WAY

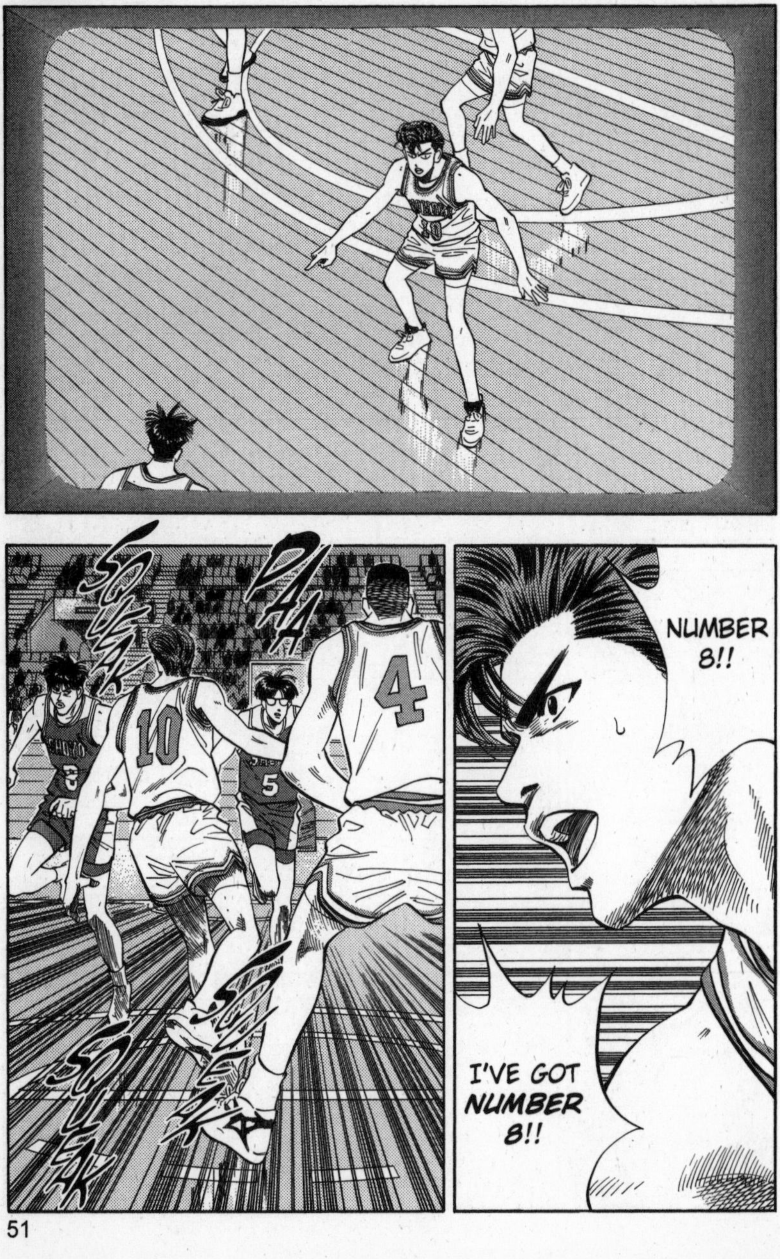
NUMBER 8!!
I'VE GOT NUMBER 8!!
DAA
SQUEAK
SQUEAK
SQUEAK

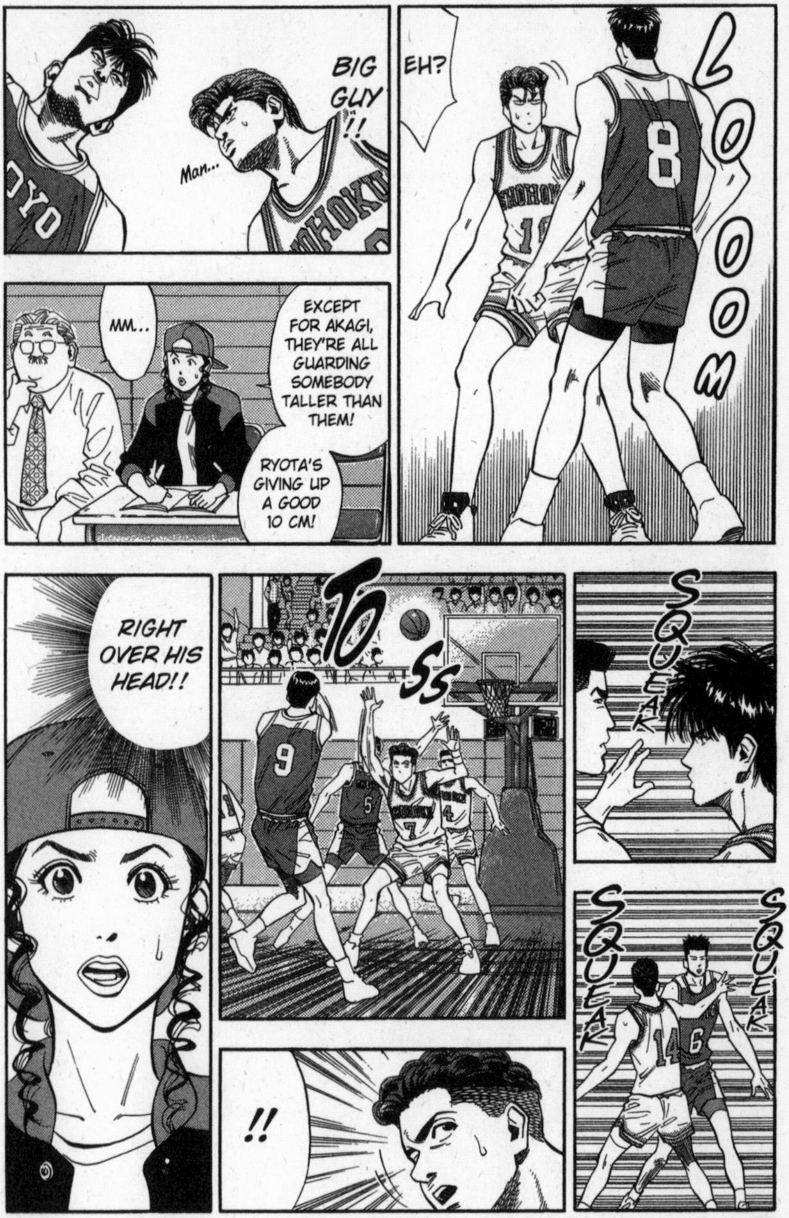
EH?
LOOOOM
BIG GUY!!
Man...
EXCEPT FOR AKAGI, THEY'RE ALL GUARDING SOMEBODY TALLER THAN THEM!
MM...
RYOTA'S GIVING UP A GOOD 10 CM!
SQUEAK
SQUEAK
SQUEAK
TOSS
!!
RIGHT OVER HIS HEAD!!

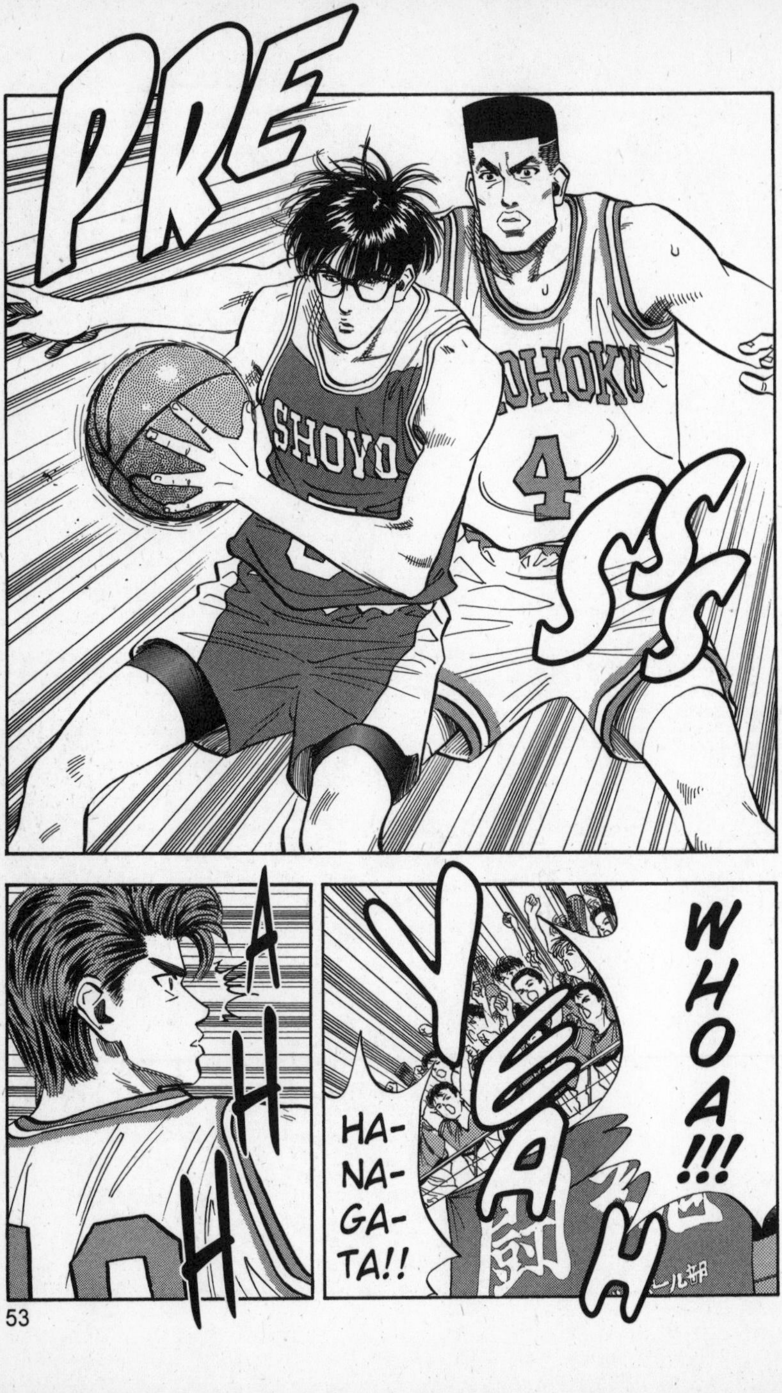
PRE
SSSS
WHOA!!!
YEAAH
HANAGATA!!
AHH

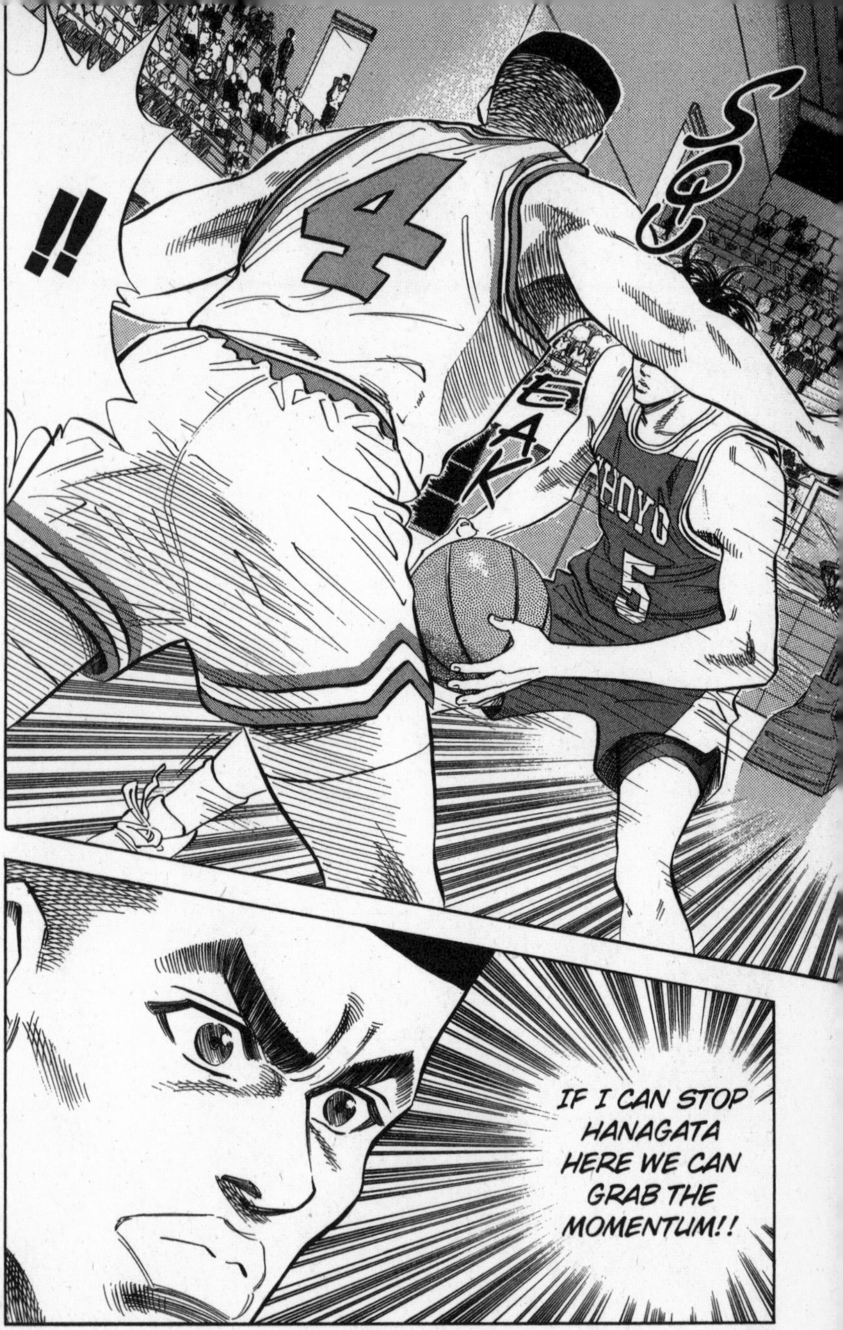
SQU
EAK
!!
IF I CAN STOP HANAGATA HERE WE CAN GRAB THE MOMENTUM!!

READ THIS WAY

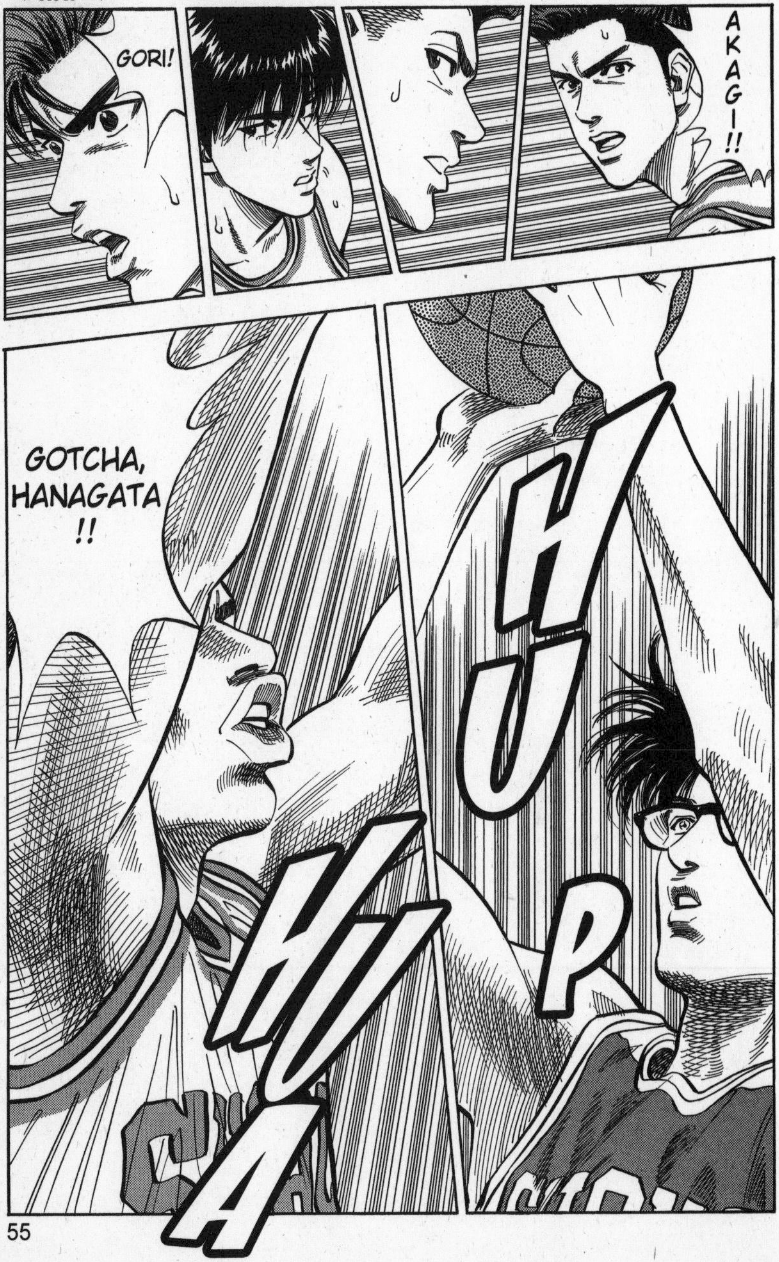
AKAGI!!
GORI!
HUP
GOTCHA, HANAGATA!!
HUA

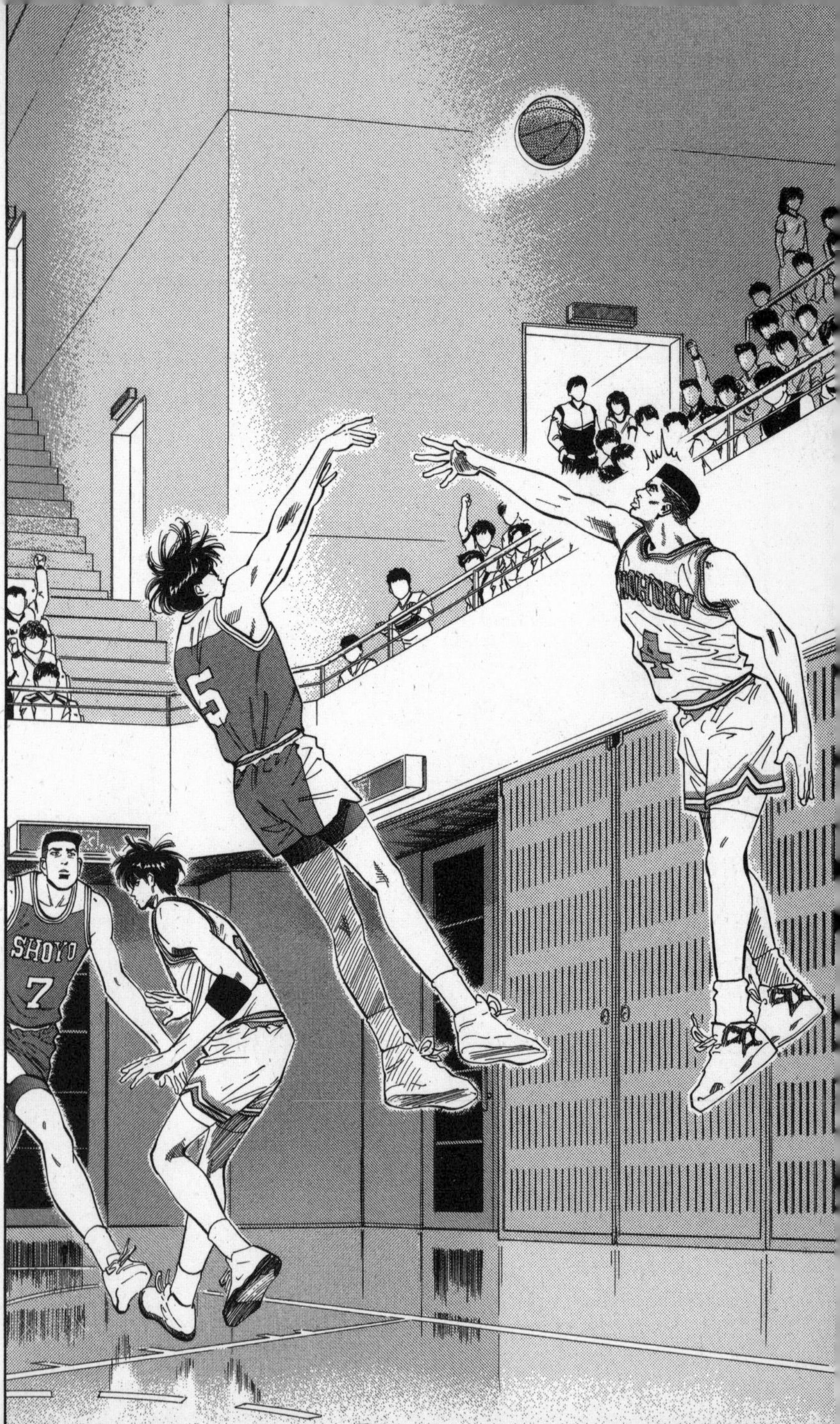
SHOYO
7

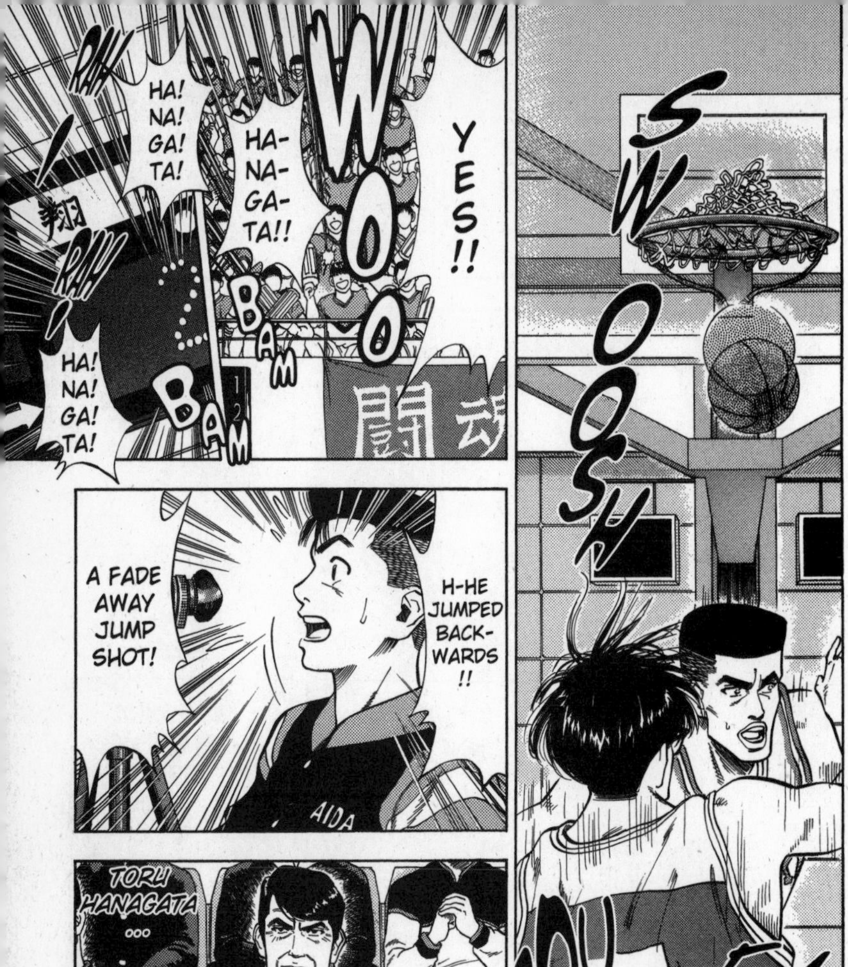
SWOOSH
SQUEAK
YES!!
WOO
HA-NA-GA-TA!!
BAM BAM
HA! NA! GA! TA!
RAH! RAH!
HA! NA! GA! TA!
H-HE JUMPED BACKWARDS!!
A FADE AWAY JUMP SHOT!
AIDA
TORU HANAGATA...

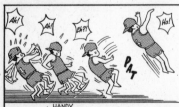

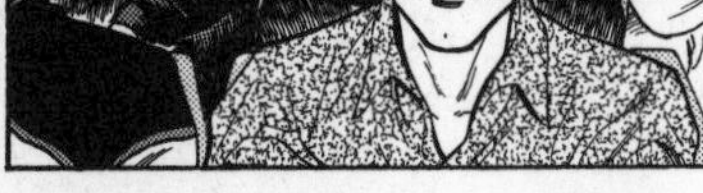
Ah!
Ah!
Eh?!
Ha!
PAT

FADE AWAY JUMP SHOT

A SHOT TAKEN WHILE JUMPING BACKWARDS. THIS TECHNIQUE HELPS AVOID DEFENDERS. LEAN TOO FAR BACK, HOWEVER, AND YOU'LL LOSE YOUR GROUND AS WELL AS YOUR BALANCE.

DR. T'S HANDY BASKETBALL TIPS

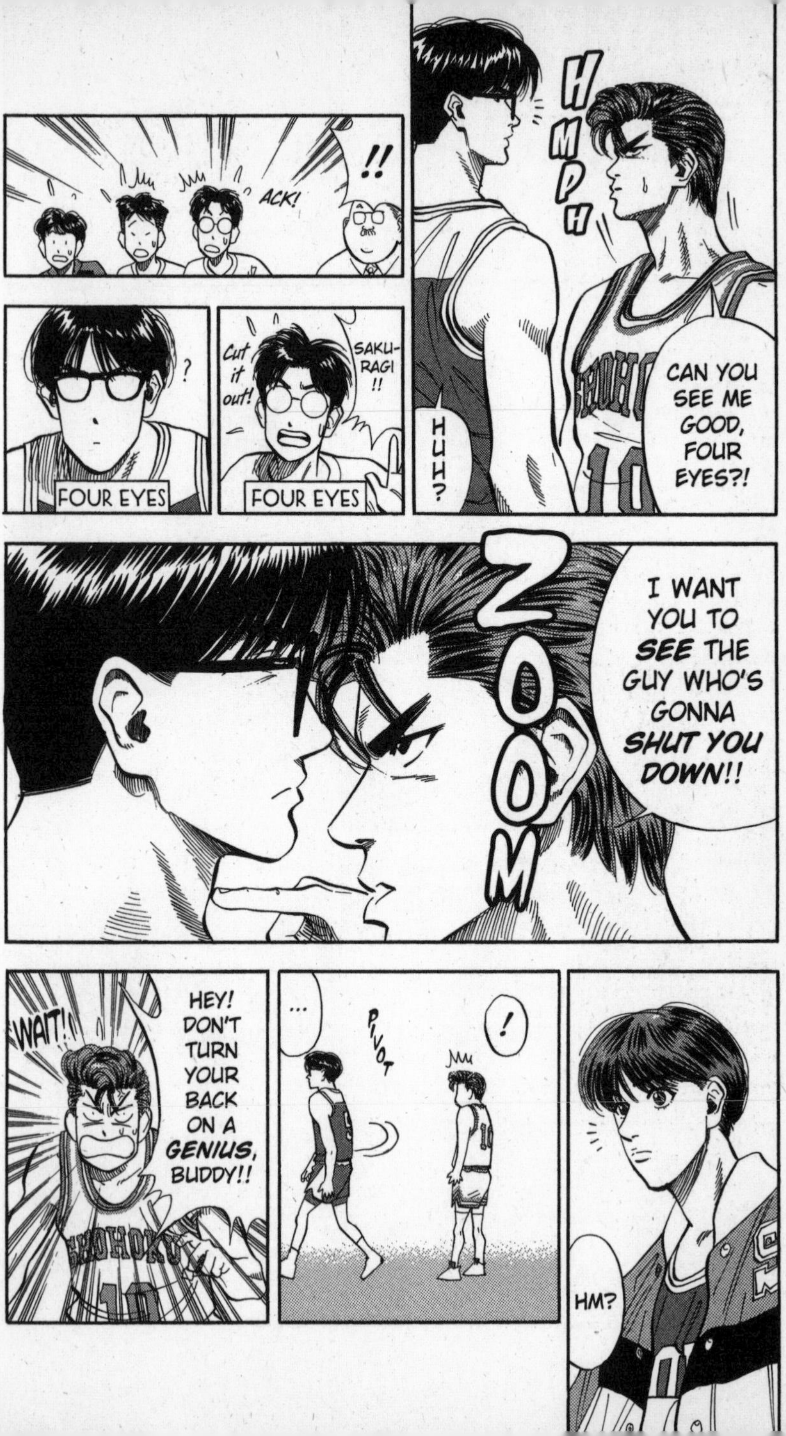

HMPH
CAN YOU SEE ME GOOD, FOUR EYES?!
HUH?
!!
ACK!
SAKU-RAGI!!
Cut it out!
FOUR EYES
?
FOUR EYES
ZOOM
I WANT YOU TO SEE THE GUY WHO'S GONNA SHUT YOU DOWN!!
!
HM?
...
PIVOT
HEY! DON'T TURN YOUR BACK ON A GENIUS, BUDDY!!
WAIT!!

READ THIS WAY

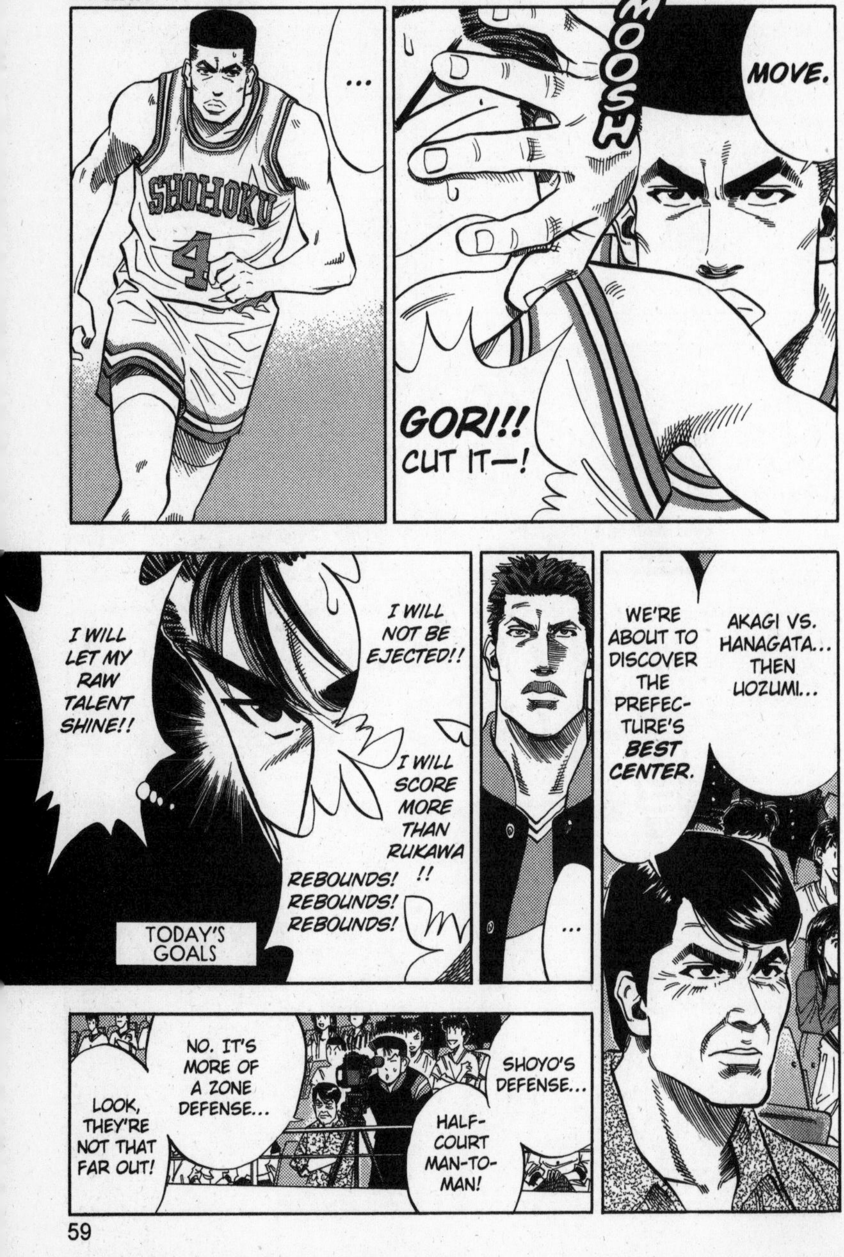
SMOOSH
MOVE.
GORI!! CUT IT—!
...
AKAGI VS. HANAGATA... THEN UOZUMI...
WE'RE ABOUT TO DISCOVER THE PREFECTURE'S BEST CENTER.
...
I WILL NOT BE EJECTED!!
I WILL LET MY RAW TALENT SHINE!!
I WILL SCORE MORE THAN RUKAWA!!
REBOUNDS! REBOUNDS! REBOUNDS!
TODAY'S GOALS
SHOYO'S DEFENSE...
HALF-COURT MAN-TO-MAN!
NO. IT'S MORE OF A ZONE DEFENSE...
LOOK, THEY'RE NOT THAT FAR OUT!

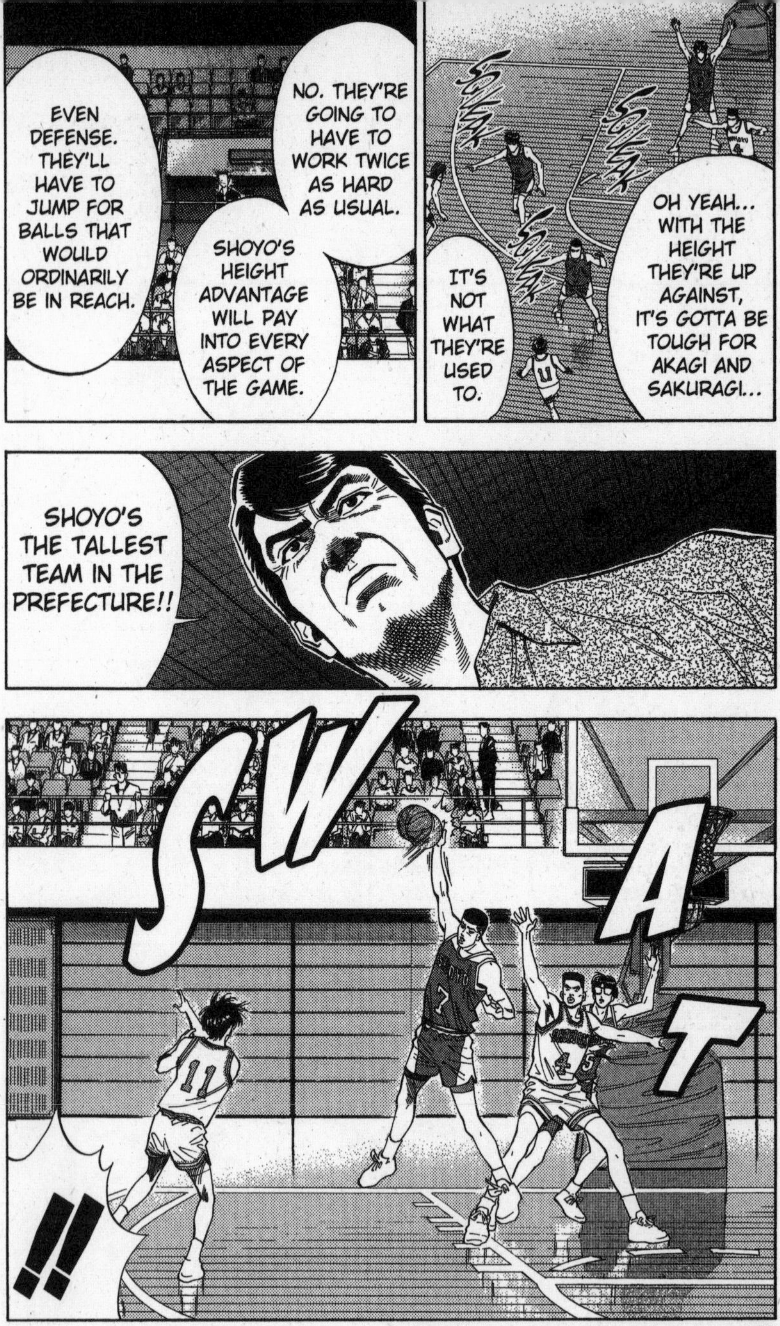
OH YEAH... WITH THE HEIGHT THEY'RE UP AGAINST, IT'S GOTTA BE TOUGH FOR AKAGI AND SAKURAGI...
IT'S NOT WHAT THEY'RE USED TO.
NO. THEY'RE GOING TO HAVE TO WORK TWICE AS HARD AS USUAL.
SHOYO'S HEIGHT ADVANTAGE WILL PAY INTO EVERY ASPECT OF THE GAME.
EVEN DEFENSE. THEY'LL HAVE TO JUMP FOR BALLS THAT WOULD ORDINARILY BE IN REACH.
SHOYO'S THE TALLEST TEAM IN THE PREFECTURE!!
SWAT
!!

READ THIS WAY

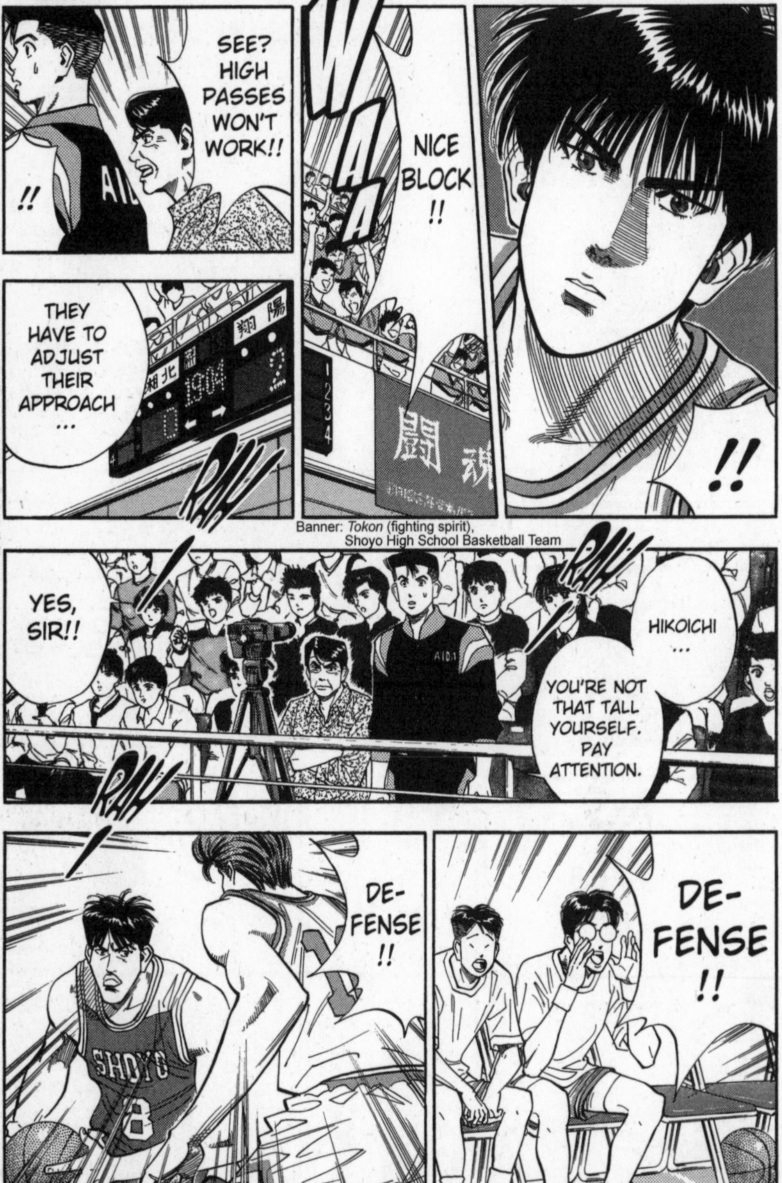
!!
WAAA
NICE BLOCK!!
SEE? HIGH PASSES WON'T WORK!!
!!
THEY HAVE TO ADJUST THEIR APPROACH...
RAH
RAH
HIKOICHI...
YOU'RE NOT THAT TALL YOURSELF. PAY ATTENTION.
YES, SIR!!
RAH
DE-FENSE!!
DE-FENSE!!

Scoreboard: Shohoku 1st Half 2nd Half Shoyo

Banner: *Tokon* (fighting spirit), Shoyo High School Basketball Team

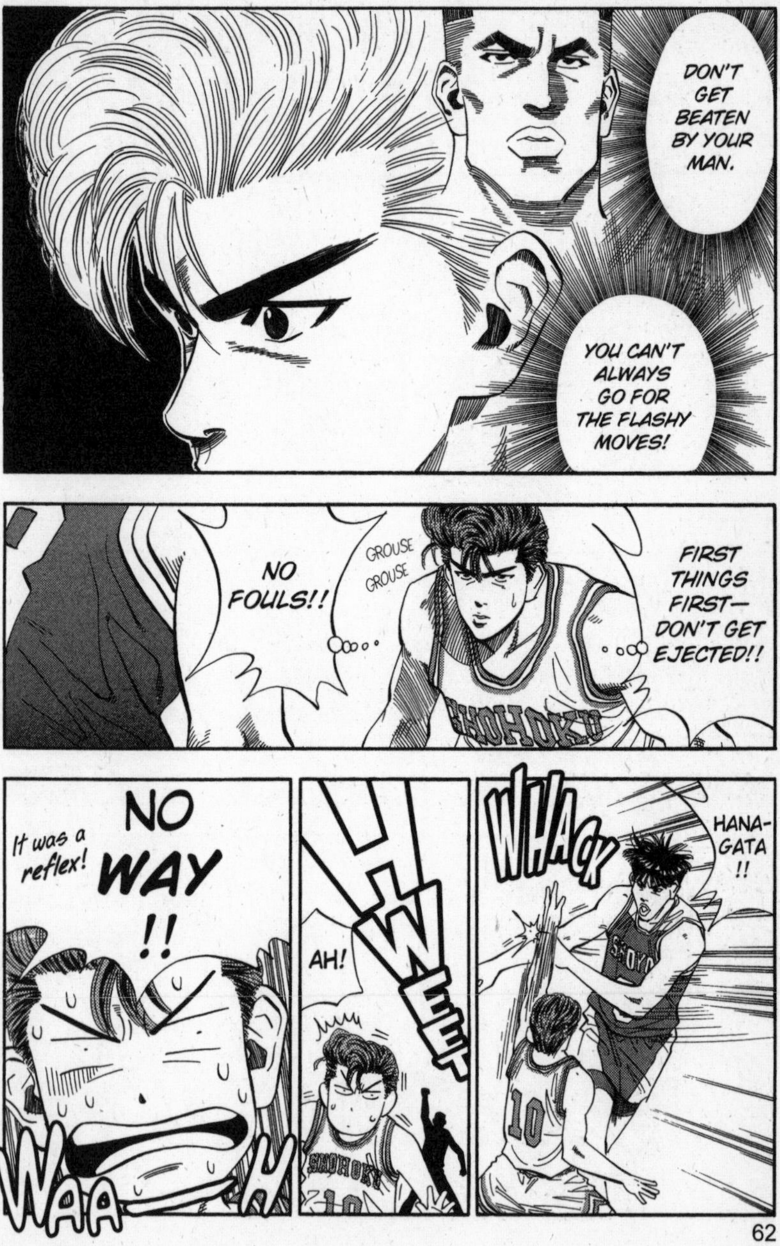
DON'T GET BEATEN BY YOUR MAN.
YOU CAN'T ALWAYS GO FOR THE FLASHY MOVES!
FIRST THINGS FIRST— DON'T GET EJECTED!!
GROUSE GROUSE
NO FOULS!!
HANA-GATA !!
WHACK
FWEET
AH!
NO WAY !!
It was a reflex!
WAAH

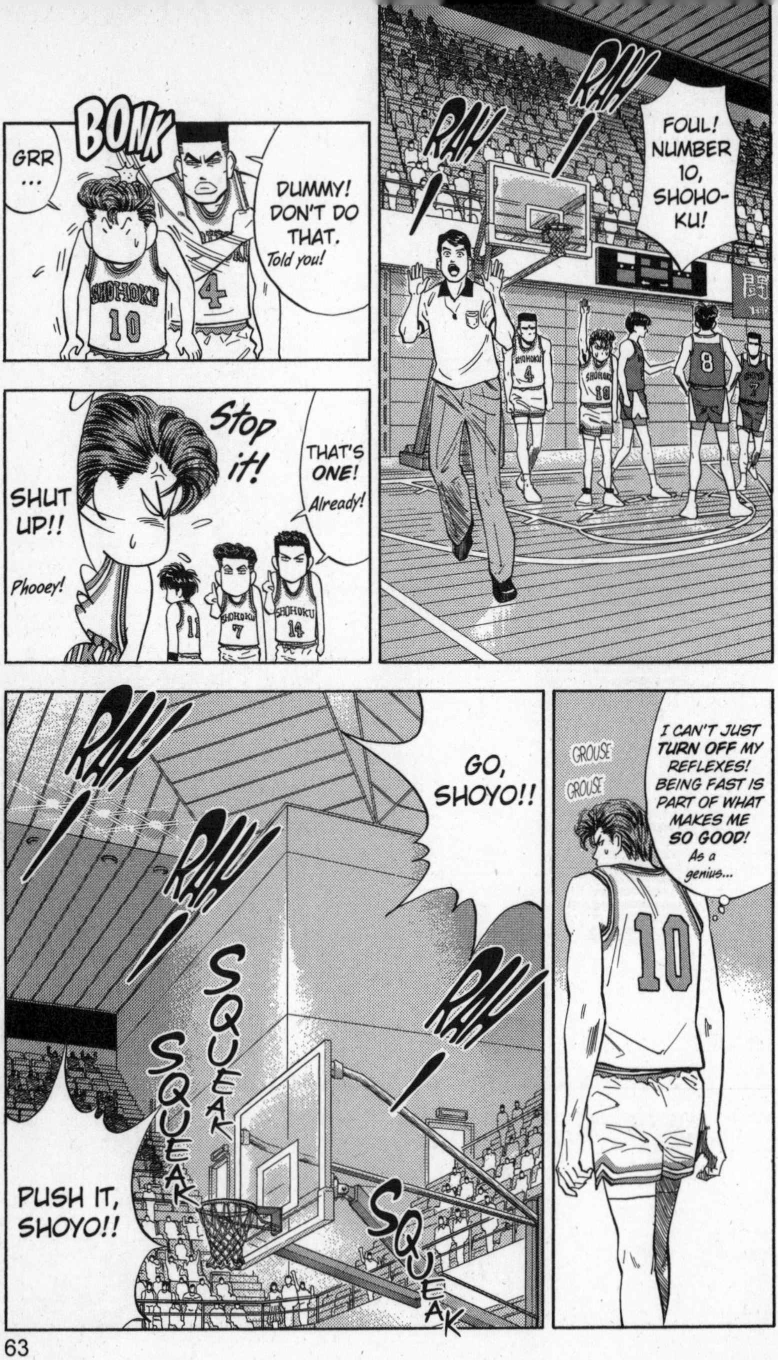
RAH!
RAH!
FOUL! NUMBER 10, SHOHOKU!
BONK
DUMMY! DON'T DO THAT.
Told you!
GRR ...
THAT'S ONE!
Already!
Stop it!
SHUT UP!!
Phooey!
GROUSE
GROUSE
I CAN'T JUST TURN OFF MY REFLEXES! BEING FAST IS PART OF WHAT MAKES ME SO GOOD!
As a genius...
RAH!
RAH!
GO, SHOYO!!
SQUEAK
SQUEAK
RAH!
SQUEAK
PUSH IT, SHOYO!!

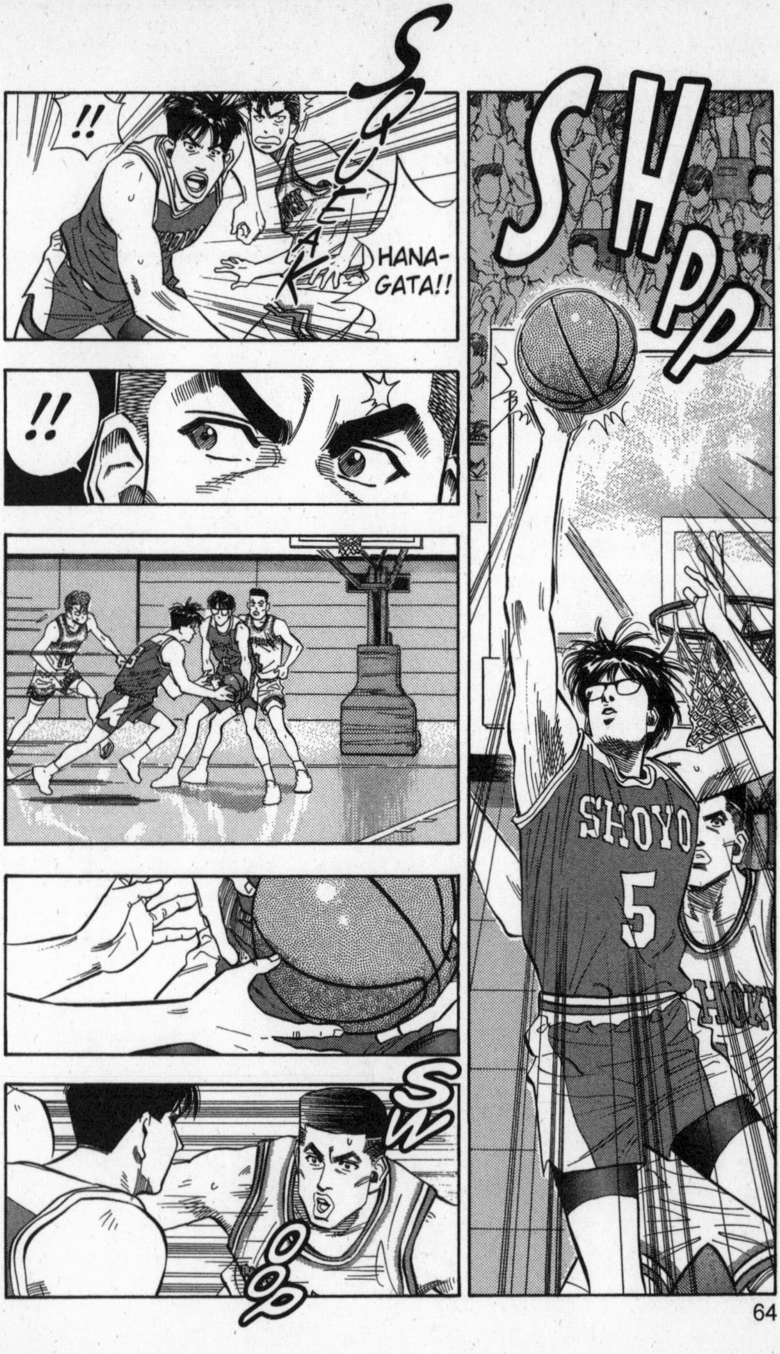
SHPP
SQUEAK
!!
HANA-GATA!!
!!
SWOOP

READ THIS WAY

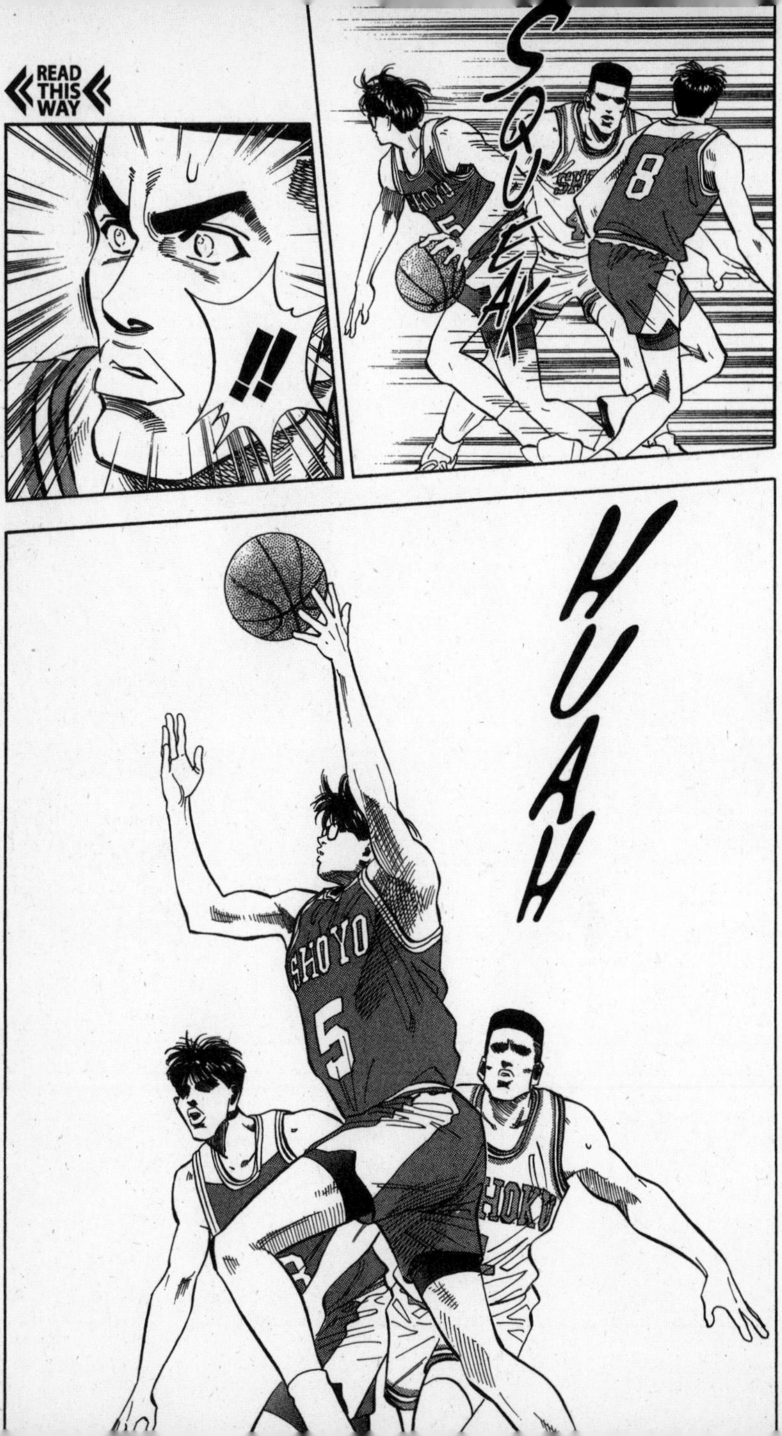
SQUEAK
!!
HUAAH

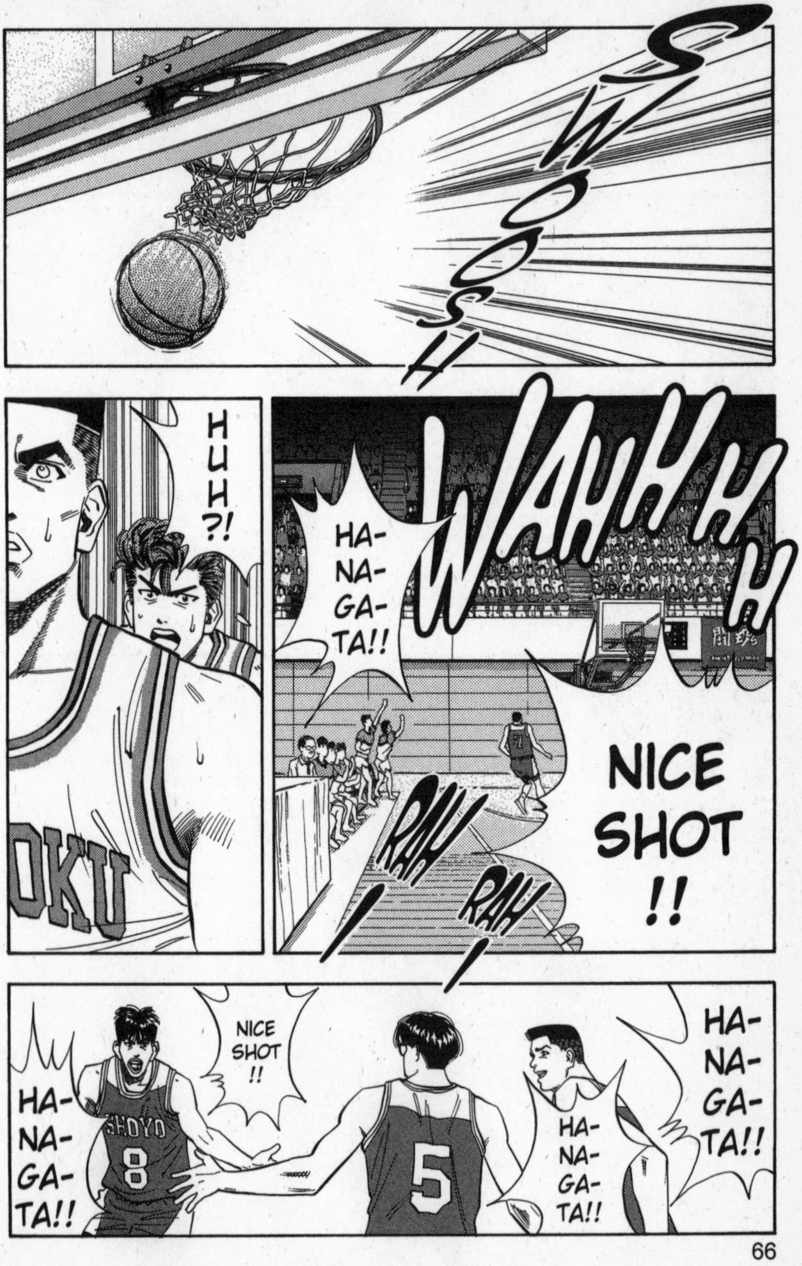
SWOOSH
WAHHHHH
HA-NA-GA-TA!!
NICE SHOT!!
RAH! RAH!
HUH?!
HA-NA-GA-TA!!
HA-NA-GA-TA!!
NICE SHOT!!
HA-NA-GA-TA!!

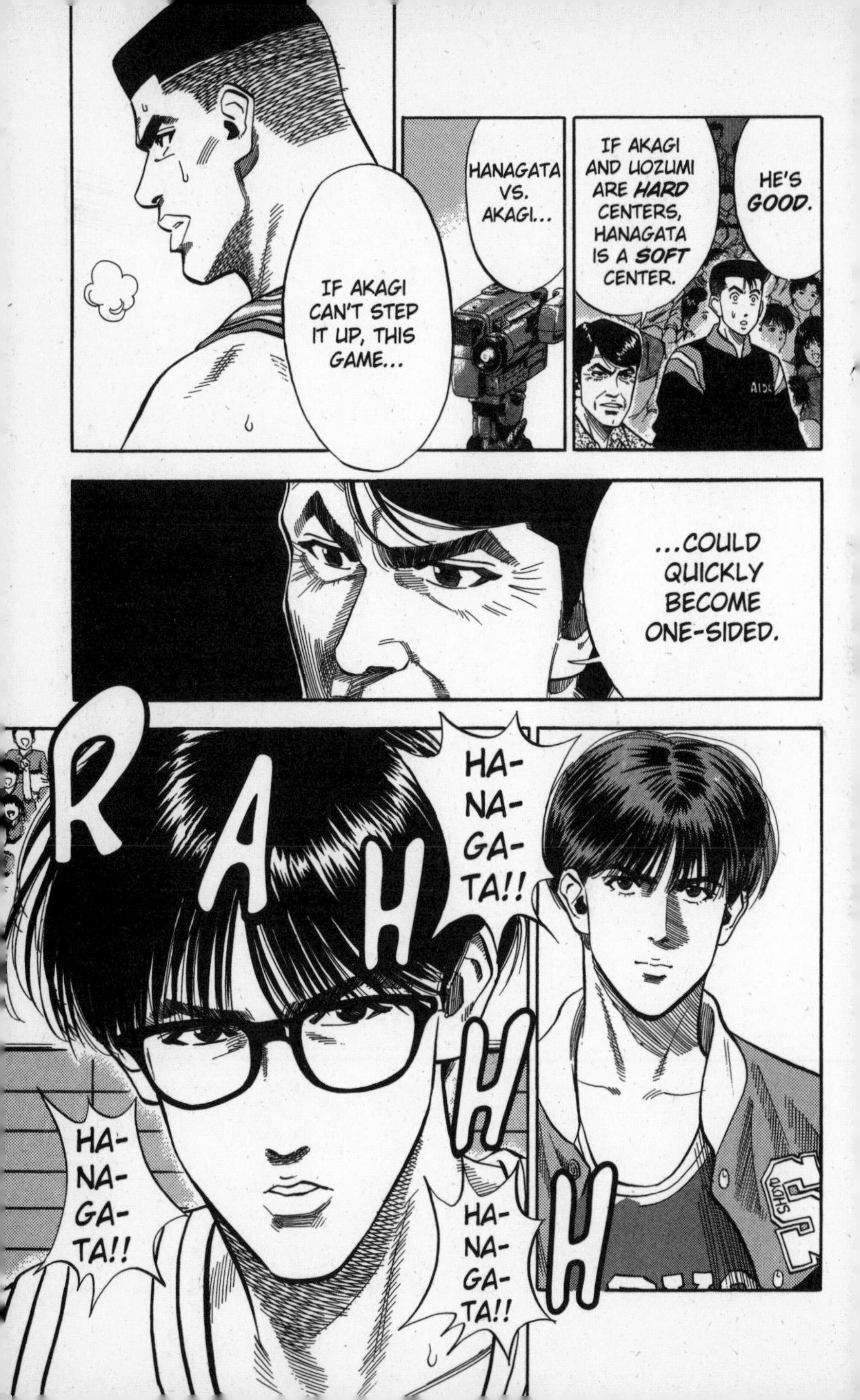
HE'S **GOOD**.
IF AKAGI AND UOZUMI ARE ***HARD*** CENTERS, HANAGATA IS A ***SOFT*** CENTER.
HANAGATA VS. AKAGI...
IF AKAGI CAN'T STEP IT UP, THIS GAME...
...COULD QUICKLY BECOME ONE-SIDED.
HA-NA-GA-TA!!
HA-NA-GA-TA!!
RAHHHH
HA-NA-GA-TA!!

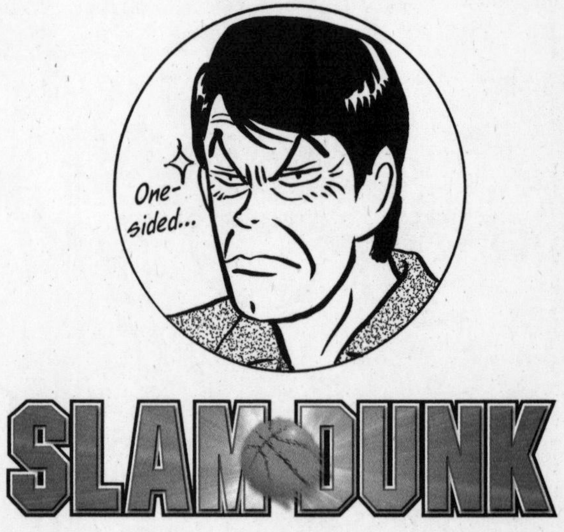
One-sided...

SLAM DUNK

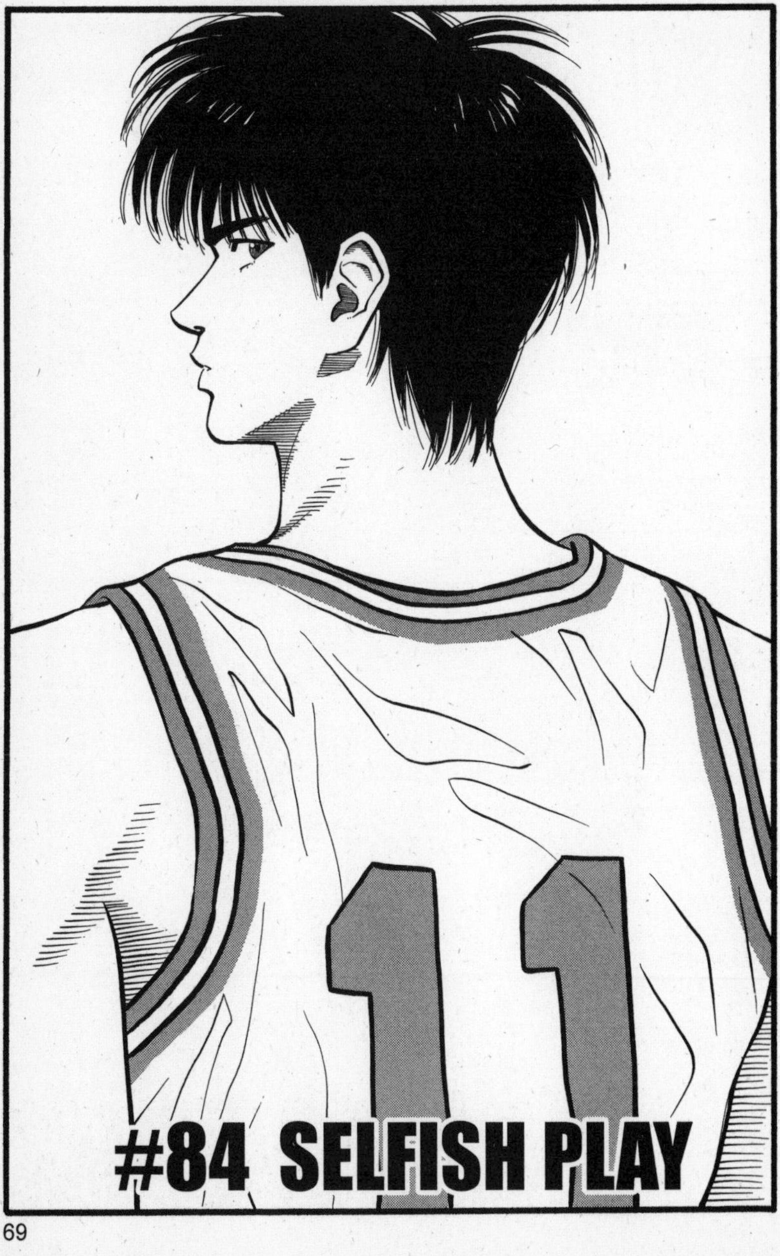
#84 SELFISH PLAY

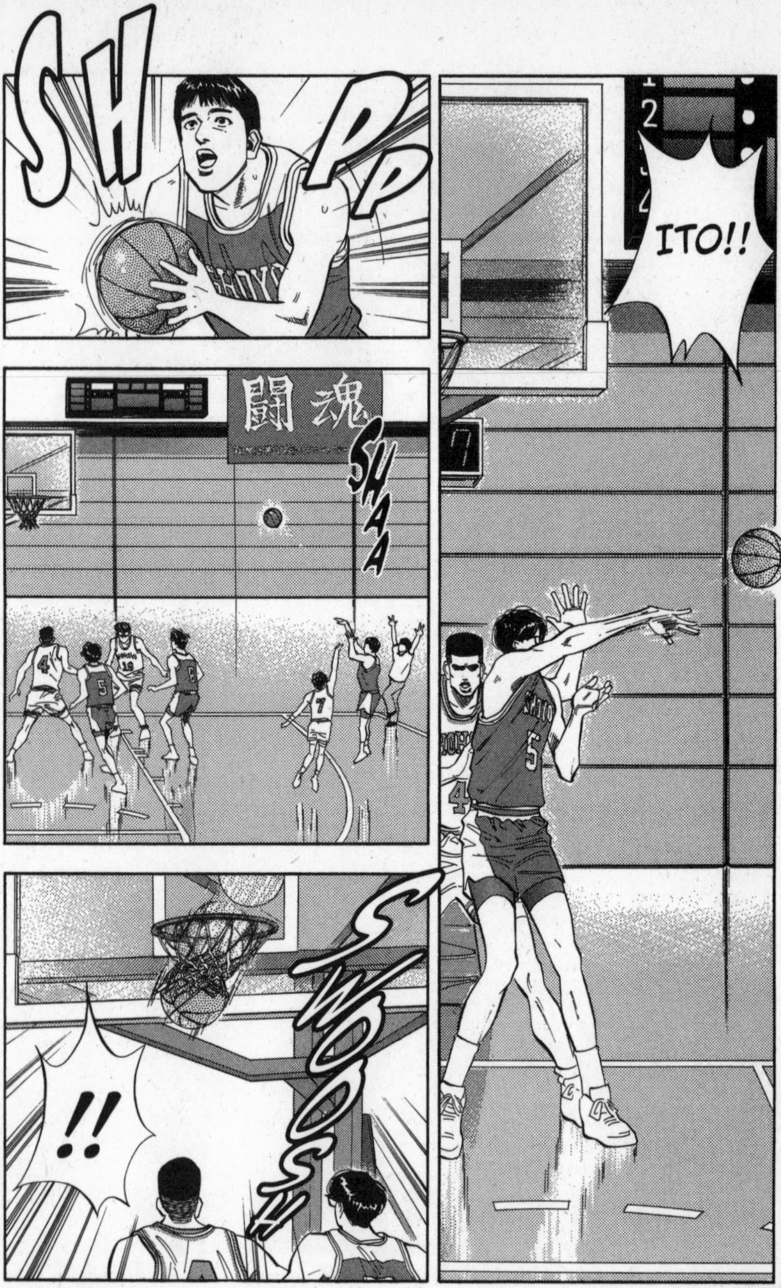
ITO!!
SHPP
闘魂
SHAA
SWOOSH
!!

READ THIS WAY

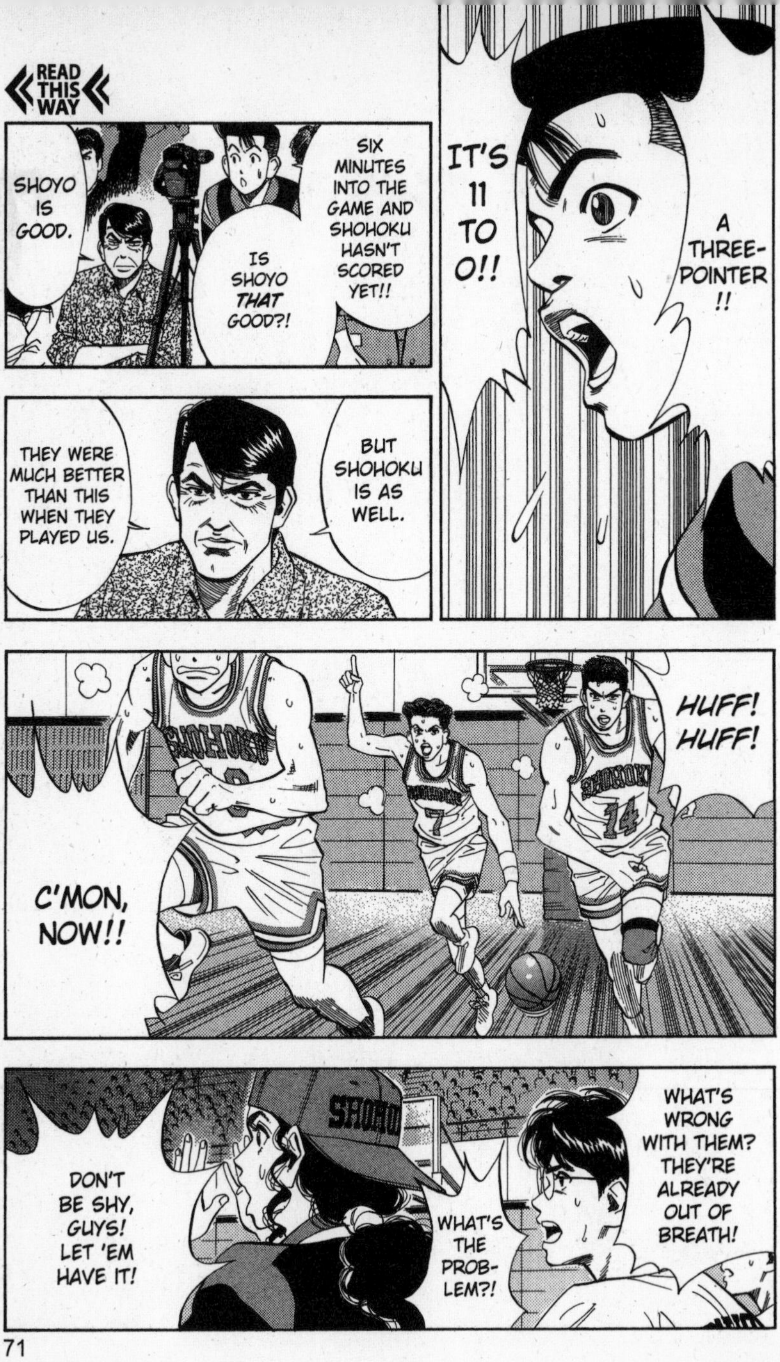
A THREE-POINTER!!
IT'S 11 TO 0!!
SIX MINUTES INTO THE GAME AND SHOHOKU HASN'T SCORED YET!!
IS SHOYO *THAT* GOOD?!
SHOYO IS GOOD.
BUT SHOHOKU IS AS WELL.
THEY WERE MUCH BETTER THAN THIS WHEN THEY PLAYED US.
HUFF! HUFF!
C'MON, NOW!!
WHAT'S WRONG WITH THEM? THEY'RE ALREADY OUT OF BREATH!
WHAT'S THE PROB-LEM?!
DON'T BE SHY, GUYS! LET 'EM HAVE IT!

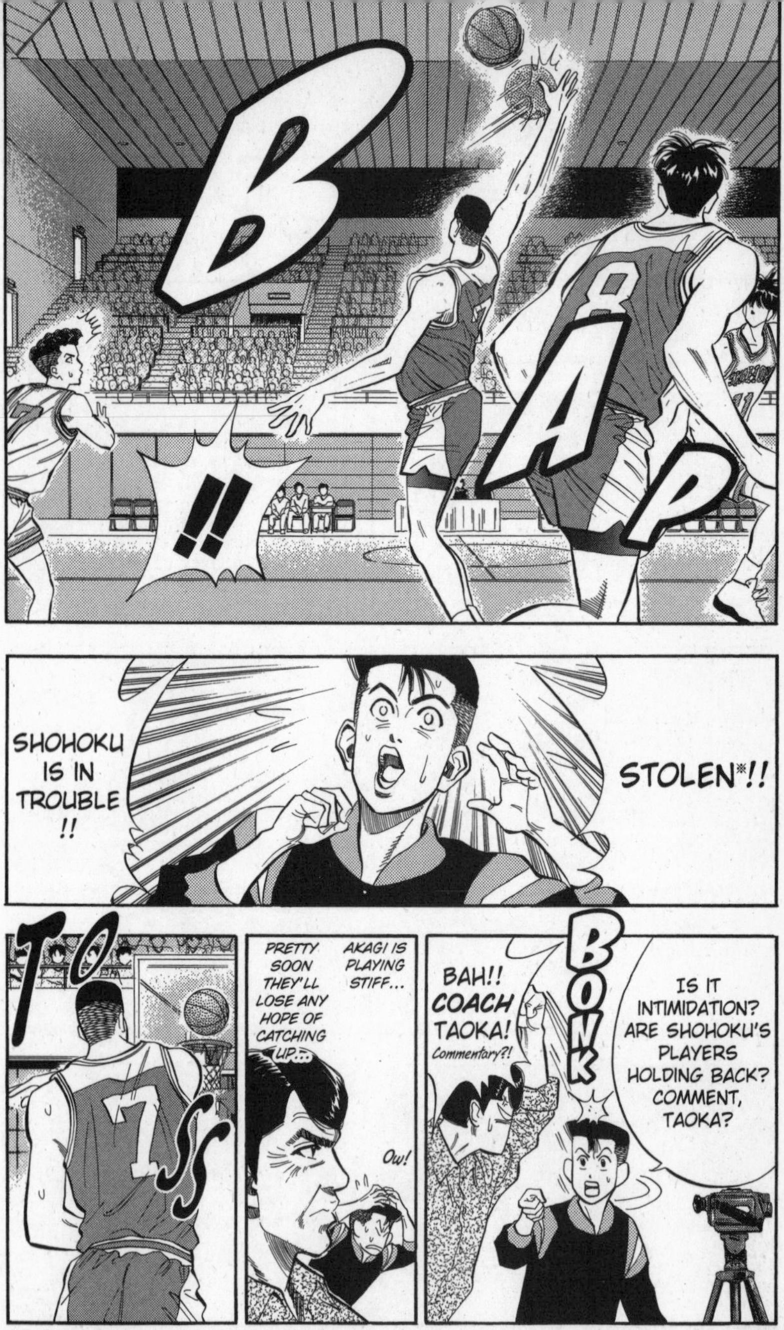
BAP
!!
STOLEN※!!
SHOHOKU IS IN TROUBLE !!
BONK
IS IT INTIMIDATION? ARE SHOHOKU'S PLAYERS HOLDING BACK? COMMENT, TAOKA?
BAH!! COACH TAOKA! Commentary?!
AKAGI IS PLAYING STIFF...
PRETTY SOON THEY'LL LOSE ANY HOPE OF CATCHING UP...
Ow!
TOSS

※ To Steal = To take possession of the ball by intercepting a pass or knocking the ball away during a dribble.

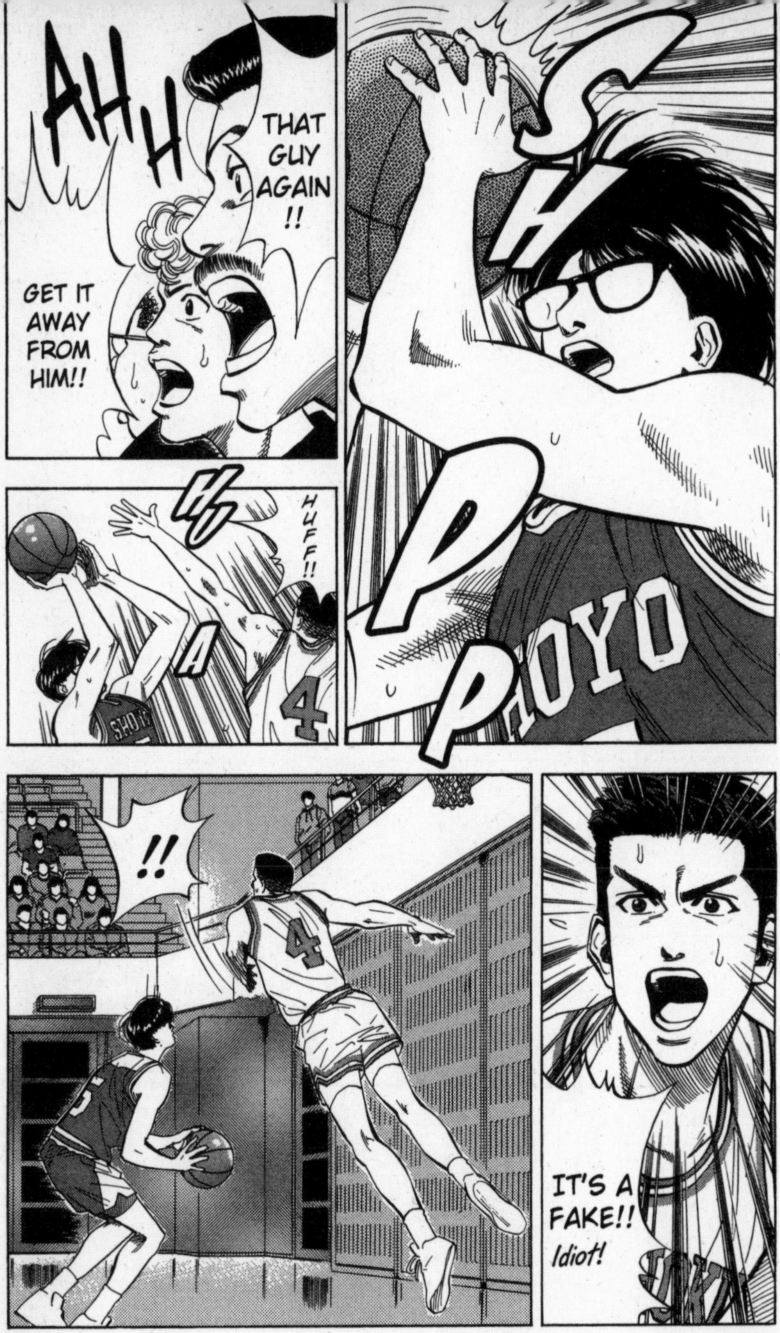
SH
PP
SHOYO
THAT GUY AGAIN!!
AHH
GET IT AWAY FROM HIM!!
HUFF!!
HA
SHOYO
IT'S A FAKE!!
Idiot!
!!

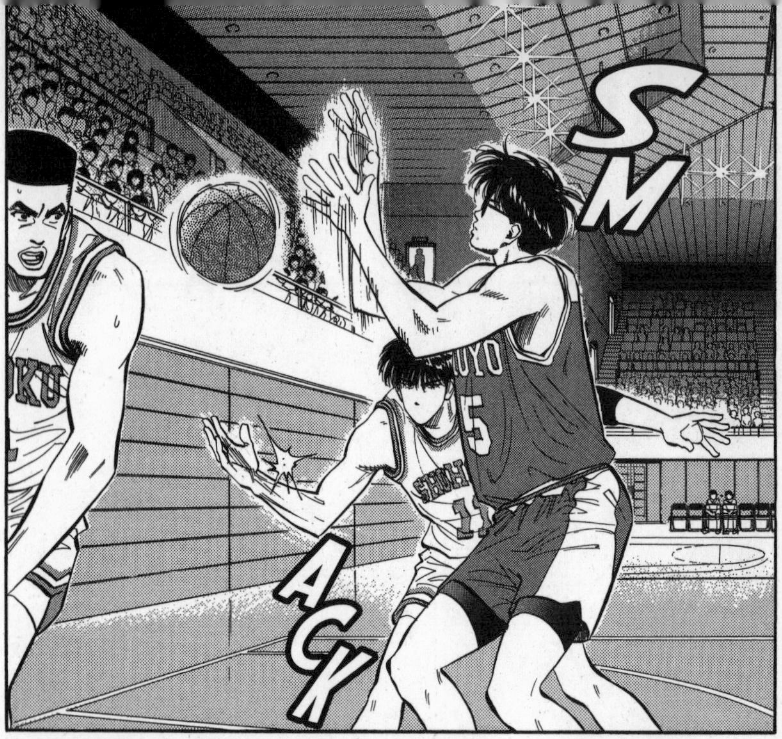
SMACK
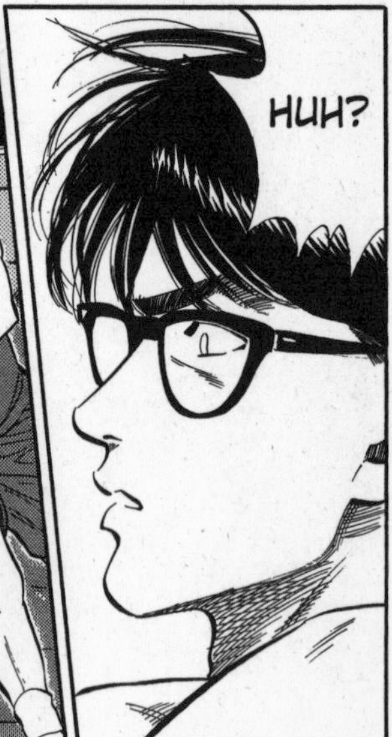
HUH?
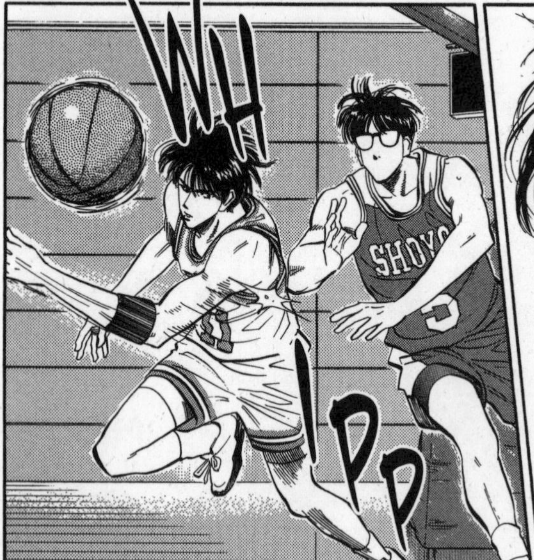
WHIPP
SHOYO

READ THIS WAY

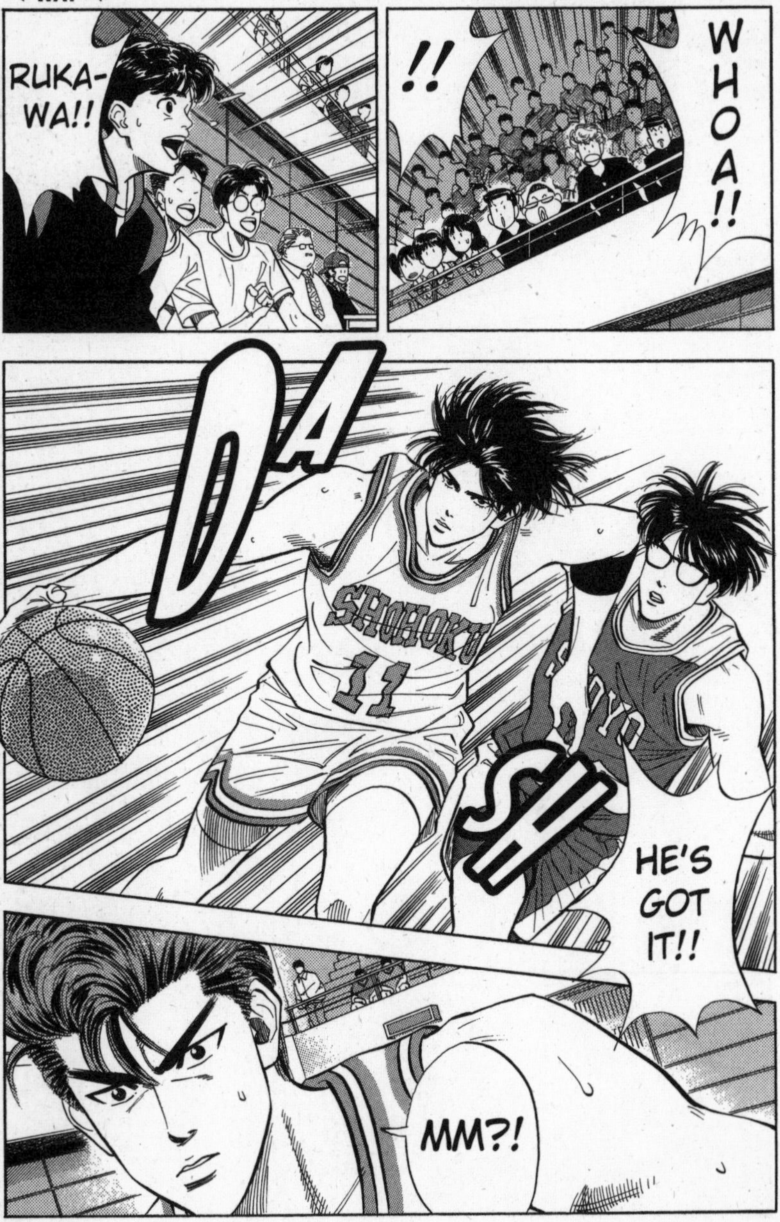

!!
WHOA!!
RUKA-WA!!
DA
SH
HE'S GOT IT!!
MM?!

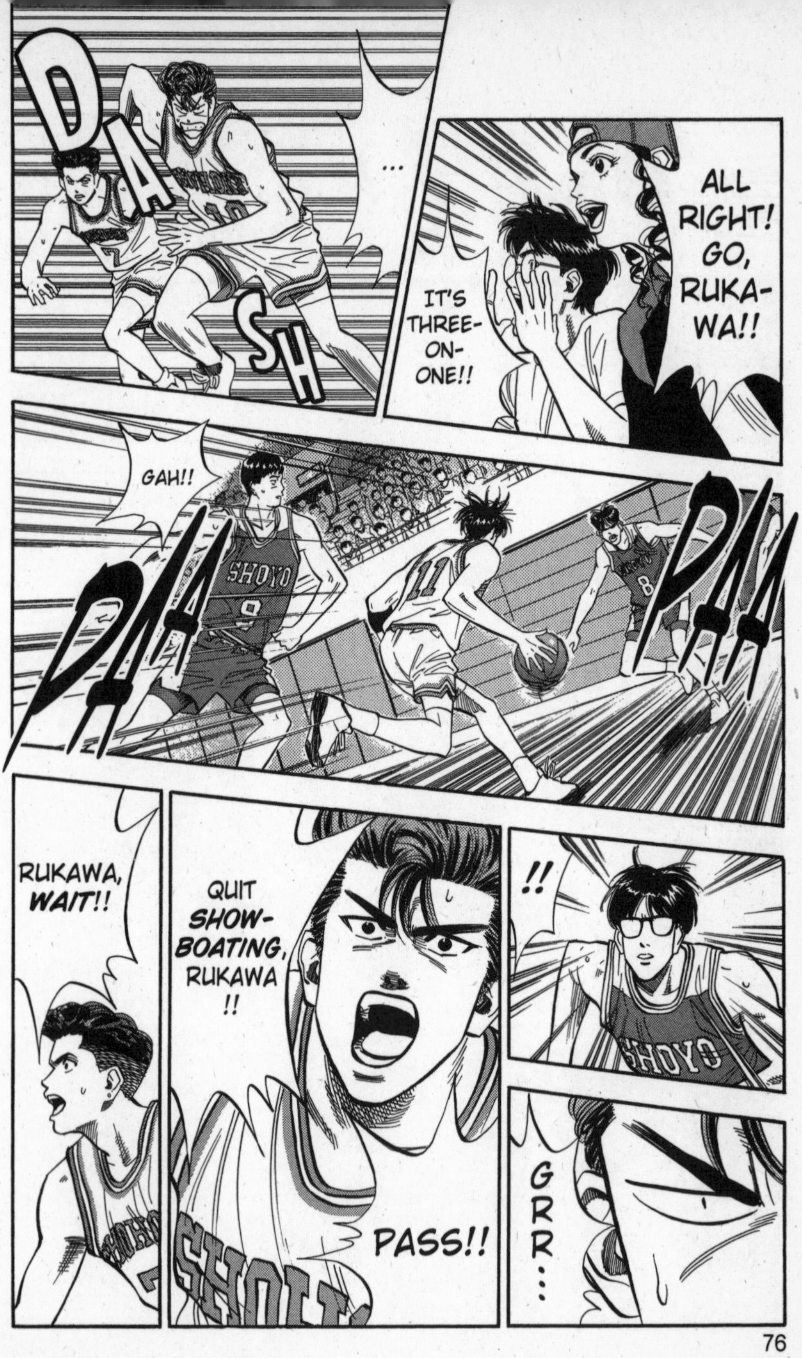
ALL RIGHT! GO, RUKAWA!!
IT'S THREE-ON-ONE!!
...
DASH
GAH!!
DAA
DAA
!!
GRR...
QUIT SHOWBOATING, RUKAWA!!
PASS!!
RUKAWA, WAIT!!

READ THIS WAY

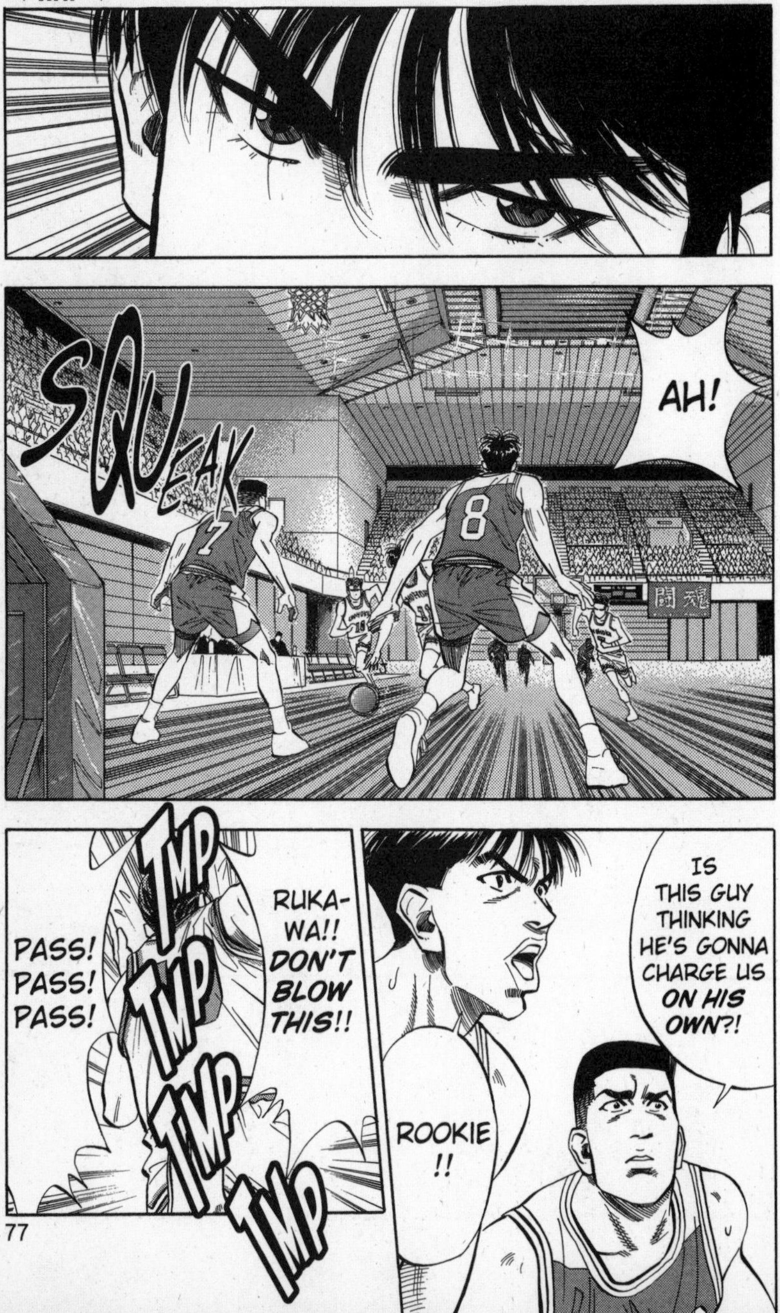
AH!
SQUEAK
IS THIS GUY THINKING HE'S GONNA CHARGE US ON HIS OWN?!
ROOKIE!!
RUKA-WA!! DON'T BLOW THIS!!
PASS! PASS! PASS!
TMP TMP TMP TMP

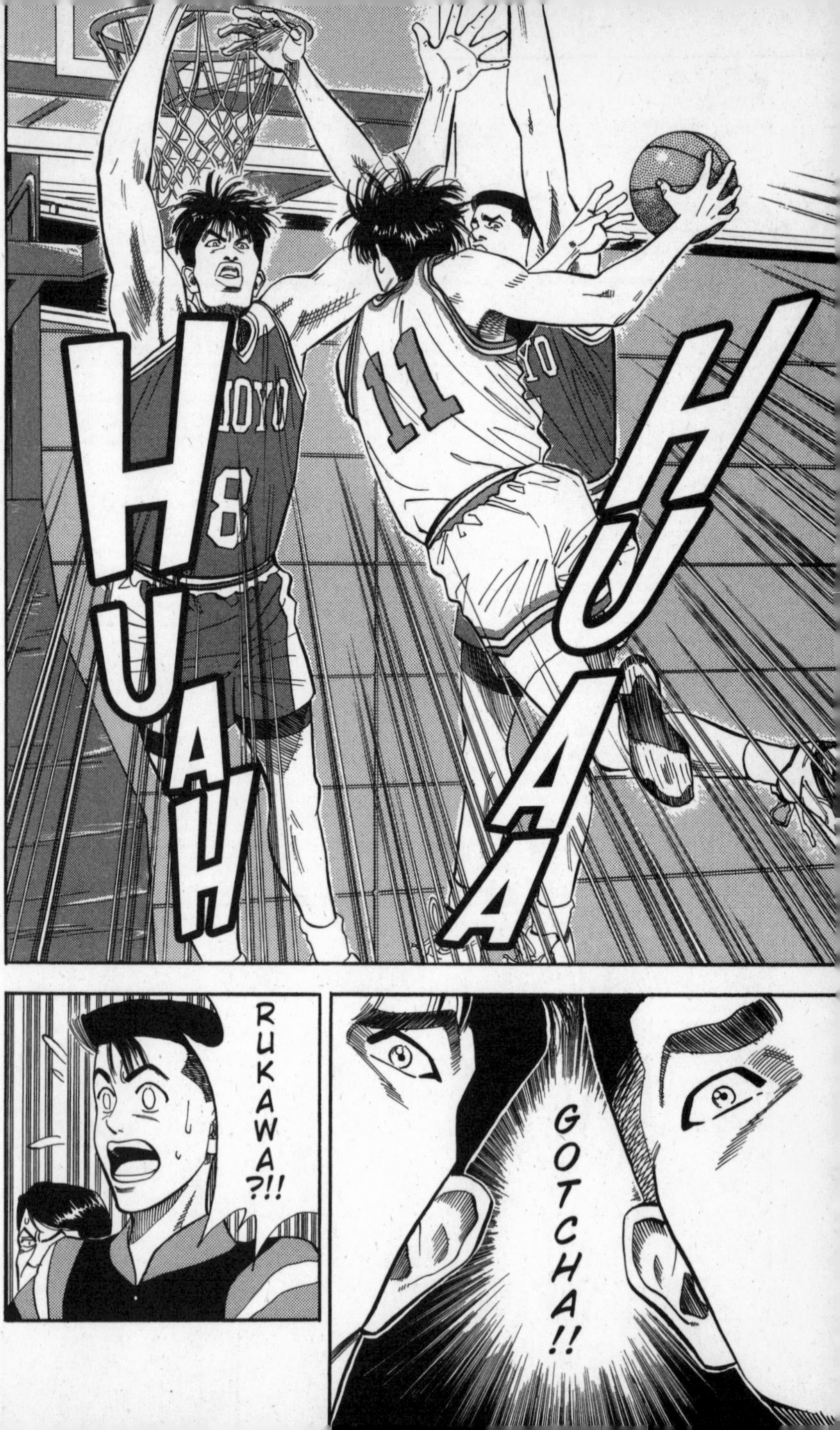
HUAAA
HUAUH
GOTCHA!!
RUKAWA?!!

READ THIS WAY

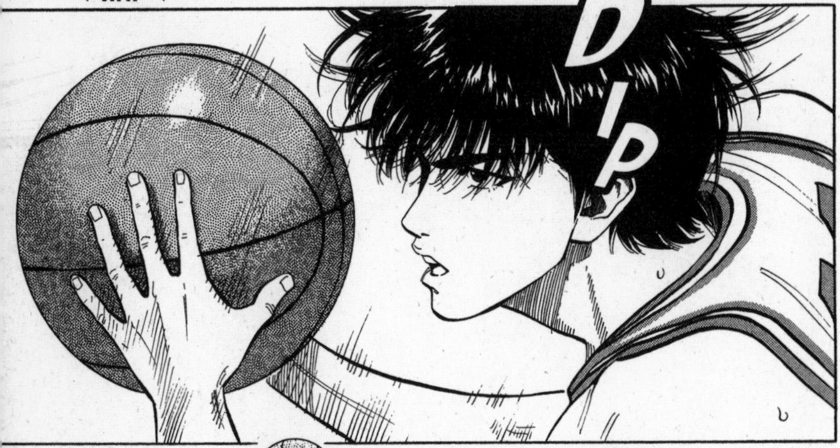
DIP

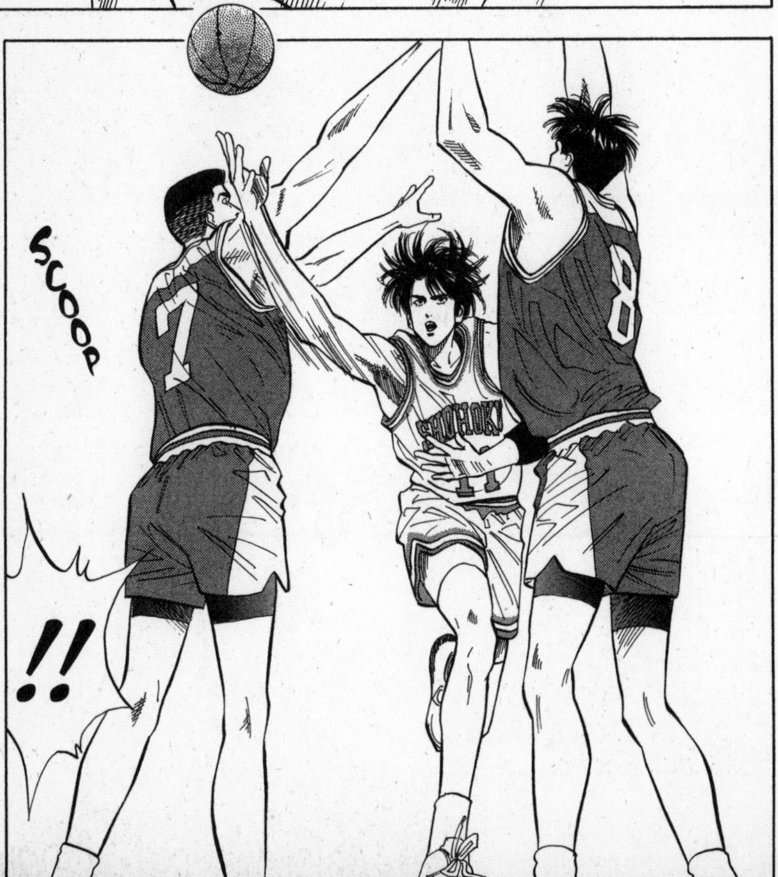
SCOOP
!!

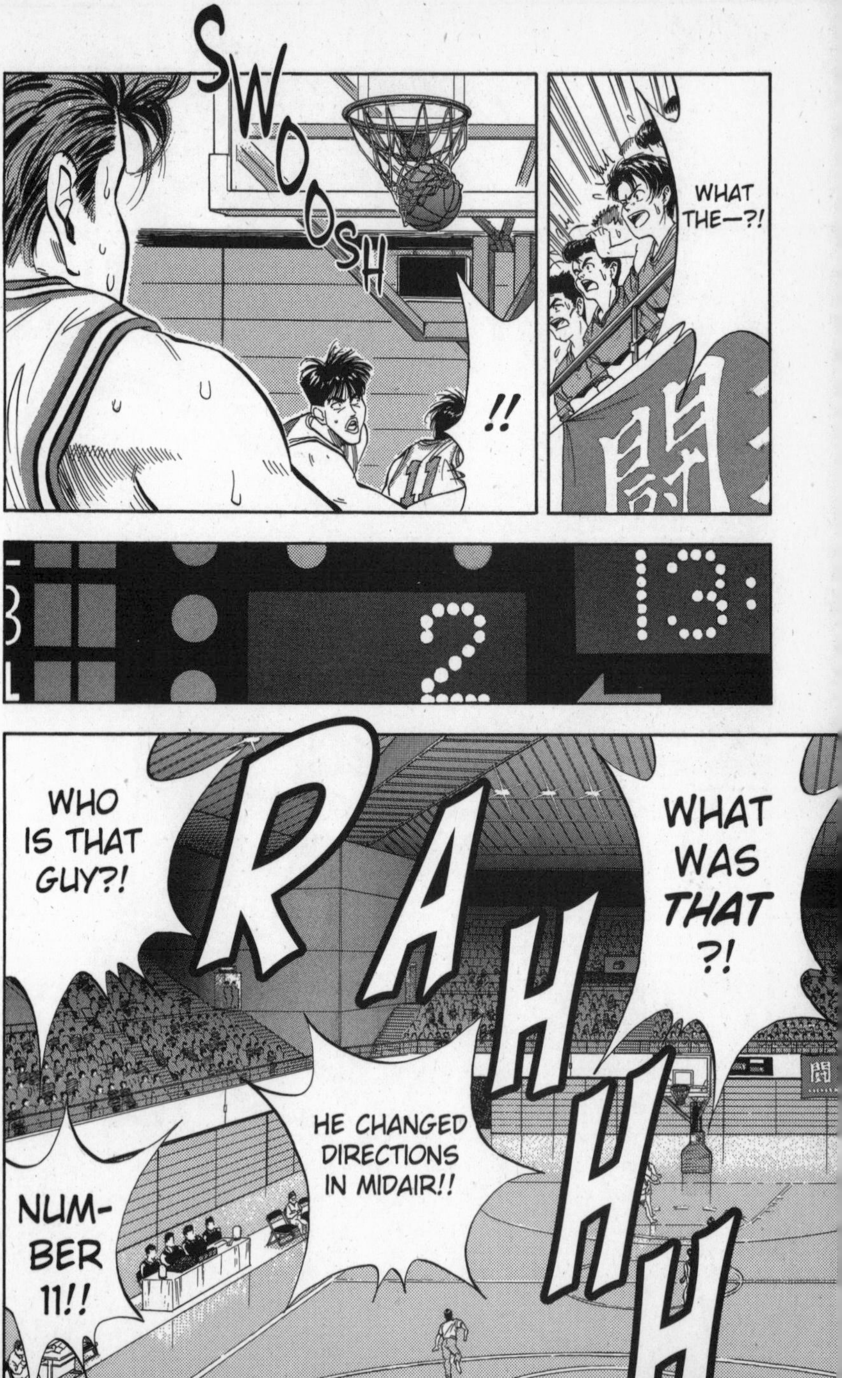
WHAT THE—?!
SWOOSH
!!
13:
2
WHAT WAS THAT?!
RAHHHHH
WHO IS THAT GUY?!
HE CHANGED DIRECTIONS IN MIDAIR!!
NUMBER 11!!

READ THIS WAY

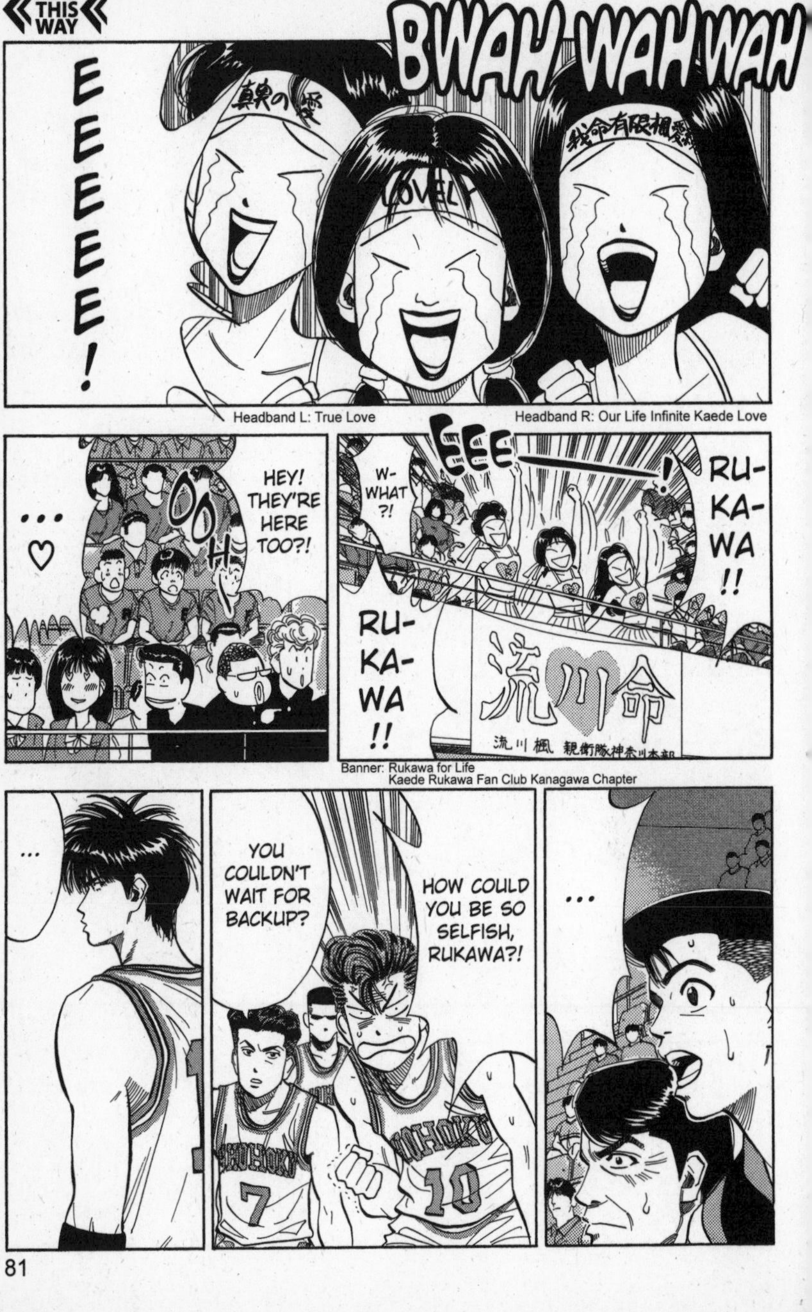
BWAH WAH WAH
EEEEEE!
Headband L: True Love
LOVELY
Headband R: Our Life Infinite Kaede Love
RU-KA-WA!!
EEE—!
W-WHAT?!
RU-KA-WA!!
流川命
流川楓 親衛隊神奈川本部
Banner: Rukawa for Life
Kaede Rukawa Fan Club Kanagawa Chapter
HEY! THEY'RE HERE TOO?!
OOH
...♡
...
HOW COULD YOU BE SO SELFISH, RUKAWA?!
YOU COULDN'T WAIT FOR BACKUP?
...

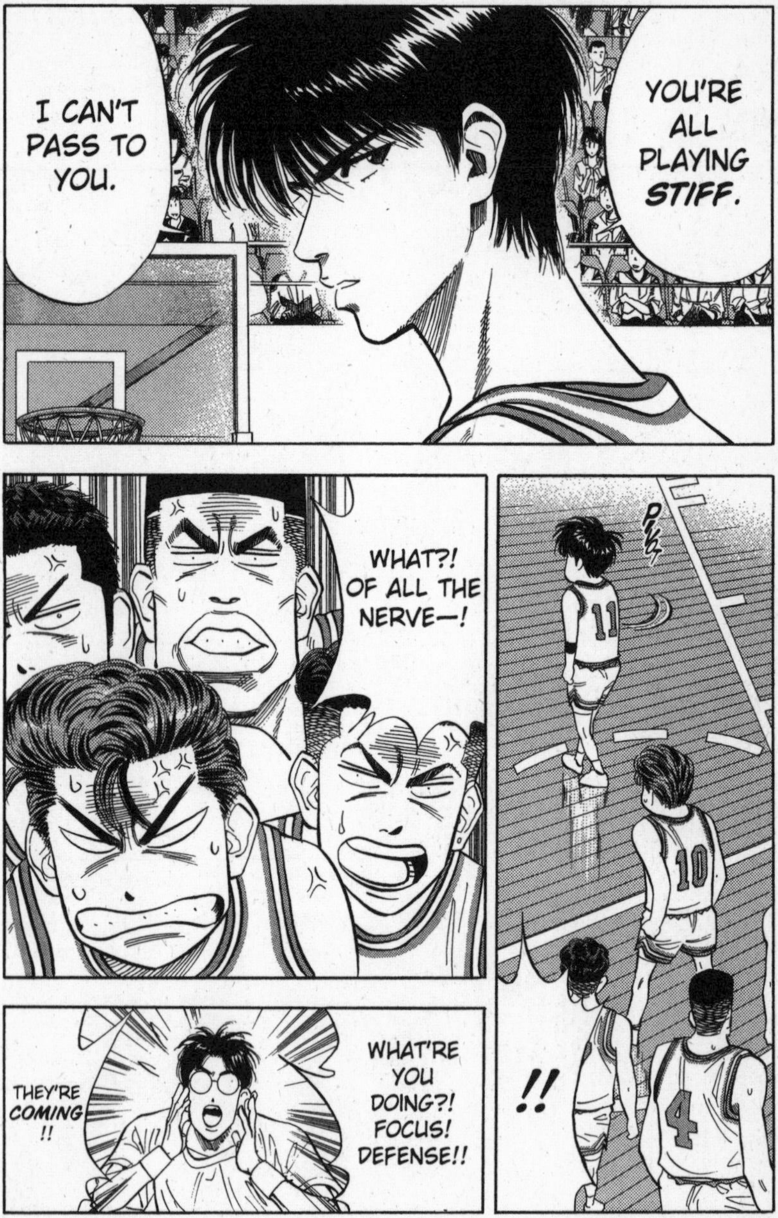
YOU'RE ALL PLAYING STIFF.
I CAN'T PASS TO YOU.
!!
WHAT?! OF ALL THE NERVE—!
WHAT'RE YOU DOING?! FOCUS! DEFENSE!!
THEY'RE COMING!!

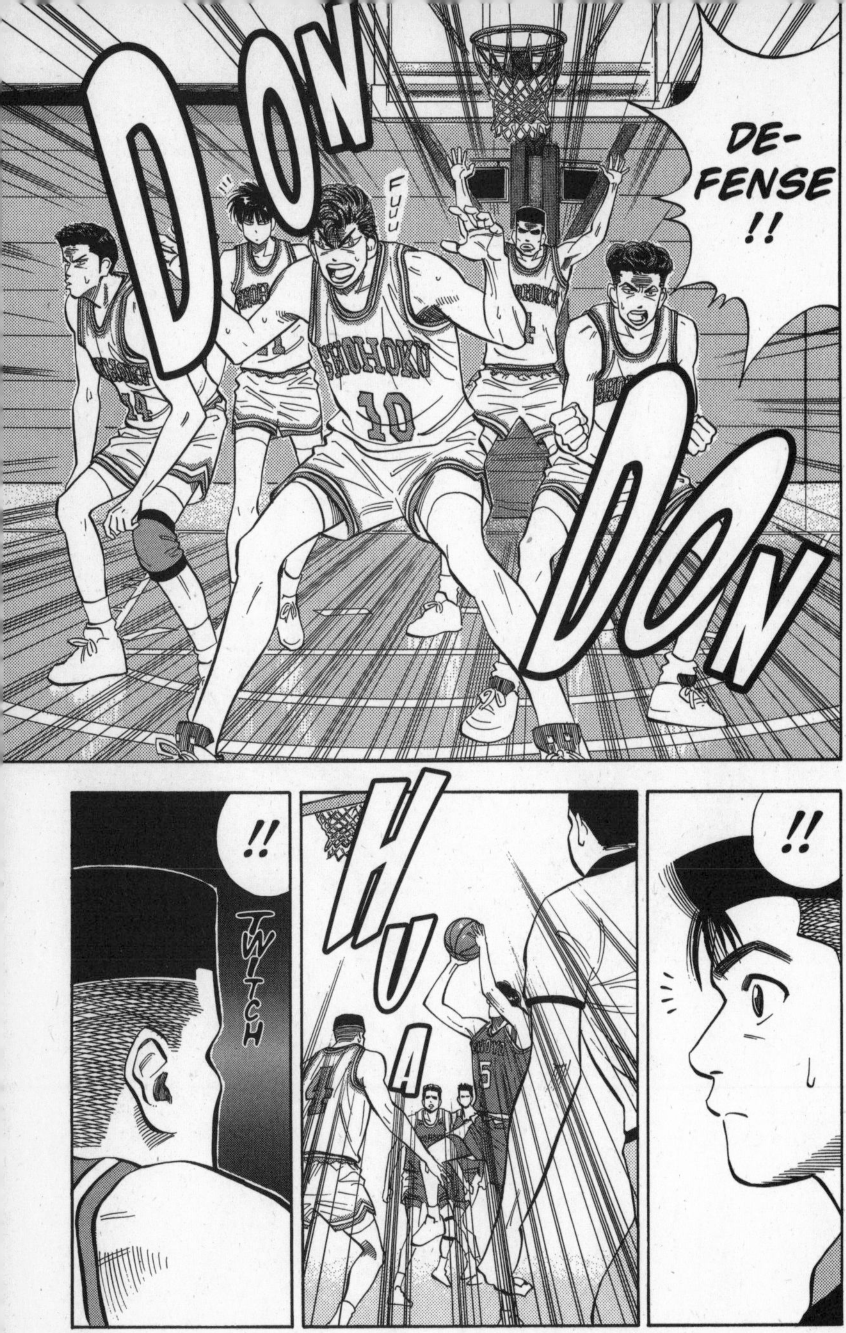
DE-
FENSE
!!
DON
FUUU
DON
!!
HUA
!!
TWITCH

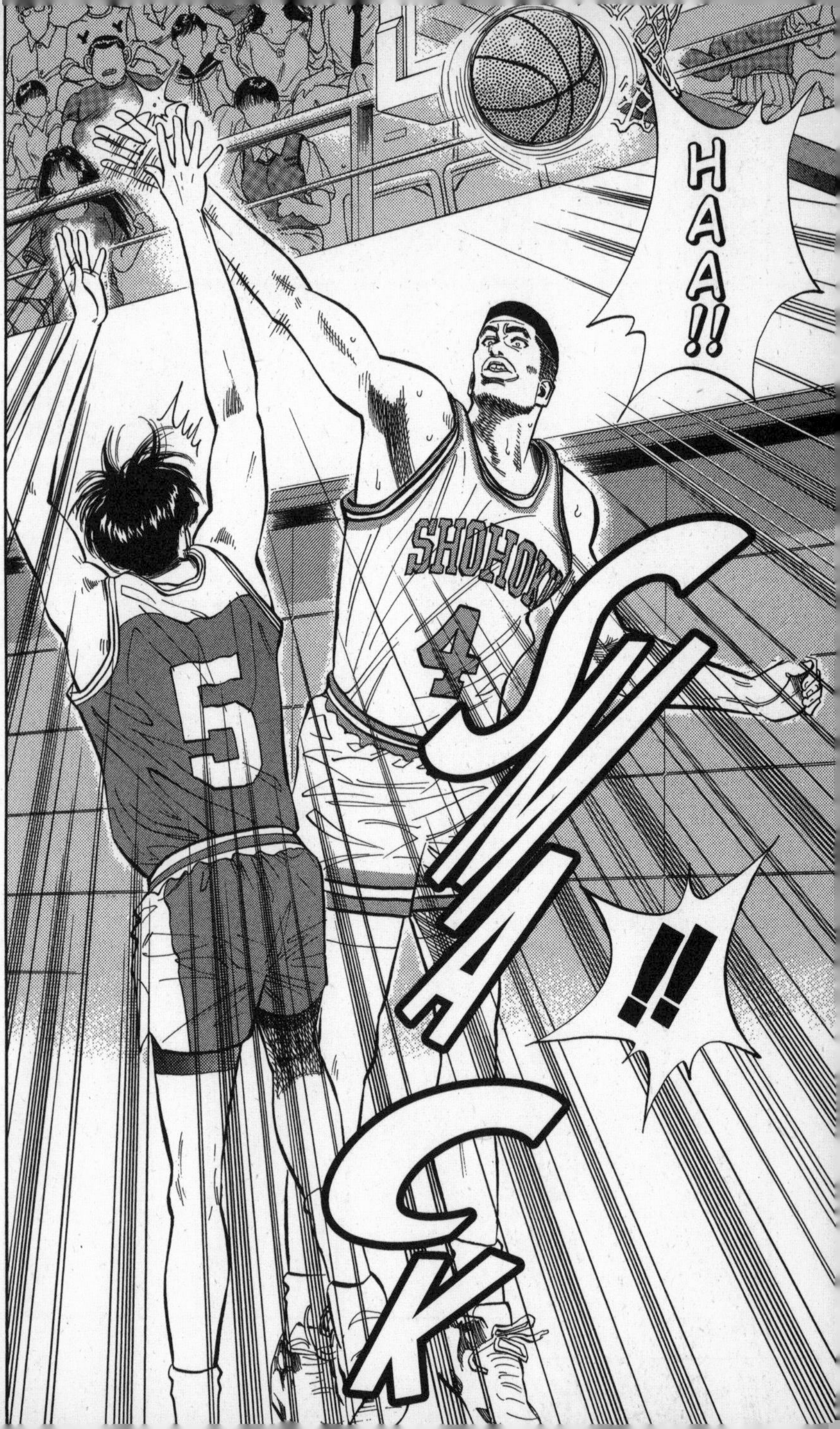
HAAA!!
SMACK!!

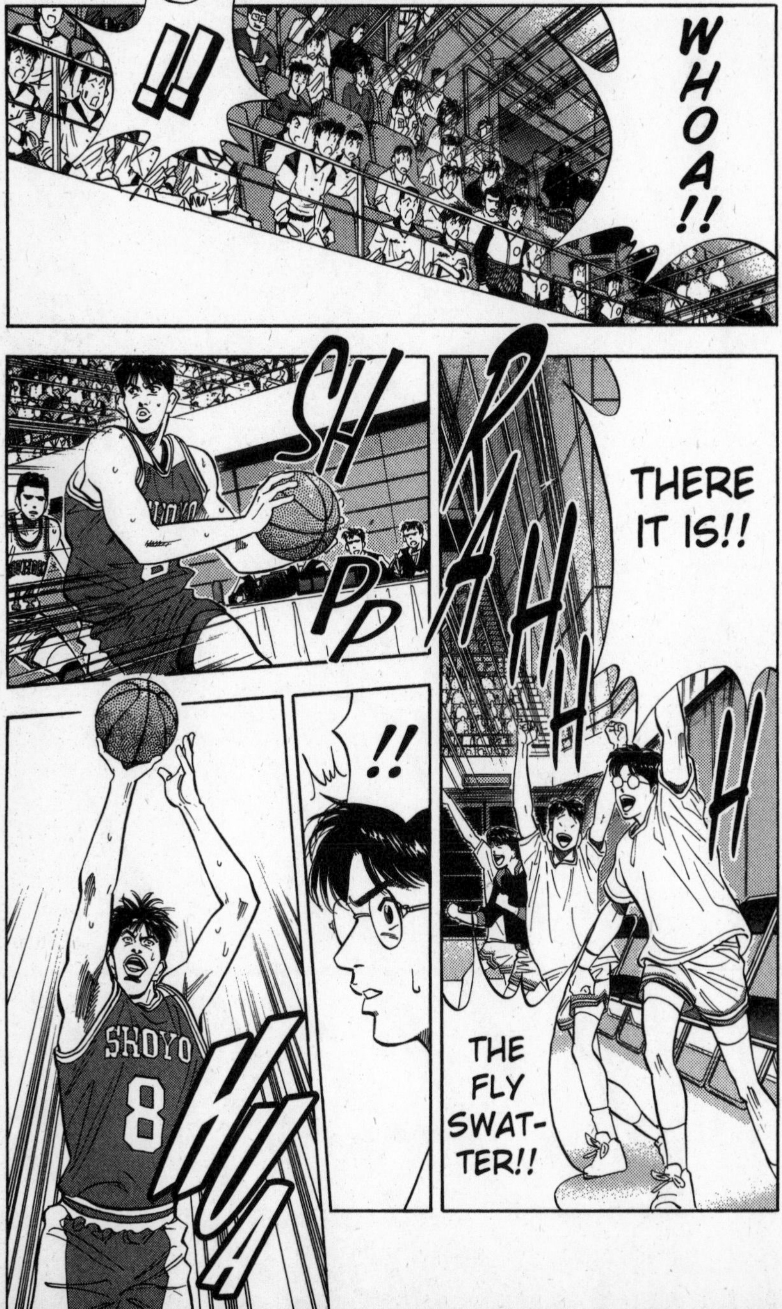
WHOA!!
!!
THERE IT IS!!
RAHHH
THE FLY SWATTER!!
SHPP
!!
SHOYO
8
WHUA

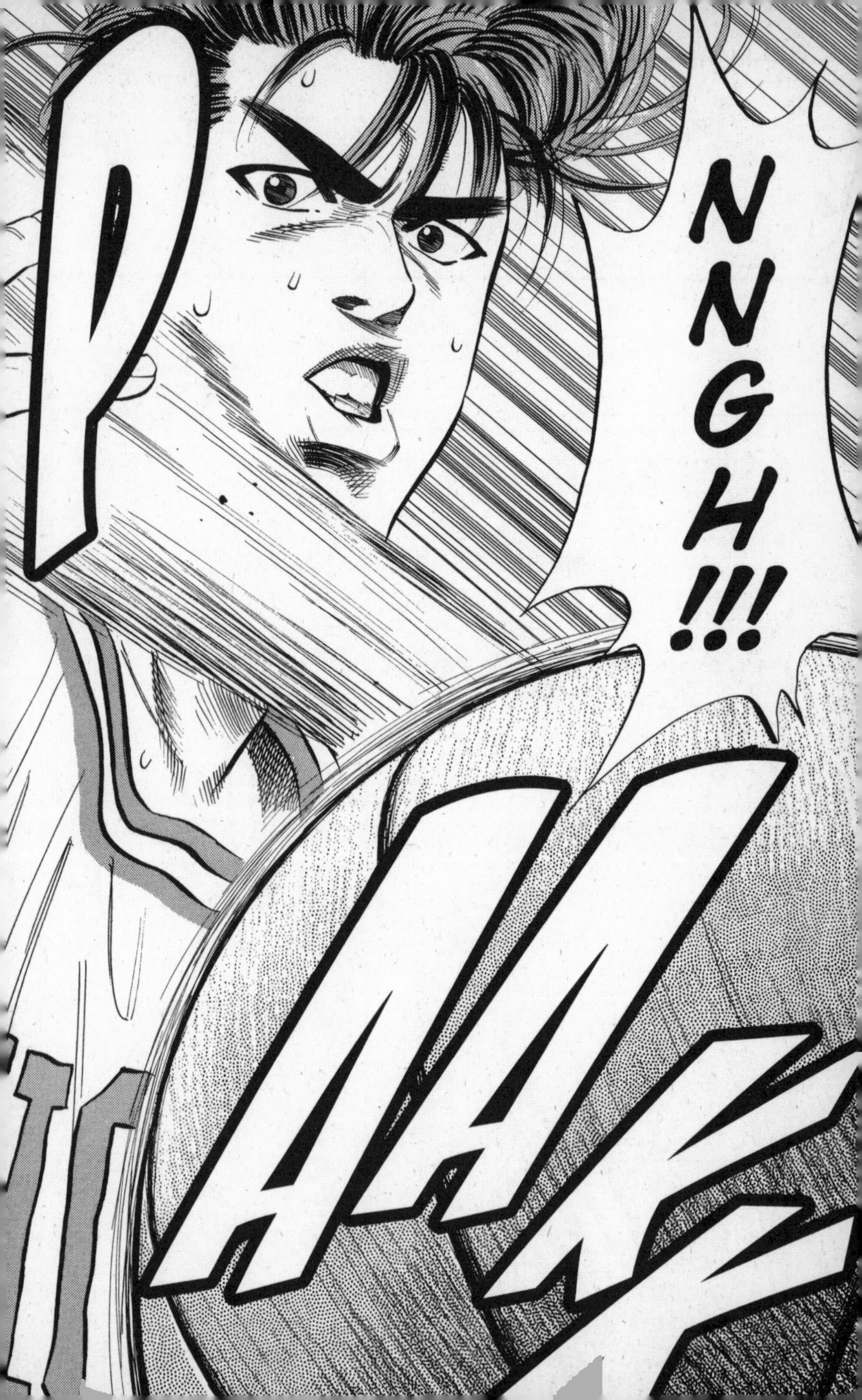
NNGH!!!

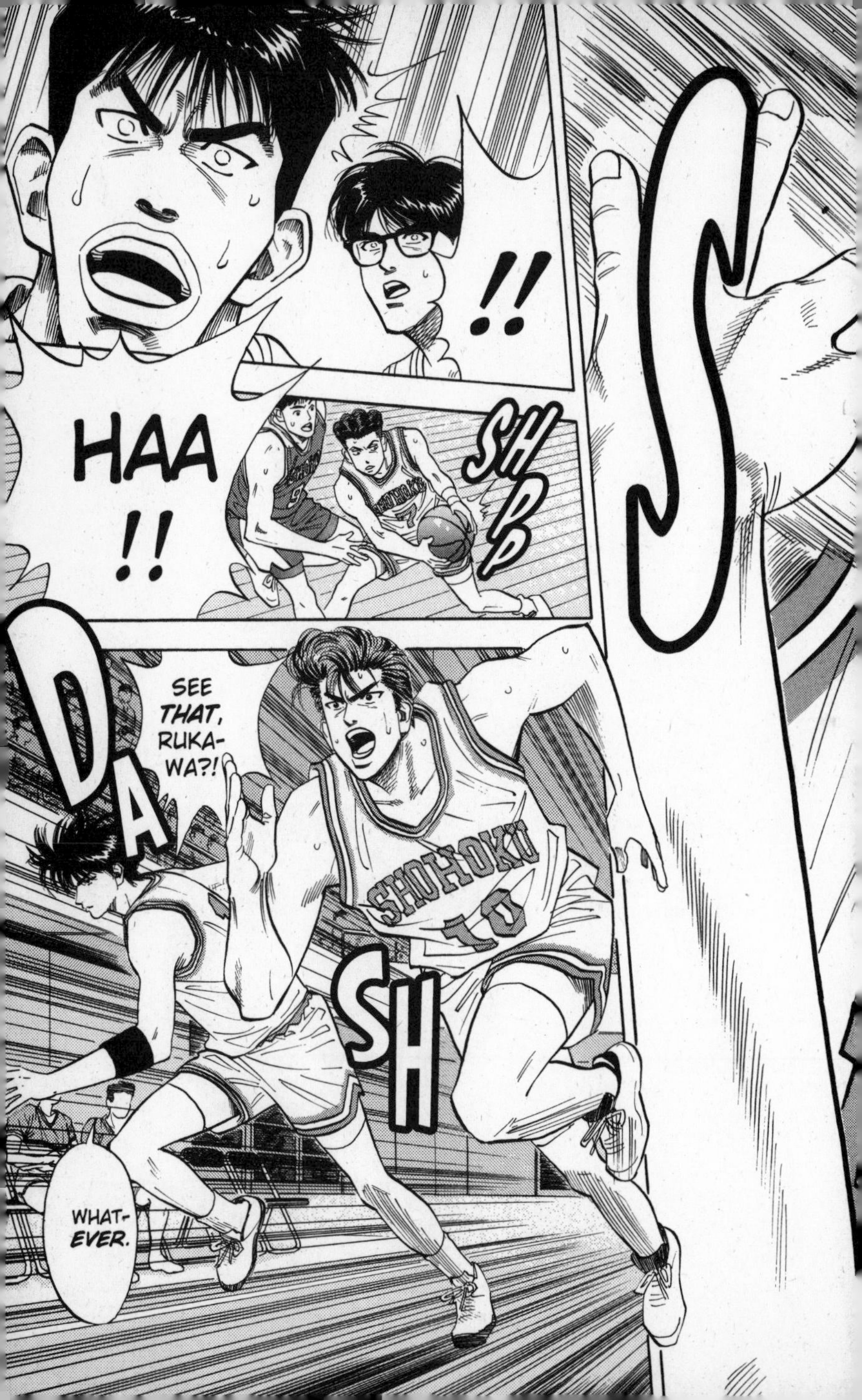

S
!!
HAA !!
SHPP
DA
SEE THAT, RUKAWA?!
SH
WHATEVER.

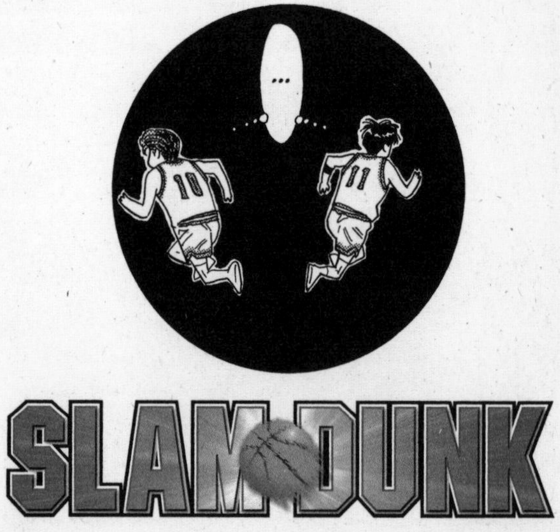
...

SLAM DUNK

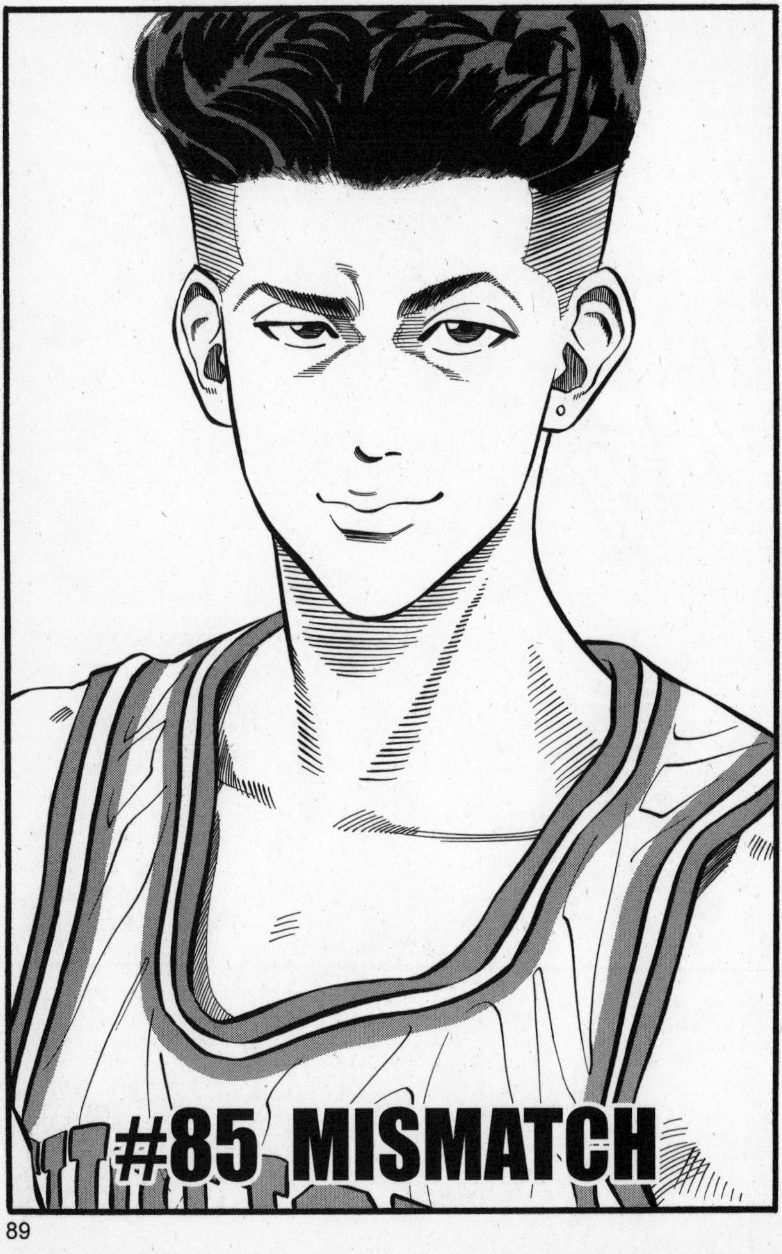
#85 MISMATCH

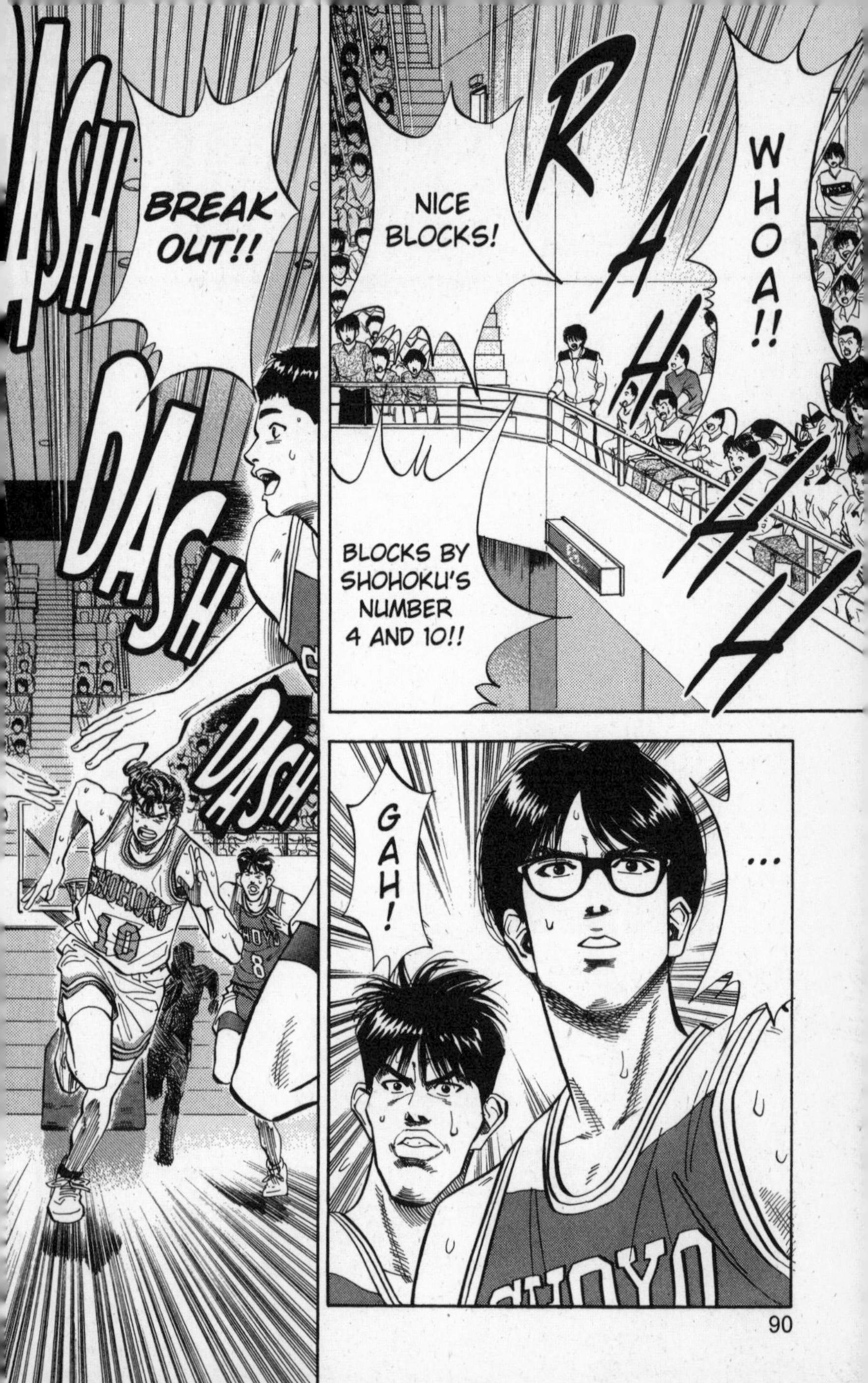
WHOA!!
RAHHHH
NICE BLOCKS!
BLOCKS BY SHOHOKU'S NUMBER 4 AND 10!!
...
GAH!
ASH
BREAK OUT!!
DASH
DASH

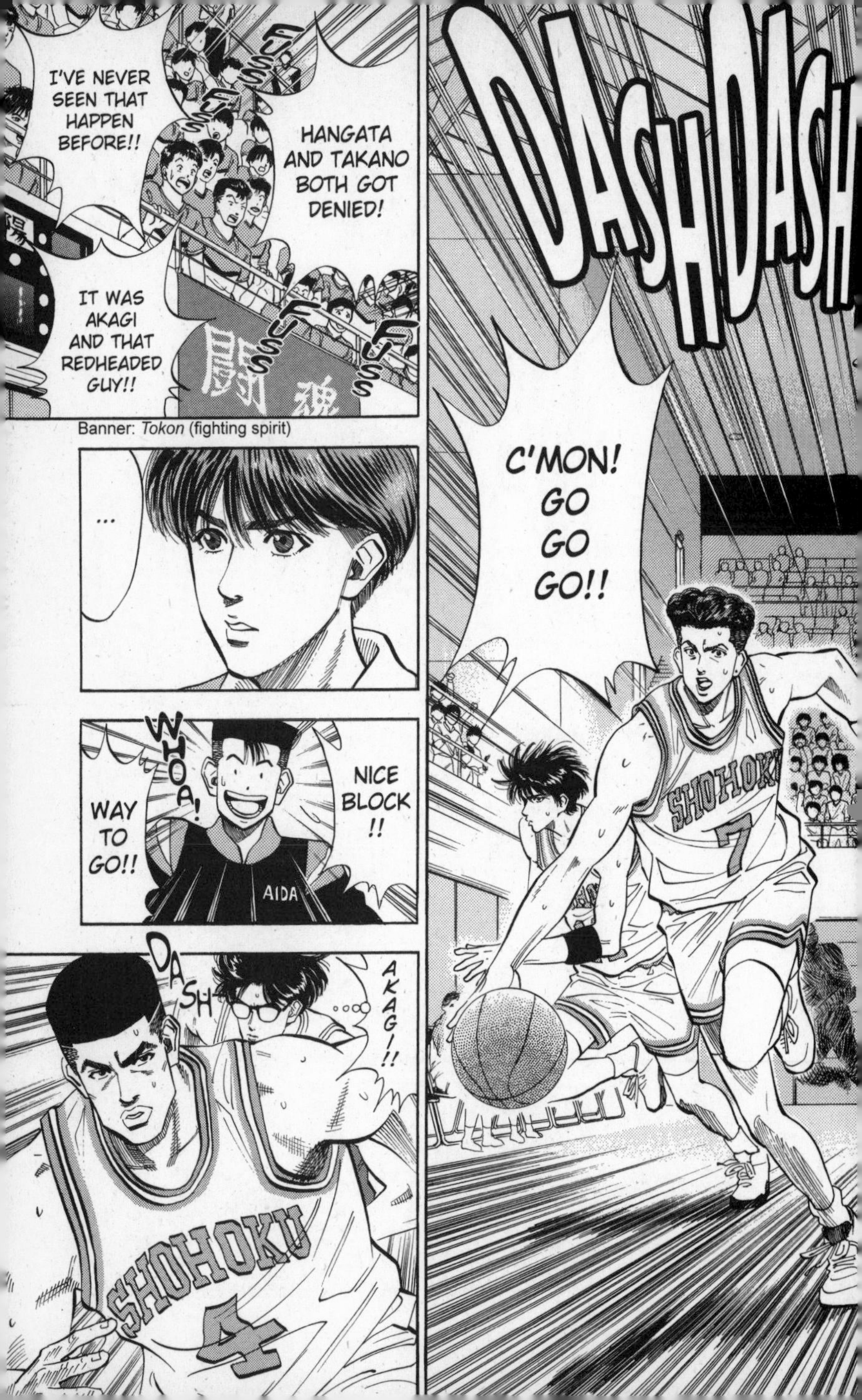
DASH DASH
C'MON! GO GO GO!!
HANGATA AND TAKANO BOTH GOT DENIED!
FUSS FUSS
I'VE NEVER SEEN THAT HAPPEN BEFORE!!
FUSS FUSS
IT WAS AKAGI AND THAT REDHEADED GUY!!
...
NICE BLOCK!!
WHOA!
WAY TO GO!!
AIDA
AKAGI!!
DASH
Banner: *Tokon* (fighting spirit)

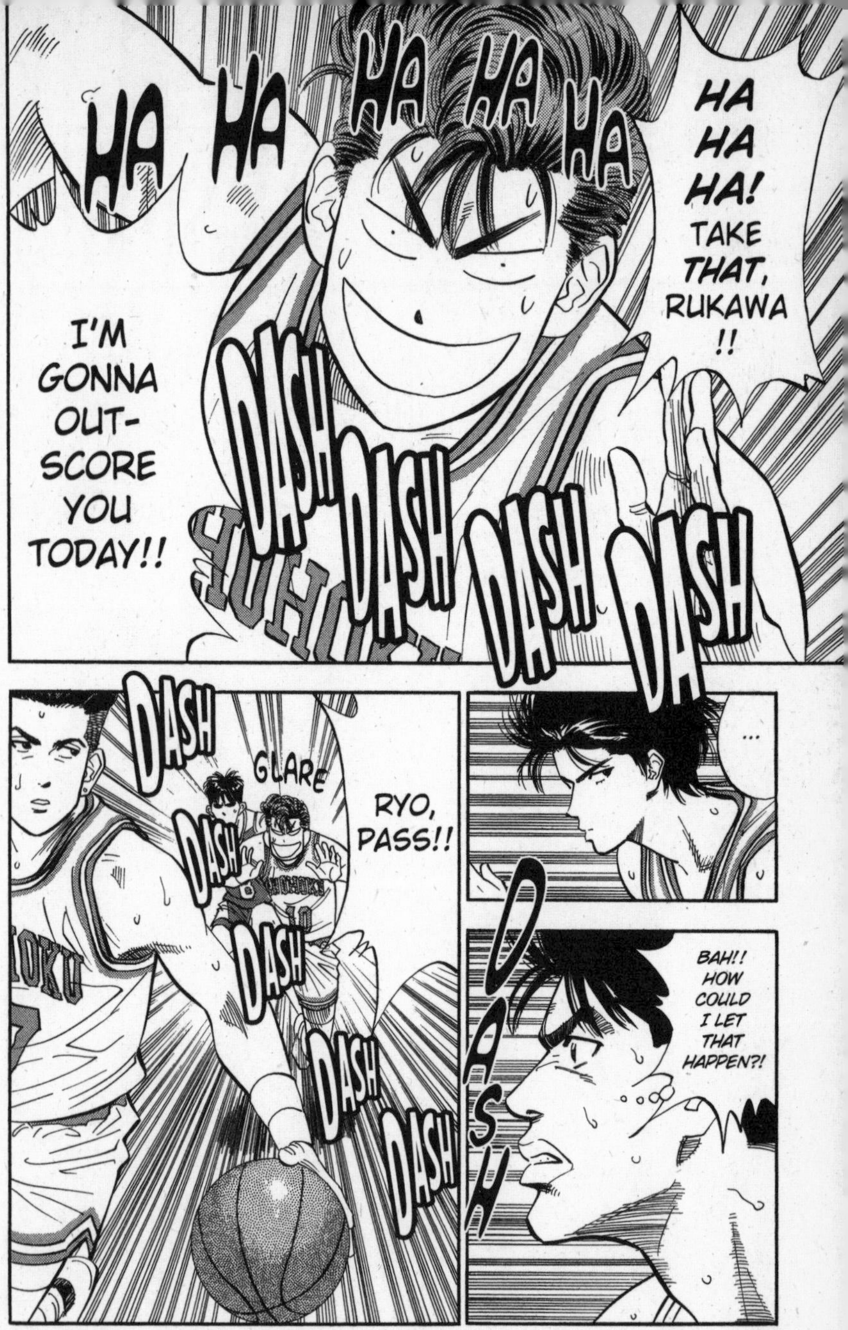
HA HA HA HA HA HA
HA HA HA! TAKE THAT, RUKAWA!!
I'M GONNA OUT-SCORE YOU TODAY!!
DASH DASH DASH DASH
...
DASH
BAH!! HOW COULD I LET THAT HAPPEN?!
DASH
GLARE
RYO, PASS!!
DASH DASH DASH DASH

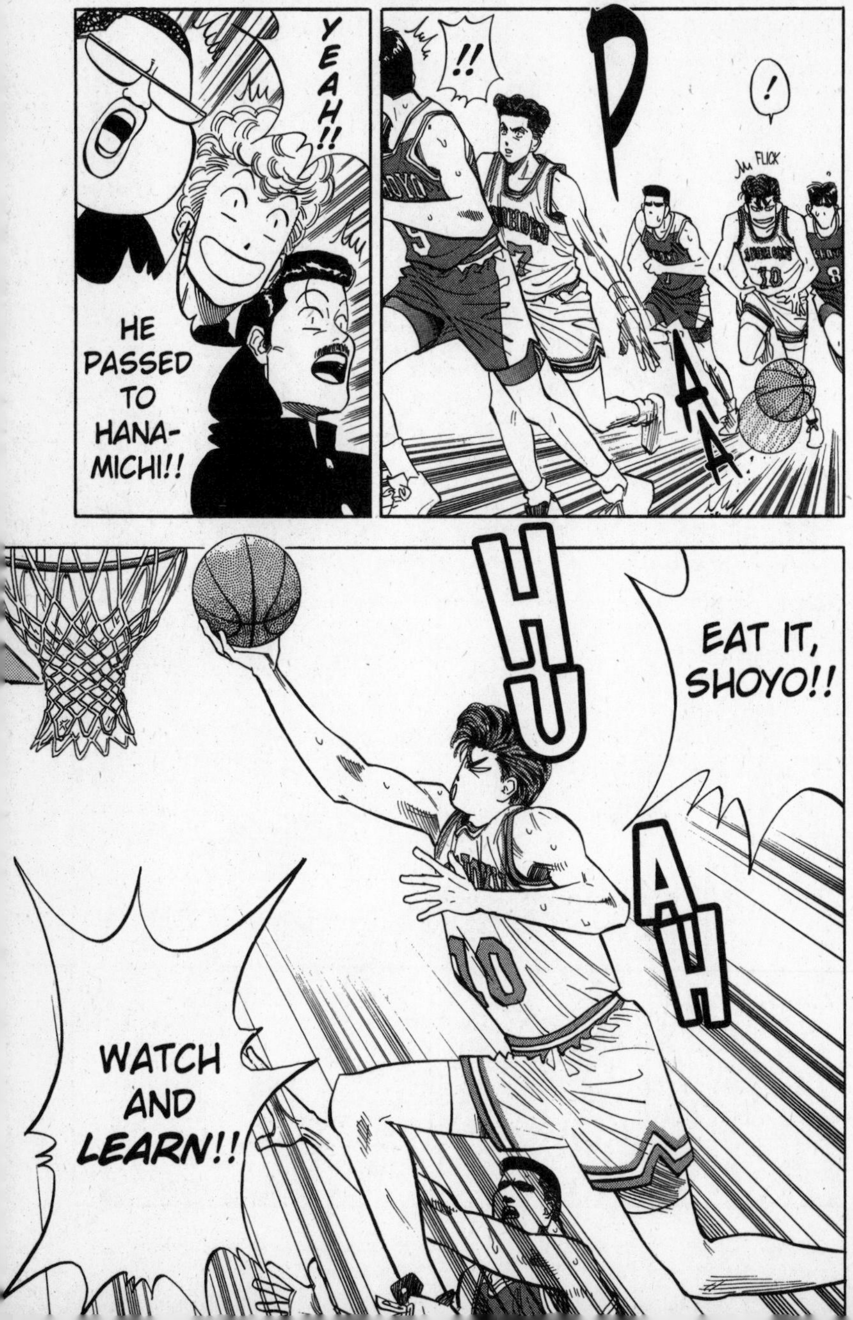

P
!!
!
FLICK
AA
YEAH!!
HE PASSED TO HANA-MICHI!!
EAT IT, SHOYO!!
HU
AH
WATCH AND LEARN!!

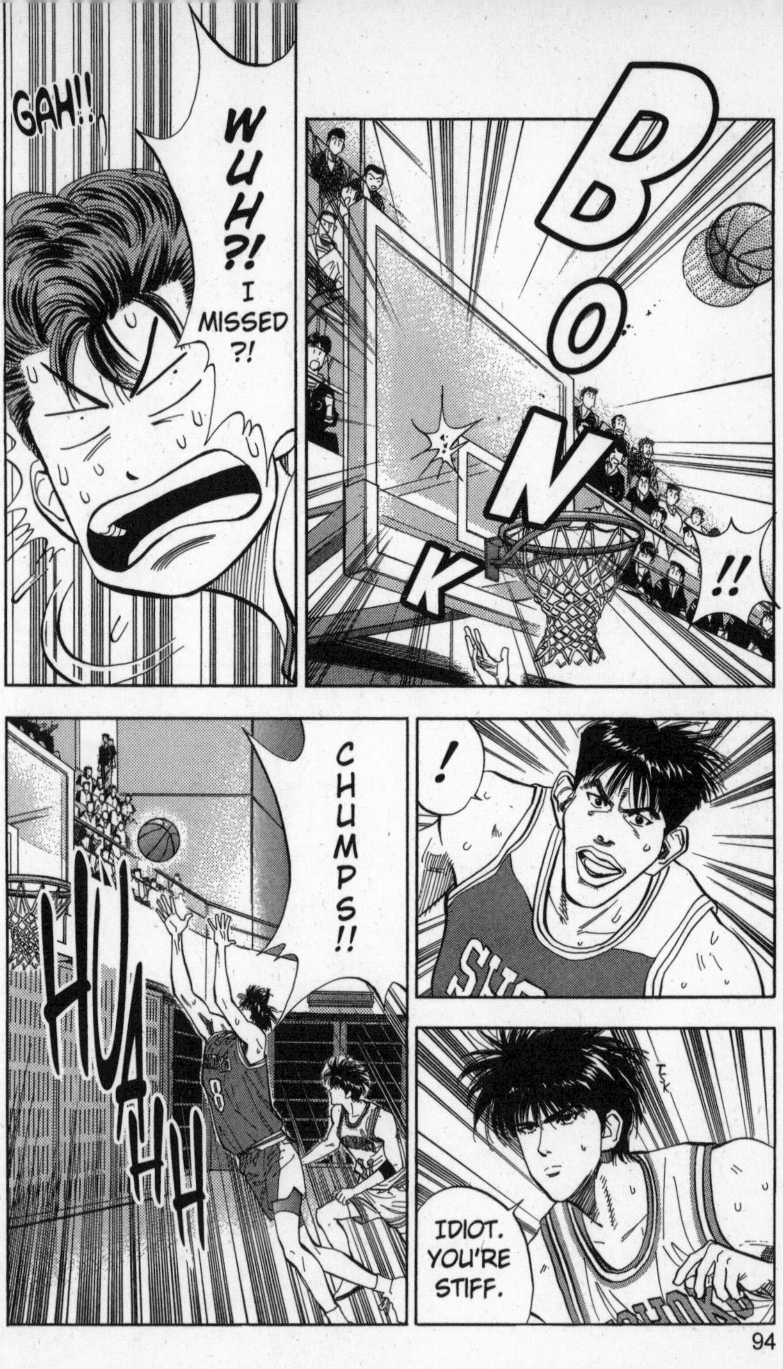
BONK
!!
GAH!!
WUH?!
I MISSED?!
!
TSK
IDIOT. YOU'RE STIFF.
CHUMPS!!
HUHHH

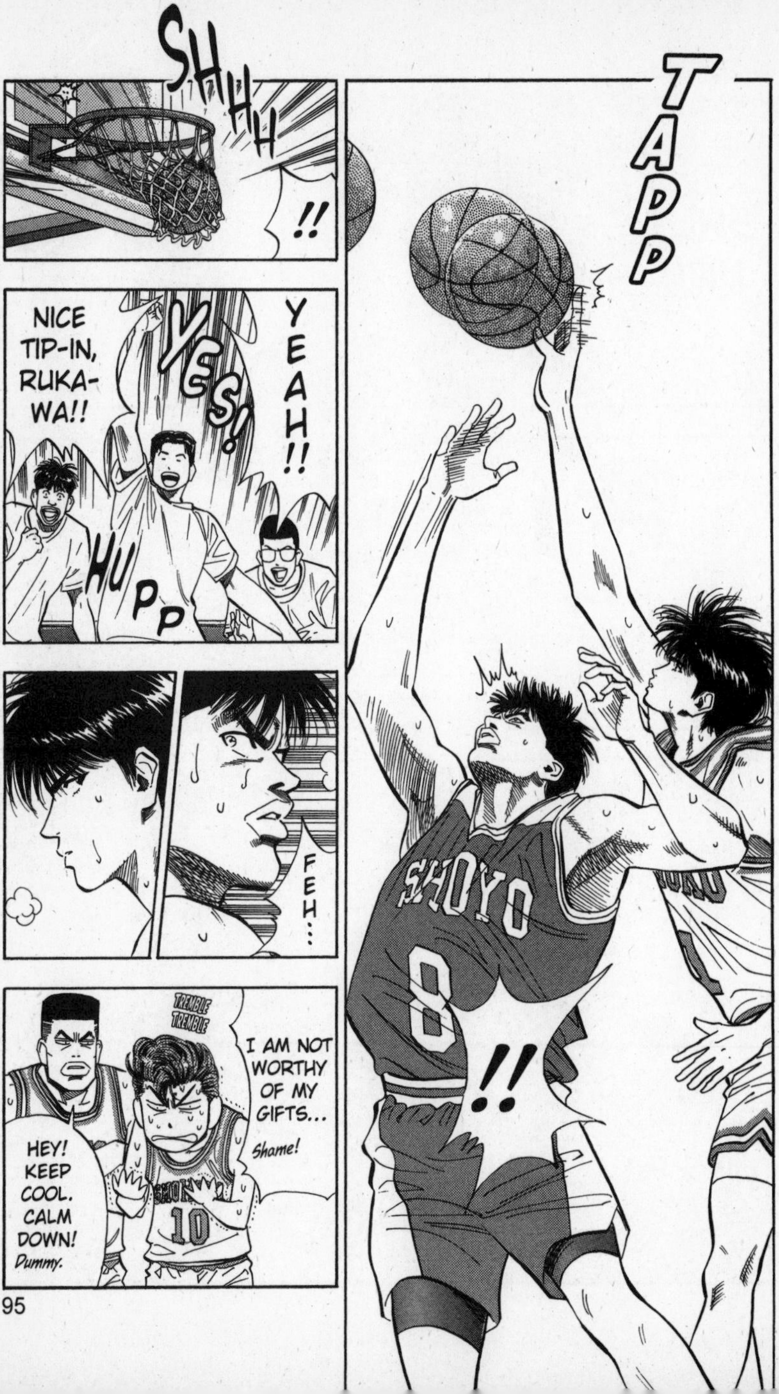
TAPP
!!
SHHHH
!!
YEAH!!
YES!
NICE TIP-IN, RUKAWA!!
HUPP
FEH...
TREMBLE TREMBLE
I AM NOT WORTHY OF MY GIFTS...
Shame!
HEY! KEEP COOL. CALM DOWN!
Dummy.

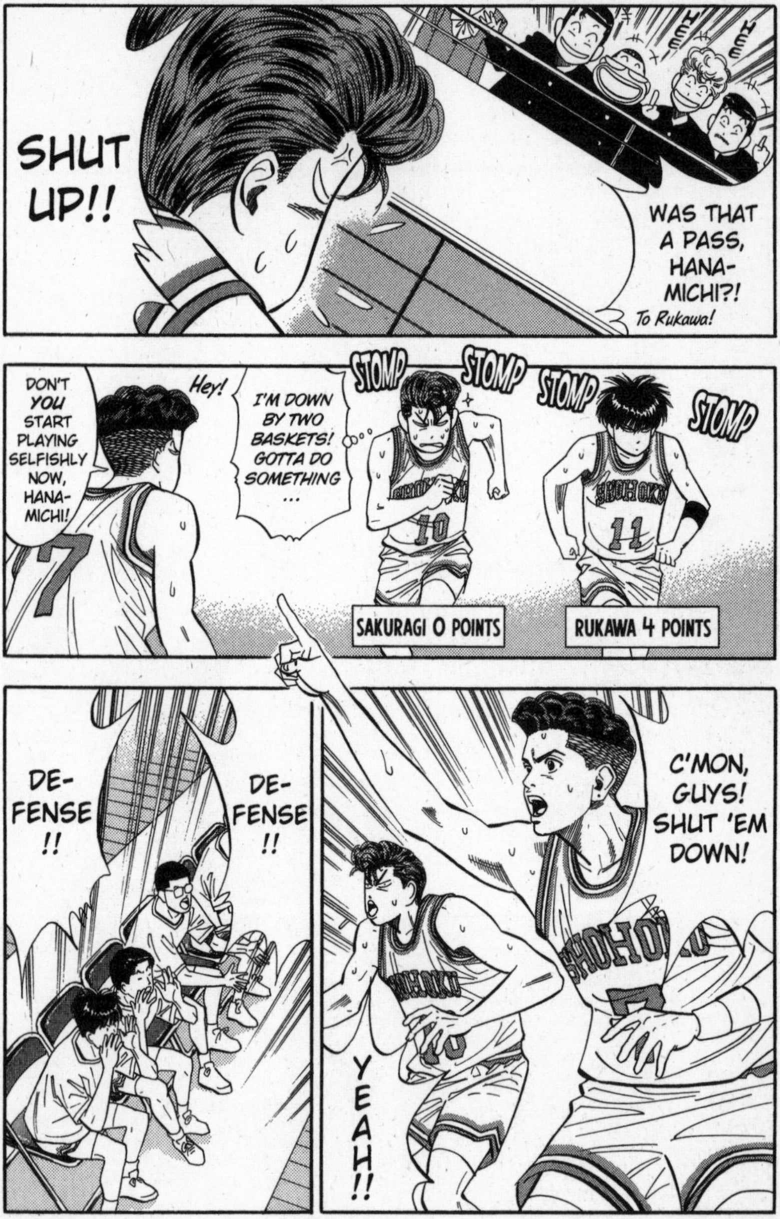
HEE HEE
WAS THAT A PASS, HANA-MICHI?!
To Rukawa!
SHUT UP!!
STOMP STOMP STOMP STOMP
RUKAWA 4 POINTS
SAKURAGI 0 POINTS
I'M DOWN BY TWO BASKETS! GOTTA DO SOMETHING ...
Hey!
DON'T YOU START PLAYING SELFISHLY NOW, HANA-MICHI!
C'MON, GUYS! SHUT 'EM DOWN!
YEAH!!
DE-FENSE!!
DE-FENSE!!

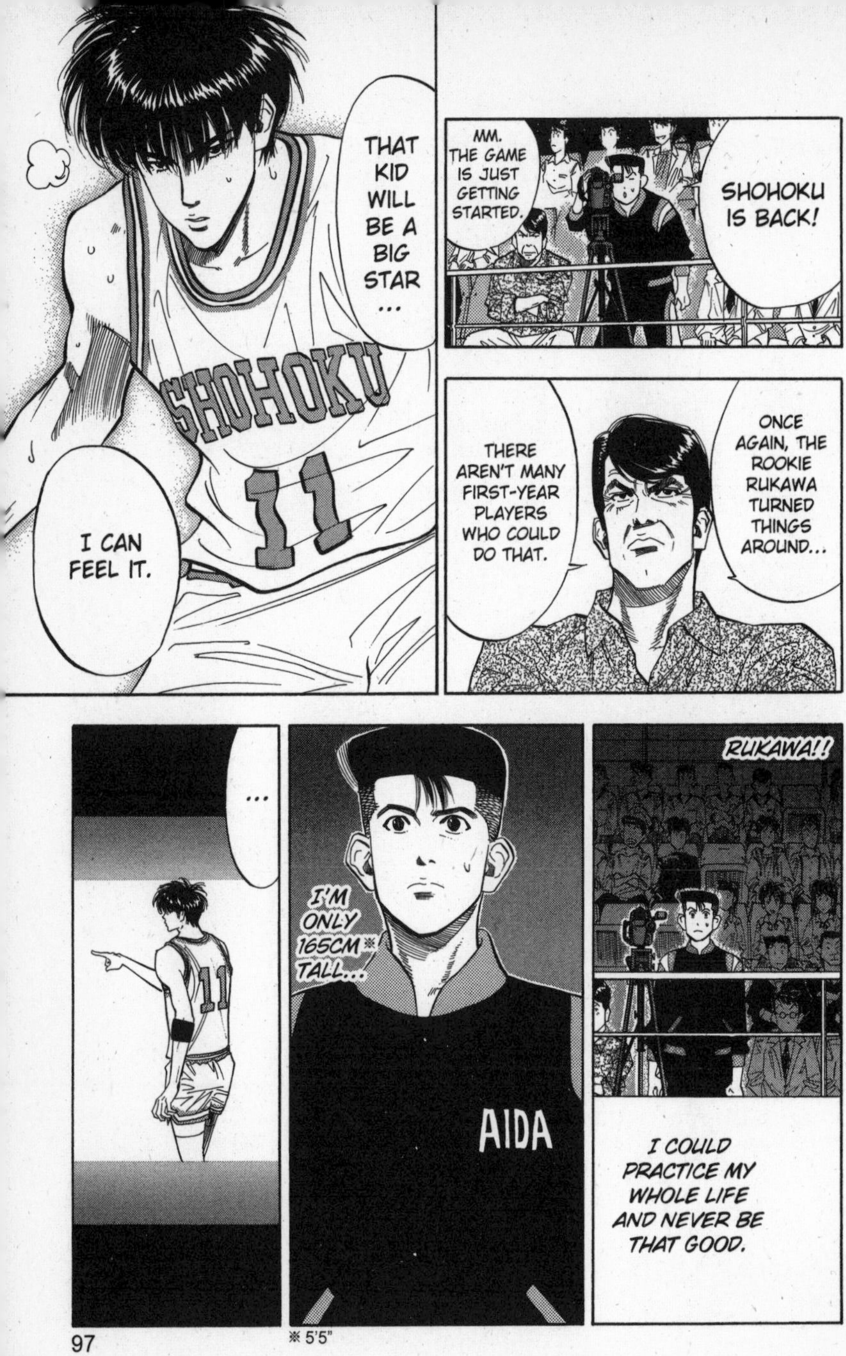
SHOHOKU IS BACK!
MM. THE GAME IS JUST GETTING STARTED.
ONCE AGAIN, THE ROOKIE RUKAWA TURNED THINGS AROUND...
THERE AREN'T MANY FIRST-YEAR PLAYERS WHO COULD DO THAT.
THAT KID WILL BE A BIG STAR...
I CAN FEEL IT.
SHOHOKU
11
RUKAWA!!
I COULD PRACTICE MY WHOLE LIFE AND NEVER BE THAT GOOD.
I'M ONLY 165CM※ TALL...
AIDA
...

※ 5'5"

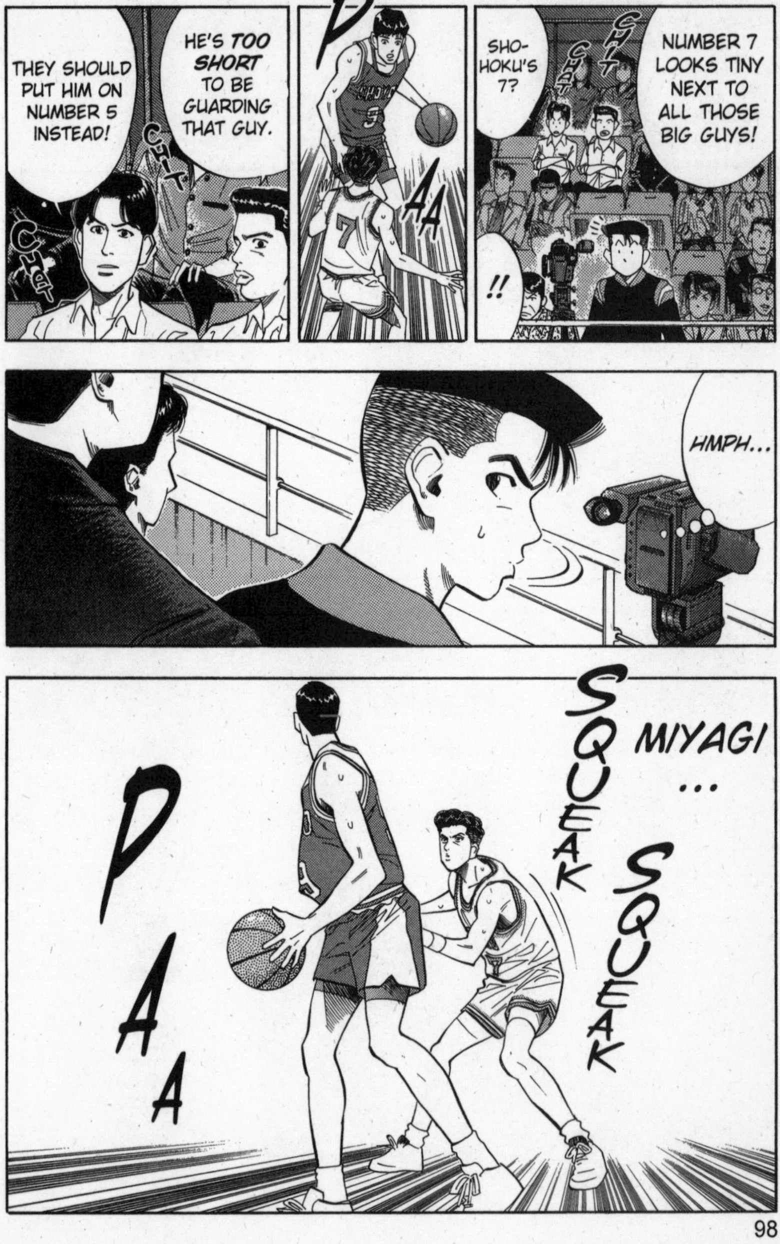

NUMBER 7 LOOKS TINY NEXT TO ALL THOSE BIG GUYS!
CHIT
CHAT
SHO-HOKU'S 7?
!!
DAA
HE'S TOO SHORT TO BE GUARDING THAT GUY.
CHIT
THEY SHOULD PUT HIM ON NUMBER 5 INSTEAD!
CHAT
HMPH...
MIYAGI ...
SQUEAK
SQUEAK
DAAA

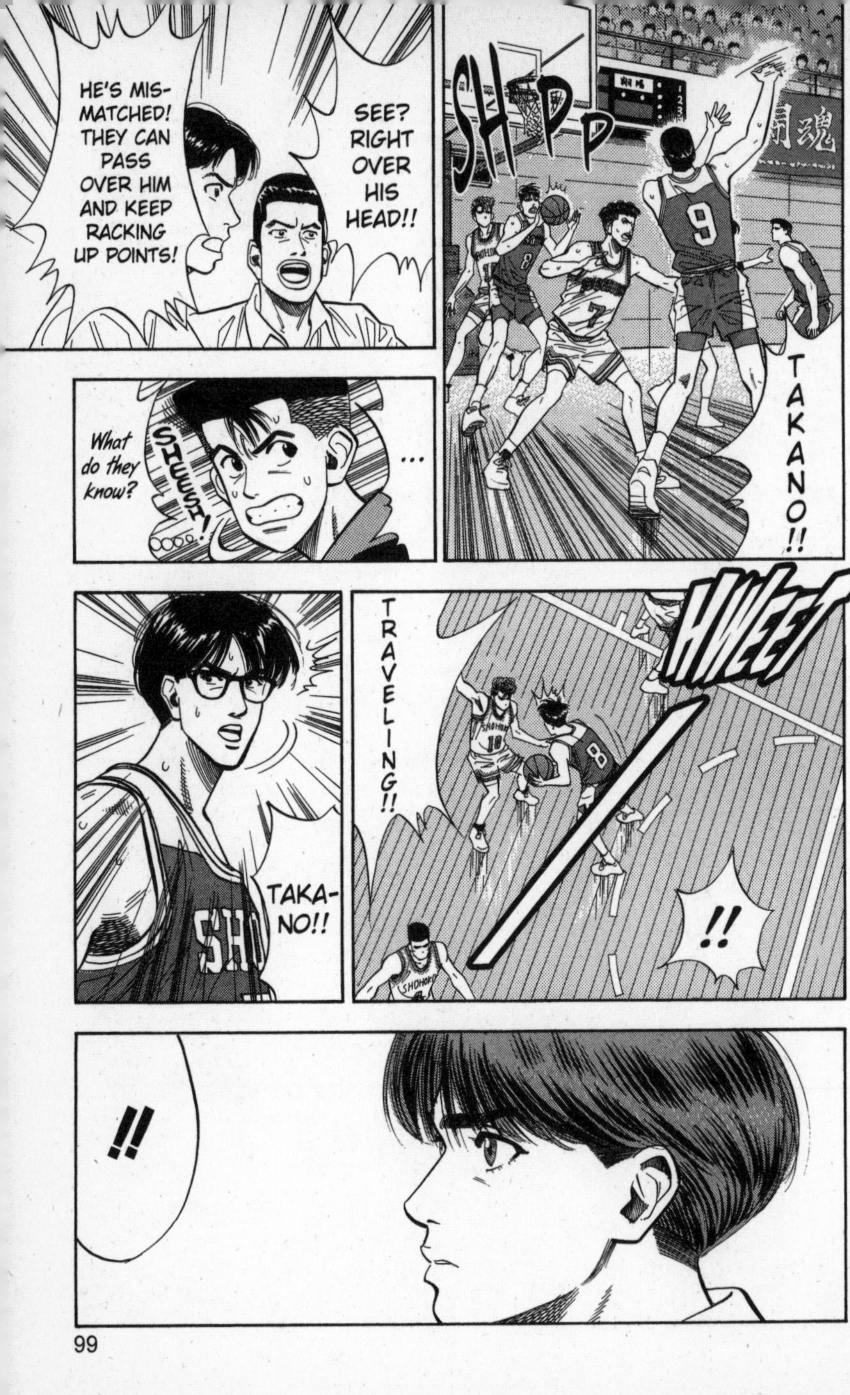
SHPP
TAKANO!!
SEE? RIGHT OVER HIS HEAD!!
HE'S MIS-MATCHED! THEY CAN PASS OVER HIM AND KEEP RACKING UP POINTS!
...
SHEESH!
What do they know?
HWEET
TRAVELING!!
!!
TAKA-NO!!
!!

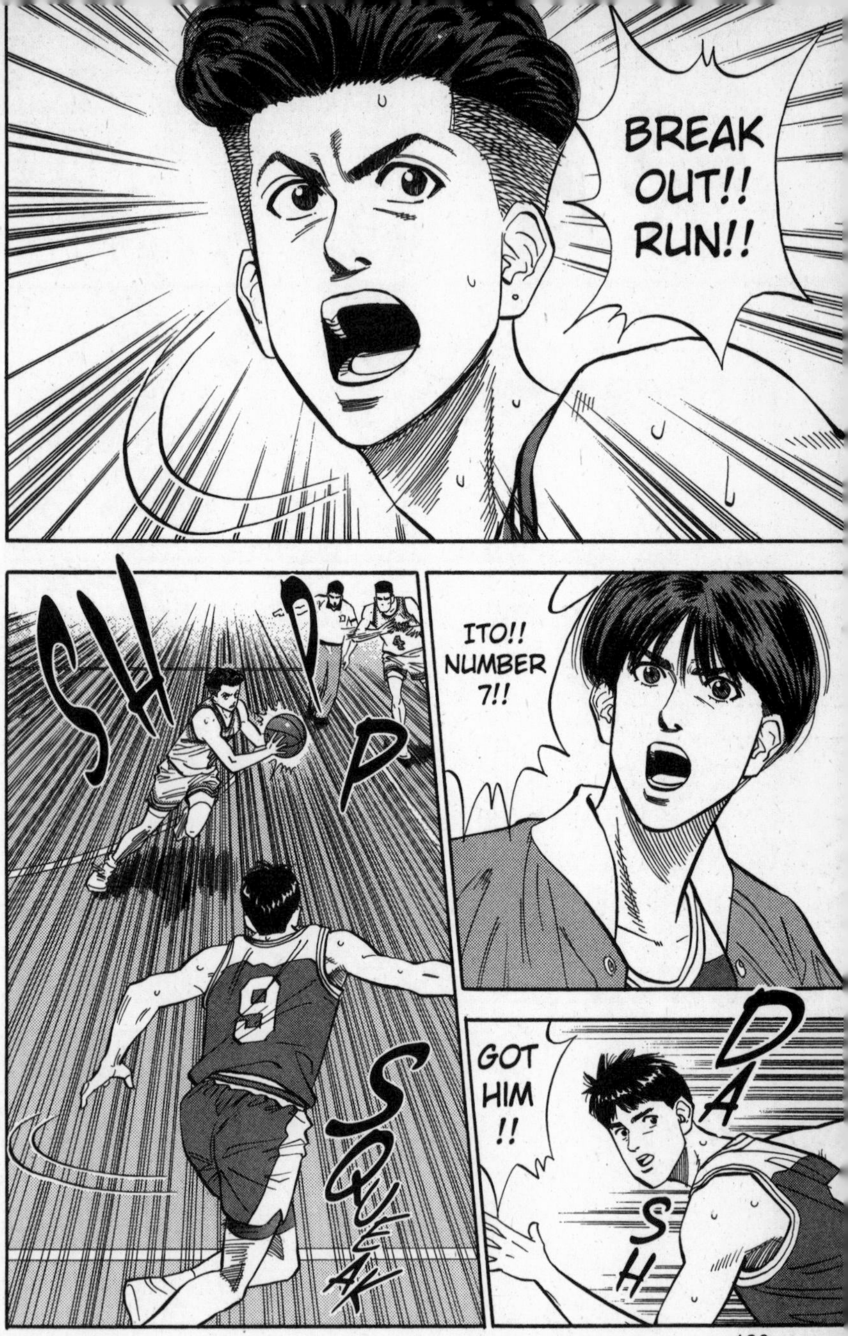
BREAK OUT!! RUN!!
ITO!! NUMBER 7!!
GOT HIM!!
DASH
SHPP
SQUEAK

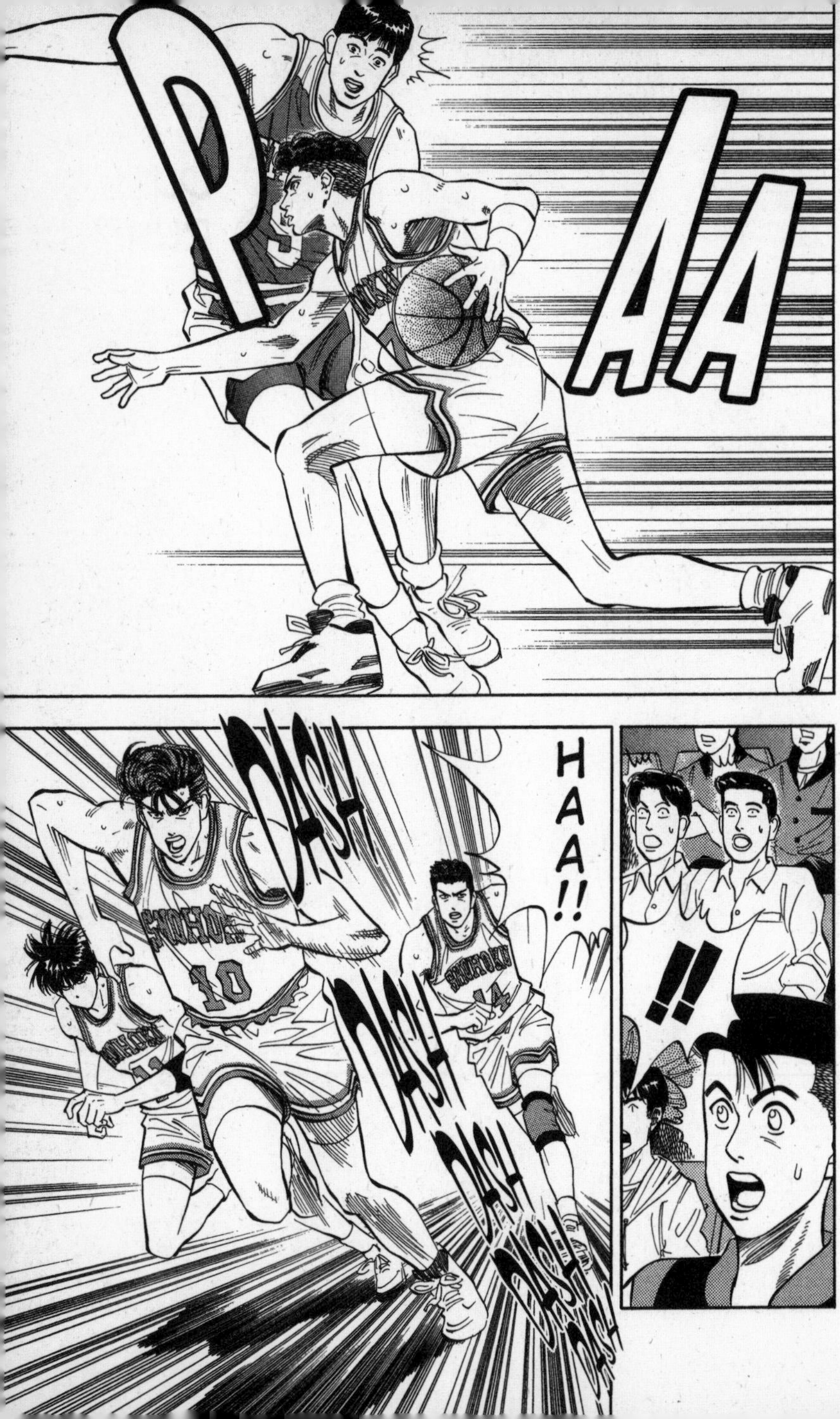

PAA
!!
DASH
HAAA!!
DASH
DASH
DASH
DASH

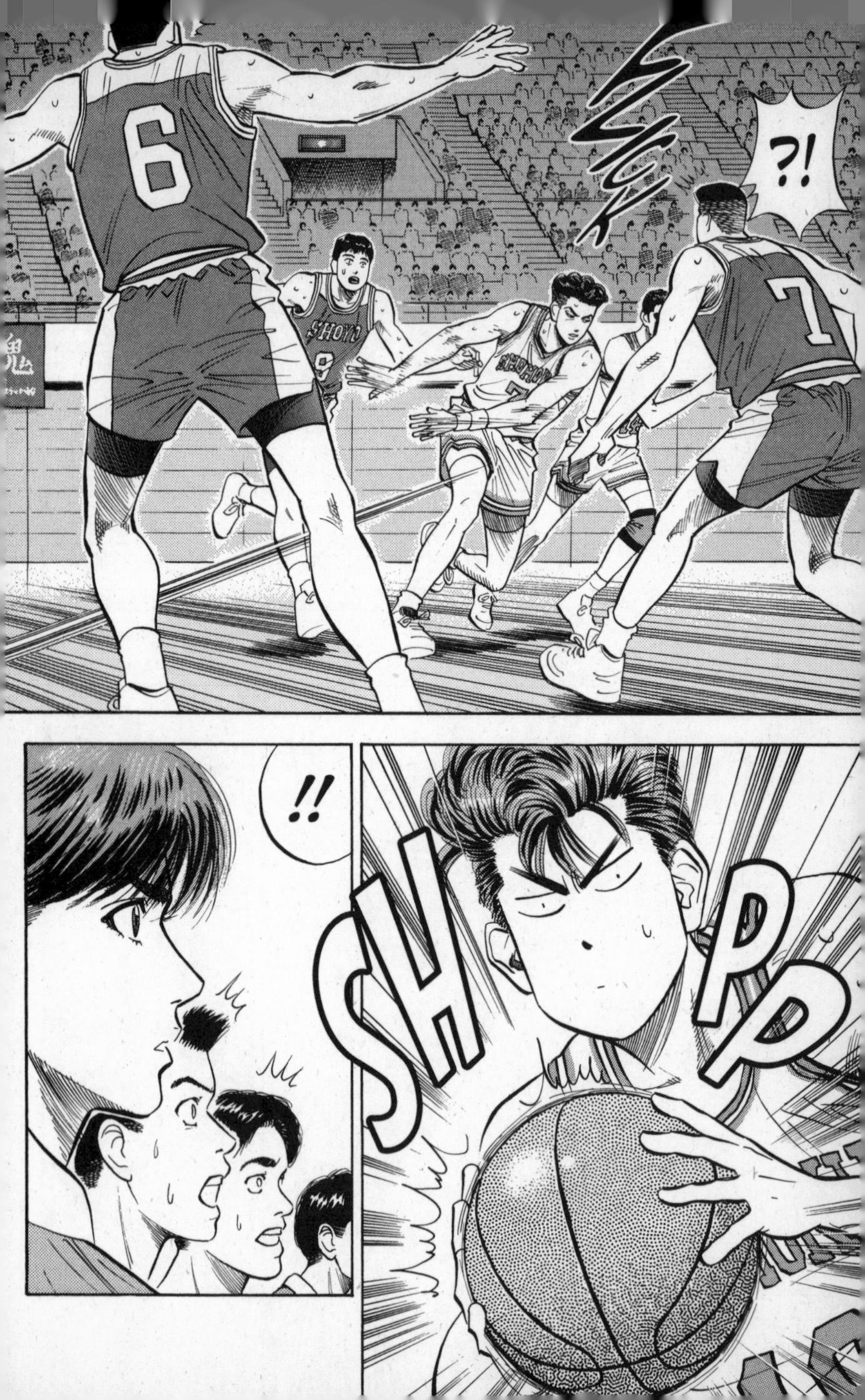
?!
SH
PP
!!

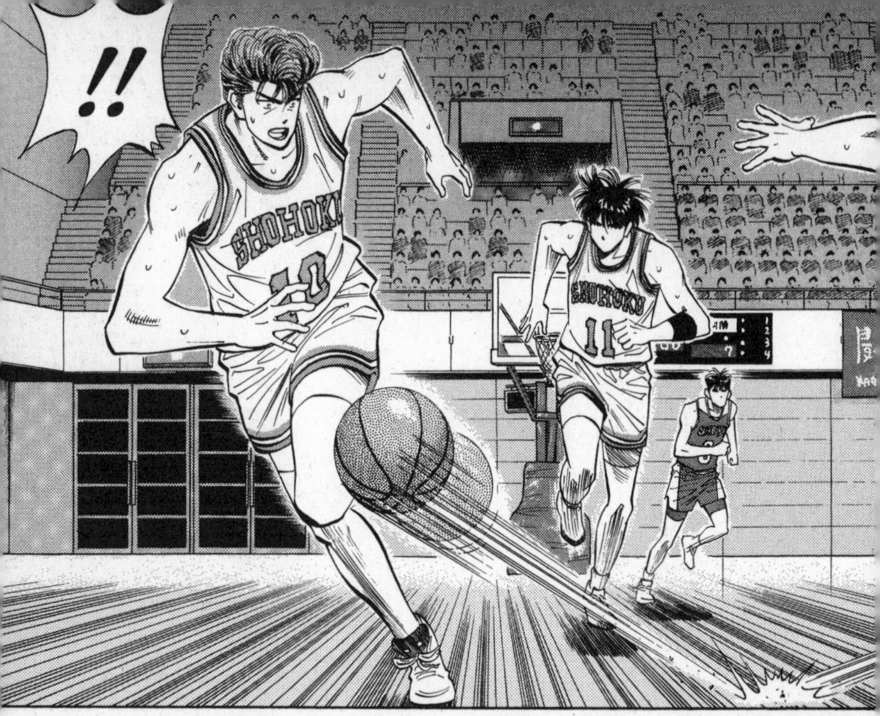
!!

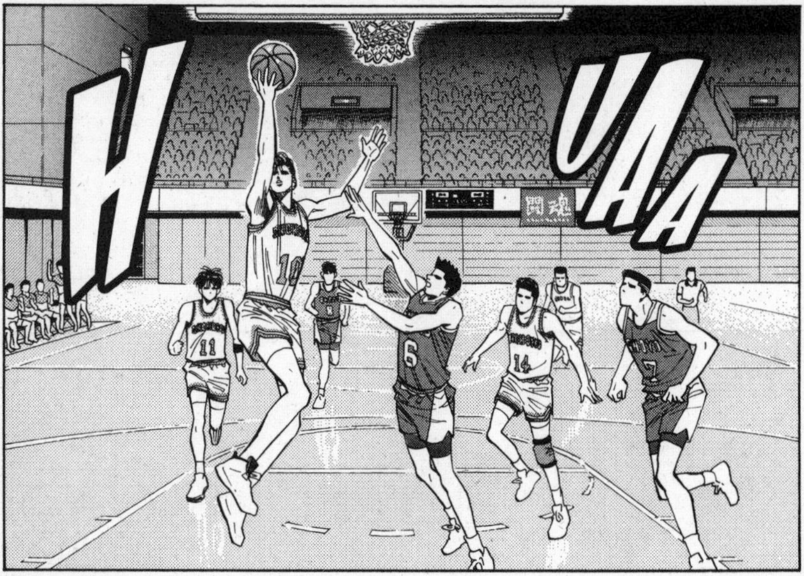
HUAA

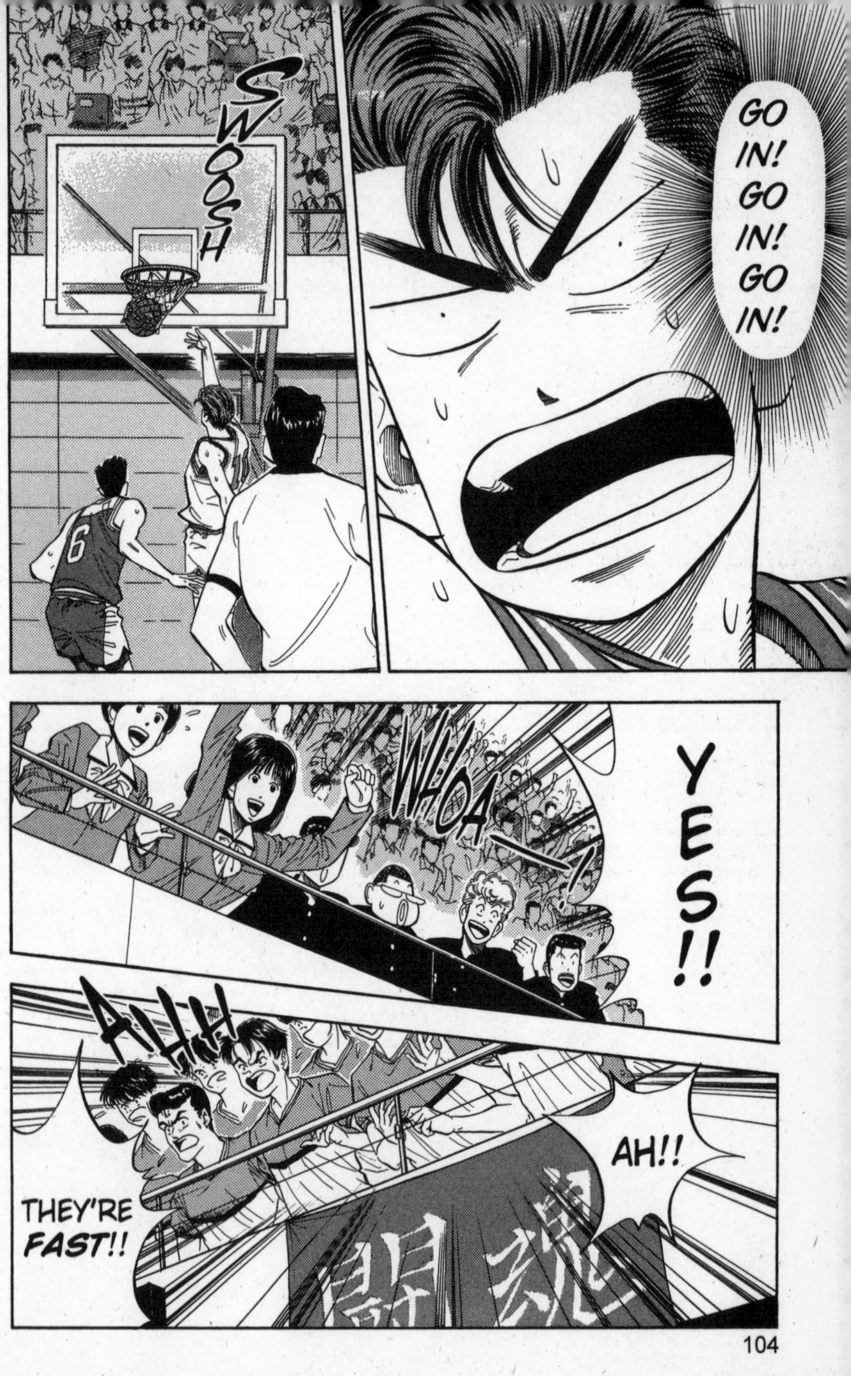
GO IN! GO IN! GO IN!
SWOOSH
YES!!
WHOA—!
AH!!
AHH
THEY'RE *FAST*!!

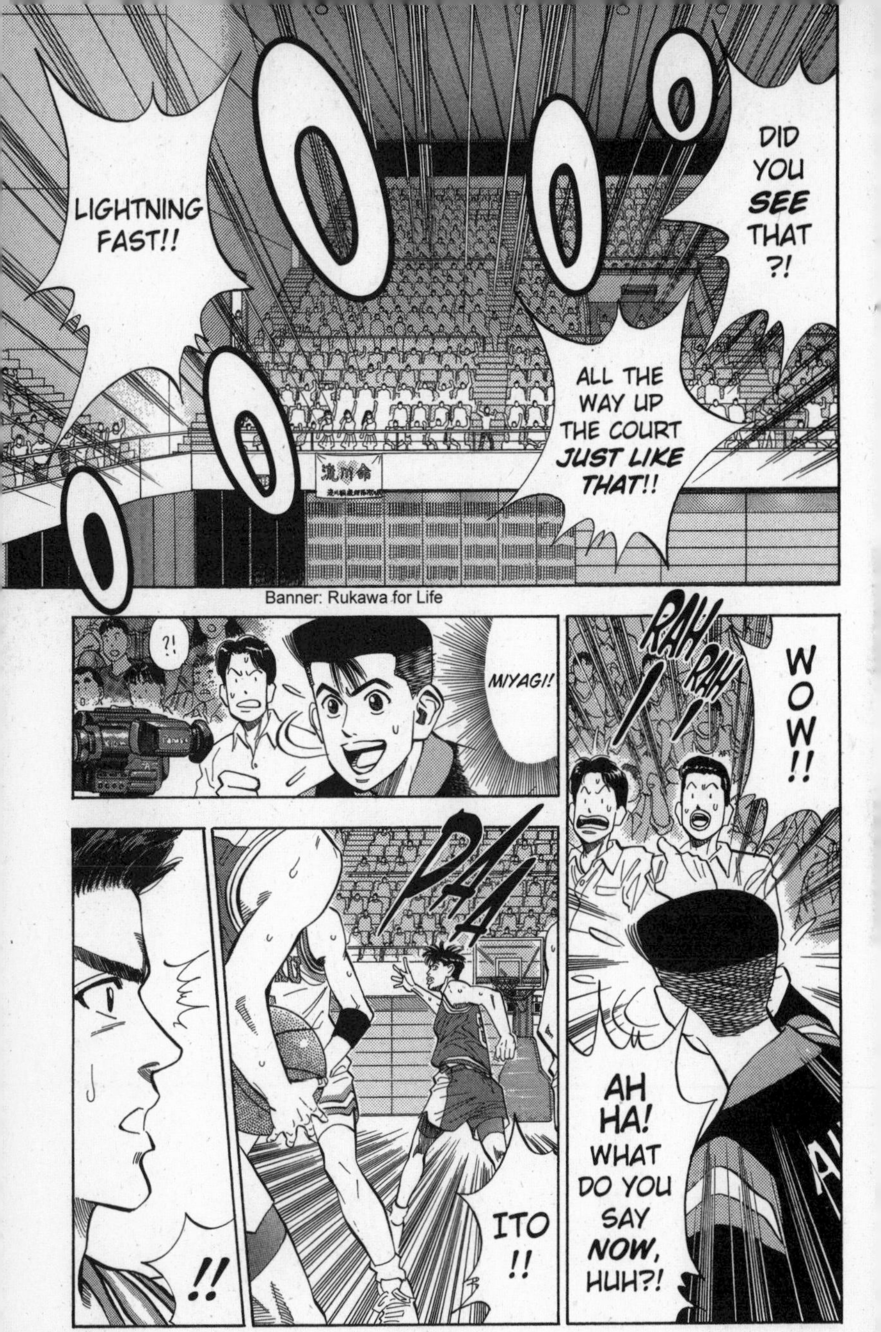
DID YOU SEE THAT ?!
ALL THE WAY UP THE COURT JUST LIKE THAT!!
LIGHTNING FAST!!
Banner: Rukawa for Life
RAH RAH
RAH RAH
WOW!!
AH HA! WHAT DO YOU SAY NOW, HUH?!
MIYAGI!
?!
PA
ITO!!
!!

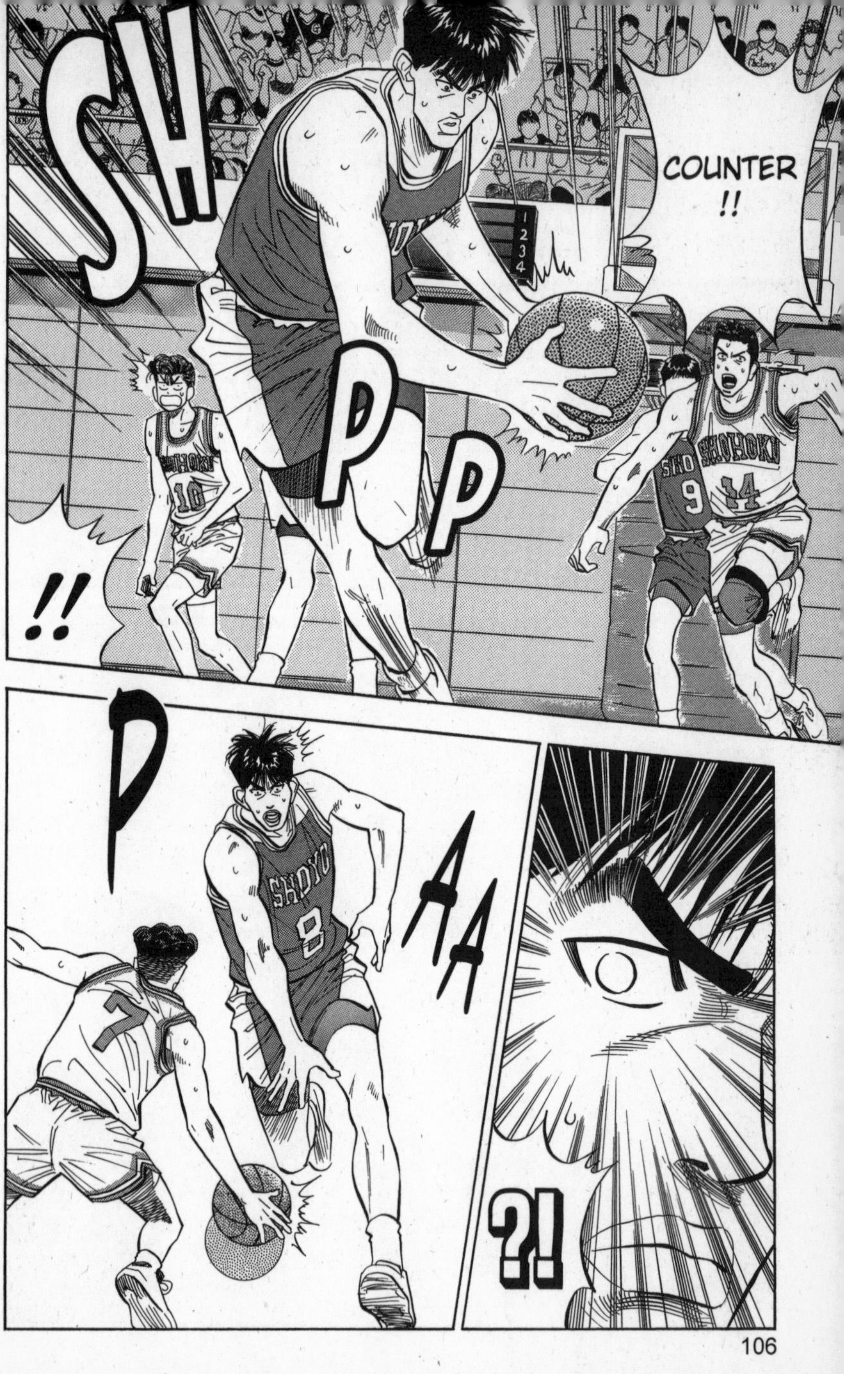
COUNTER !!
SH
P
P
!!
?!
P
AA
A

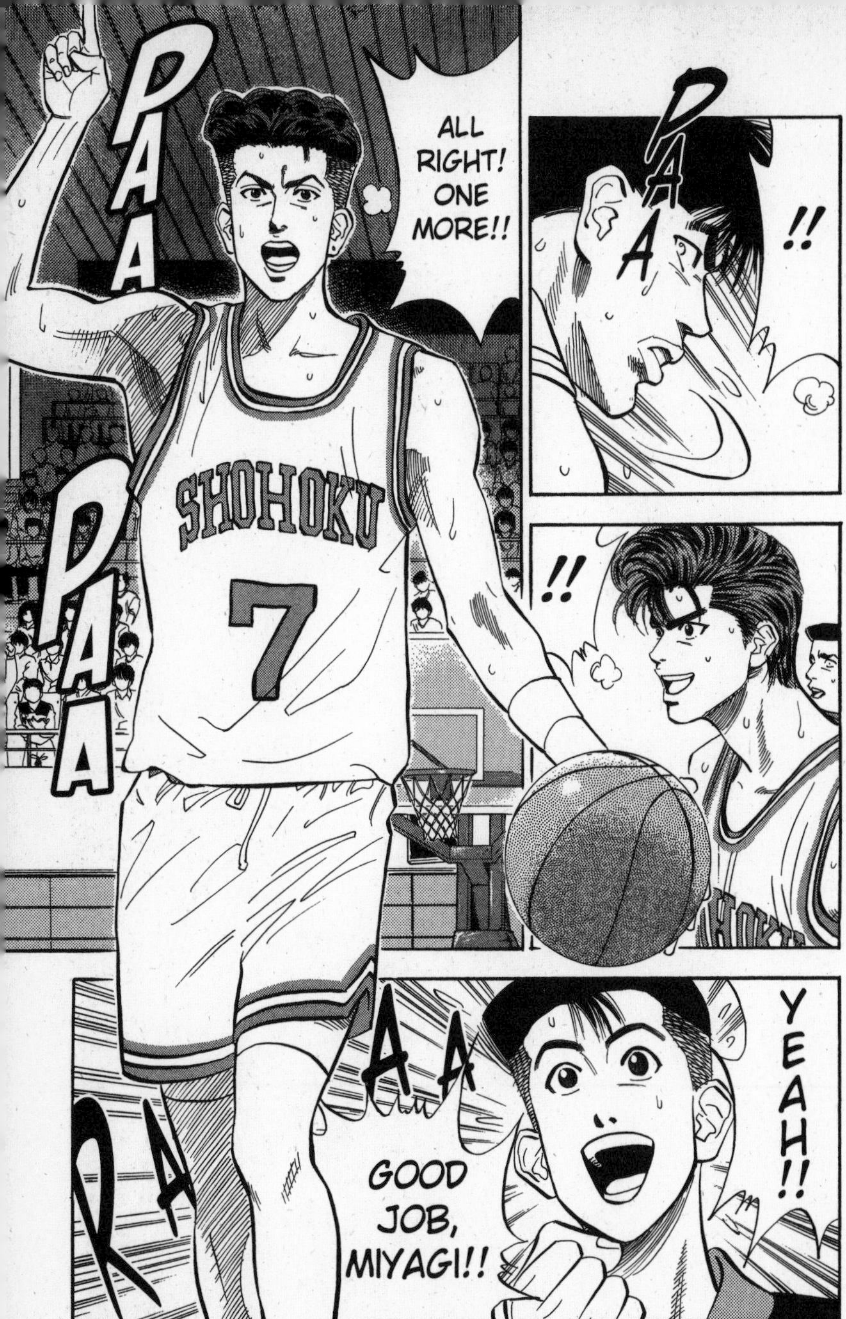
ALL RIGHT! ONE MORE!!
PAA
PAA
!!
PAA
!!
YEAH!!
GOOD JOB, MIYAGI!!
AA
RA

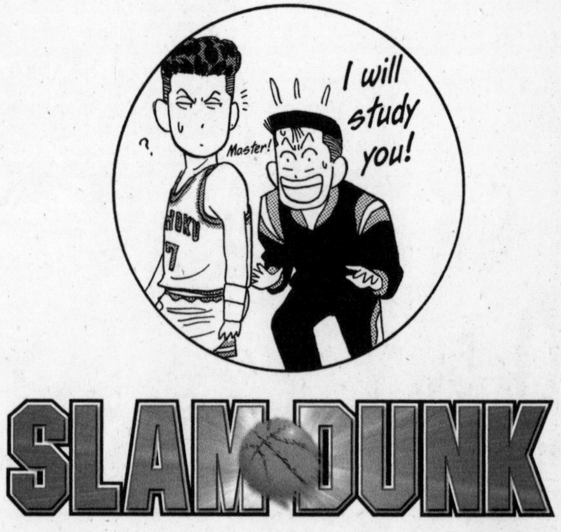
I will study you!
Master!

SLAM DUNK

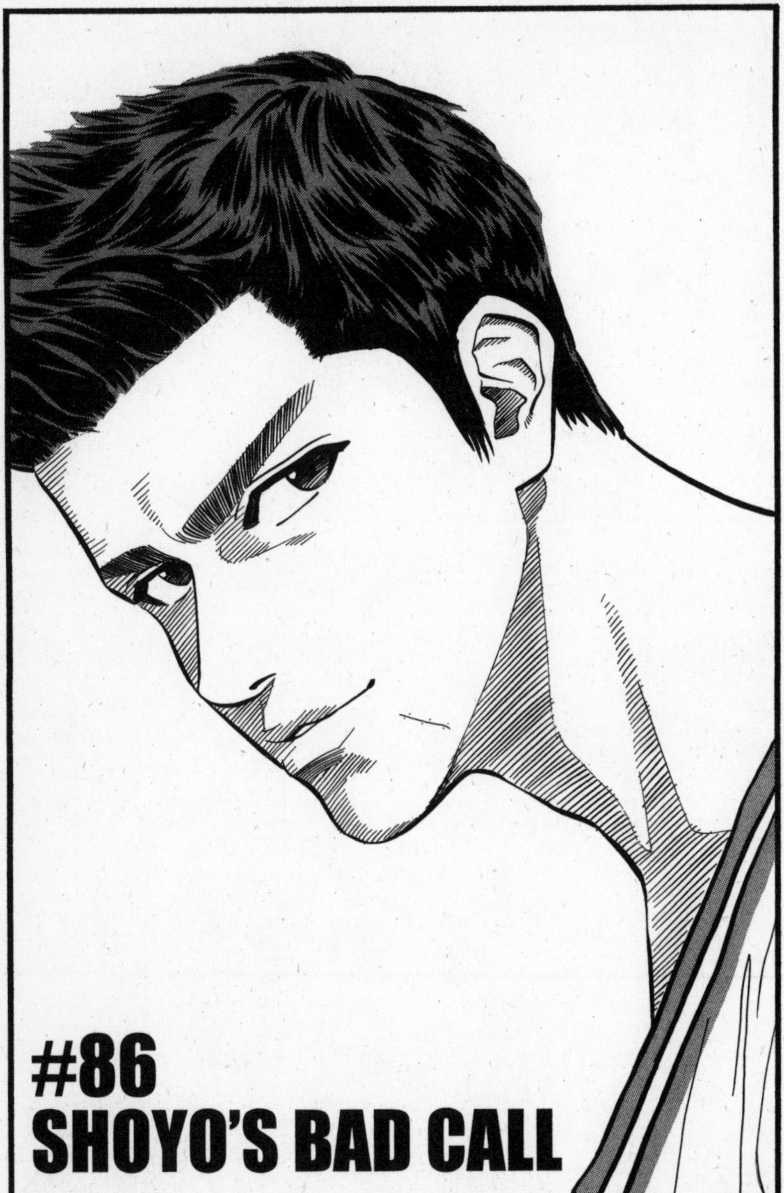

#86
SHOYO'S BAD CALL

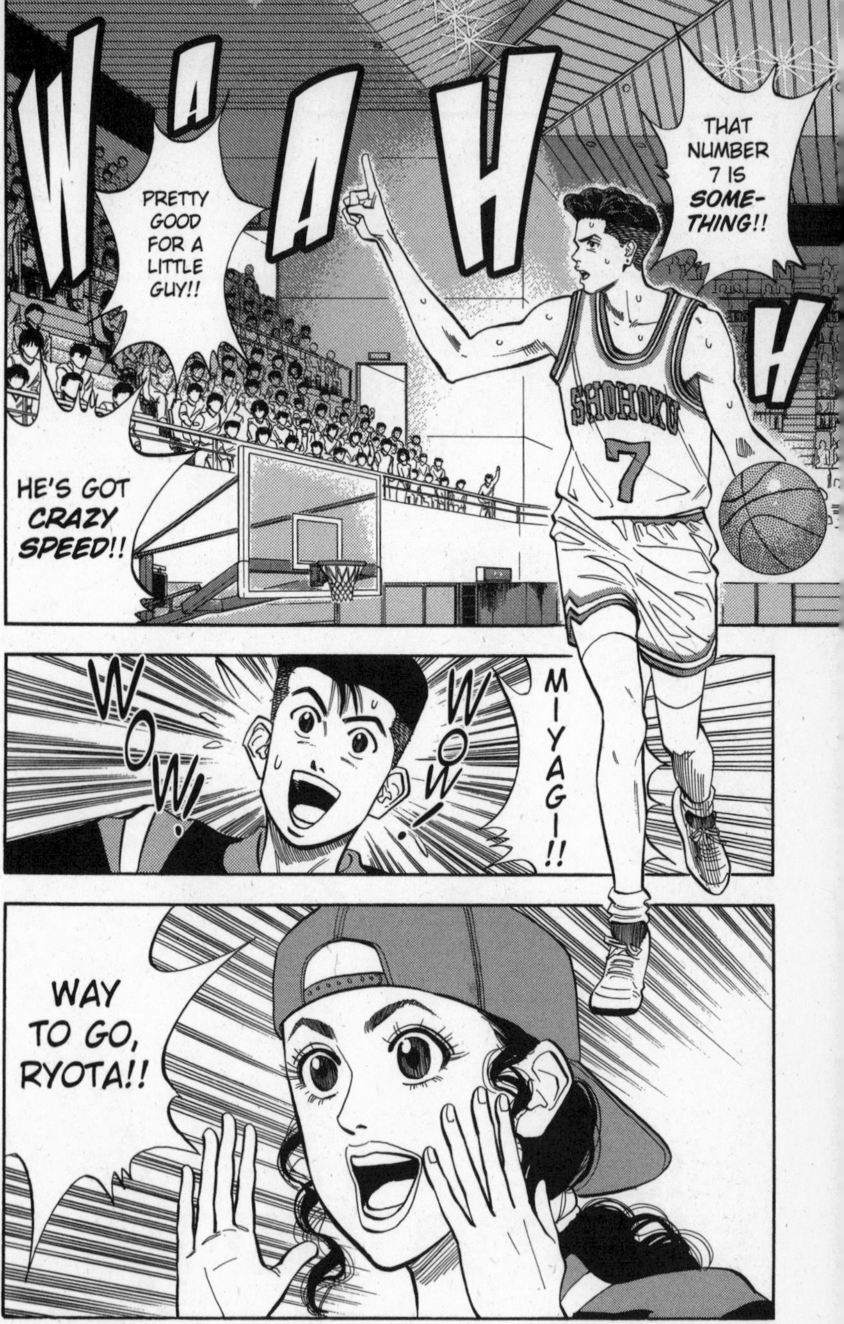
THAT NUMBER 7 IS SOMETHING!!
WAAHH
PRETTY GOOD FOR A LITTLE GUY!!
HE'S GOT CRAZY SPEED!!
SHOHOKU 7
MIYAGI!!
WOW!
WOW!
WAY TO GO, RYOTA!!

READ THIS WAY

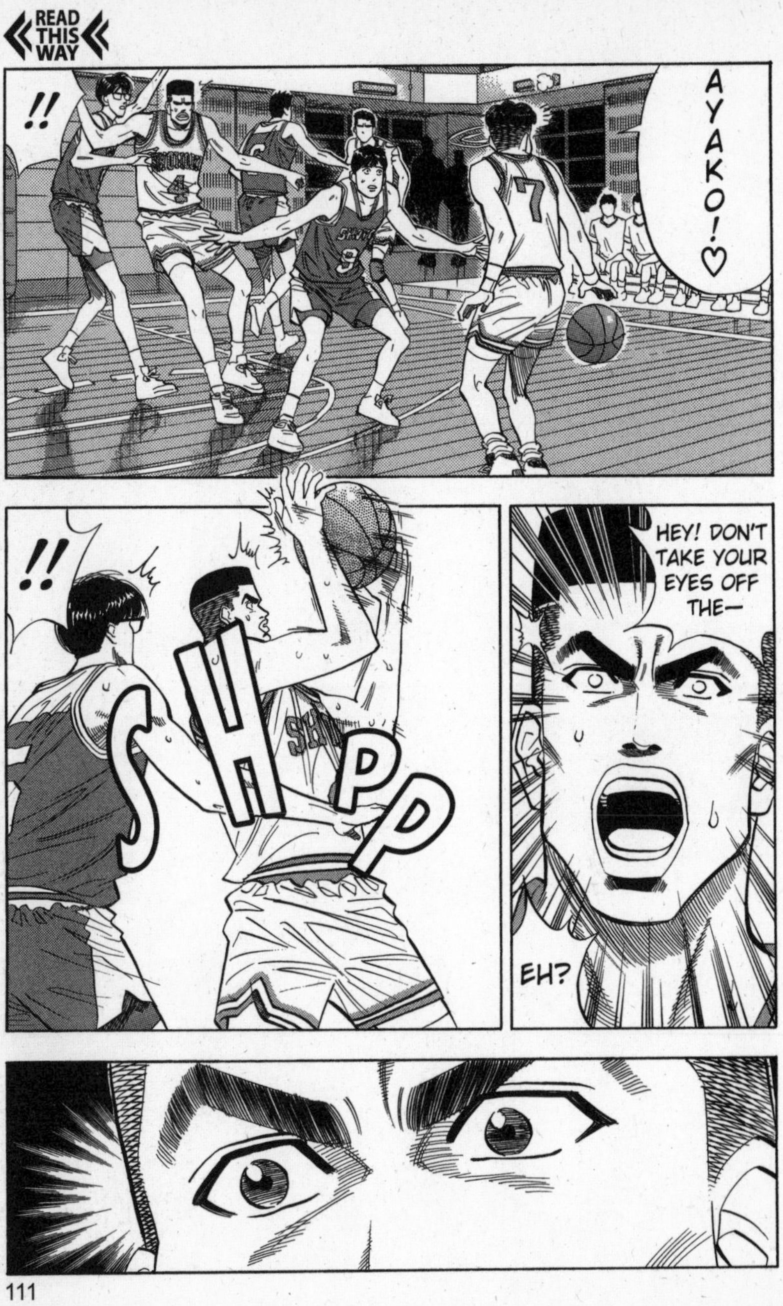
AYAKO!♥
!!
HEY! DON'T TAKE YOUR EYES OFF THE—
EH?
!!
SHPP

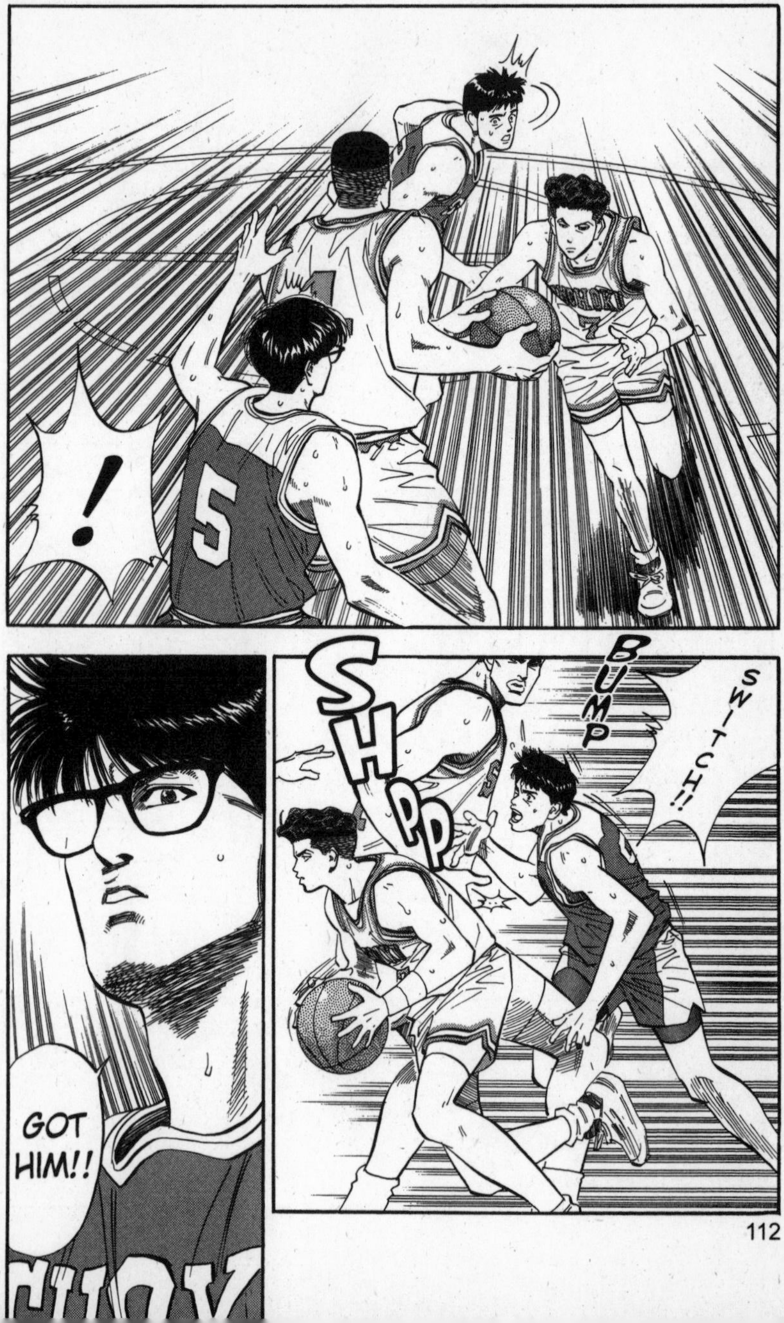
!
SWITCH!!
BUMP
SHPP
GOT HIM!!

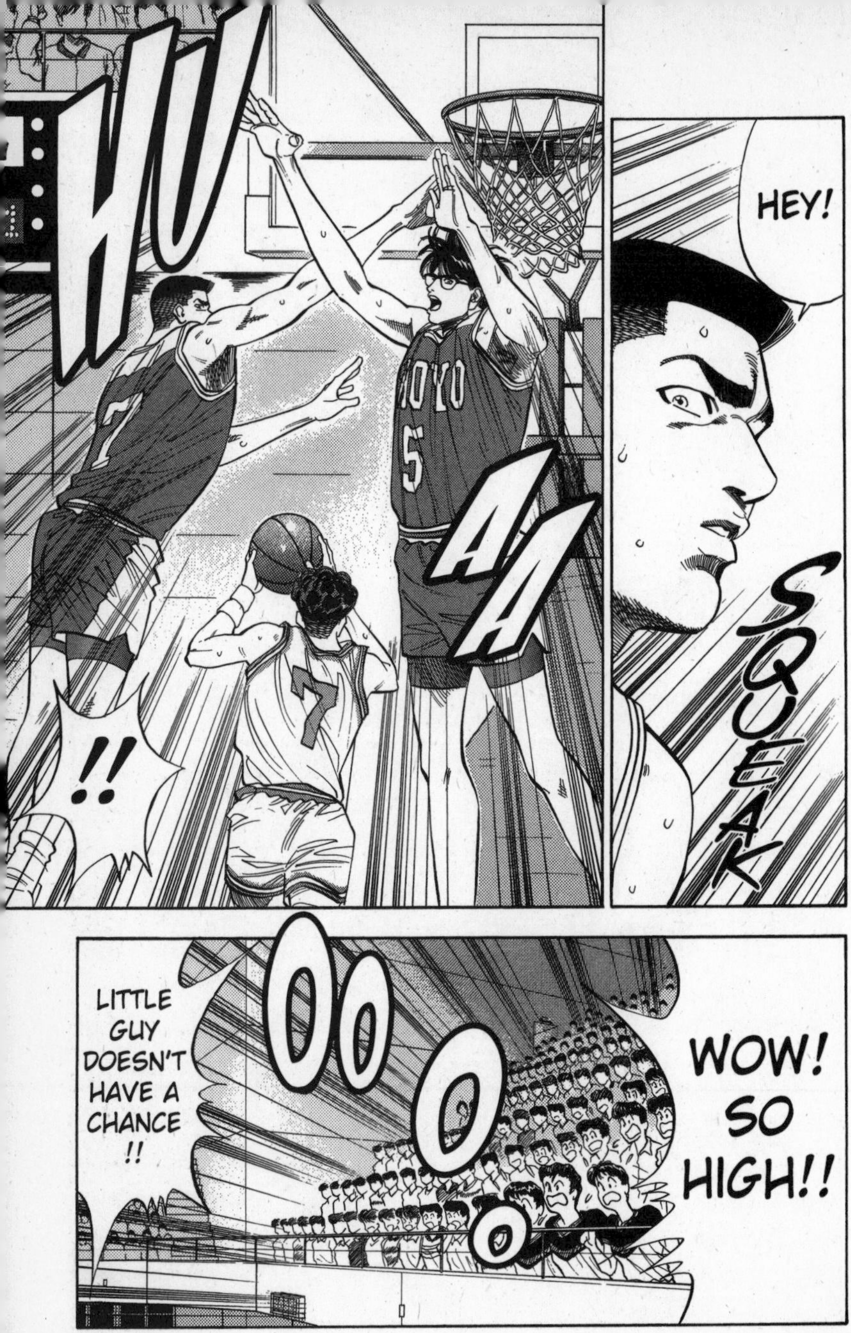
HEY!
SQUEAK
HU
AA
!!
WOW! SO HIGH!!
OOOO
LITTLE GUY DOESN'T HAVE A CHANCE !!

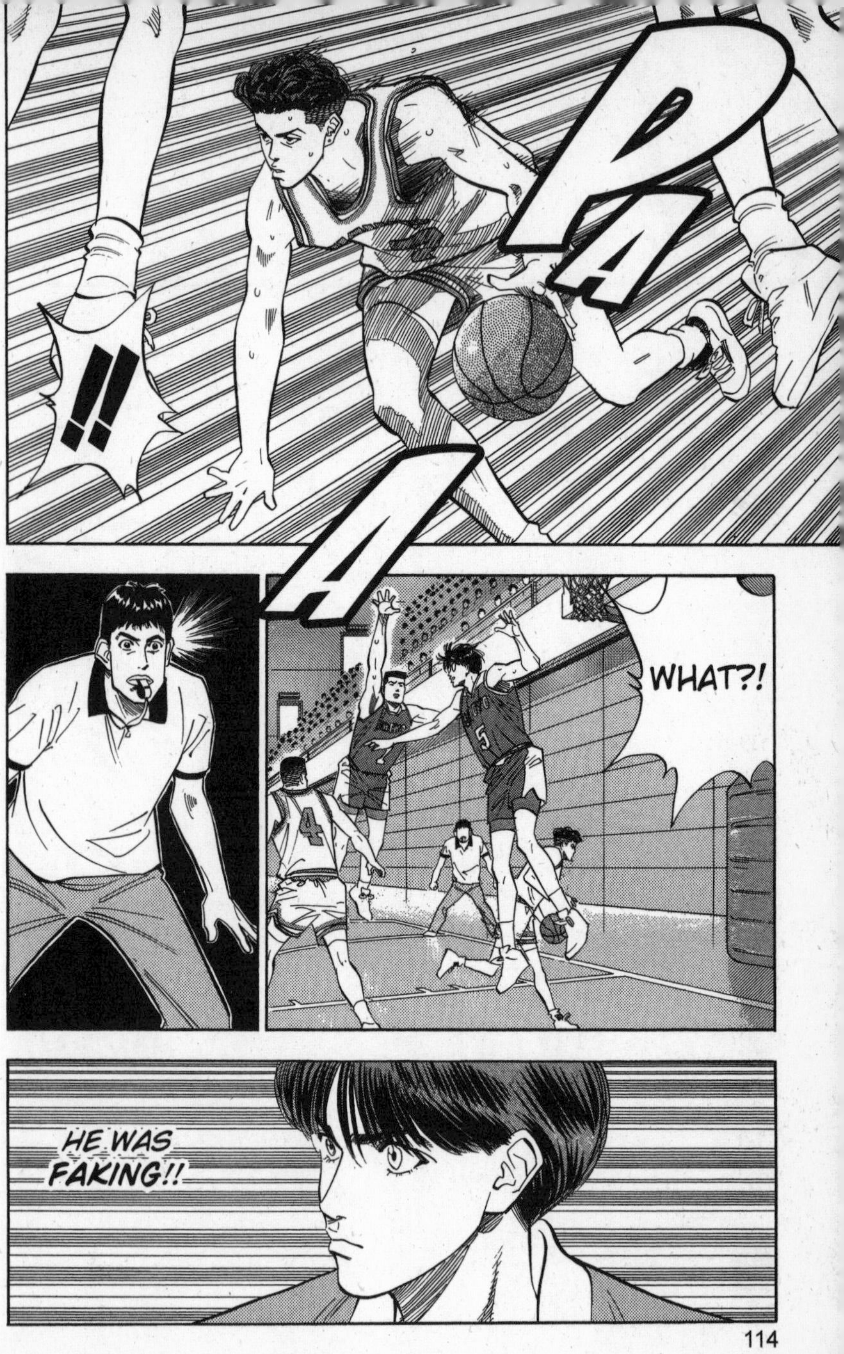
PAA
!!
WHAT?!
HE WAS FAKING!!

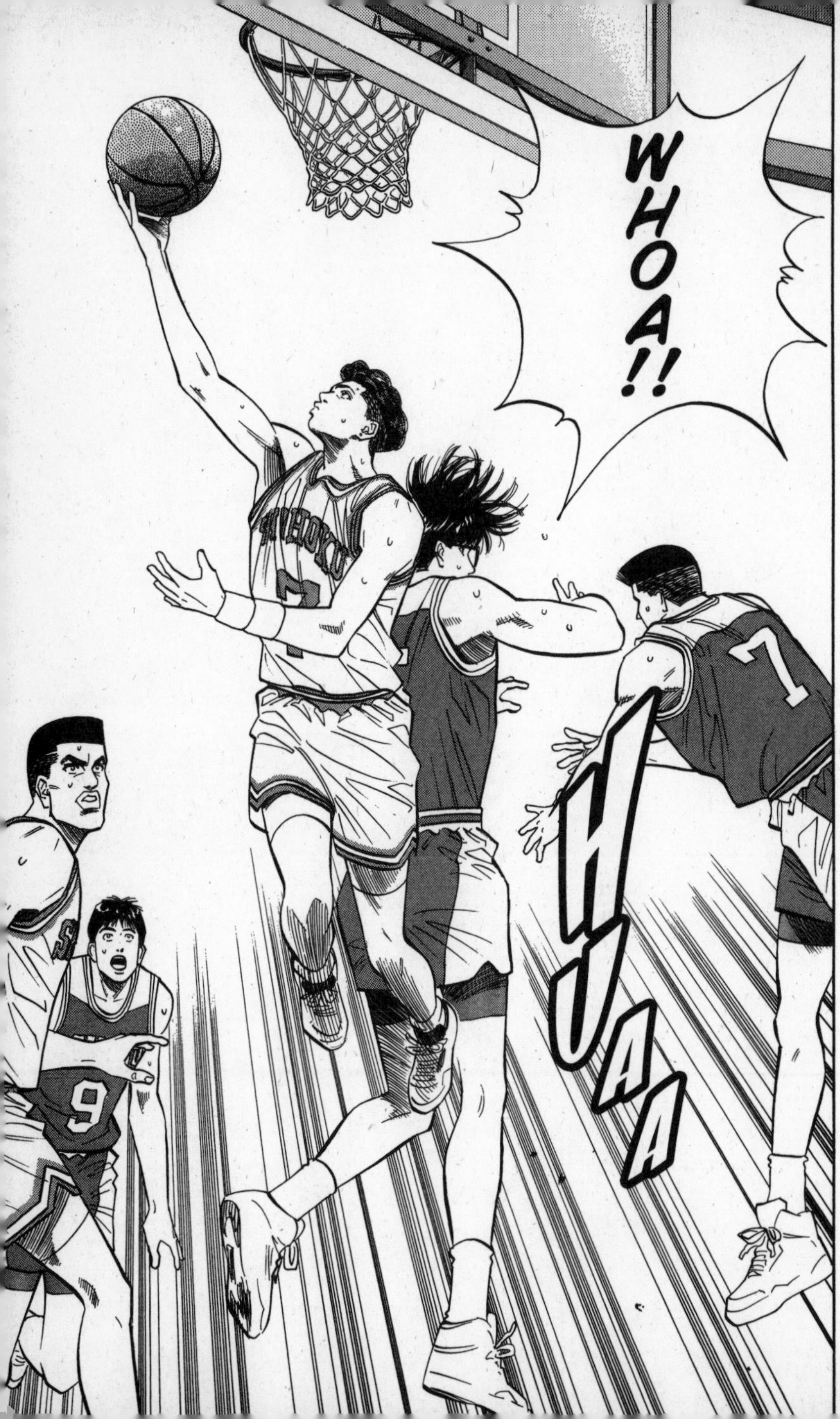
WHOA!!
HUWAAA

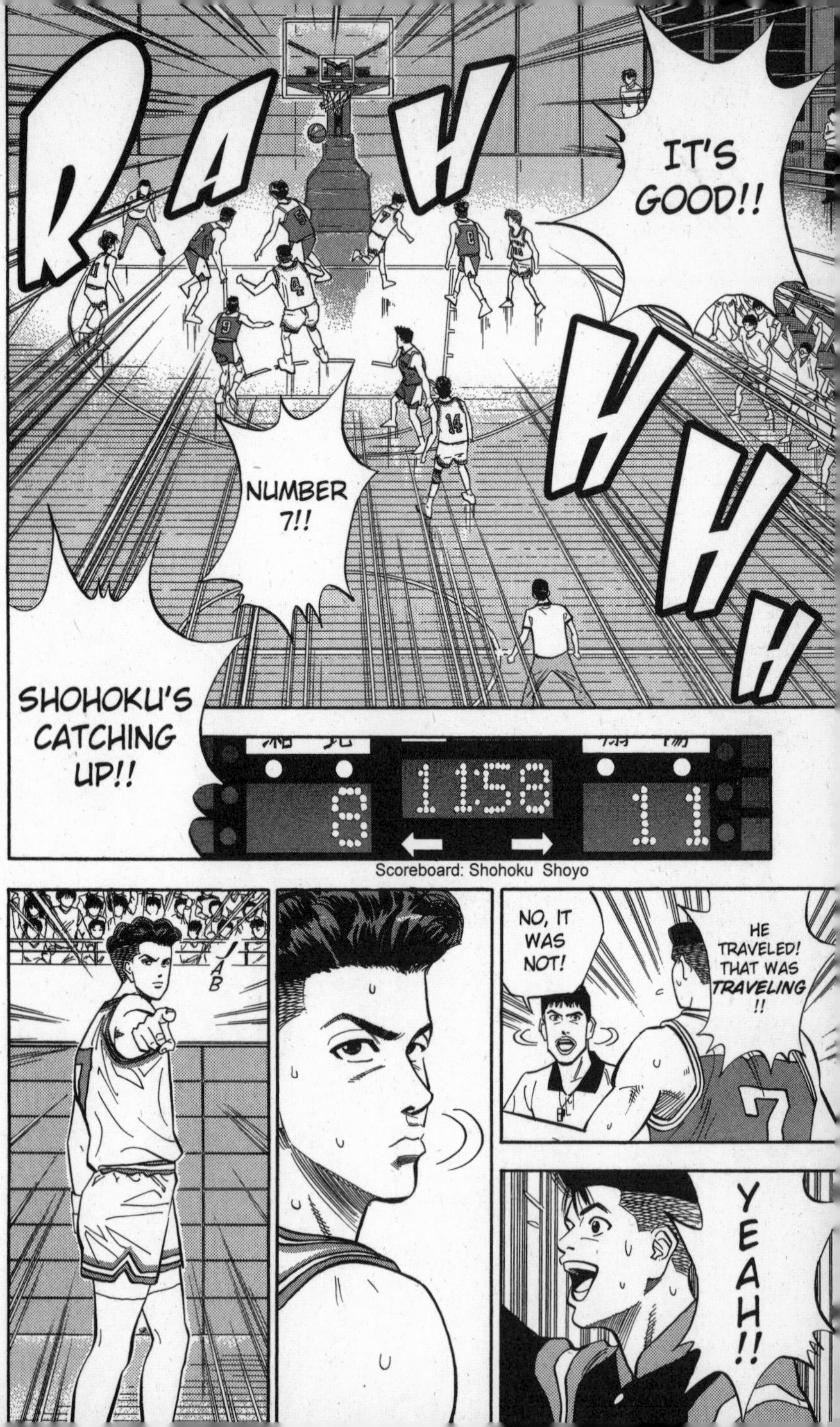
RAAHHHHH
IT'S GOOD!!
NUMBER 7!!
SHOHOKU'S CATCHING UP!!
11:58
8
11
Scoreboard: Shohoku Shoyo
HE TRAVELED! THAT WAS TRAVELING!!
NO, IT WAS NOT!
YEAH!!
JAB

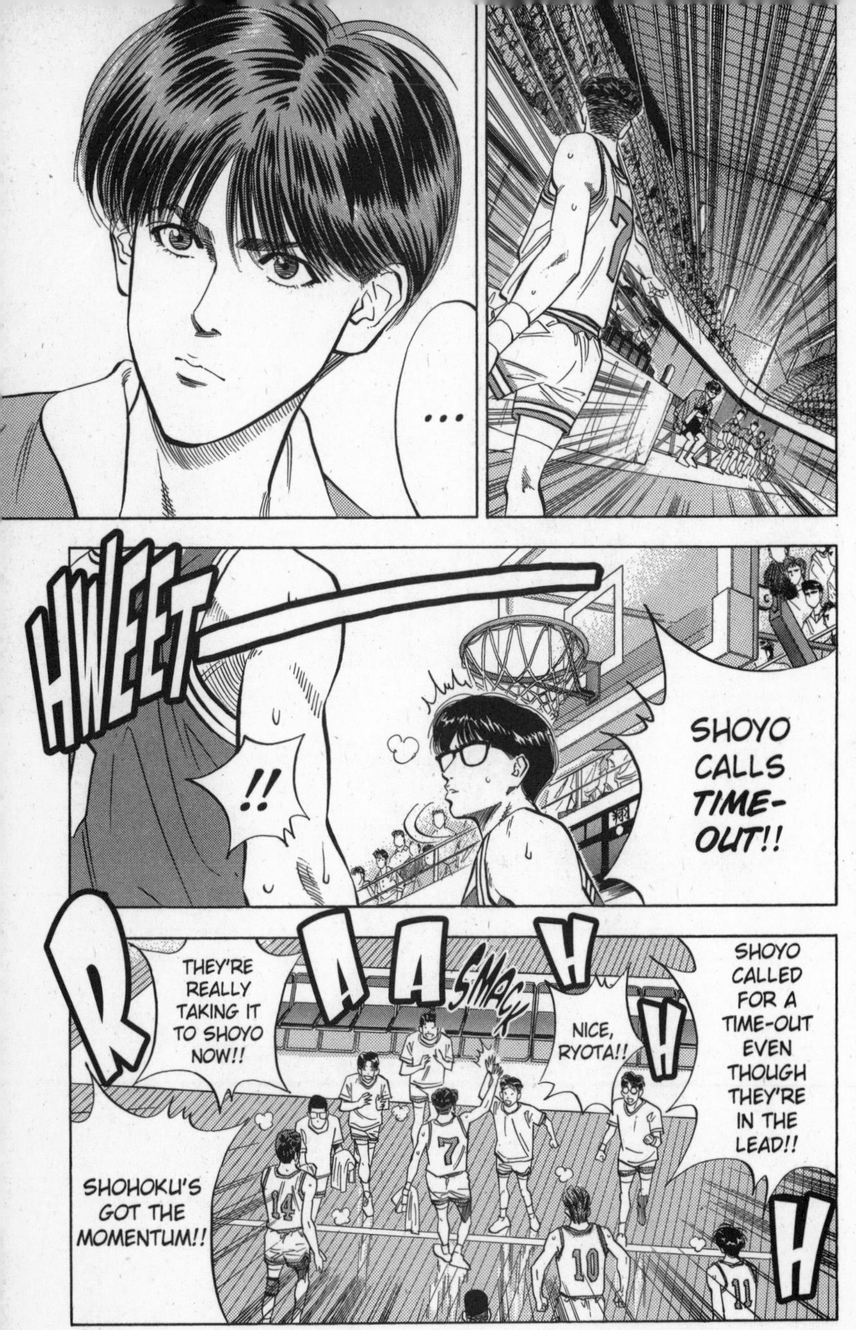
...
SHOYO CALLS TIME-OUT!!
!!
HWEET
SHOYO CALLED FOR A TIME-OUT EVEN THOUGH THEY'RE IN THE LEAD!!
NICE, RYOTA!!
SMACK
RAAHHH
THEY'RE REALLY TAKING IT TO SHOYO NOW!!
SHOHOKU'S GOT THE MOMENTUM!!

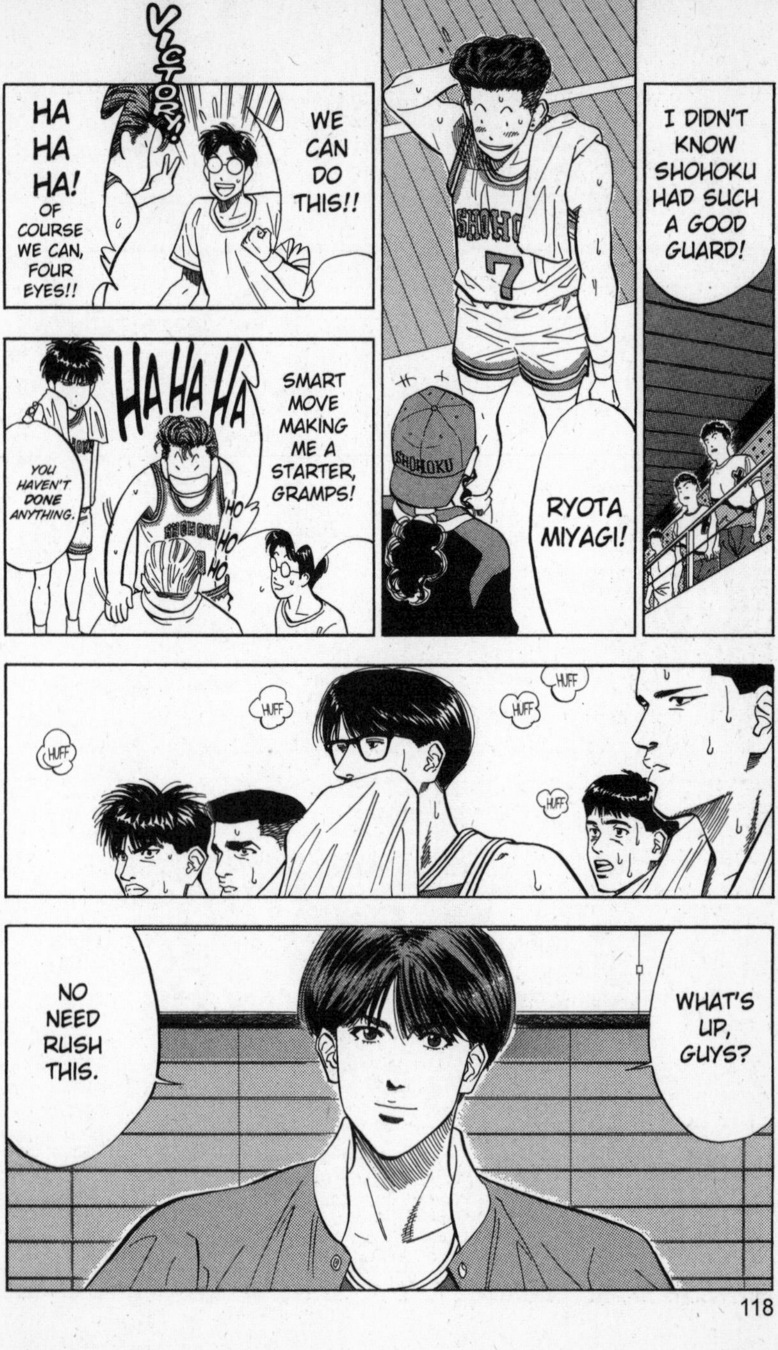
I DIDN'T KNOW SHOHOKU HAD SUCH A GOOD GUARD!
RYOTA MIYAGI!
WE CAN DO THIS!!
VICTORY!
HA HA HA! OF COURSE WE CAN, FOUR EYES!!
SMART MOVE MAKING ME A STARTER, GRAMPS!
HA HA HA
HO HO HO
YOU HAVEN'T DONE ANYTHING.
HUFF
HUFF
HUFF
HUFF
HUFF
WHAT'S UP, GUYS?
NO NEED RUSH THIS.

READ THIS WAY

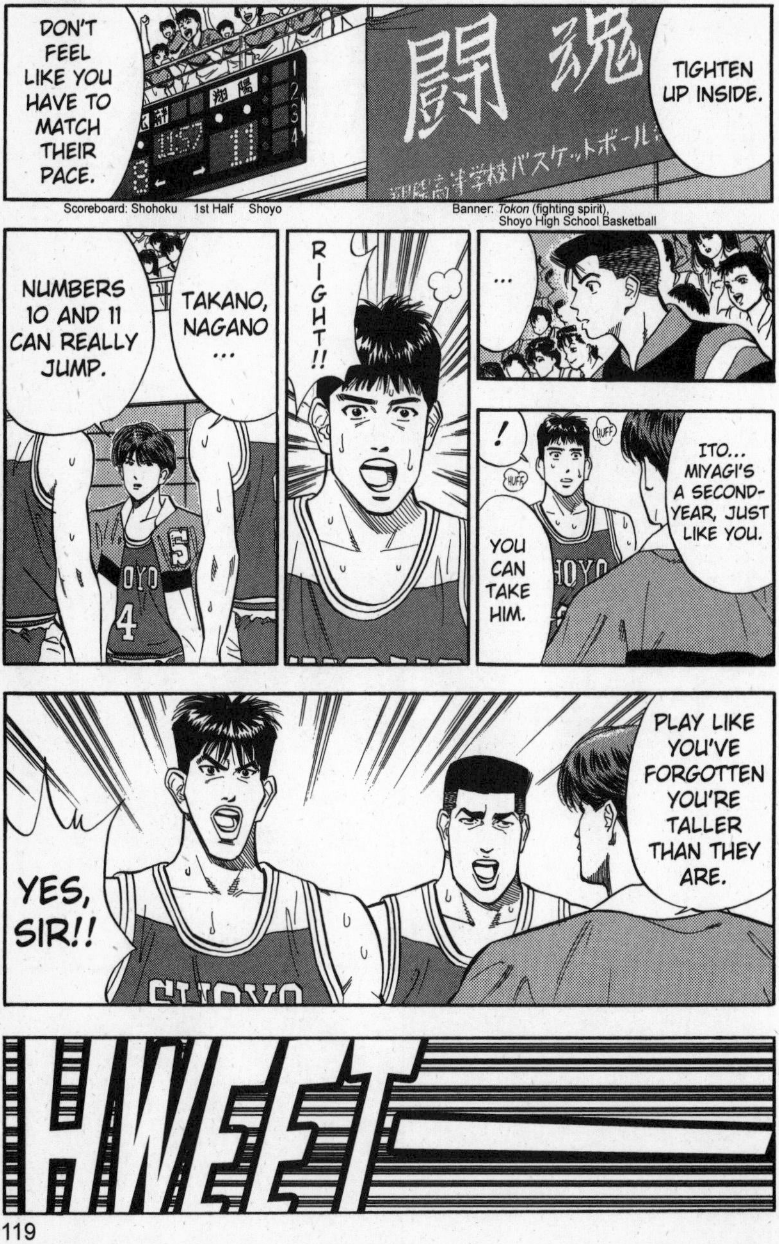
TIGHTEN UP INSIDE.
DON'T FEEL LIKE YOU HAVE TO MATCH THEIR PACE.
...
ITO... MIYAGI'S A SECOND-YEAR, JUST LIKE YOU.
HUFF
!
HUFF
YOU CAN TAKE HIM.
RIGHT!!
TAKANO, NAGANO...
NUMBERS 10 AND 11 CAN REALLY JUMP.
PLAY LIKE YOU'VE FORGOTTEN YOU'RE TALLER THAN THEY ARE.
YES, SIR!!
HWEET

Scoreboard: Shohoku 1st Half Shoyo
Banner: *Tokon* (fighting spirit), Shoyo High School Basketball

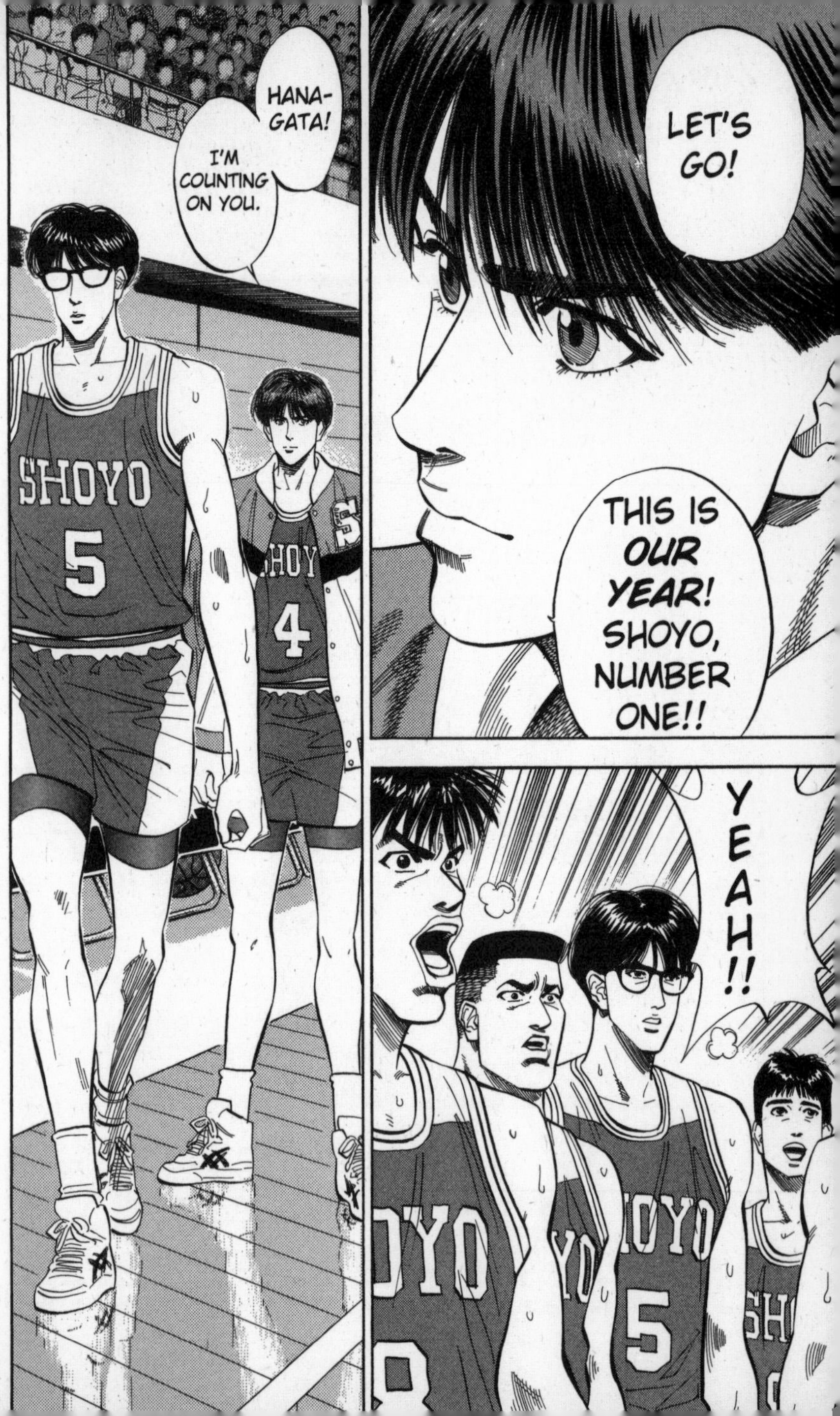
LET'S GO!
THIS IS **OUR YEAR!** SHOYO, NUMBER ONE!!
YEAH!!
HANA-GATA!
I'M COUNTING ON YOU.

READ THIS WAY

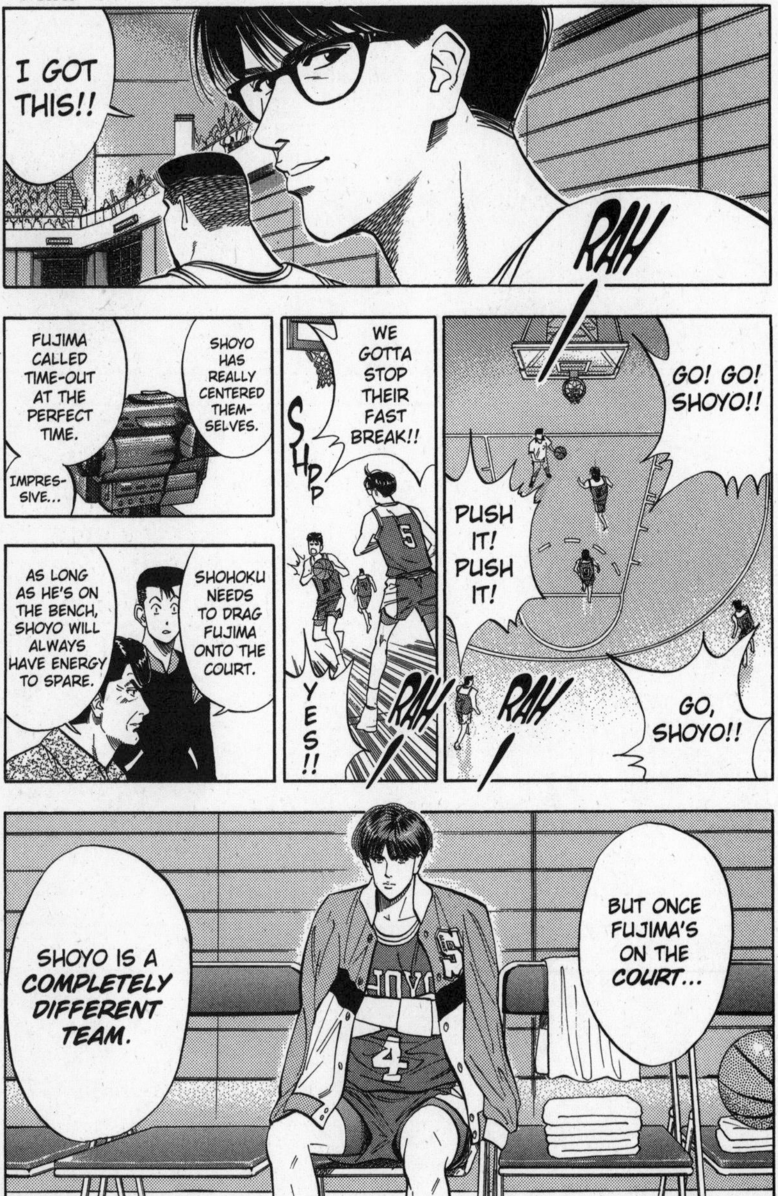
I GOT THIS!!
RAH
GO! GO! SHOYO!!
PUSH IT! PUSH IT!
RAH
RAH
GO, SHOYO!!
WE GOTTA STOP THEIR FAST BREAK!!
SHPP
YES!!
SHOYO HAS REALLY CENTERED THEMSELVES.
FUJIMA CALLED TIME-OUT AT THE PERFECT TIME.
IMPRES-SIVE...
SHOHOKU NEEDS TO DRAG FUJIMA ONTO THE COURT.
AS LONG AS HE'S ON THE BENCH, SHOYO WILL ALWAYS HAVE ENERGY TO SPARE.
BUT ONCE FUJIMA'S ON THE COURT...
SHOYO IS A COMPLETELY DIFFERENT TEAM.

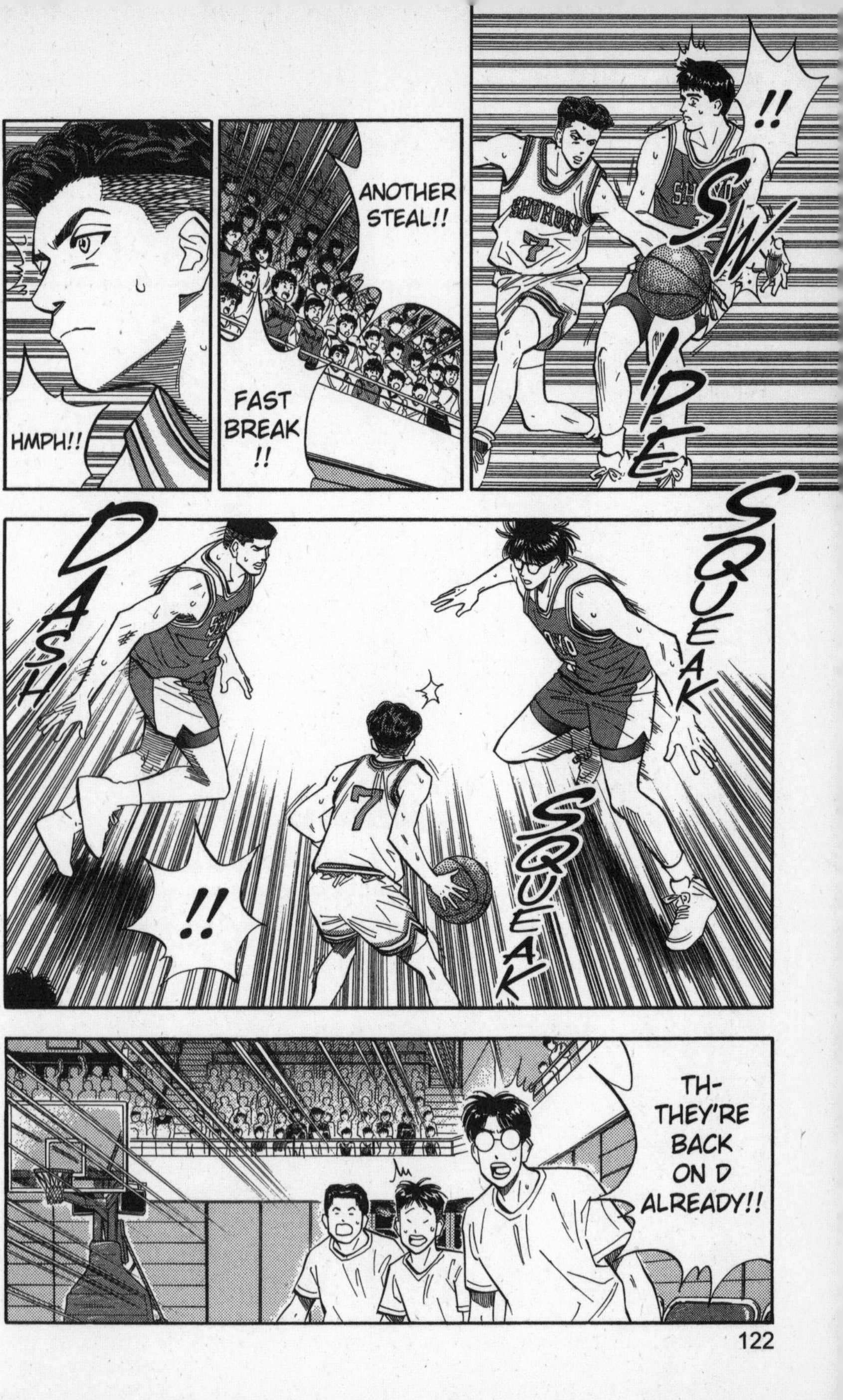
!!
SWIPE
ANOTHER STEAL!!
FAST BREAK!!
HMPH!!
SQUEAK
SQUEAK
!!
DASH
TH- THEY'RE BACK ON D ALREADY!!

READ THIS WAY

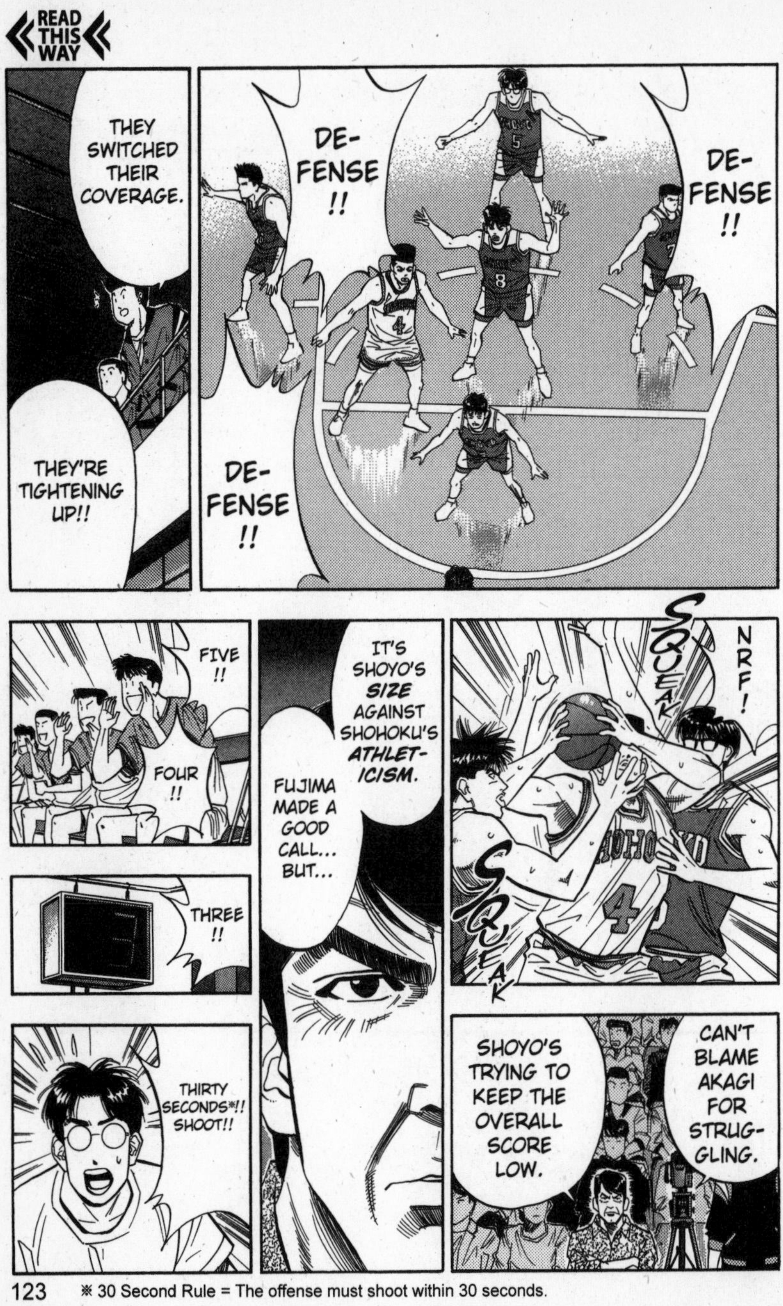
DE-FENSE!!
DE-FENSE!!
DE-FENSE!!
THEY SWITCHED THEIR COVERAGE.
THEY'RE TIGHTENING UP!!
SQUEAK
NRF!
SQUEAK
CAN'T BLAME AKAGI FOR STRUGGLING.
SHOYO'S TRYING TO KEEP THE OVERALL SCORE LOW.
IT'S SHOYO'S **SIZE** AGAINST SHOHOKU'S **ATHLETICISM**.
FUJIMA MADE A GOOD CALL... BUT...
FIVE!!
FOUR!!
THREE!!
THIRTY SECONDS※!! SHOOT!!

※ 30 Second Rule = The offense must shoot within 30 seconds.

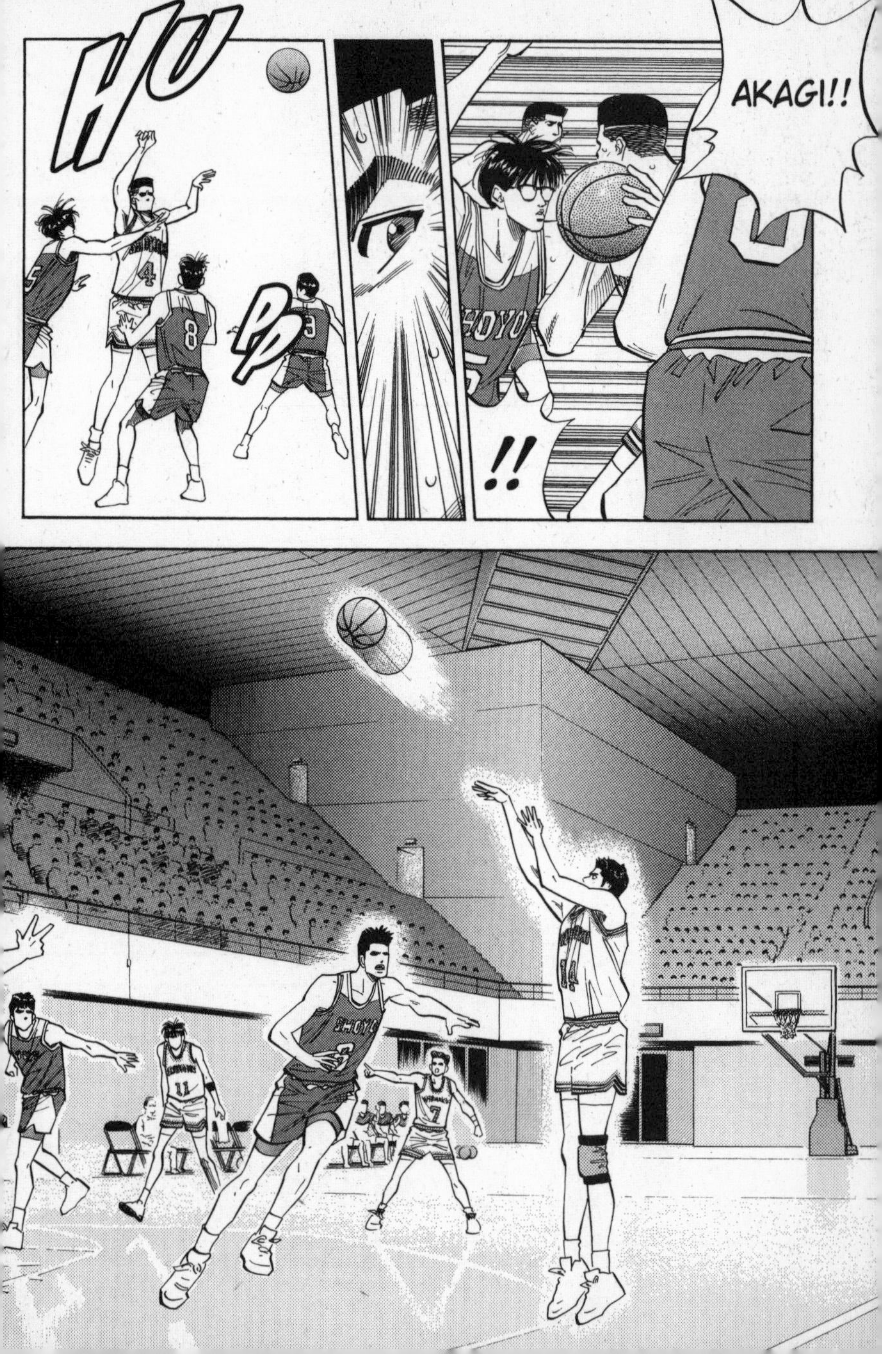
AKAGI!!
!!

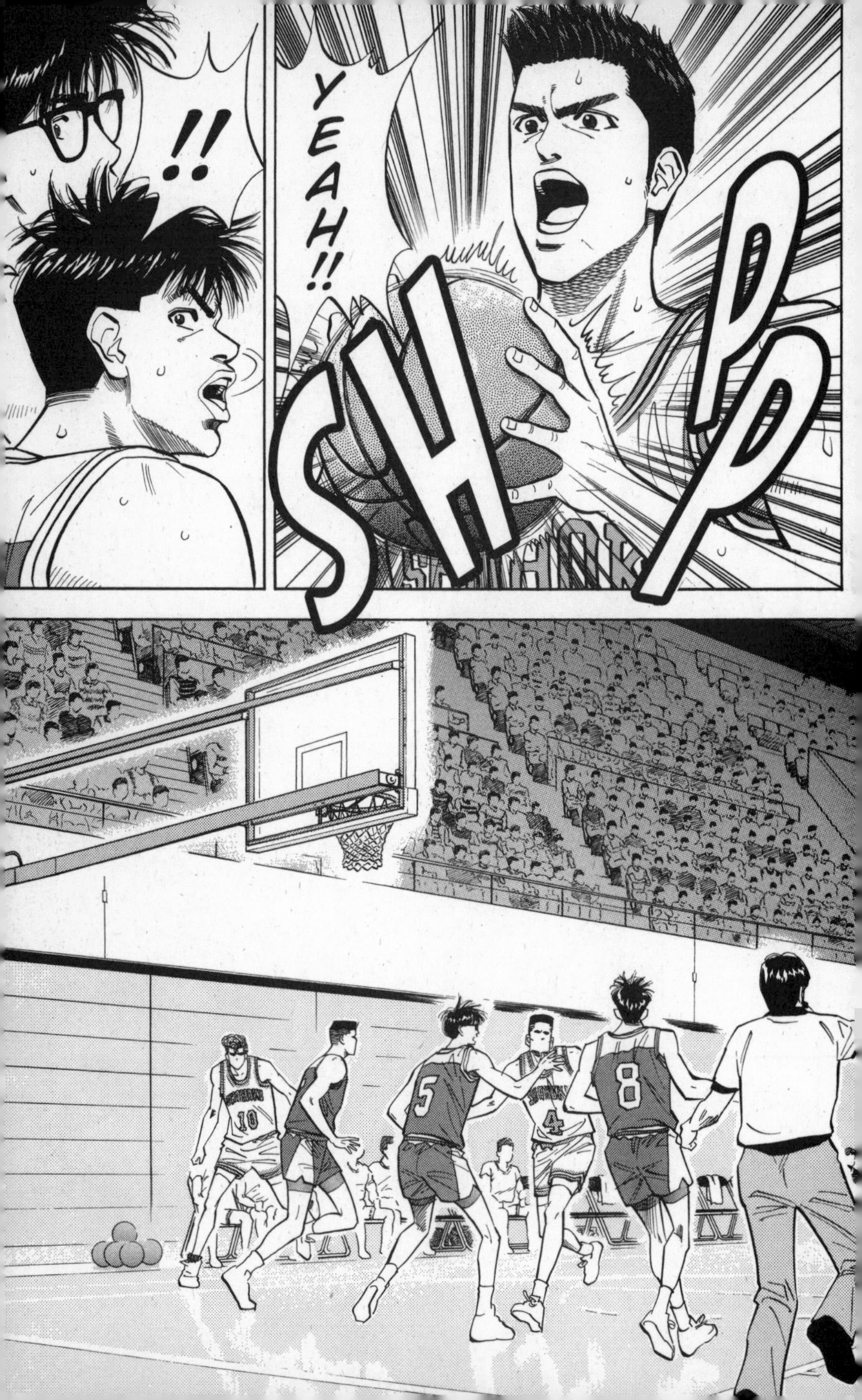
YEAH!!
SHPP
!!

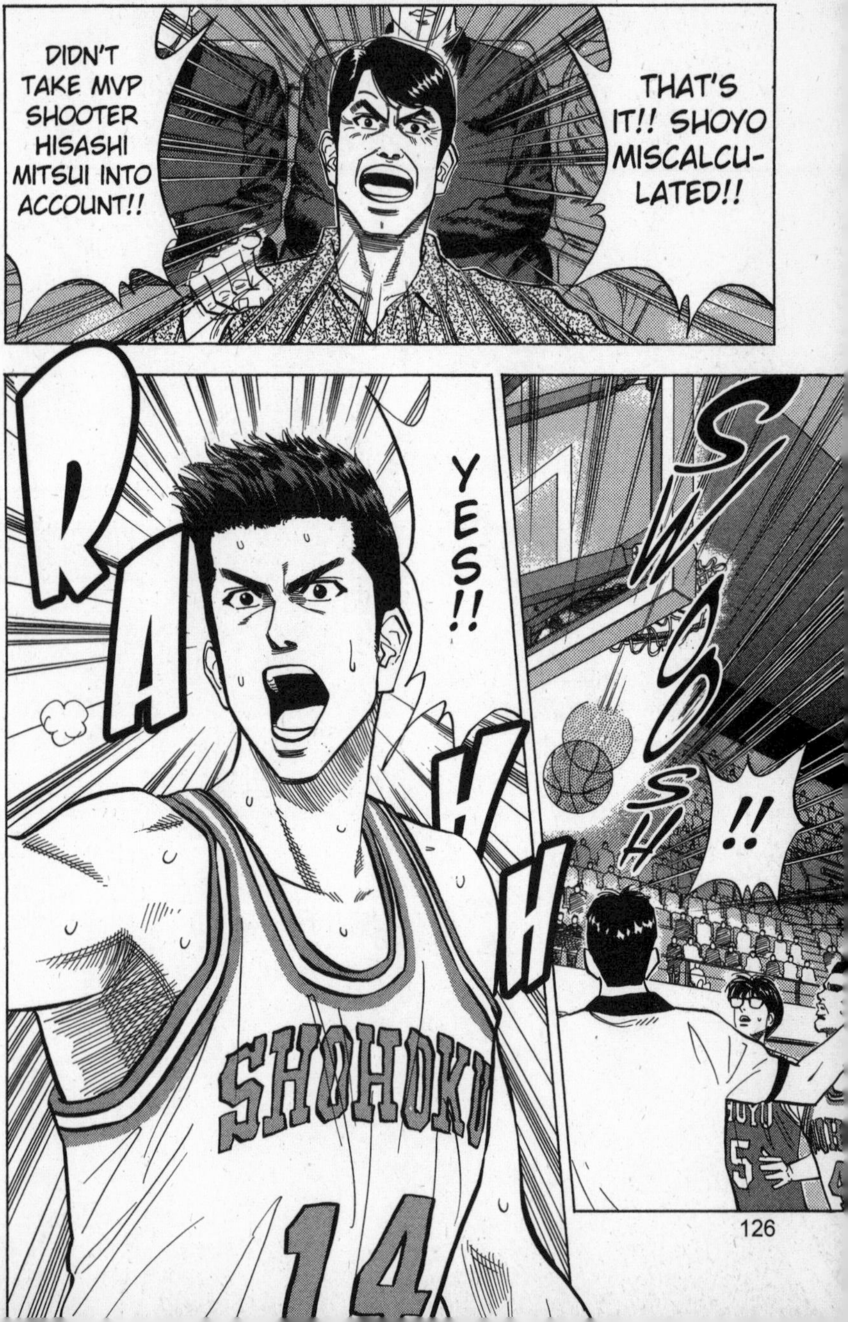
THAT'S IT!! SHOYO MISCALCULATED!!
DIDN'T TAKE MVP SHOOTER HISASHI MITSUI INTO ACCOUNT!!
SWOOSH!!
YES!!
RAHH
SHOHOKU
14

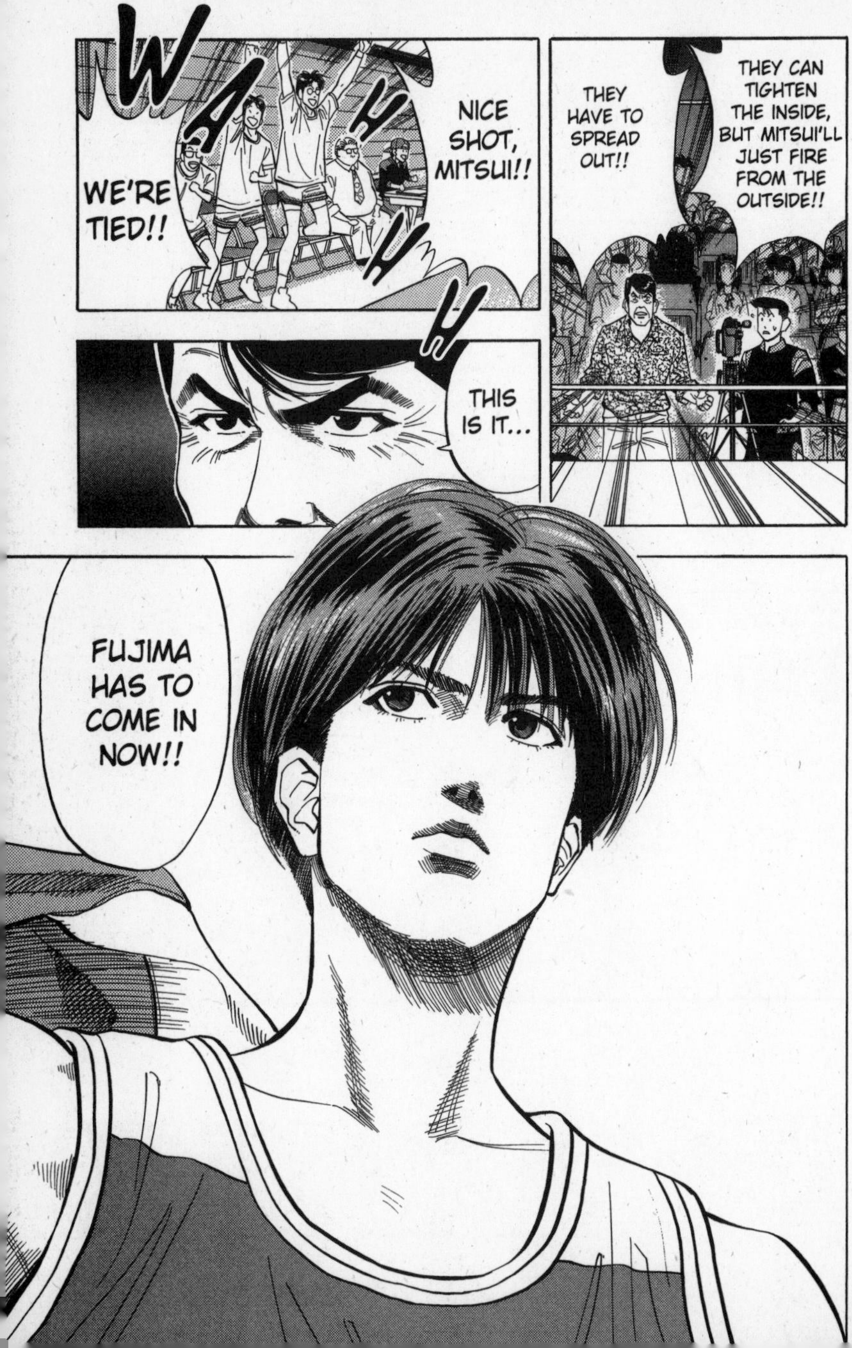
THEY CAN TIGHTEN THE INSIDE, BUT MITSUI'LL JUST FIRE FROM THE OUTSIDE!!
THEY HAVE TO SPREAD OUT!!
WAHHHH
NICE SHOT, MITSUI!!
WE'RE TIED!!
THIS IS IT...
FUJIMA HAS TO COME IN NOW!!

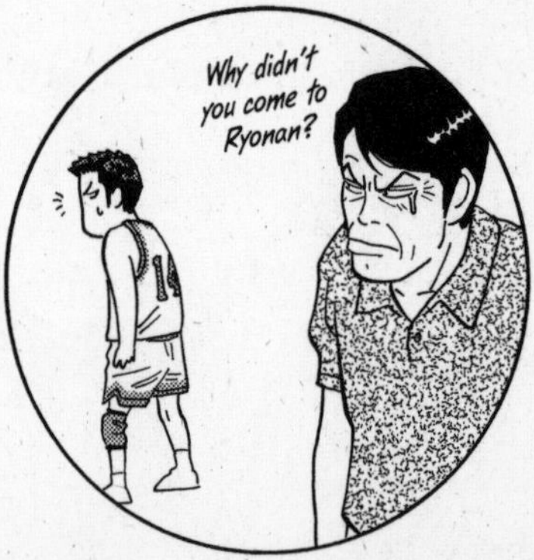
Why didn't you come to Ryonan?

SLAM DUNK

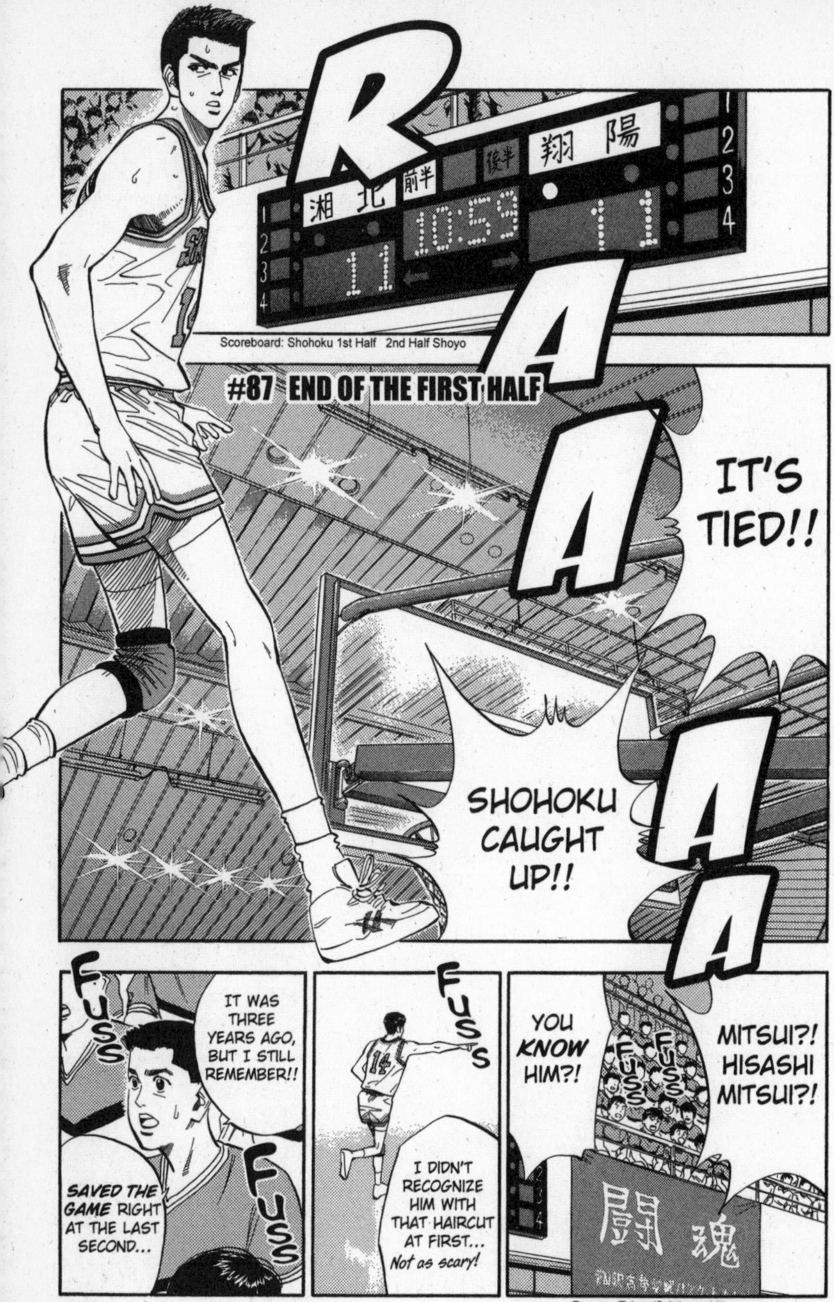
RAAAAA
#87 END OF THE FIRST HALF
湘北 前半 後半 翔陽
10:59
11 11
IT'S TIED!!
SHOHOKU CAUGHT UP!!
MITSUI?! HISASHI MITSUI?!
FUSS FUSS
YOU KNOW HIM?!
闘魂
FUSS
I DIDN'T RECOGNIZE HIM WITH THAT HAIRCUT AT FIRST... Not as scary!
FUSS
IT WAS THREE YEARS AGO, BUT I STILL REMEMBER!!
FUSS
SAVED THE GAME RIGHT AT THE LAST SECOND...

Scoreboard: Shohoku 1st Half 2nd Half Shoyo

Banner: *Tokon* (fighting spirit)
Shoyo High School Basketball

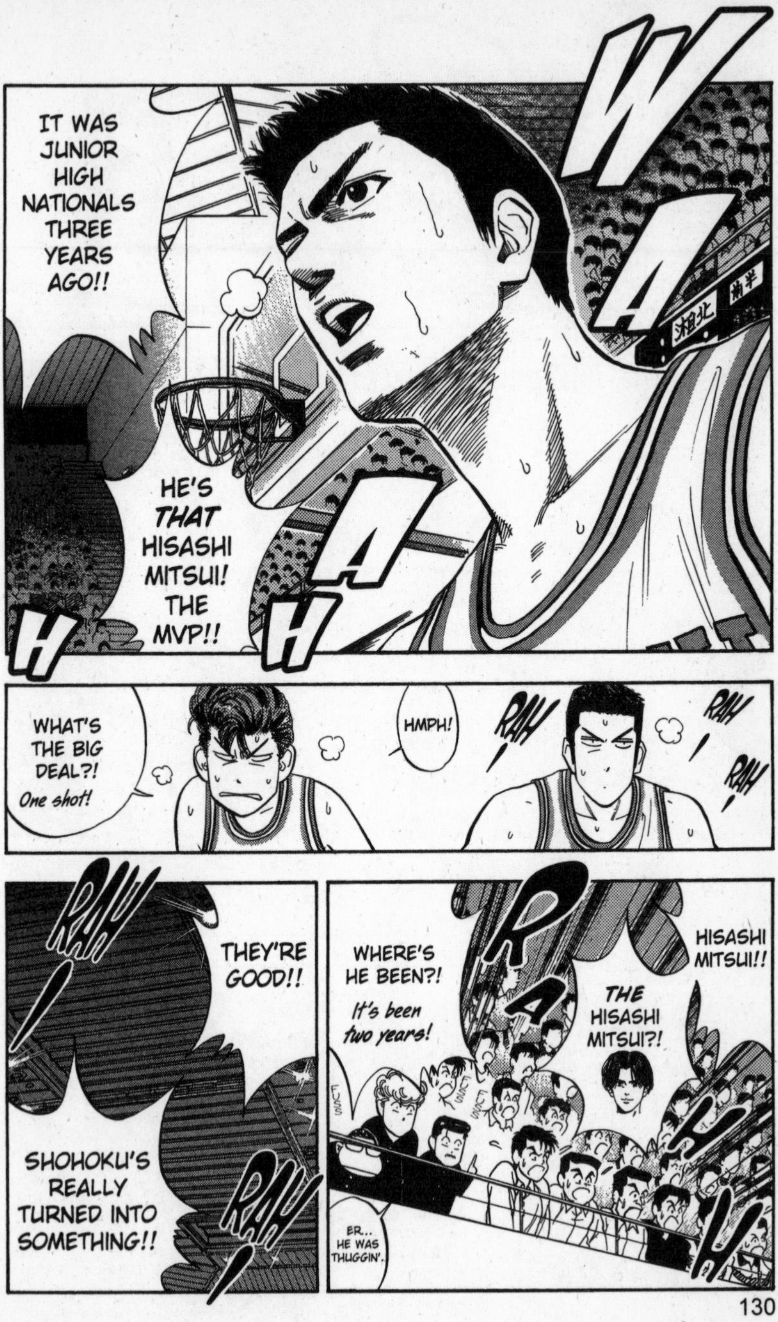
WAAHH
IT WAS JUNIOR HIGH NATIONALS THREE YEARS AGO!!
HE'S *THAT* HISASHI MITSUI! THE MVP!!
HAH
RAH! RAH! RAH!
HMPH!
WHAT'S THE BIG DEAL?! *One shot!*
RAAHH
HISASHI MITSUI!!
WHERE'S HE BEEN?! *It's been two years!*
THE HISASHI MITSUI?!
FUSS
ER... HE WAS THUGGIN'.
RAH!
THEY'RE GOOD!!
SHOHOKU'S REALLY TURNED INTO SOMETHING!!
RAH!

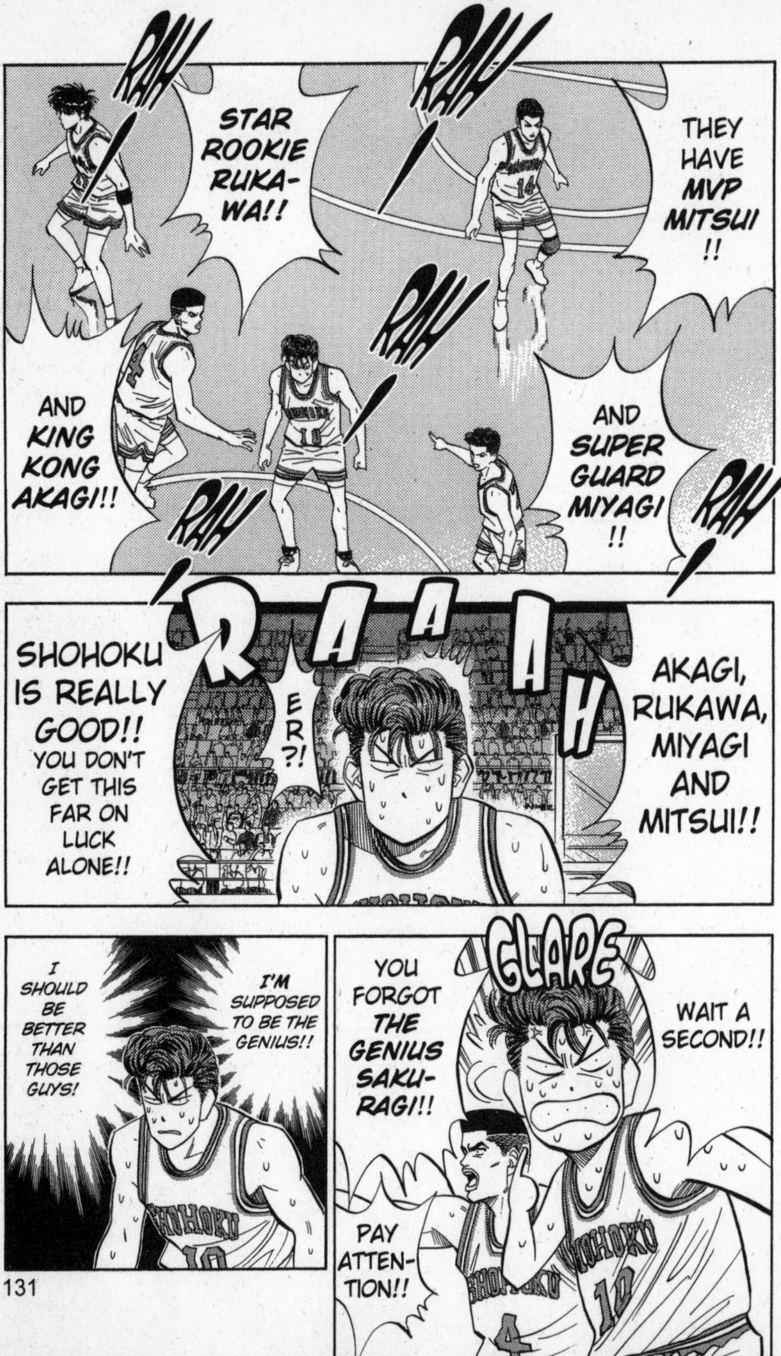

RAH!
THEY HAVE MVP MITSUI!!
RAH!
STAR ROOKIE RUKA-WA!!
RAH!
AND SUPER GUARD MIYAGI!!
AND KING KONG AKAGI!!
RAH!
RAH!
AKAGI, RUKAWA, MIYAGI AND MITSUI!!
RAAAH
ER?!
SHOHOKU IS REALLY GOOD!!
YOU DON'T GET THIS FAR ON LUCK ALONE!!
GLARE
WAIT A SECOND!!
YOU FORGOT THE GENIUS SAKU-RAGI!!
PAY ATTEN-TION!!
I'M SUPPOSED TO BE THE GENIUS!!
I SHOULD BE BETTER THAN THOSE GUYS!

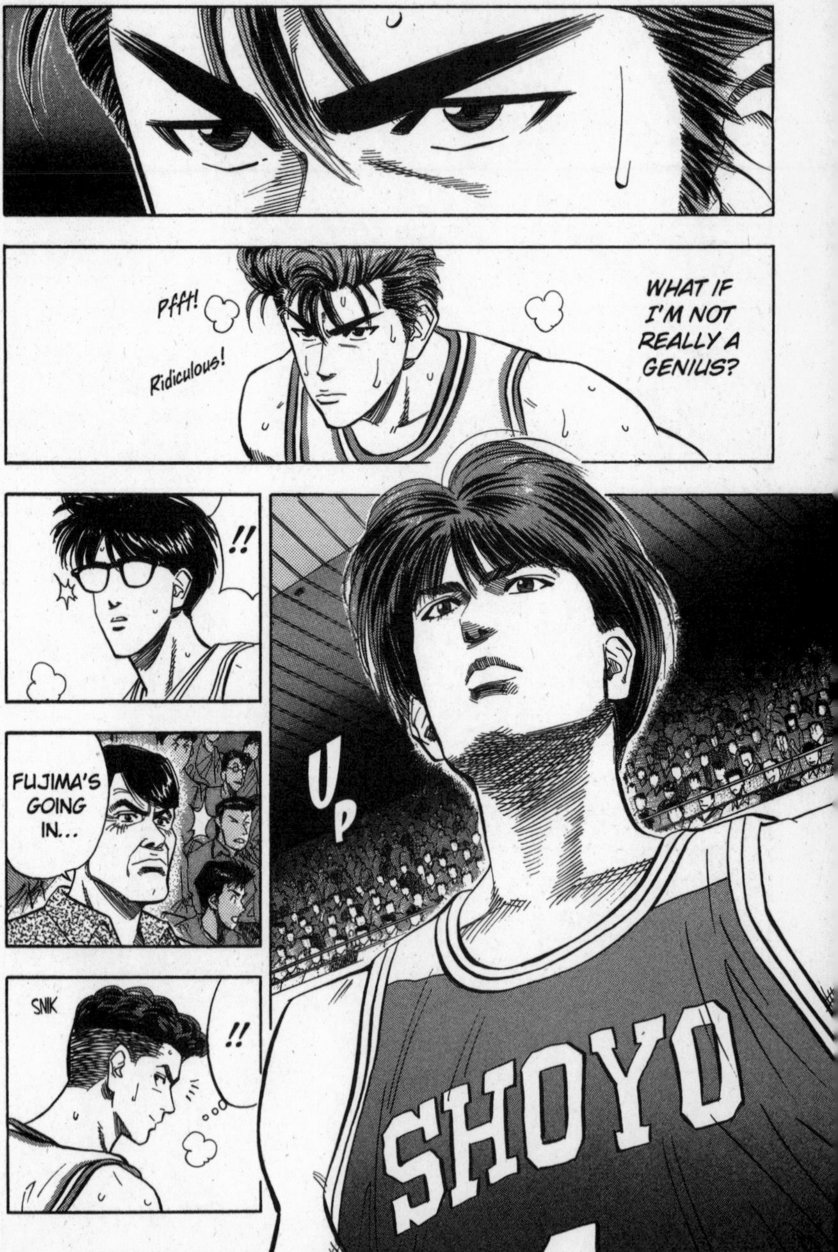
WHAT IF I'M NOT REALLY A GENIUS?
Pfft!
Ridiculous!
UP
!!
FUJIMA'S GOING IN...
SNIK
!!

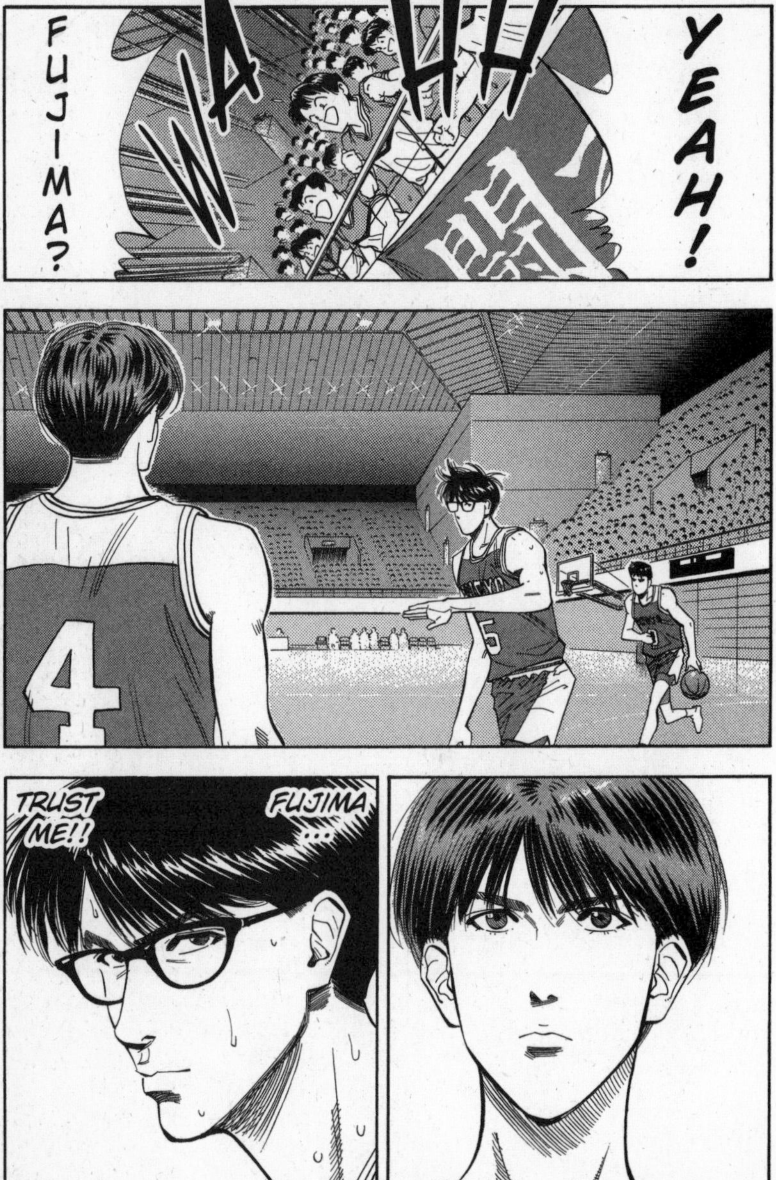
YEAH!
WAHHH
FUJIMA?
FUJIMA...
TRUST ME!!

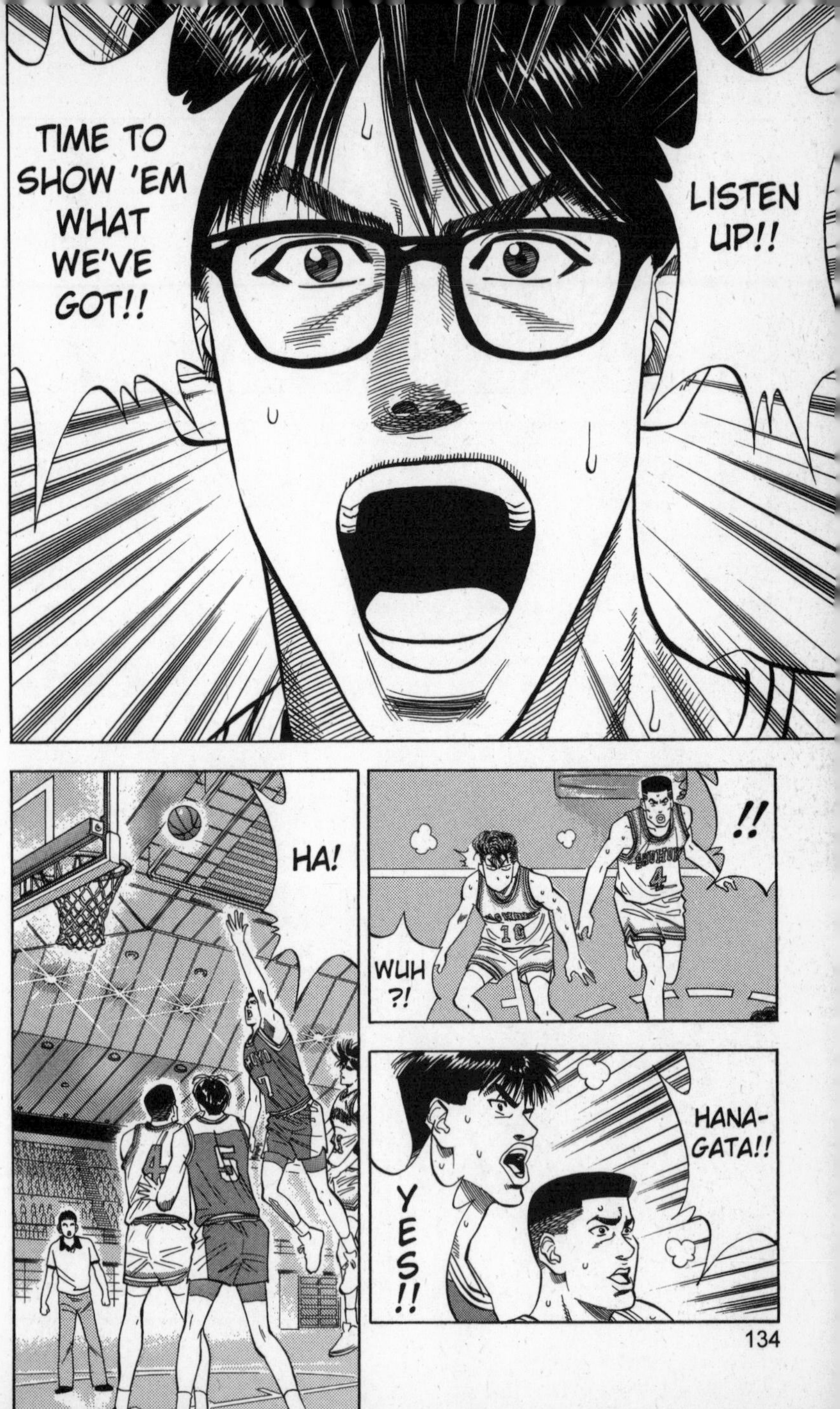

LISTEN UP!!
TIME TO SHOW 'EM WHAT WE'VE GOT!!
!!
WUH ?!
HANA-GATA!!
YES!!
HA!

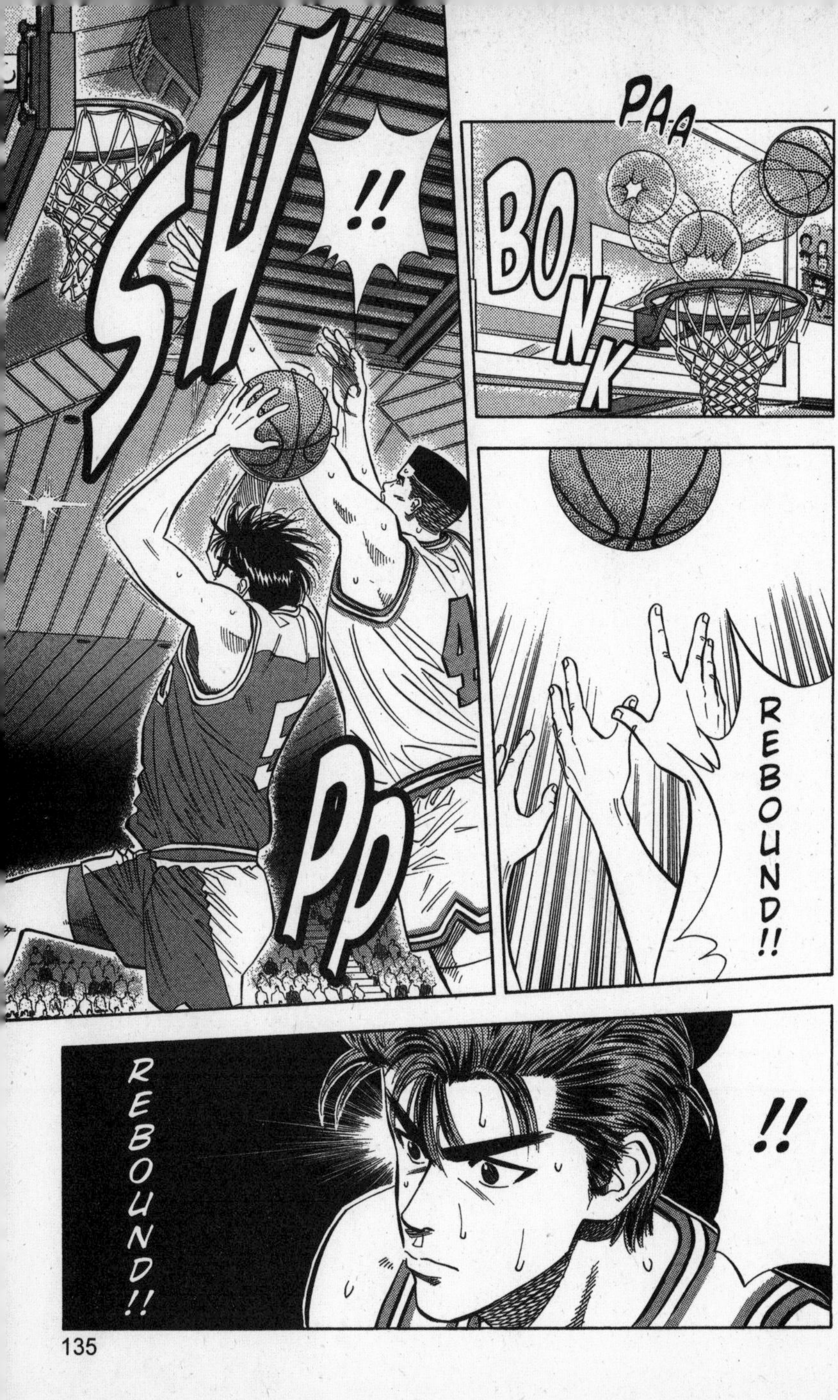
PAA
BONK
REBOUND!!
SH
!!
Pp
!!
REBOUND!!

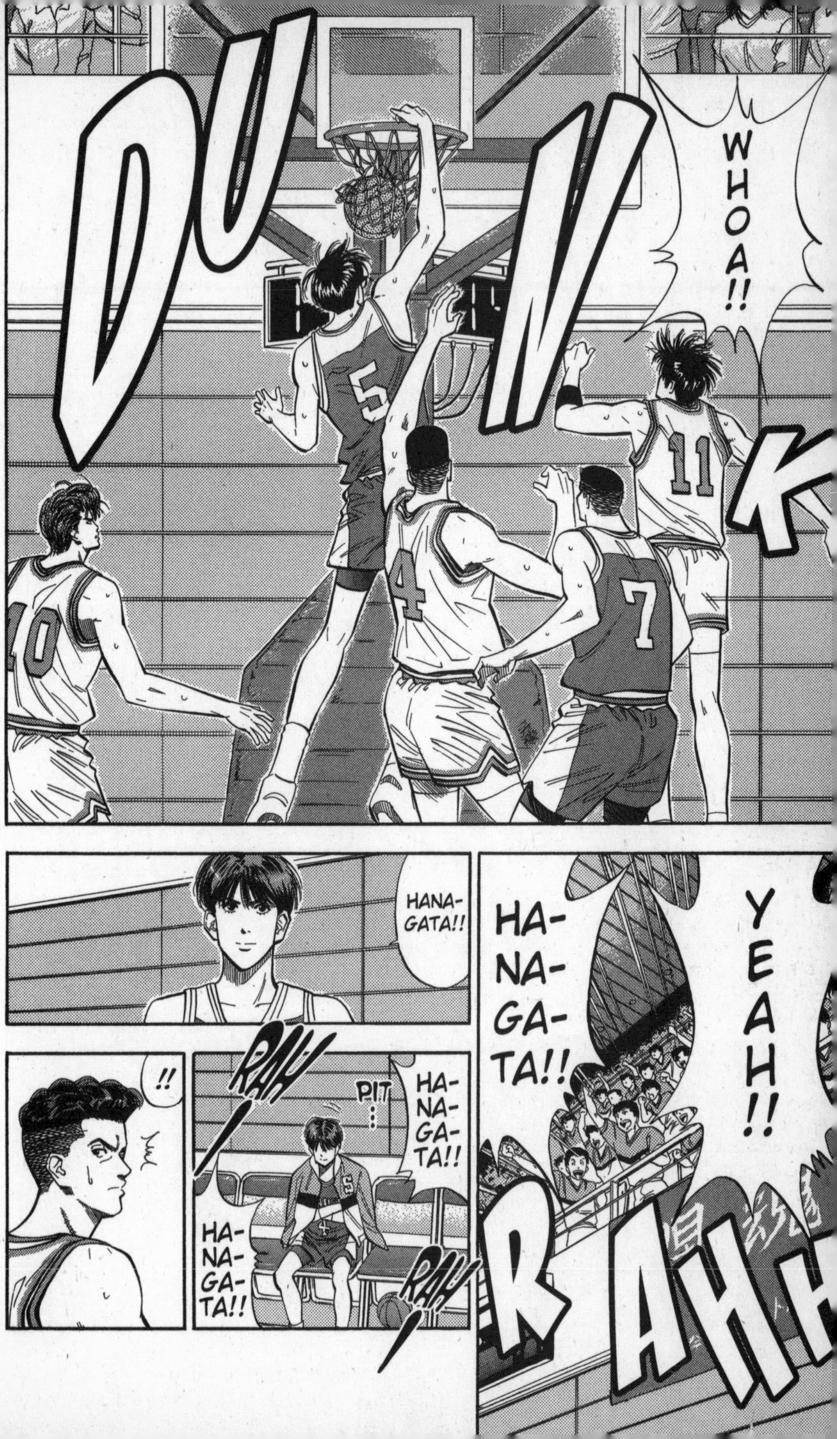
WHOA!!
DUNK
YEAH!!
HA-NA-GA-TA!!
RAHH
HANA-GATA!!
HA-NA-GA-TA!!
PIT...
RAH
HA-NA-GA-TA!!
RAH
!!

READ THIS WAY

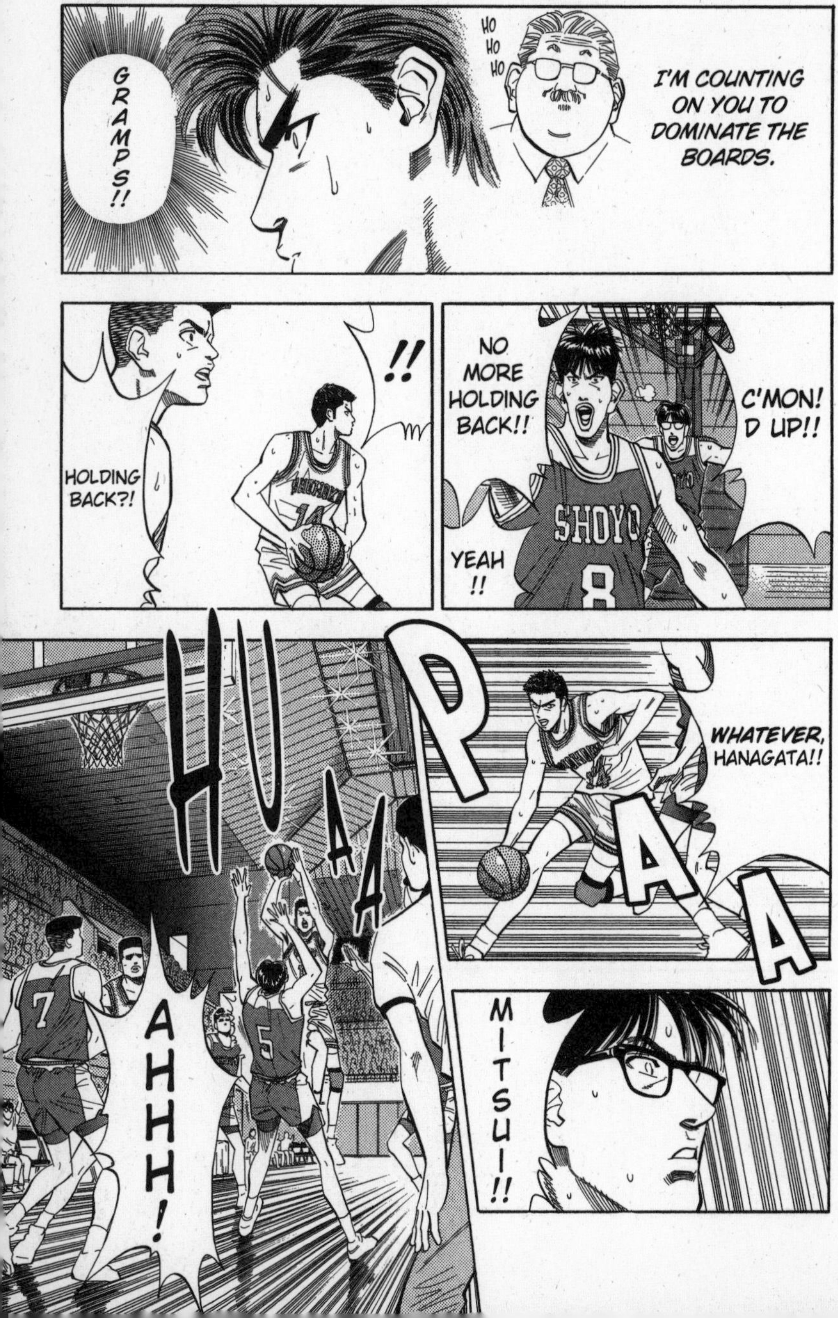
I'M COUNTING ON YOU TO DOMINATE THE BOARDS.
HO HO HO
GRAMPS!!
C'MON! D UP!!
NO MORE HOLDING BACK!!
YEAH !!
!!
HOLDING BACK?!
WHATEVER, HANAGATA!!
HUPAAAA
MITSUI!!
AHHH!

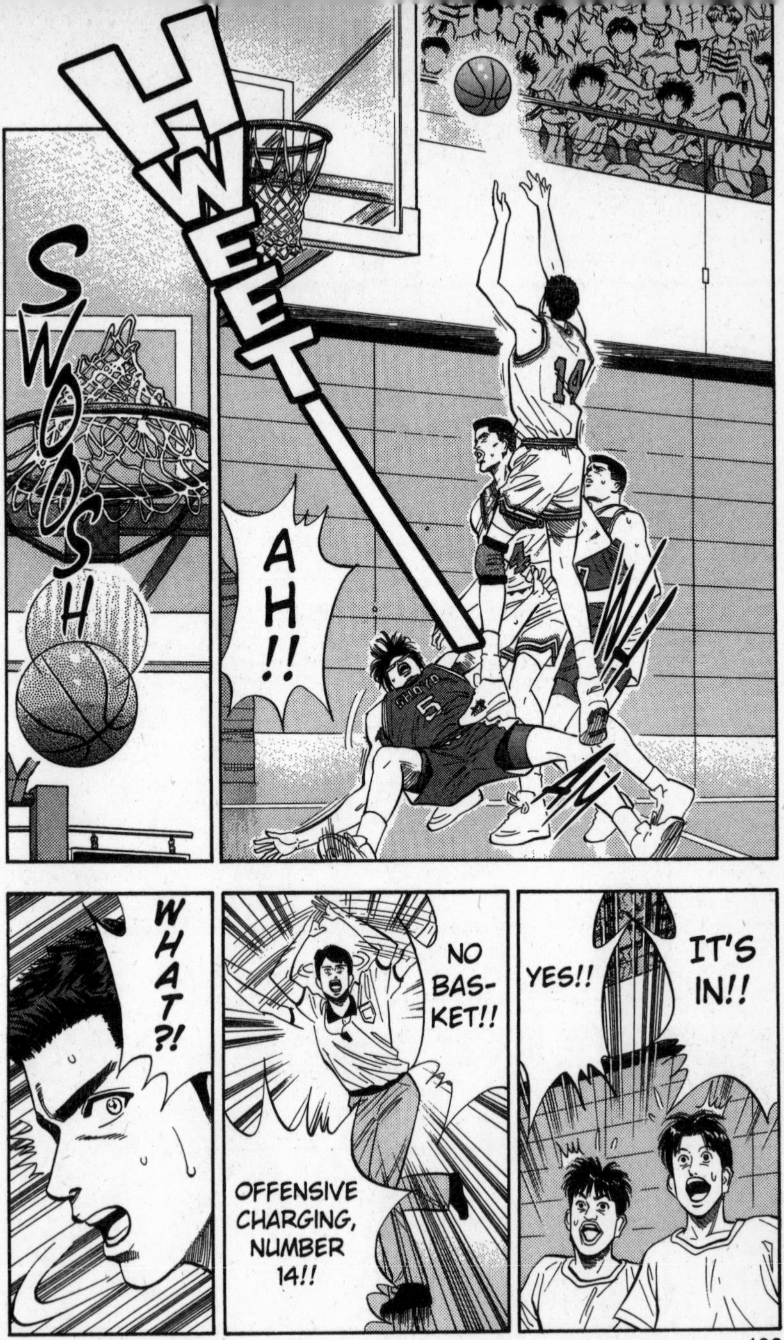
HWEET
AH!!
SWOOSH
IT'S IN!!
YES!!
NO BAS-KET!!
OFFENSIVE CHARGING, NUMBER 14!!
WHAT?!

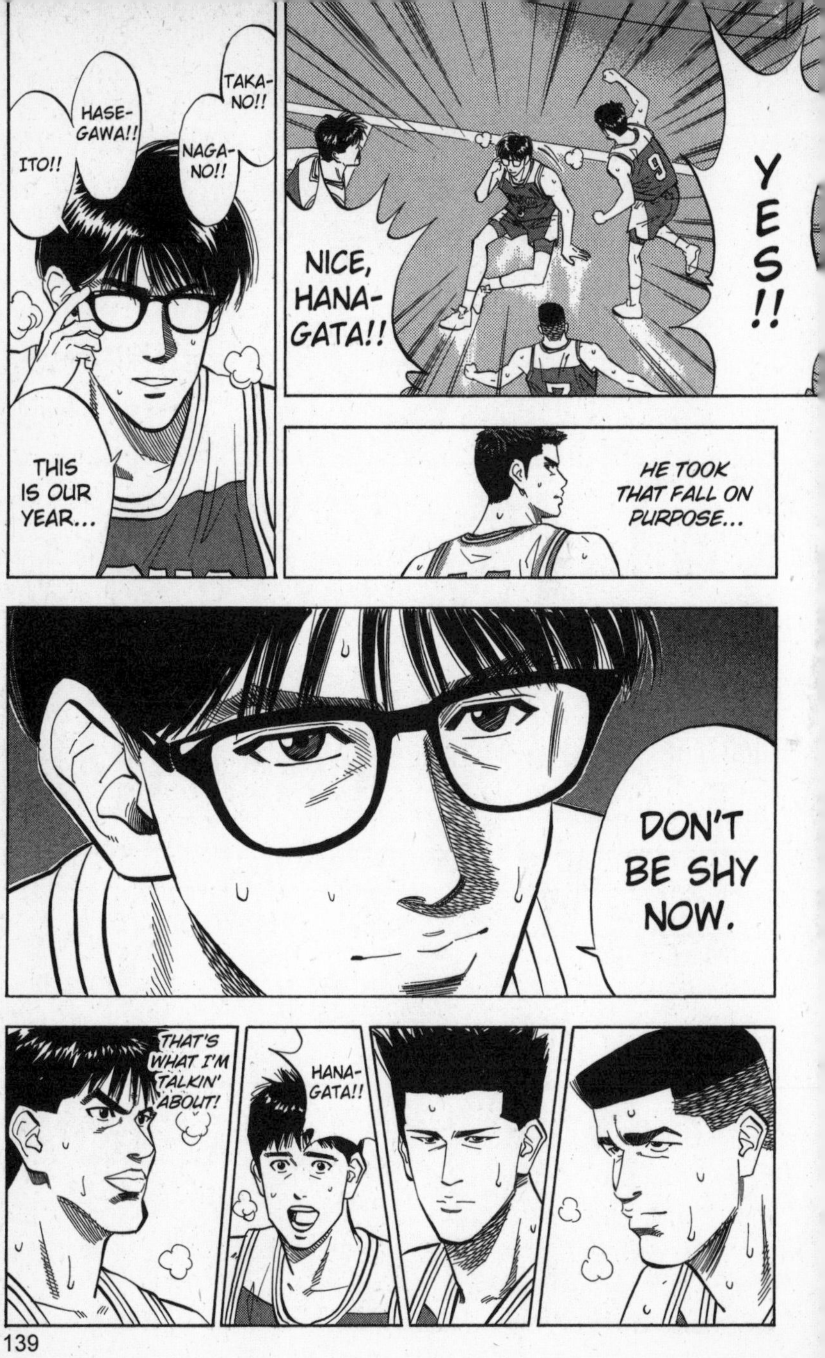
YES!!
NICE, HANA-GATA!!
HE TOOK THAT FALL ON PURPOSE...
TAKA-NO!!
NAGA-NO!!
HASE-GAWA!!
ITO!!
THIS IS OUR YEAR...
DON'T BE SHY NOW.
HANA-GATA!!
THAT'S WHAT I'M TALKIN' ABOUT!

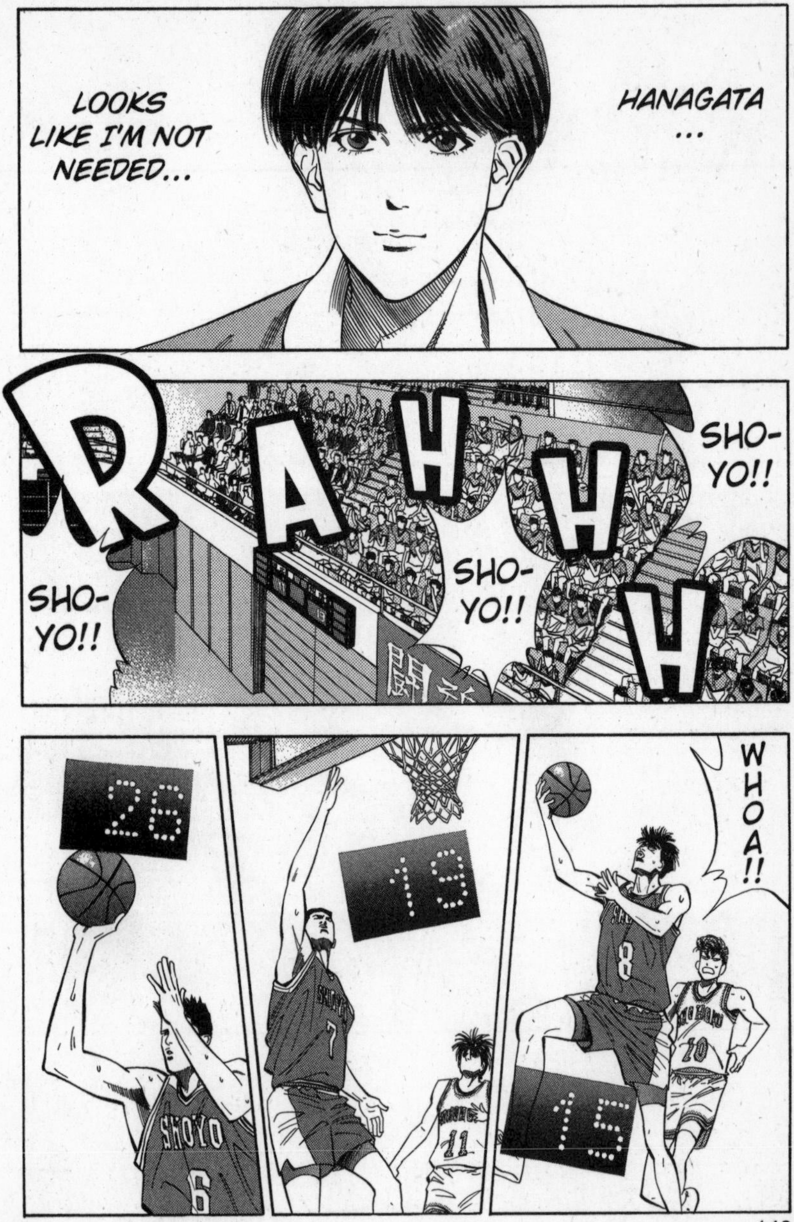
HANAGATA...
LOOKS LIKE I'M NOT NEEDED...
RAHHHH
SHO-YO!!
SHO-YO!!
SHO-YO!!
WHOA!!
15
19
26

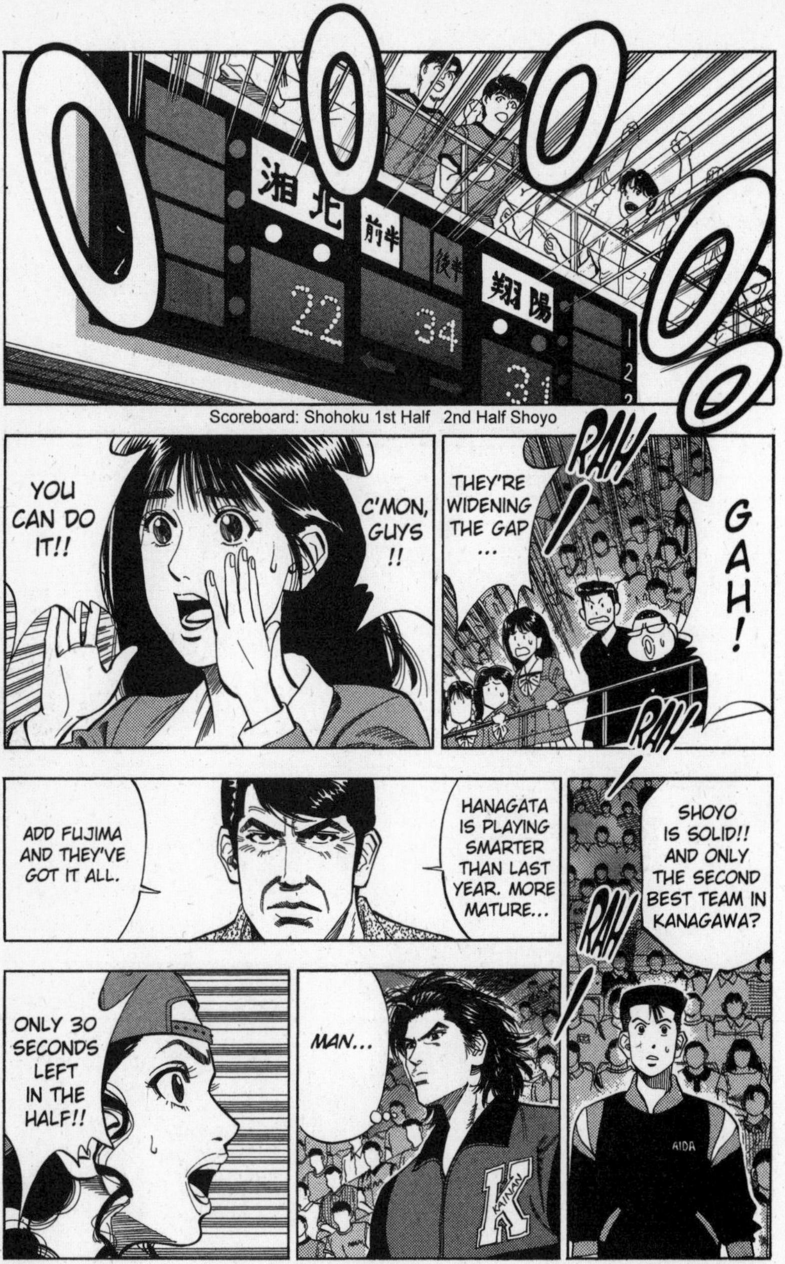
湘北
前半
後半
翔陽
22
34
31
RAH!
GAH!
THEY'RE WIDENING THE GAP...
C'MON, GUYS!!
YOU CAN DO IT!!
SHOYO IS SOLID!! AND ONLY THE SECOND BEST TEAM IN KANAGAWA?
RAH!
RAH!
HANAGATA IS PLAYING SMARTER THAN LAST YEAR. MORE MATURE...
ADD FUJIMA AND THEY'VE GOT IT ALL.
AIDA
MAN...
KAINAN
ONLY 30 SECONDS LEFT IN THE HALF!!
Scoreboard: Shohoku 1st Half 2nd Half Shoyo

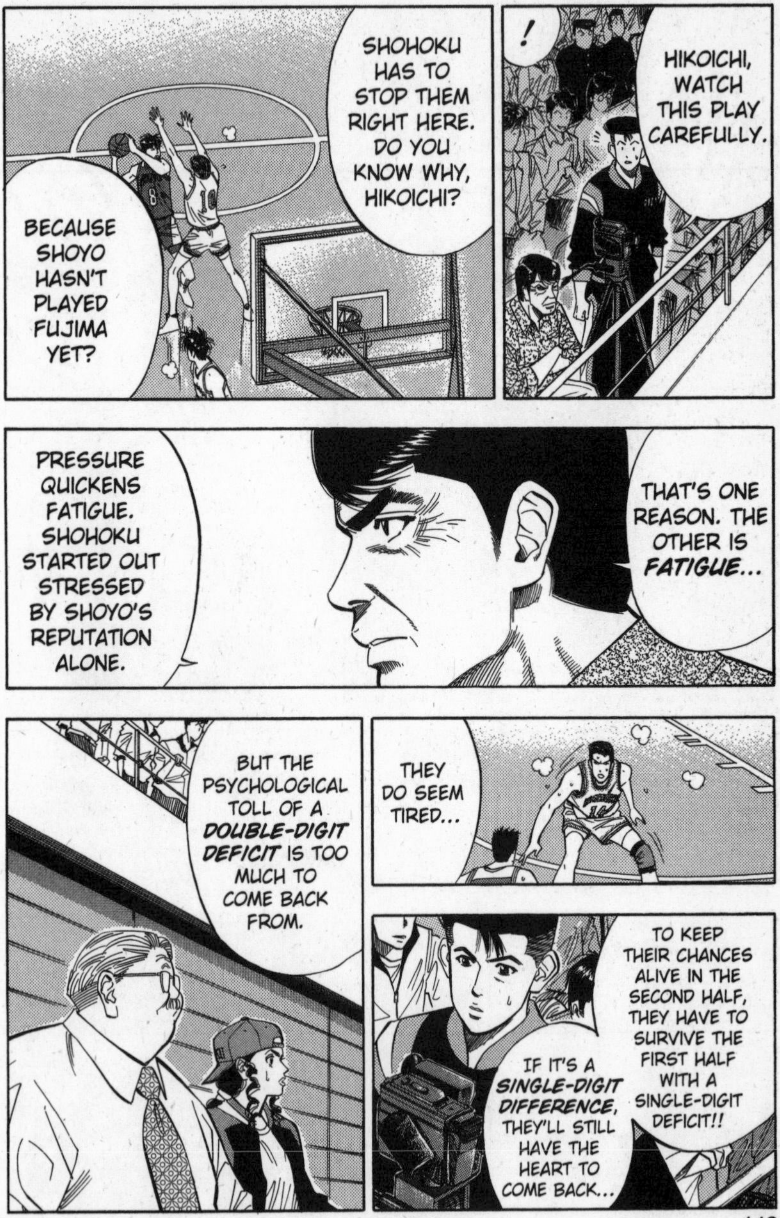
!
HIKOICHI, WATCH THIS PLAY CAREFULLY.
SHOHOKU HAS TO STOP THEM RIGHT HERE. DO YOU KNOW WHY, HIKOICHI?
BECAUSE SHOYO HASN'T PLAYED FUJIMA YET?
THAT'S ONE REASON. THE OTHER IS *FATIGUE*...
PRESSURE QUICKENS FATIGUE. SHOHOKU STARTED OUT STRESSED BY SHOYO'S REPUTATION ALONE.
THEY DO SEEM TIRED...
TO KEEP THEIR CHANCES ALIVE IN THE SECOND HALF, THEY HAVE TO SURVIVE THE FIRST HALF WITH A SINGLE-DIGIT DEFICIT!!
IF IT'S A *SINGLE-DIGIT DIFFERENCE*, THEY'LL STILL HAVE THE HEART TO COME BACK...
BUT THE PSYCHOLOGICAL TOLL OF A *DOUBLE-DIGIT DEFICIT* IS TOO MUCH TO COME BACK FROM.

READ THIS WAY

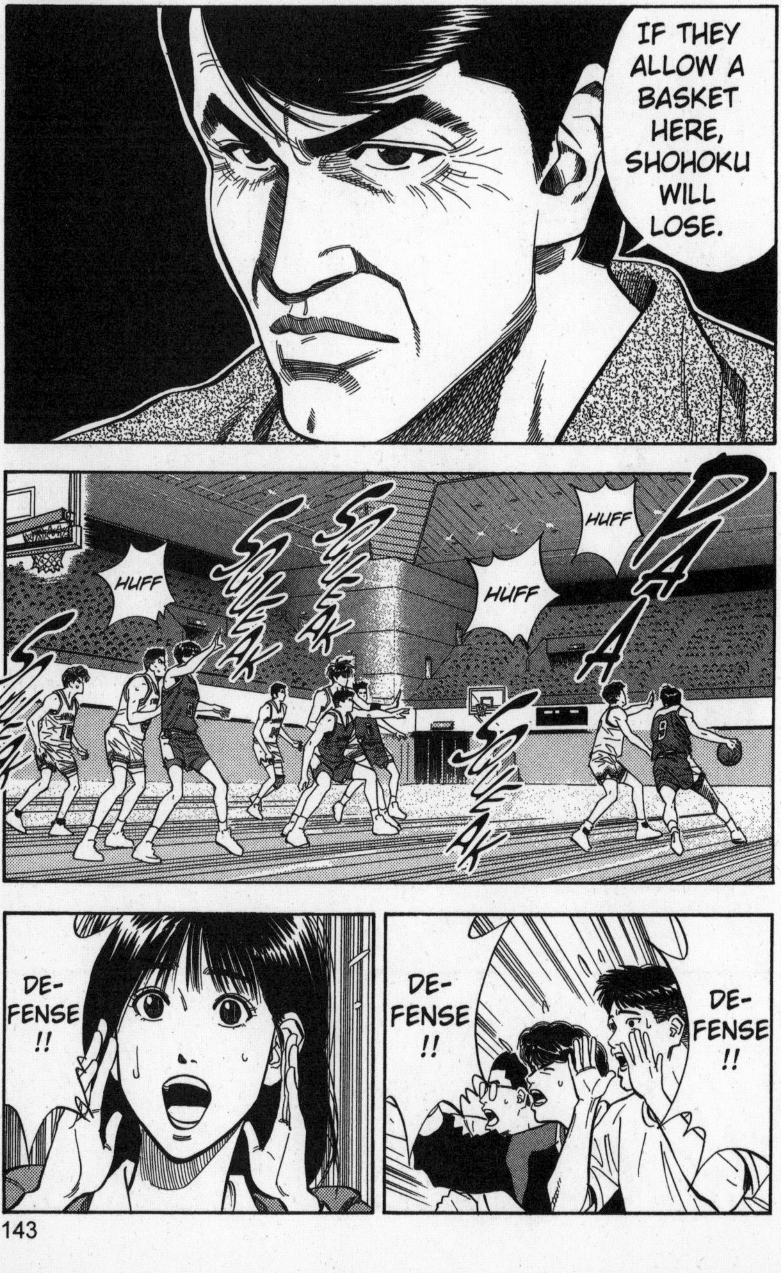
IF THEY ALLOW A BASKET HERE, SHOHOKU WILL LOSE.
DAA
HUFF
SQUEAK
HUFF
SQUEAK
SQUEAK
HUFF
SQUEAK
DE-FENSE!!
DE-FENSE!!
DE-FENSE!!

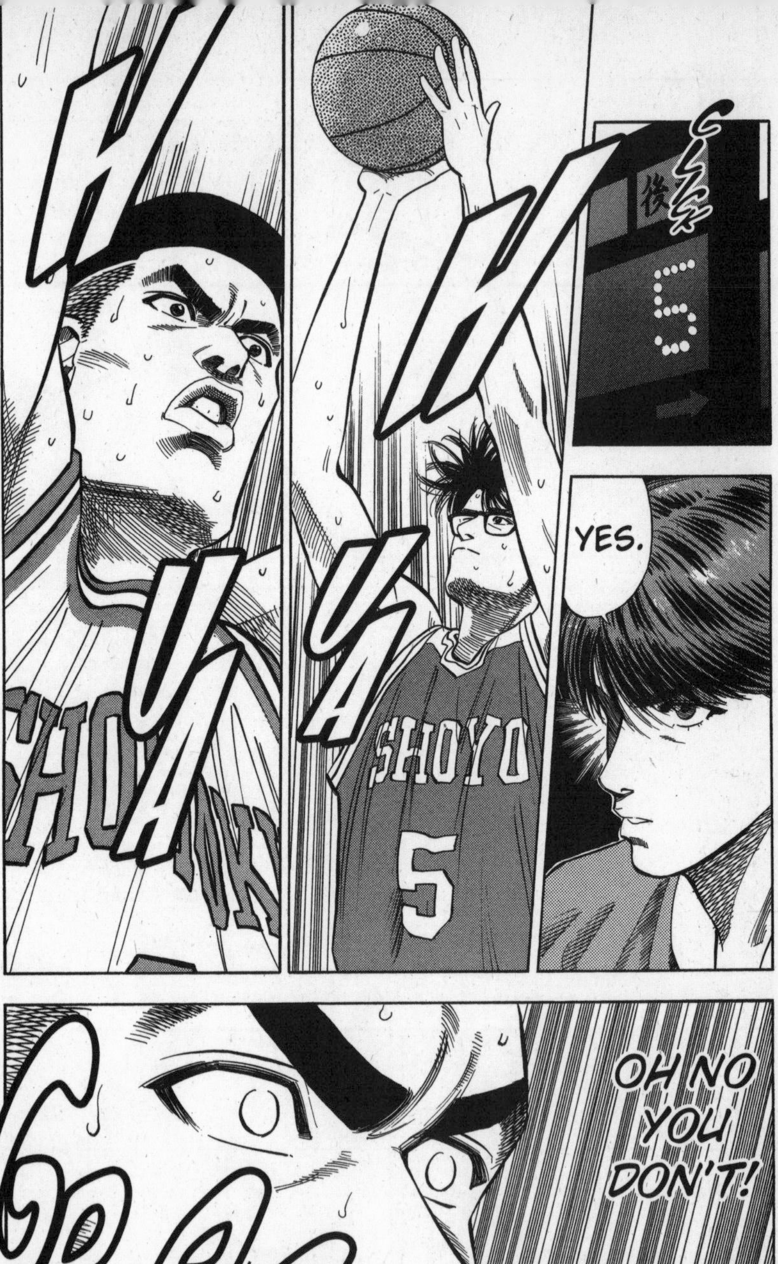
YES.
OH NO YOU DON'T!
GRAA

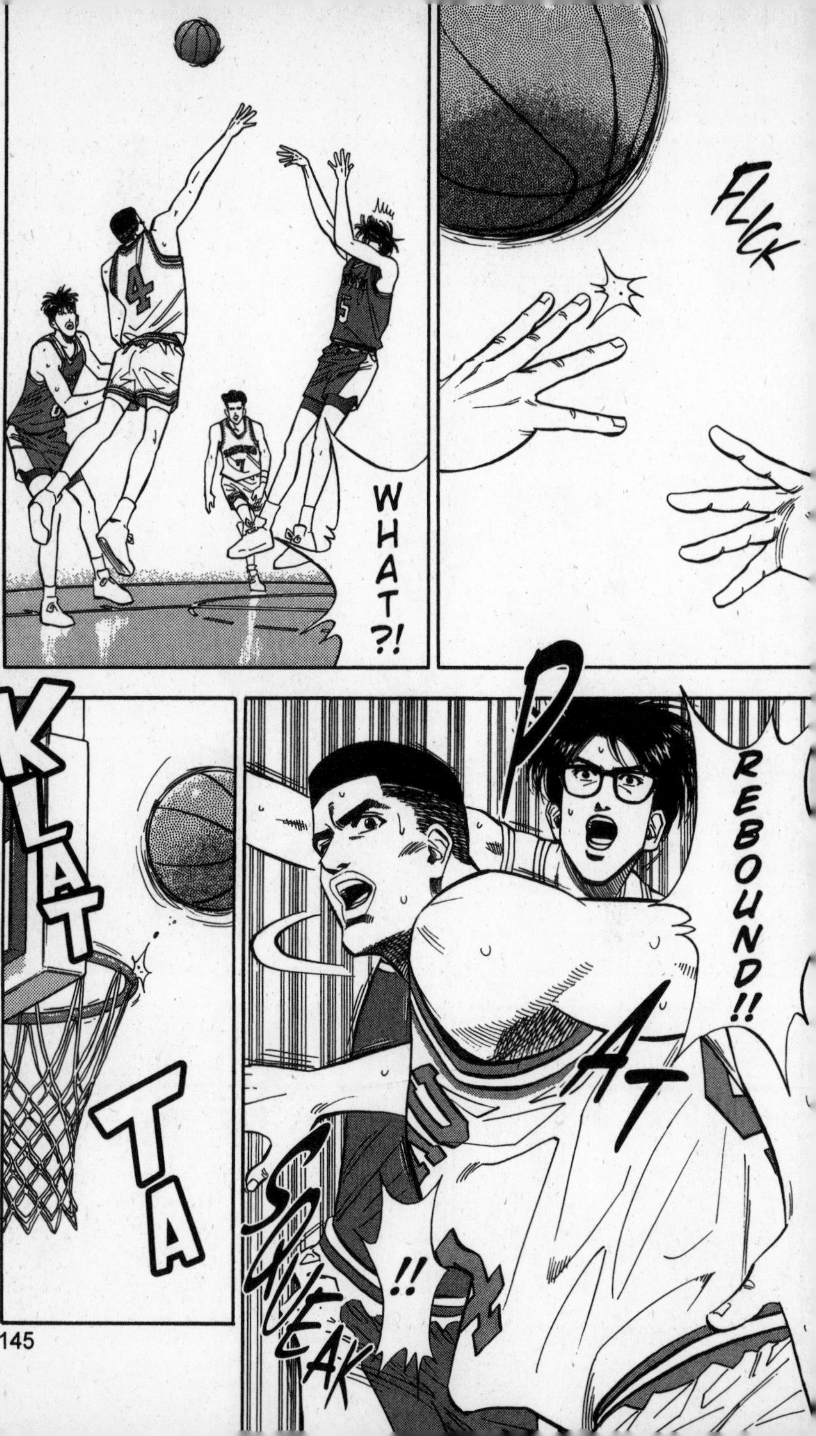
FLICK
WHAT?!
REBOUND!!
PAT
SQUEAK
!!
KLAT
TA

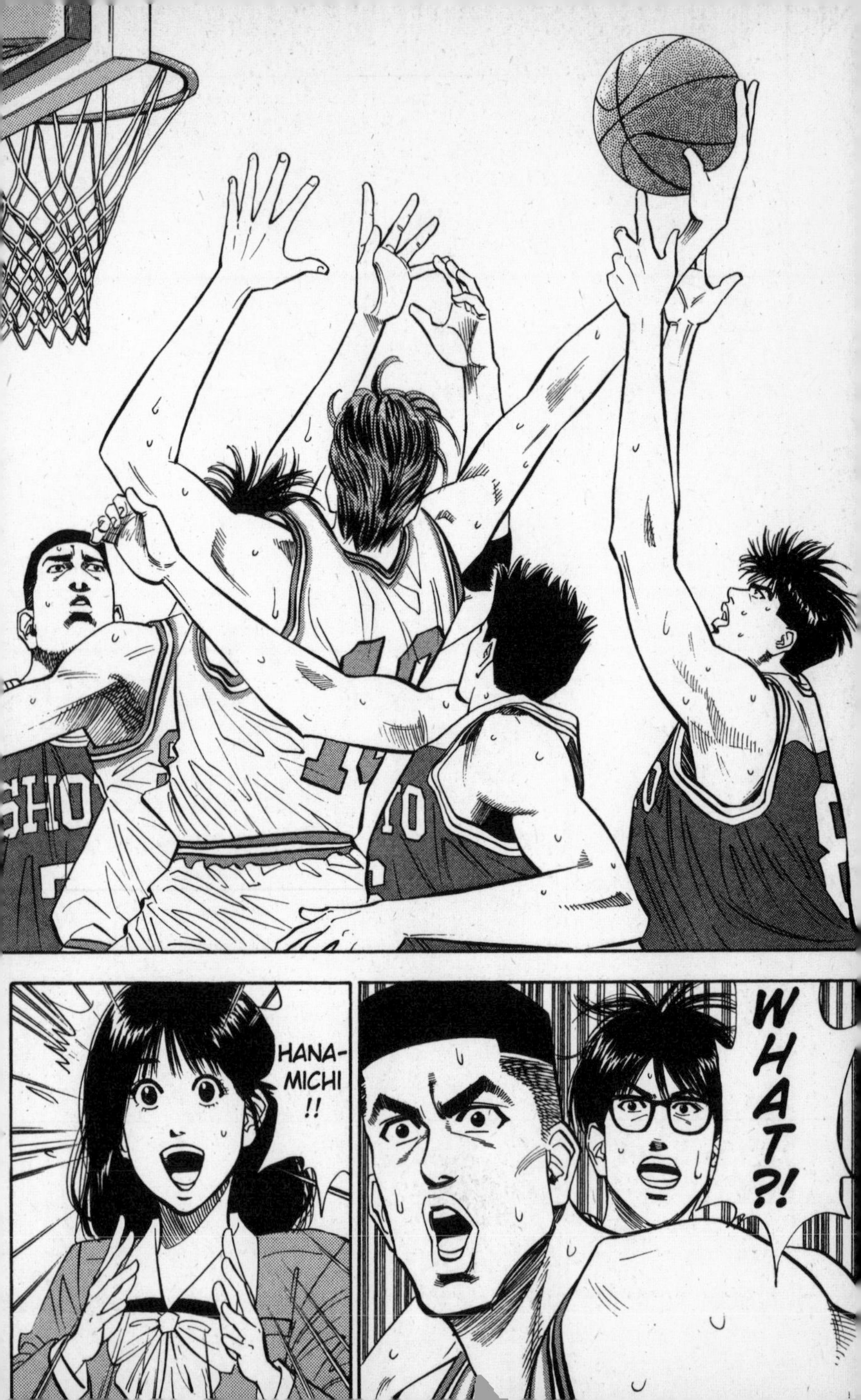
WHAT?!
HANA-MICHI!!

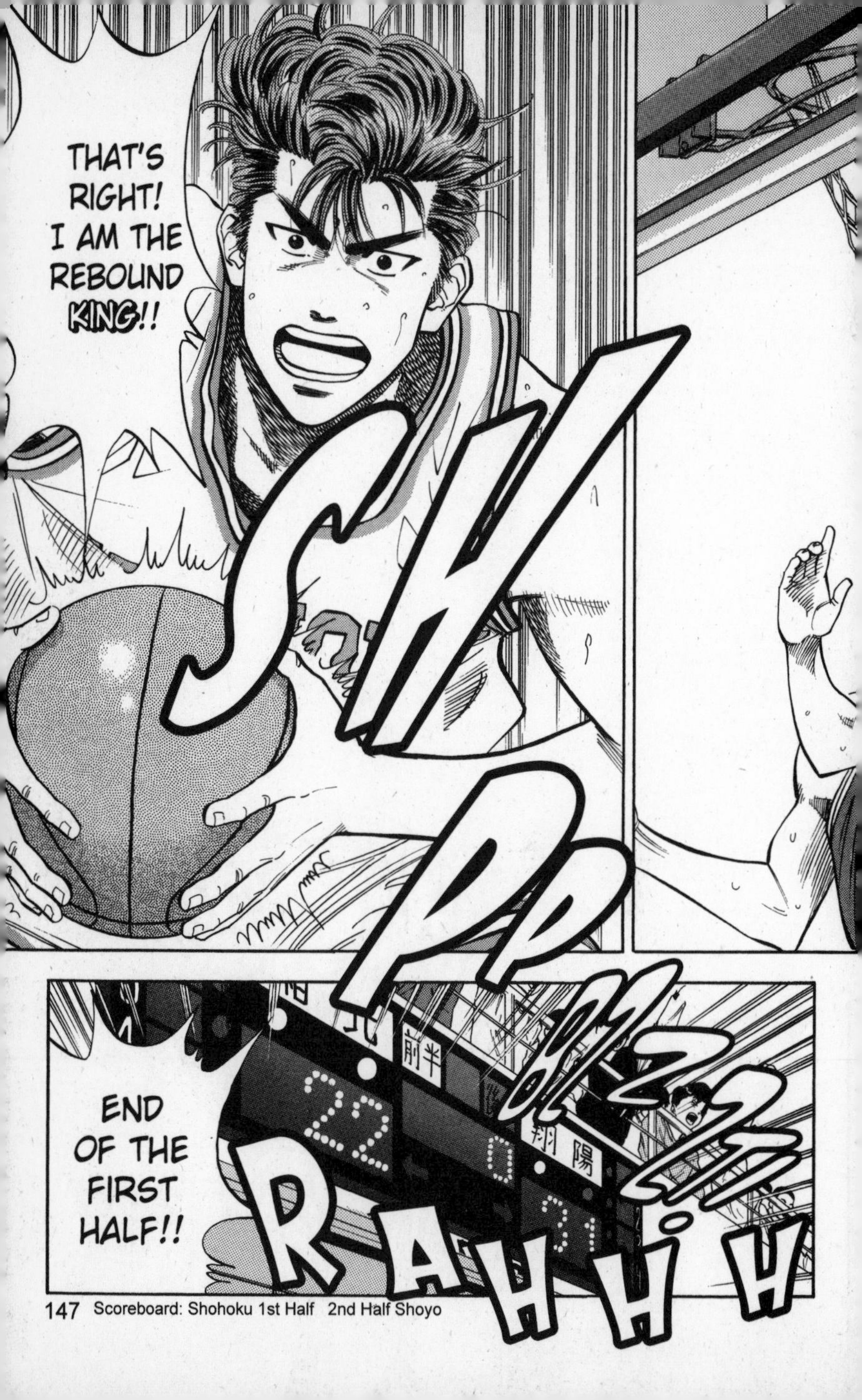
THAT'S RIGHT! I AM THE REBOUND KING!!
SHPP
END OF THE FIRST HALF!!
RAHHHH

 Scoreboard: Shohoku 1st Half 2nd Half Shoyo

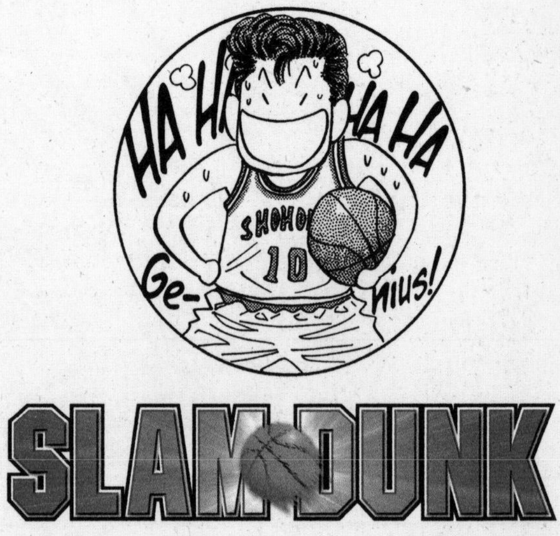
HA H
HA HA
SHOHO
10
Ge-
nius!

SLAM DUNK

#88 REBOUND KING SAKURAGI

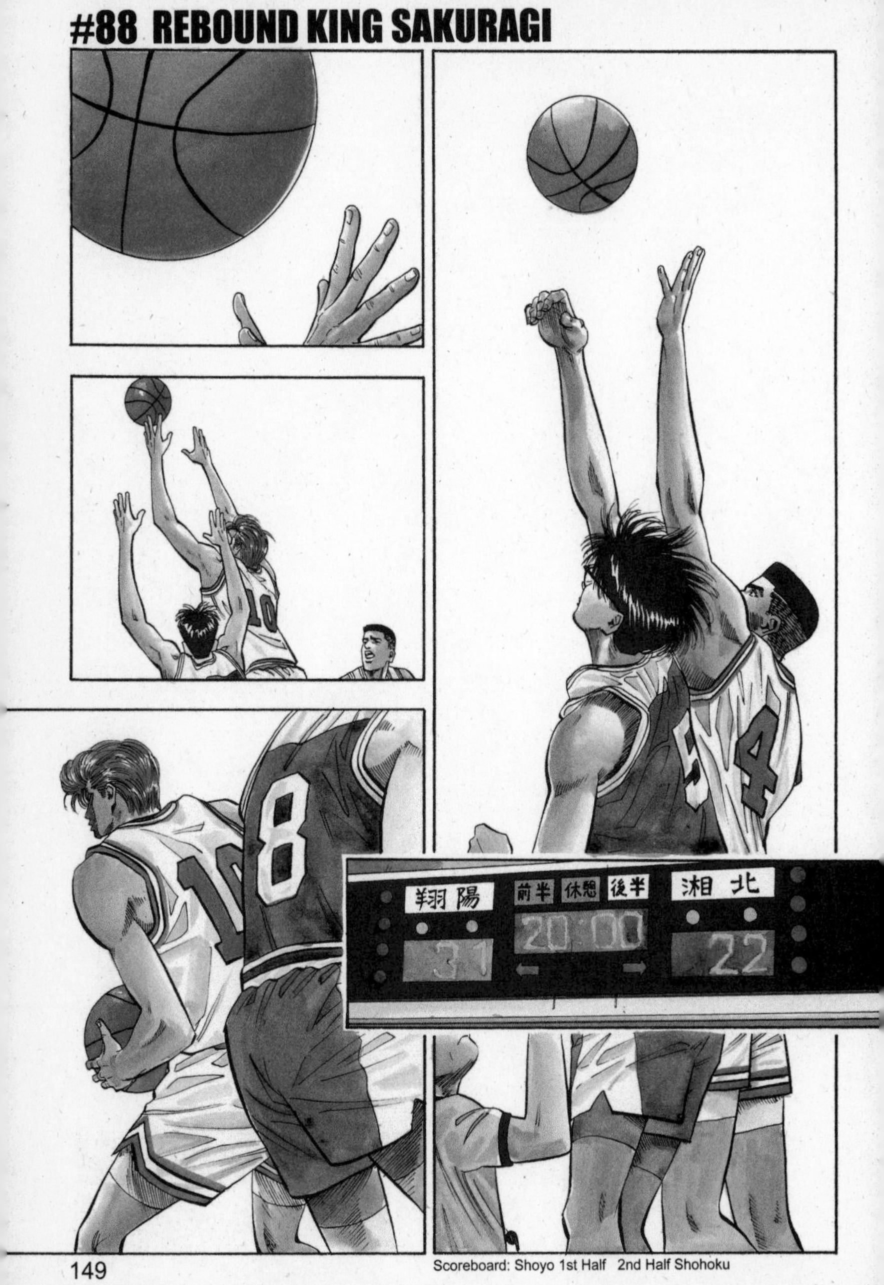
翔陽
前半 休憩 後半
湘北
20:00
31
22

Scoreboard: Shoyo 1st Half 2nd Half Shohoku

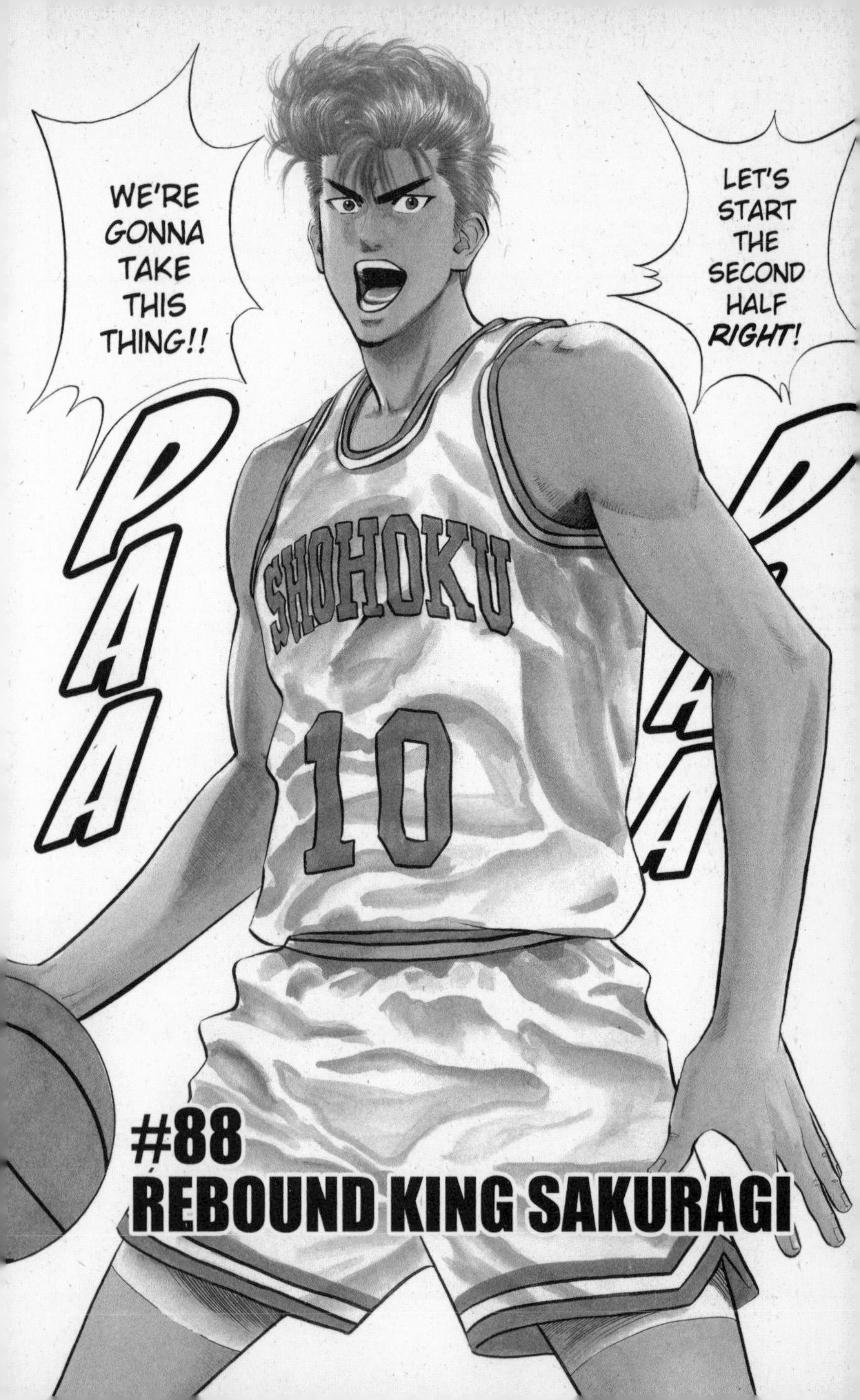
LET'S START THE SECOND HALF *RIGHT*!
WE'RE GONNA TAKE THIS THING!!
DAA
DAA

#88 REBOUND KING SAKURAGI

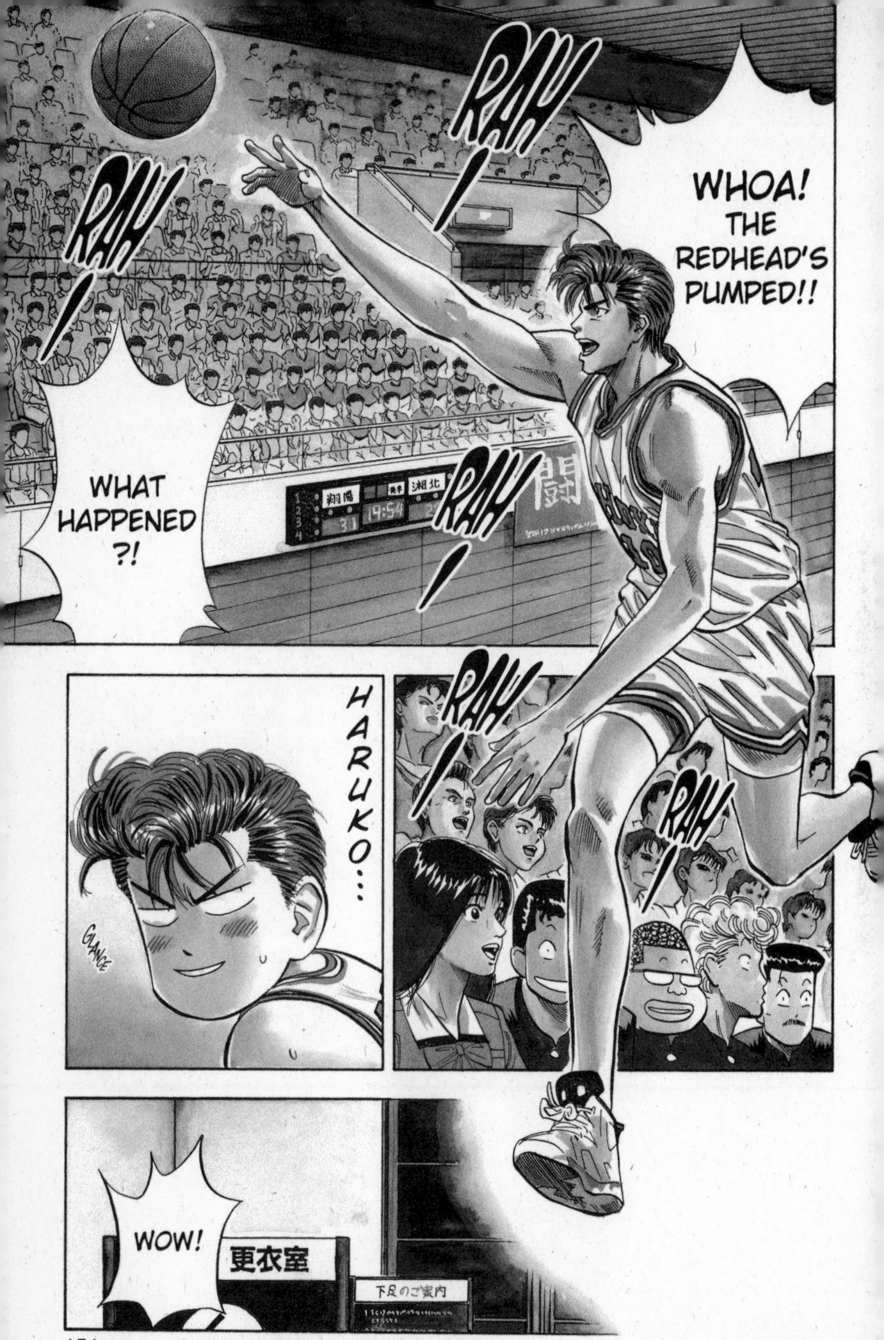
RAH!
WHOA! THE REDHEAD'S PUMPED!!
RAH!
WHAT HAPPENED?!
RAH!
RAH!
RAH!
HARUKO...
GLANCE
WOW!
更衣室
下足のご案内

Sign L: Dressing Room Sign R: Check Shoes

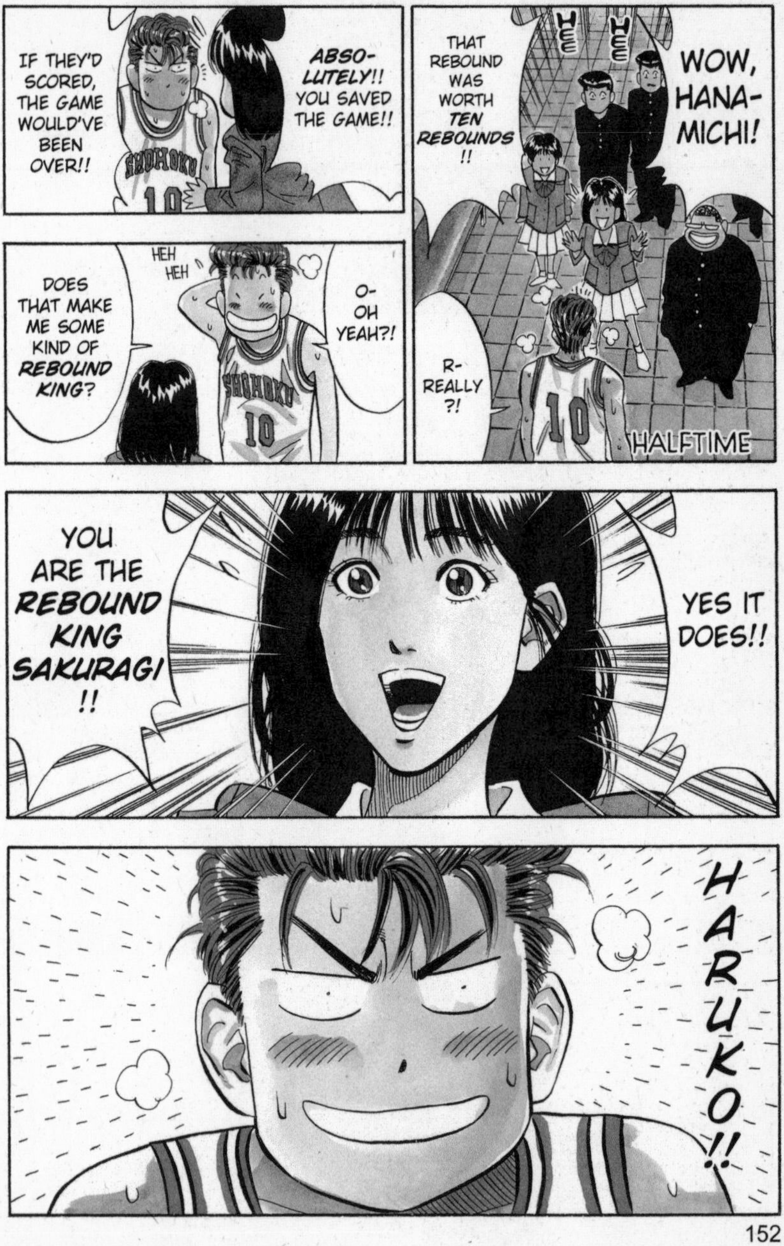
WOW, HANA-MICHI!
HEE
HEE
THAT REBOUND WAS WORTH TEN REBOUNDS!!
R-REALLY?!
HALFTIME
ABSO-LUTELY!! YOU SAVED THE GAME!!
IF THEY'D SCORED, THE GAME WOULD'VE BEEN OVER!!
O-OH YEAH?!
HEH HEH
DOES THAT MAKE ME SOME KIND OF REBOUND KING?
YES IT DOES!!
YOU ARE THE REBOUND KING SAKURAGI!!
HARUKO!!

READ THIS WAY

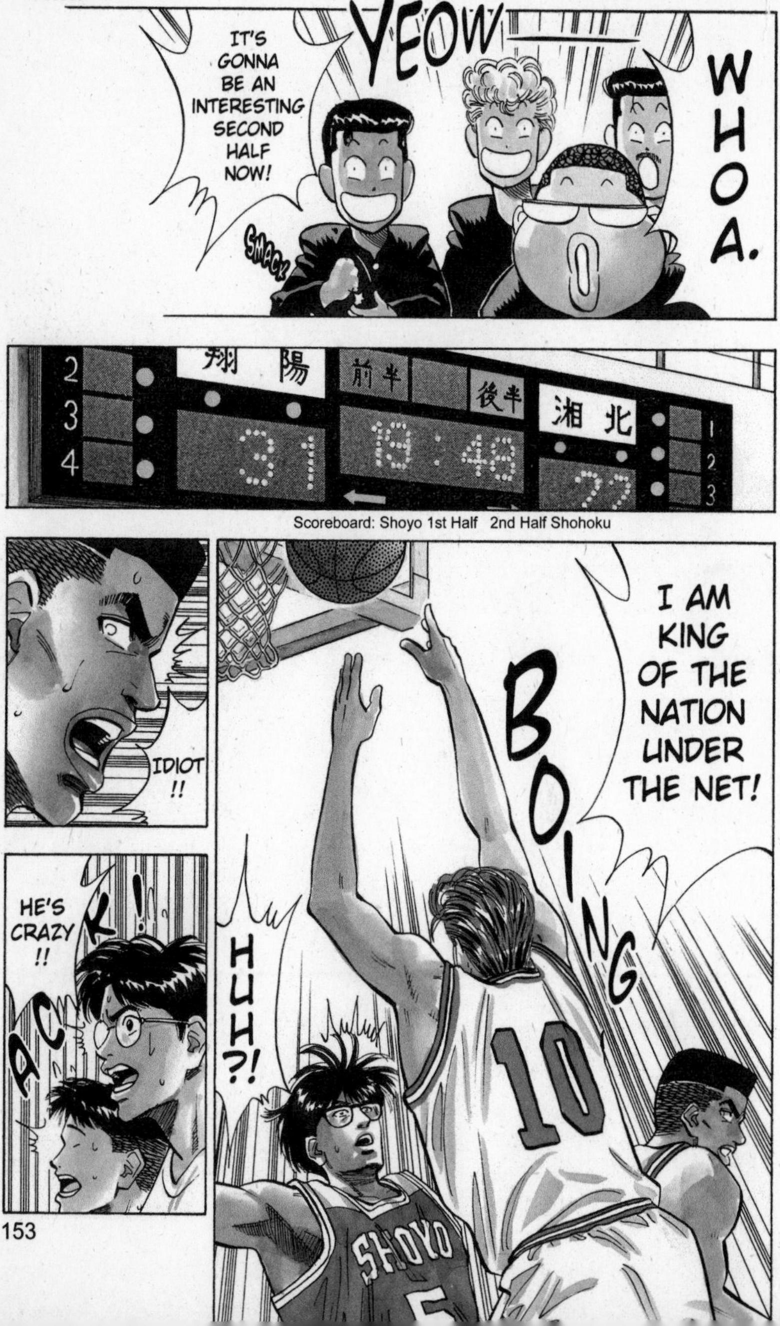
WHOA.
YEOW
IT'S GONNA BE AN INTERESTING SECOND HALF NOW!
SMACK
翔陽
前半
後半
湘北
Scoreboard: Shoyo 1st Half 2nd Half Shohoku
I AM KING OF THE NATION UNDER THE NET!
BOING
HUH?!
IDIOT!!
HE'S CRAZY!!
ACK!

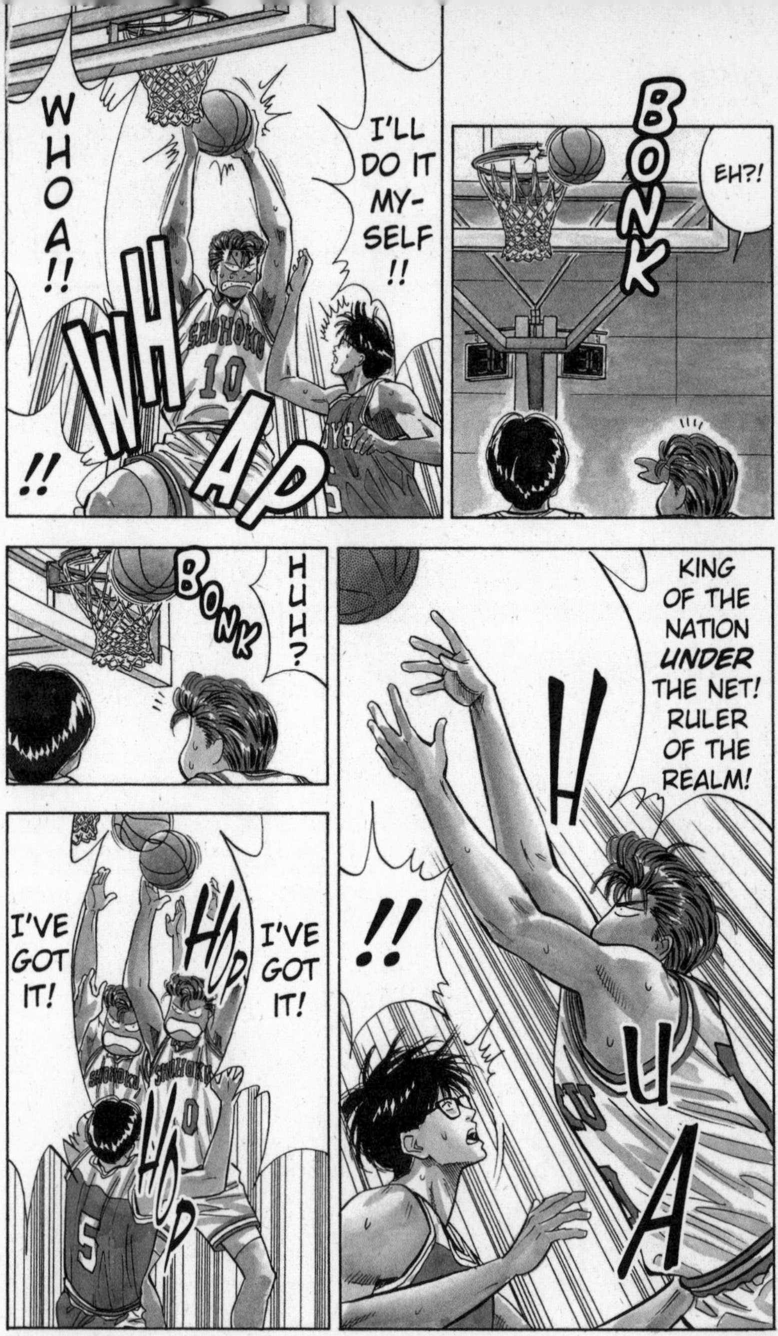

EH?!
BONK
I'LL DO IT MYSELF!!
WHOA!!
WHAP
!!
KING OF THE NATION *UNDER* THE NET! RULER OF THE REALM!
HUA
!!
HUH?
BONK
I'VE GOT IT!
HOP
I'VE GOT IT!
HOP

READ THIS WAY

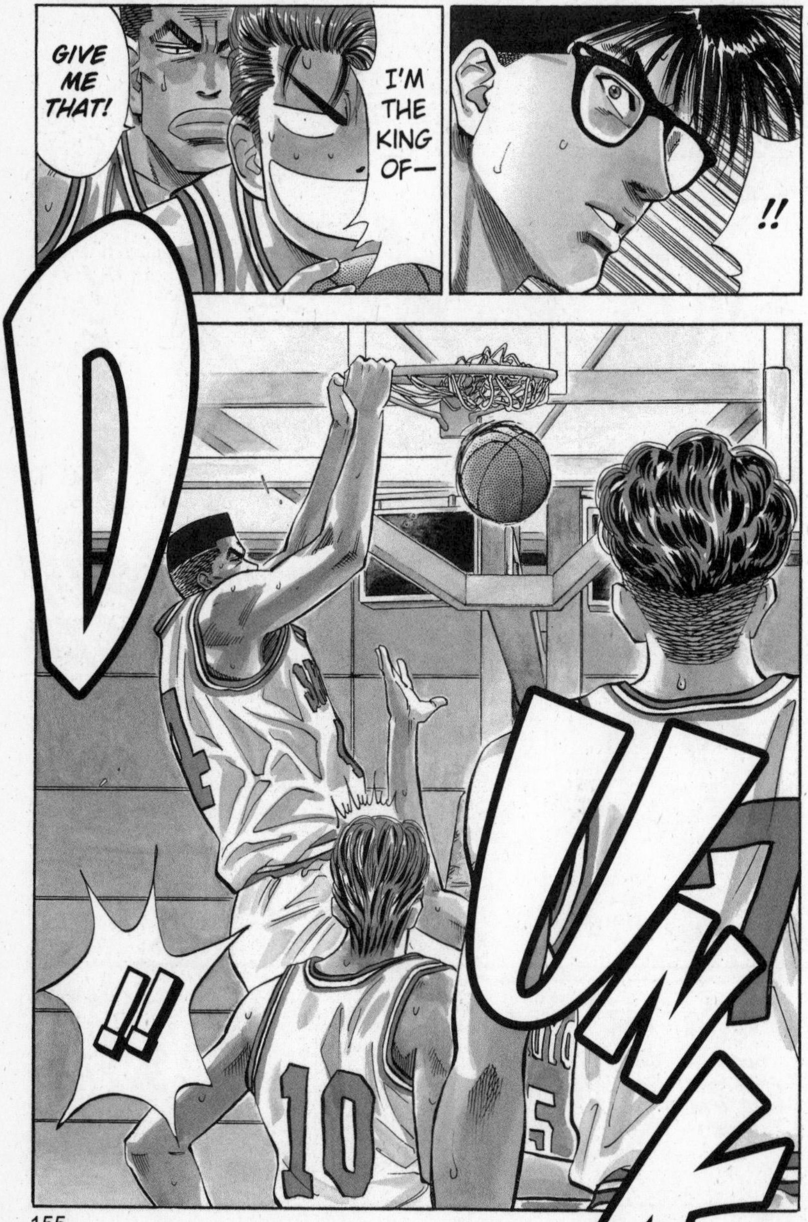
!!
I'M THE KING OF—
GIVE ME THAT!
DUNK
!!

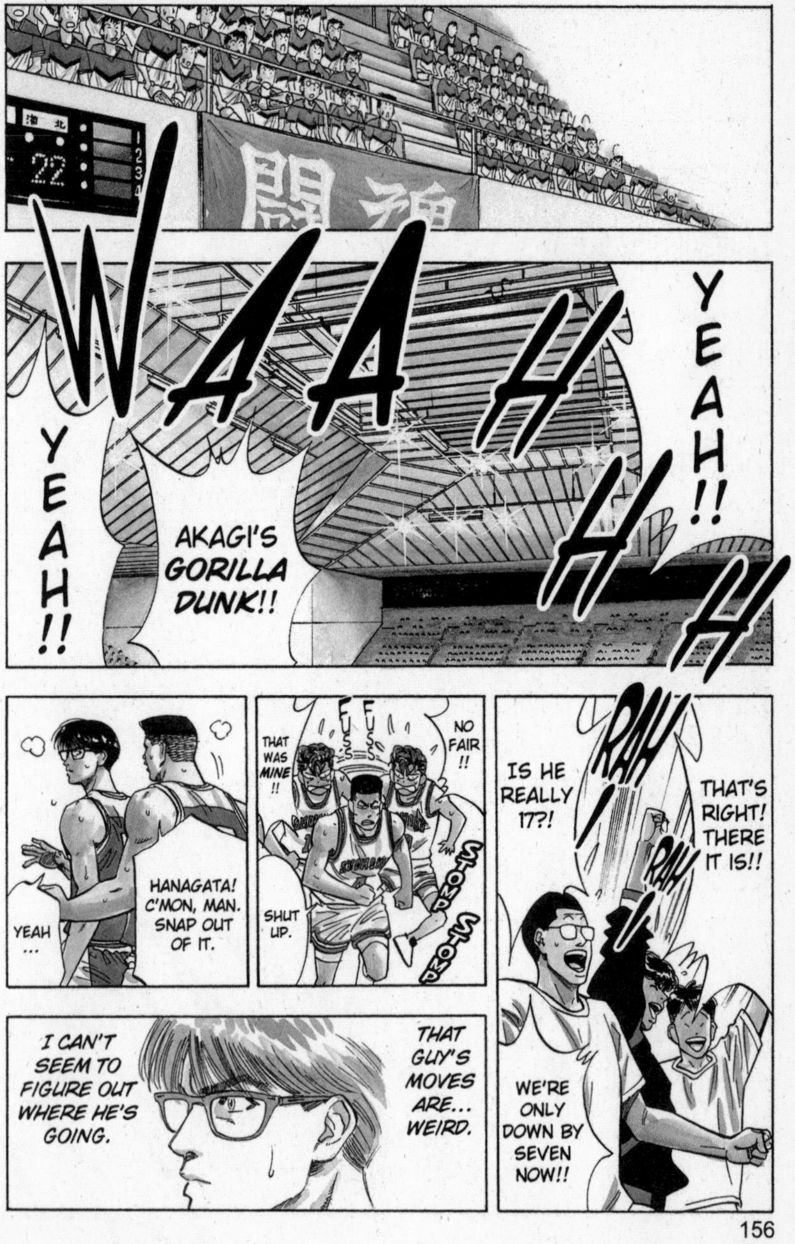
湘北
22
WAAAHHHH
YEAH!!
AKAGI'S GORILLA DUNK!!
YEAH!!
THAT'S RIGHT! THERE IT IS!!
RAH RAH
RAH RAH
IS HE REALLY 17?!
WE'RE ONLY DOWN BY SEVEN NOW!!
NO FAIR!!
FUSS FUSS
THAT WAS MINE!!
STOMP STOMP
SHUT UP.
HANAGATA! C'MON, MAN. SNAP OUT OF IT.
YEAH ...
THAT GUY'S MOVES ARE... WEIRD.
I CAN'T SEEM TO FIGURE OUT WHERE HE'S GOING.

READ THIS WAY

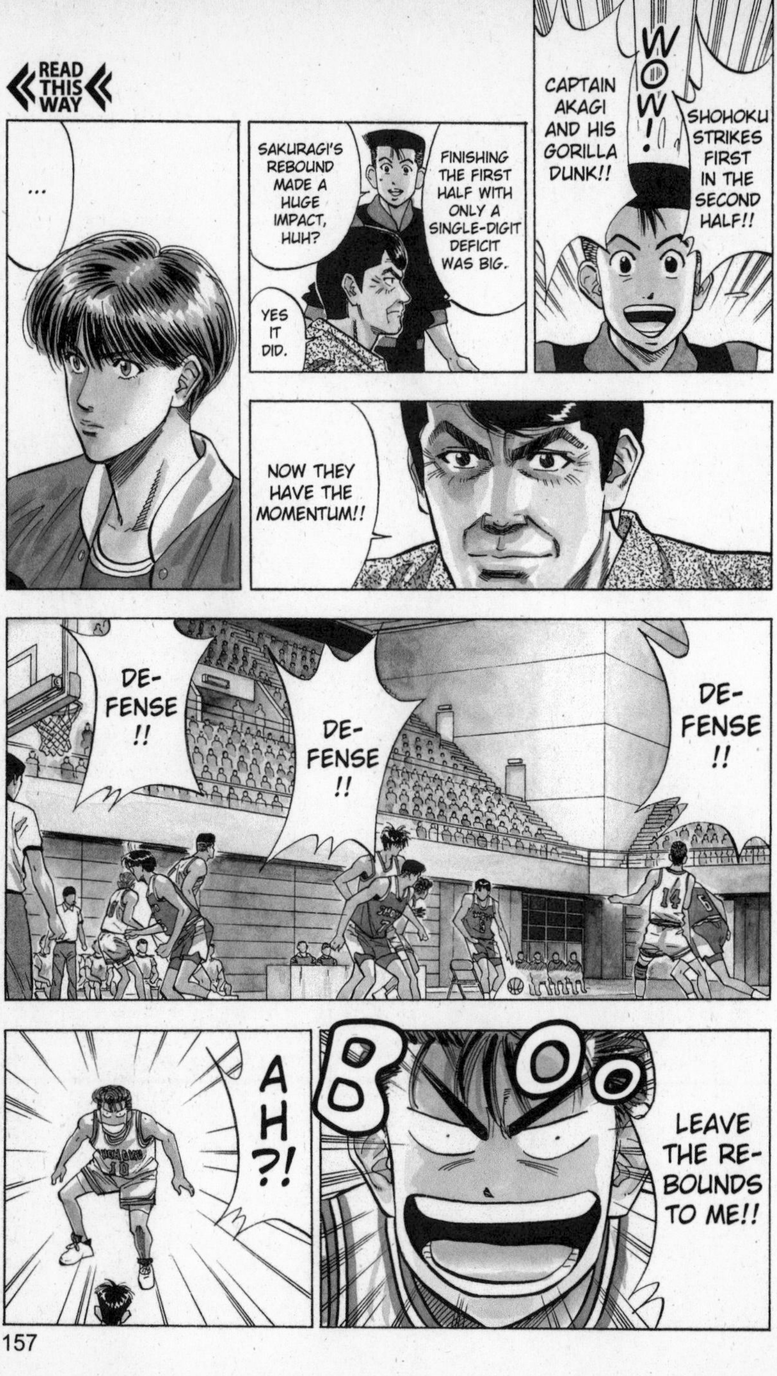
WOW!
SHOHOKU STRIKES FIRST IN THE SECOND HALF!!
CAPTAIN AKAGI AND HIS GORILLA DUNK!!
FINISHING THE FIRST HALF WITH ONLY A SINGLE-DIGIT DEFICIT WAS BIG.
SAKURAGI'S REBOUND MADE A HUGE IMPACT, HUH?
YES IT DID.
NOW THEY HAVE THE MOMENTUM!!
...
DE-FENSE!!
DE-FENSE!!
DE-FENSE!!
BOO
LEAVE THE RE-BOUNDS TO ME!!
AH?!

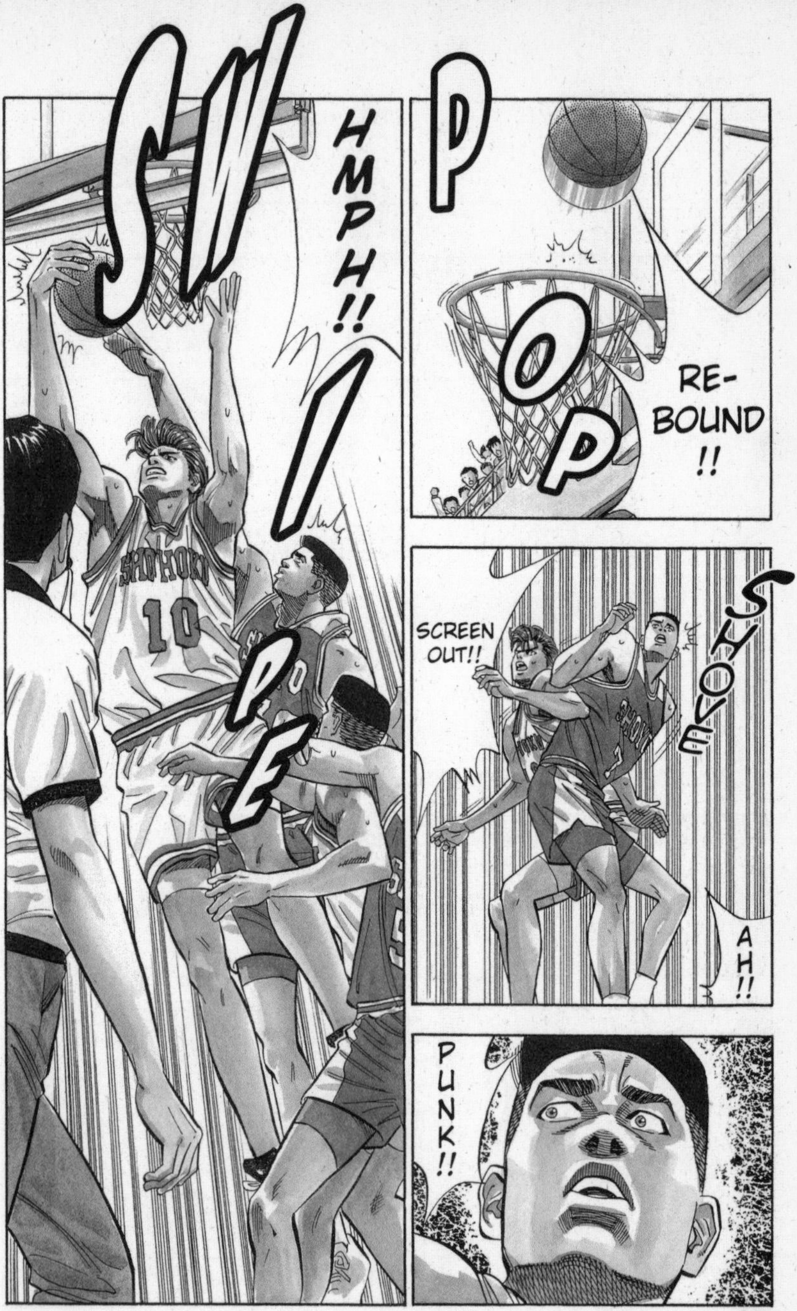
POP
RE-BOUND!!
SCREEN OUT!!
SHOVE
AH!!
PUNK!!
SWIPE
HMPH!!

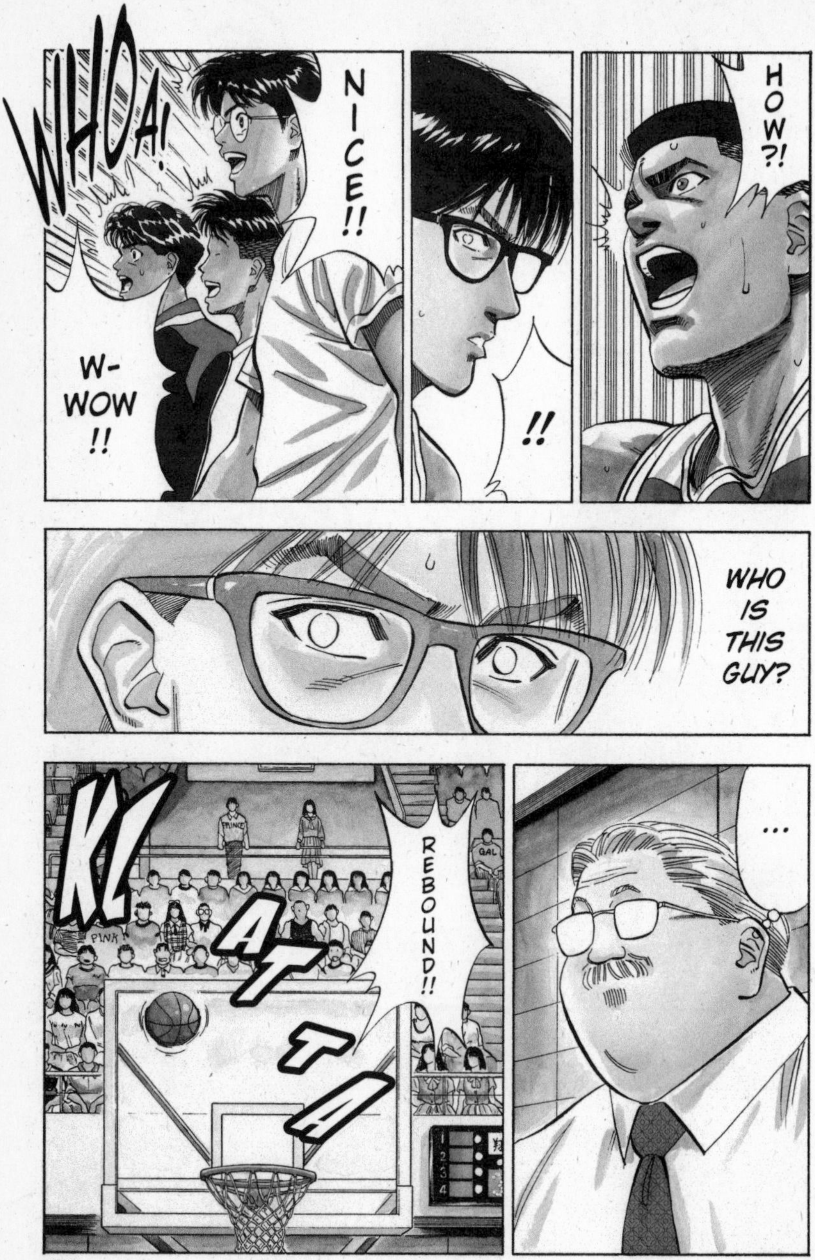
HOW?!
!!
NICE!!
WHOA!
W-WOW!!
WHO IS THIS GUY?
...
REBOUND!!
KLATTA

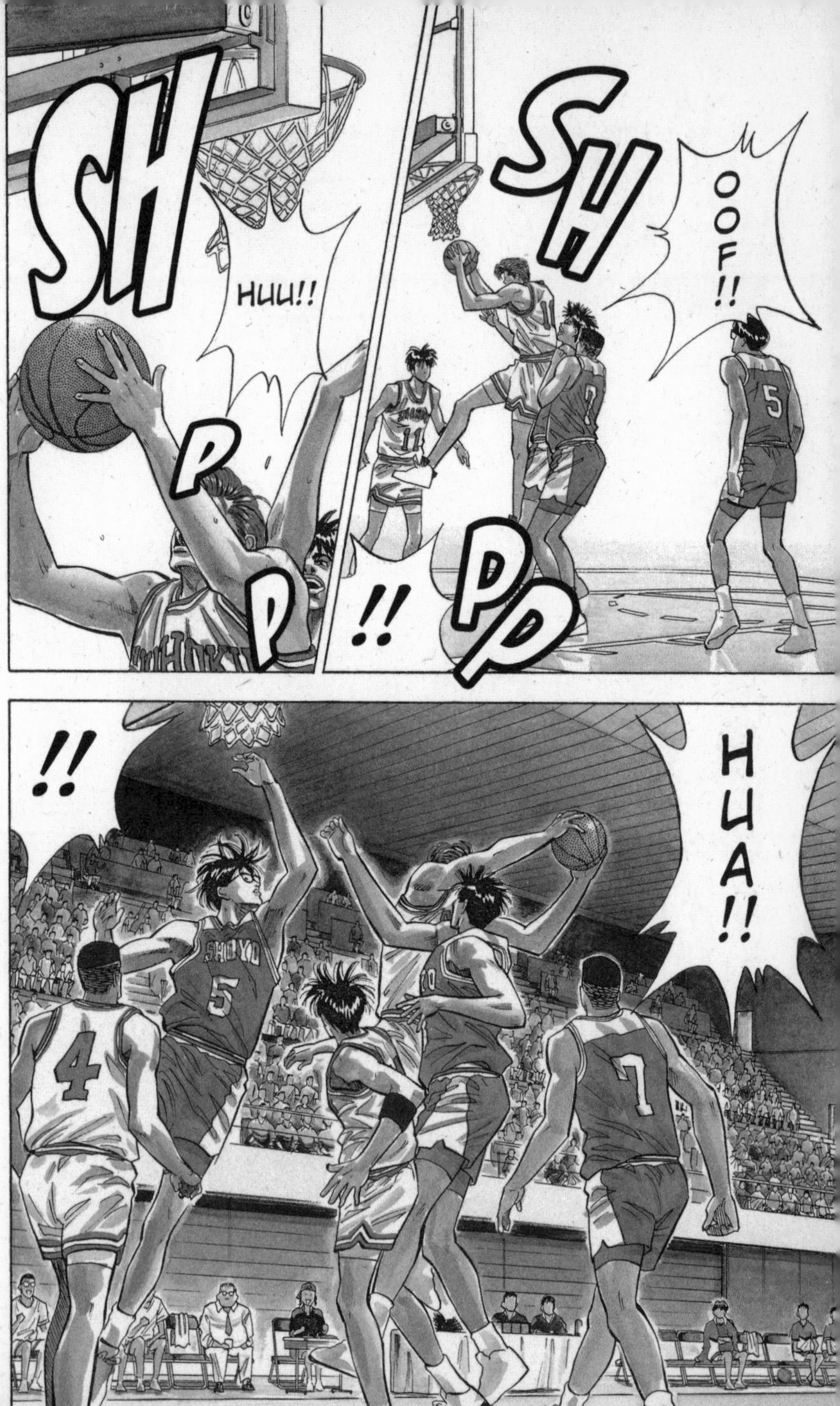
OOF!!
SH
PP
!!
SH
HUU!!
PP
HUA!!
!!

READ THIS WAY

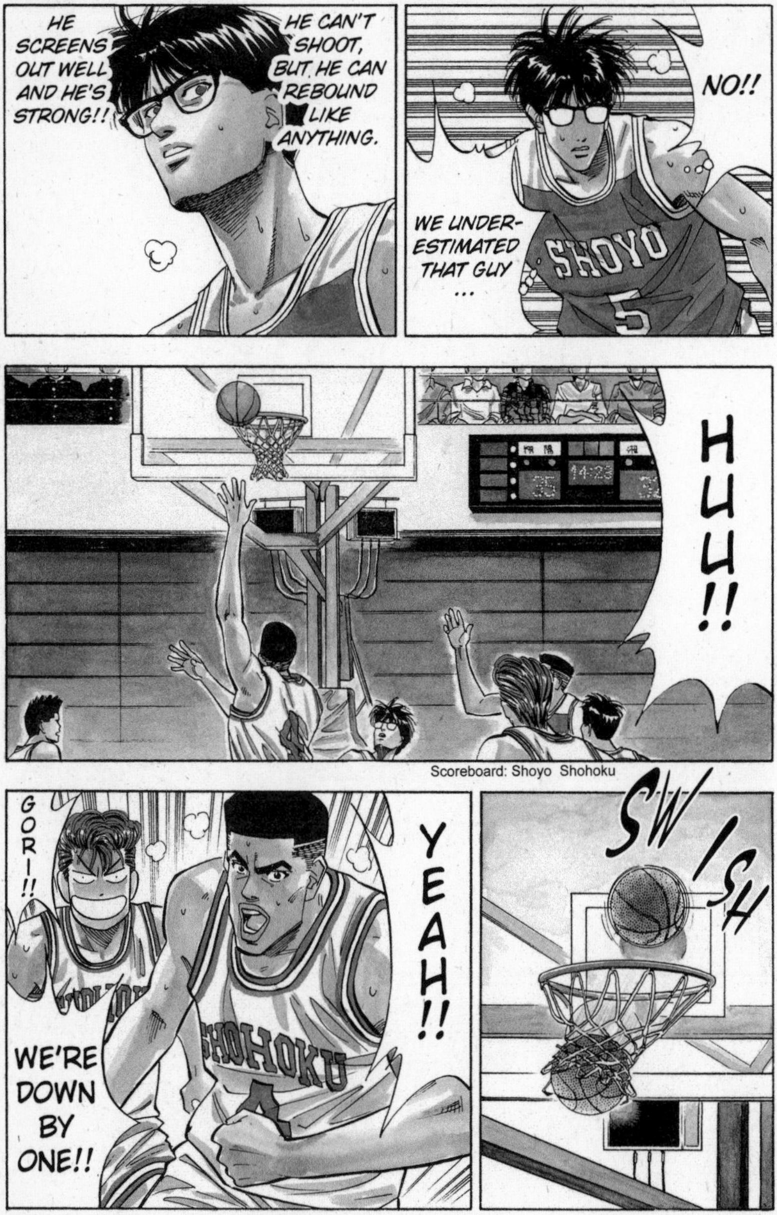
NO!!
WE UNDER-ESTIMATED THAT GUY ...
HE CAN'T SHOOT, BUT HE CAN REBOUND LIKE ANYTHING.
HE SCREENS OUT WELL AND HE'S STRONG!!
HUUU!!
Scoreboard: Shoyo Shohoku
SWISH
YEAH!!
GORI!!
WE'RE DOWN BY ONE!!

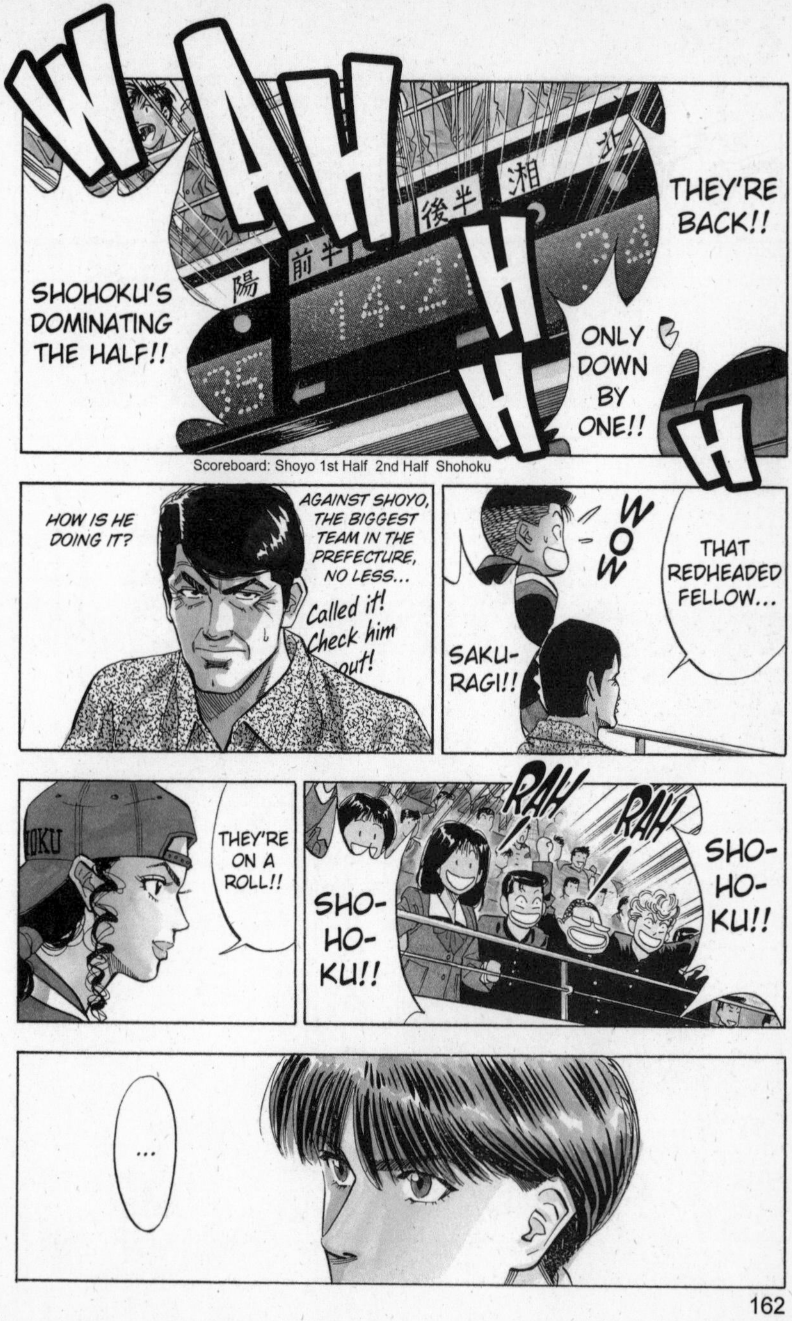
THEY'RE BACK!!
WAAHHHH
ONLY DOWN BY ONE!!
SHOHOKU'S DOMINATING THE HALF!!
THAT REDHEADED FELLOW...
WOW
SAKURAGI!!
AGAINST SHOYO, THE BIGGEST TEAM IN THE PREFECTURE, NO LESS...
Called it! Check him out!
HOW IS HE DOING IT?
SHO-HO-KU!!
RAH
RAH
SHO-HO-KU!!
THEY'RE ON A ROLL!!
...
Scoreboard: Shoyo 1st Half 2nd Half Shohoku

READ THIS WAY

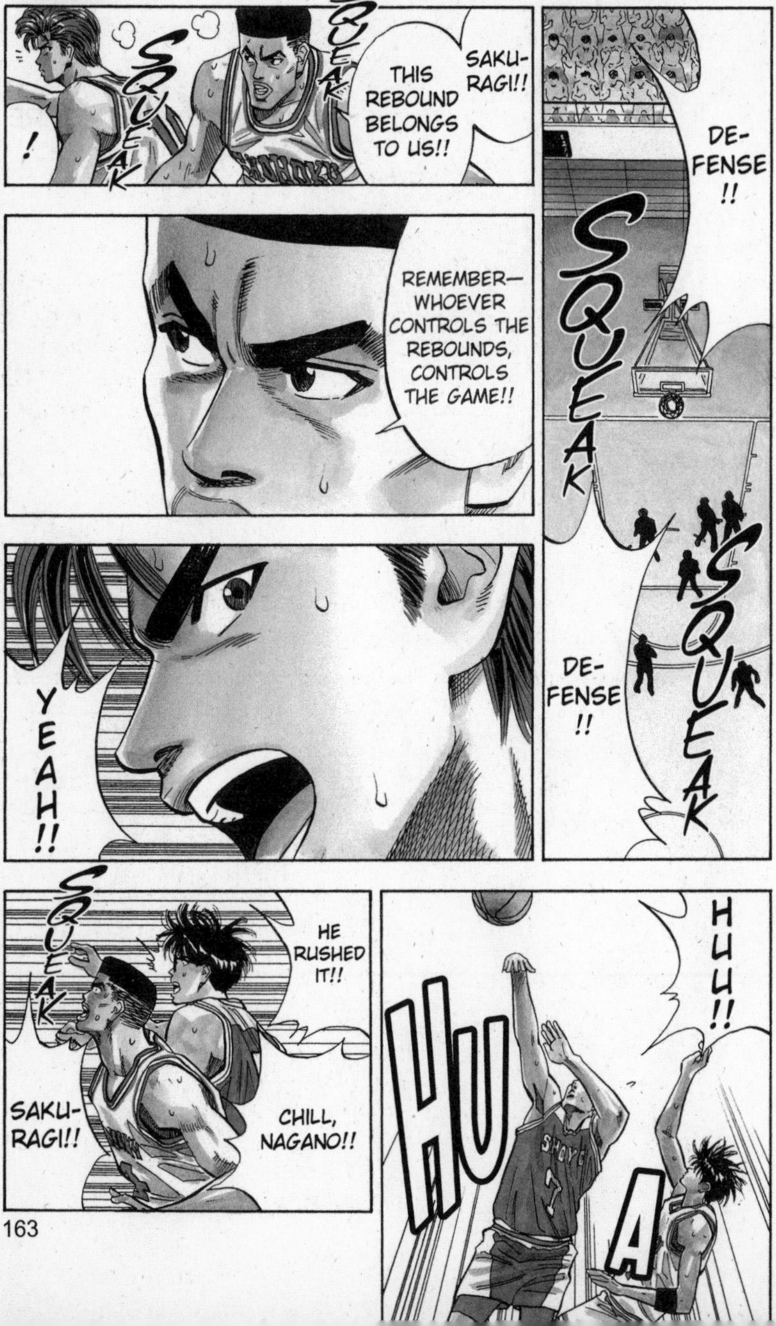
DE-FENSE!!
SQUEAK
DE-FENSE!!
SQUEAK
SAKU-RAGI!!
THIS REBOUND BELONGS TO US!!
SQUEAK
SQUEAK
!
REMEMBER—WHOEVER CONTROLS THE REBOUNDS, CONTROLS THE GAME!!
YEAH!!
HUUU!!
HU
A
HE RUSHED IT!!
SQUEAK
CHILL, NAGANO!!
SAKU-RAGI!!

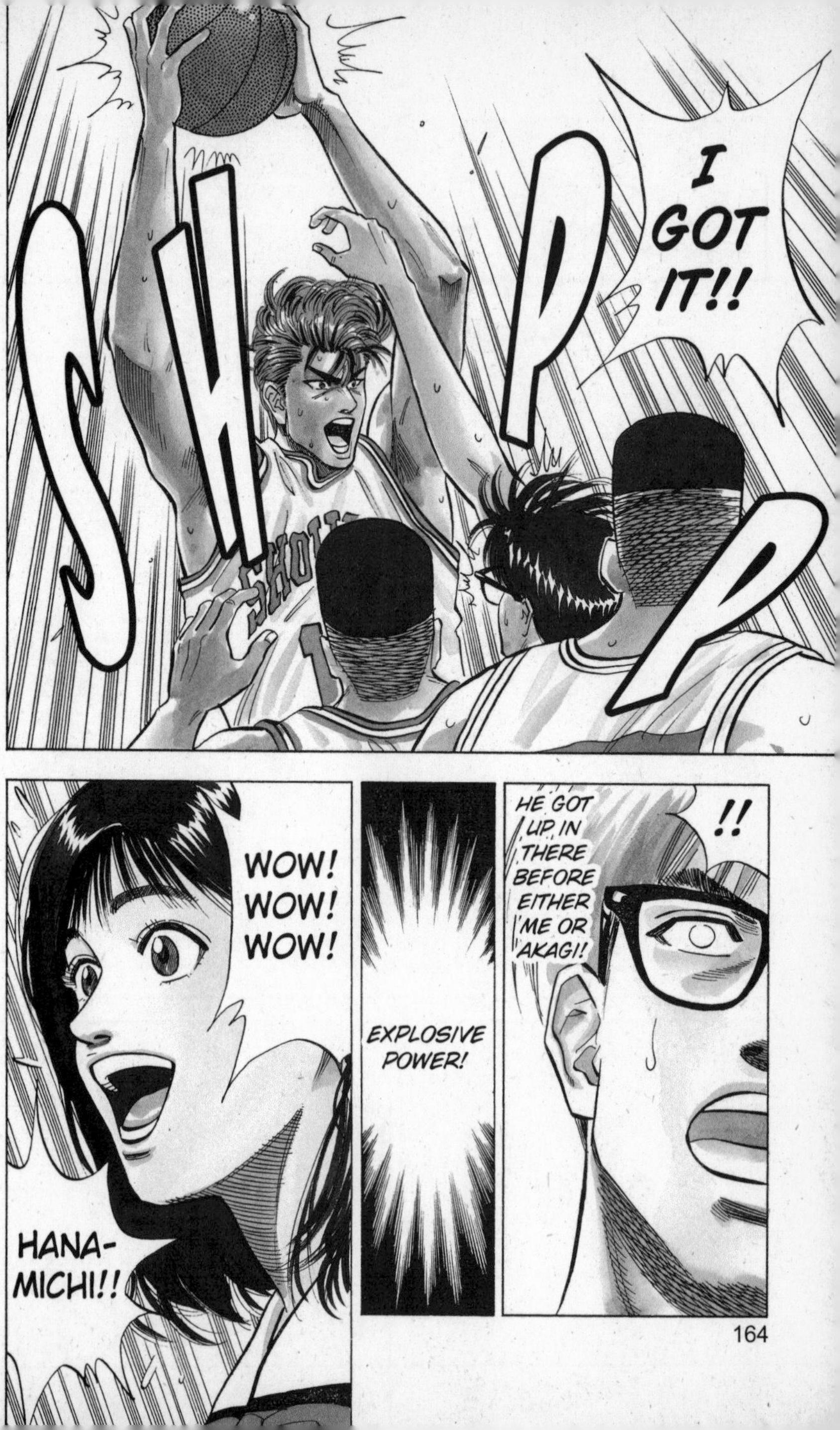
I GOT IT!!
SHPP
!!
HE GOT UP IN THERE BEFORE EITHER ME OR AKAGI!!
EXPLOSIVE POWER!
WOW! WOW! WOW!
HANA-MICHI!!

READ THIS WAY

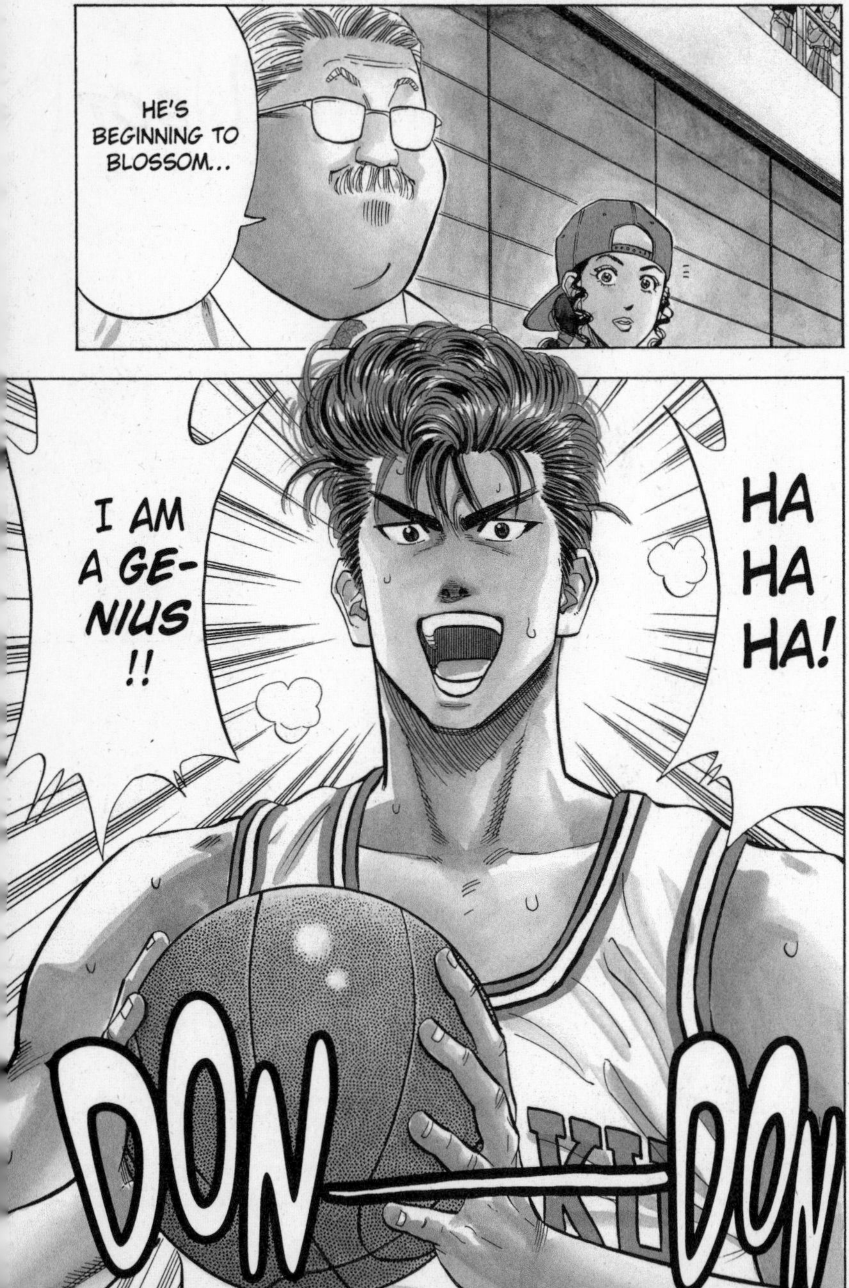
HE'S BEGINNING TO BLOSSOM...
HA HA HA!
I AM A GE-NIUS!!
DON DON

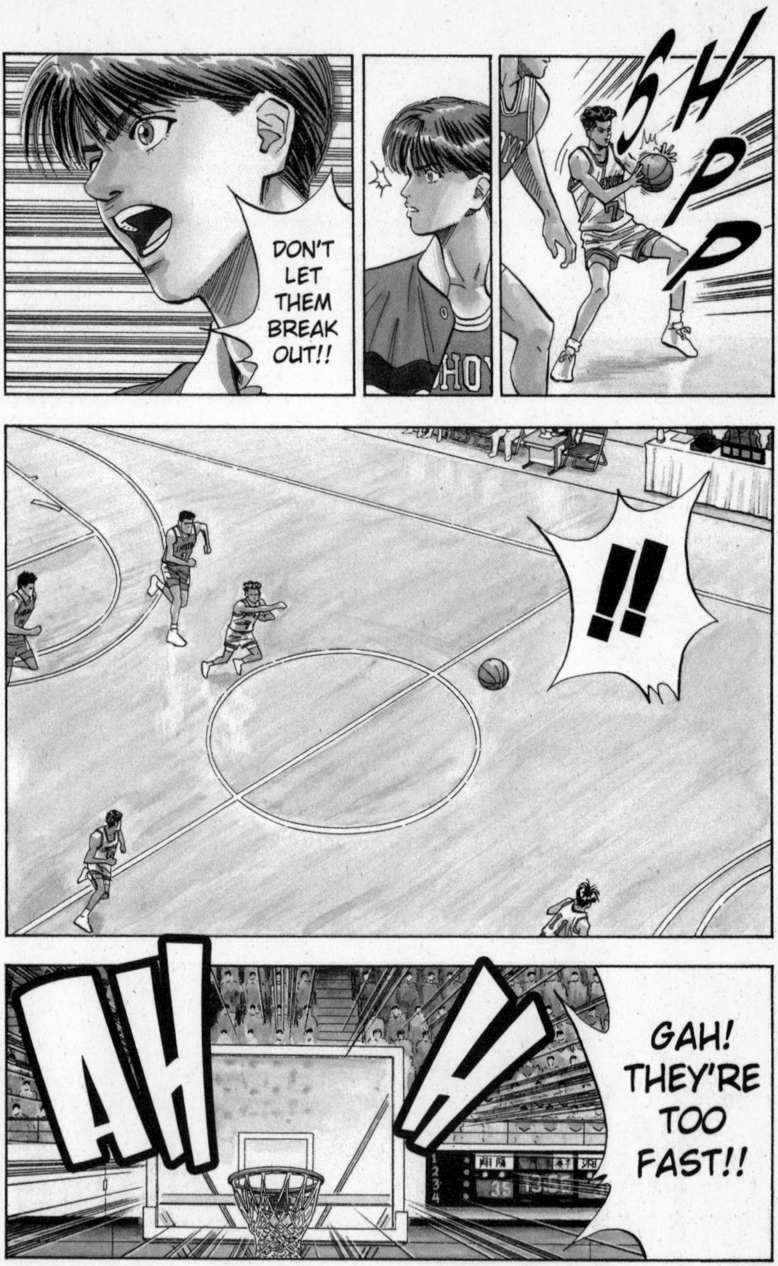
SHPP
DON'T LET THEM BREAK OUT!!
!!
GAH! THEY'RE TOO FAST!!
AHH

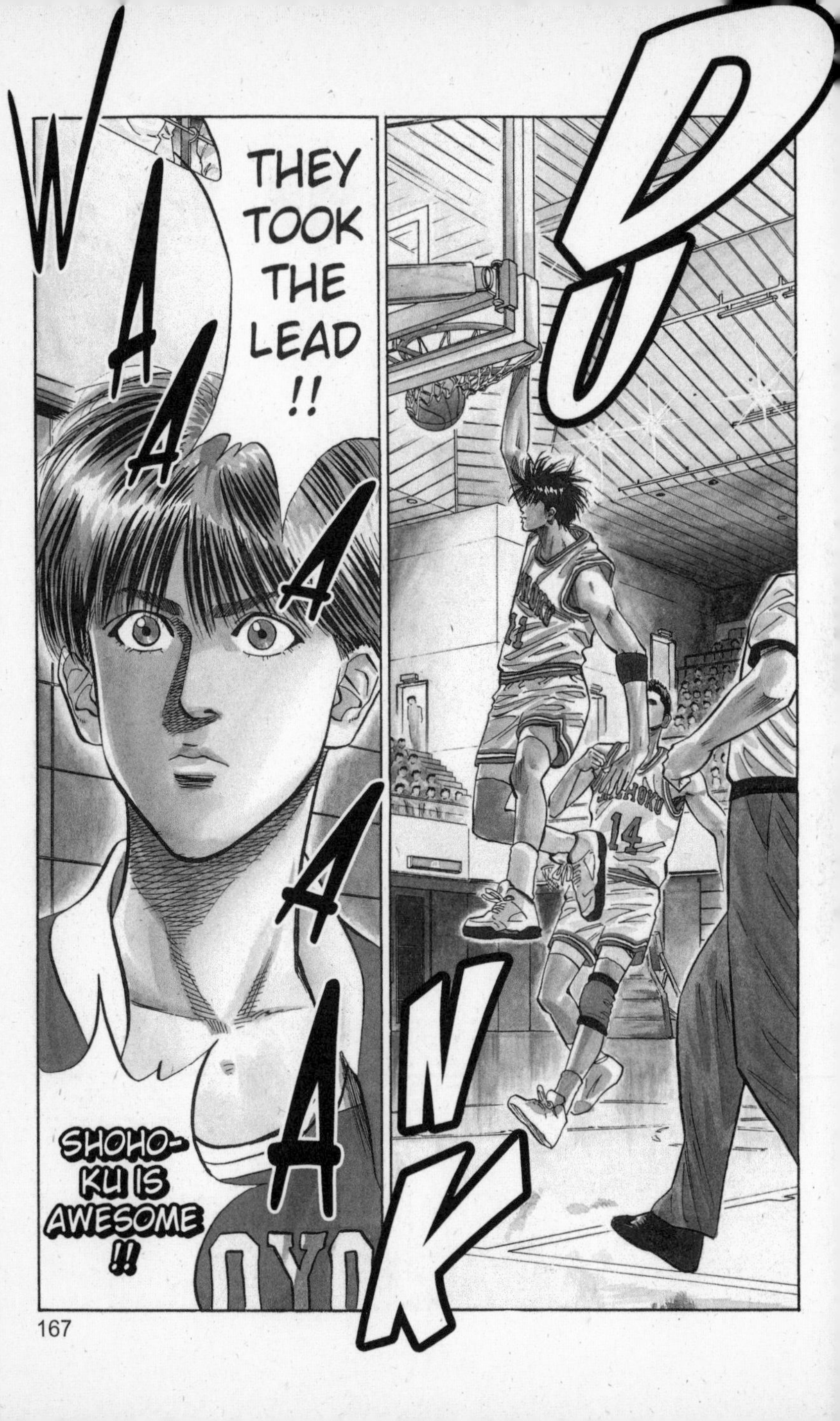
DUNK
THEY TOOK THE LEAD !!
WAAAAA
SHOHOKU IS AWESOME !!

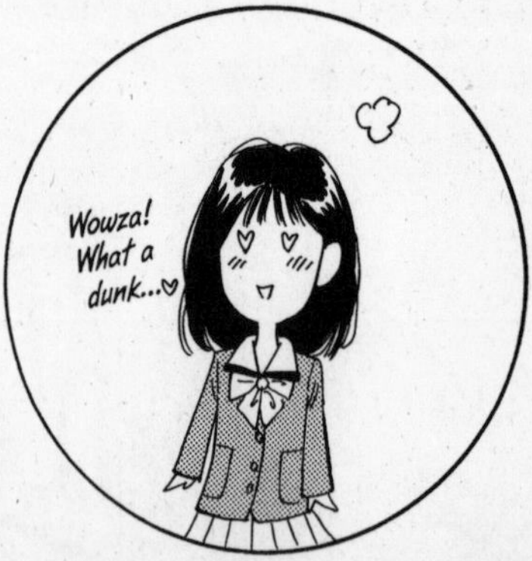
Wowza! What a dunk...♡

SLAM DUNK

READ THIS WAY

#89 SHOYO HIGH SCHOOL #4

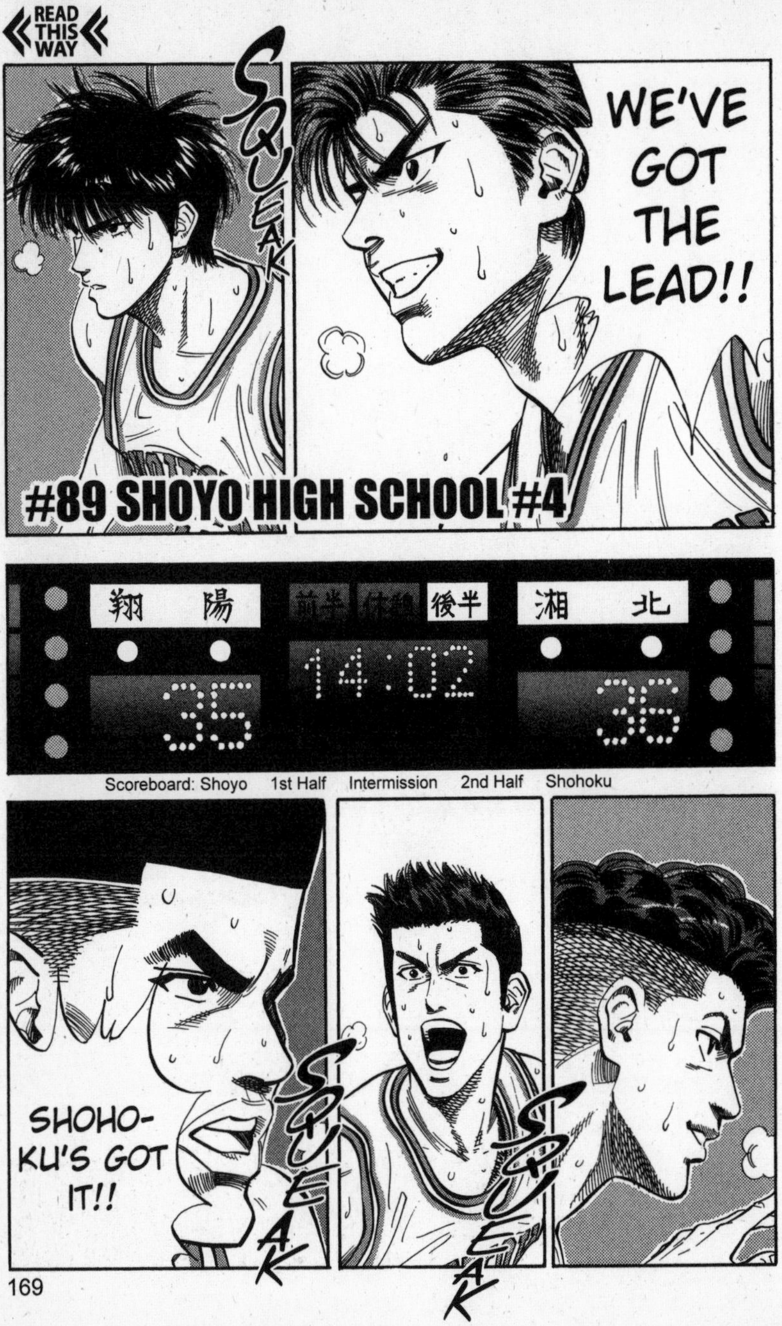
WE'VE GOT THE LEAD!!
SQUEAK
翔陽
前半
休憩
後半
湘北
14:02
35
36
Scoreboard: Shoyo 1st Half Intermission 2nd Half Shohoku
SQUEAK
SHOHOKU'S GOT IT!!
SQUEAK

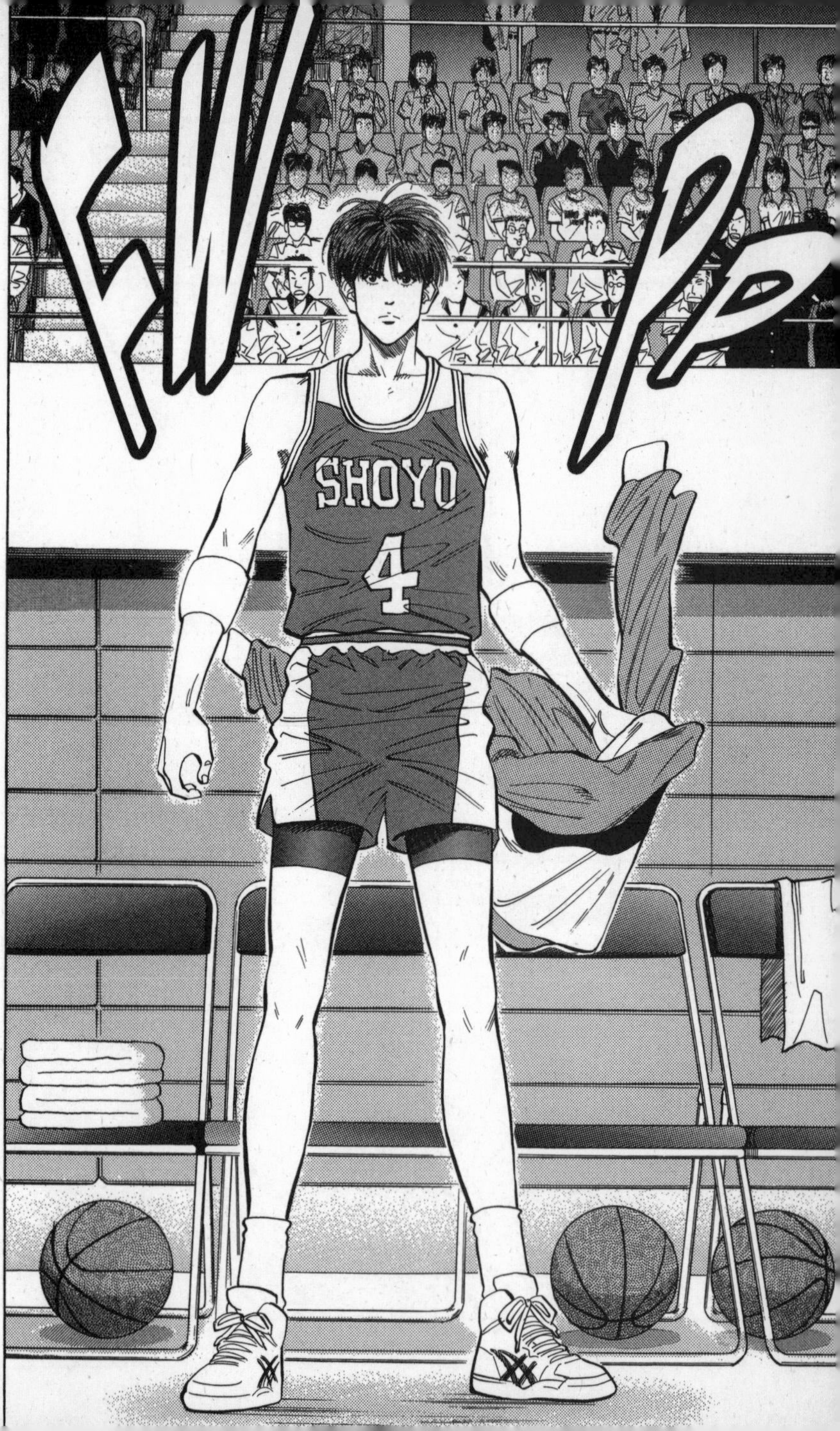
SHOYO
4

READ THIS WAY

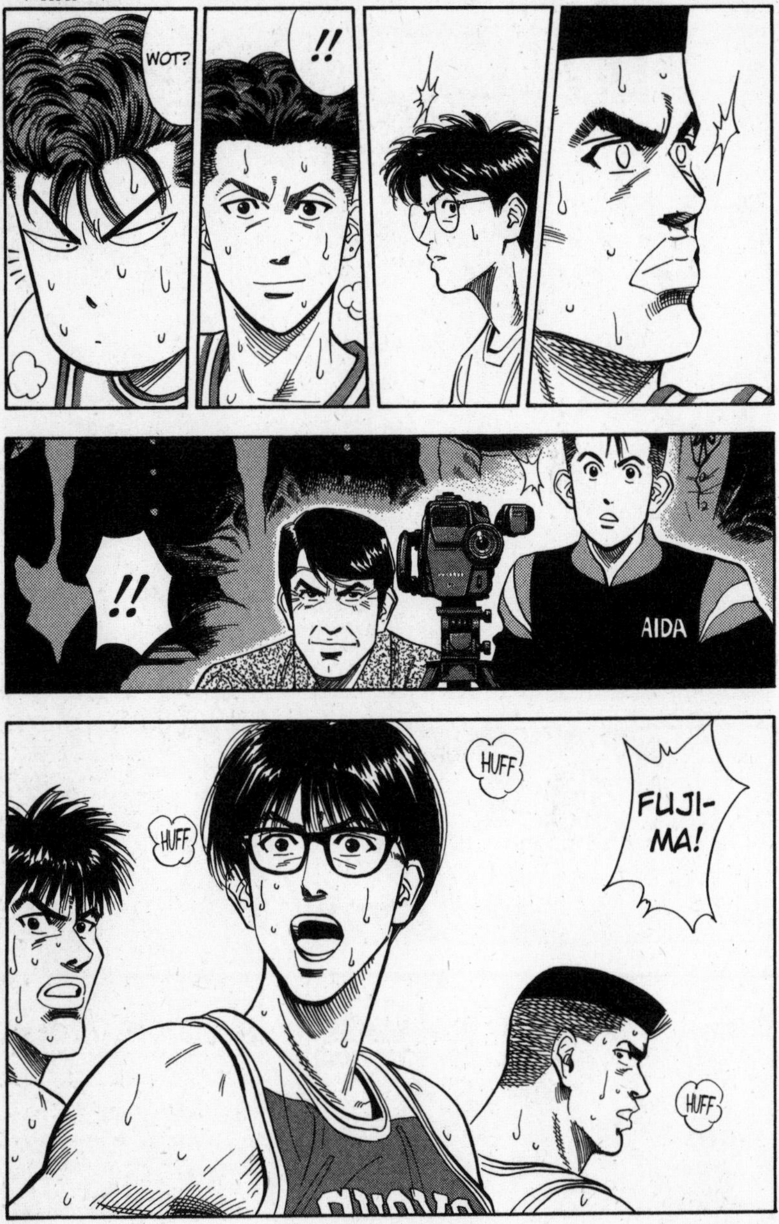
!!
WOT?
!!
AIDA
FUJI-
MA!
HUFF
HUFF
HUFF

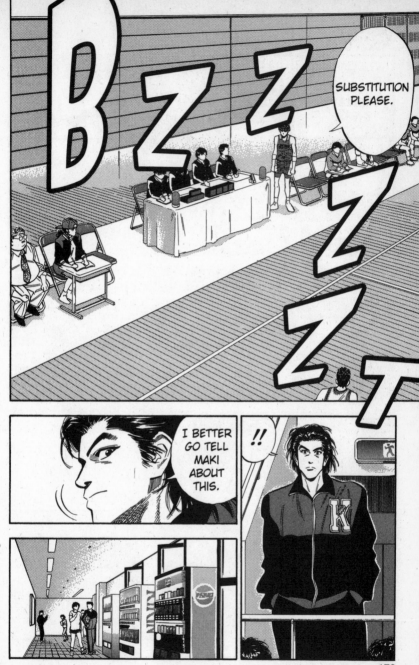

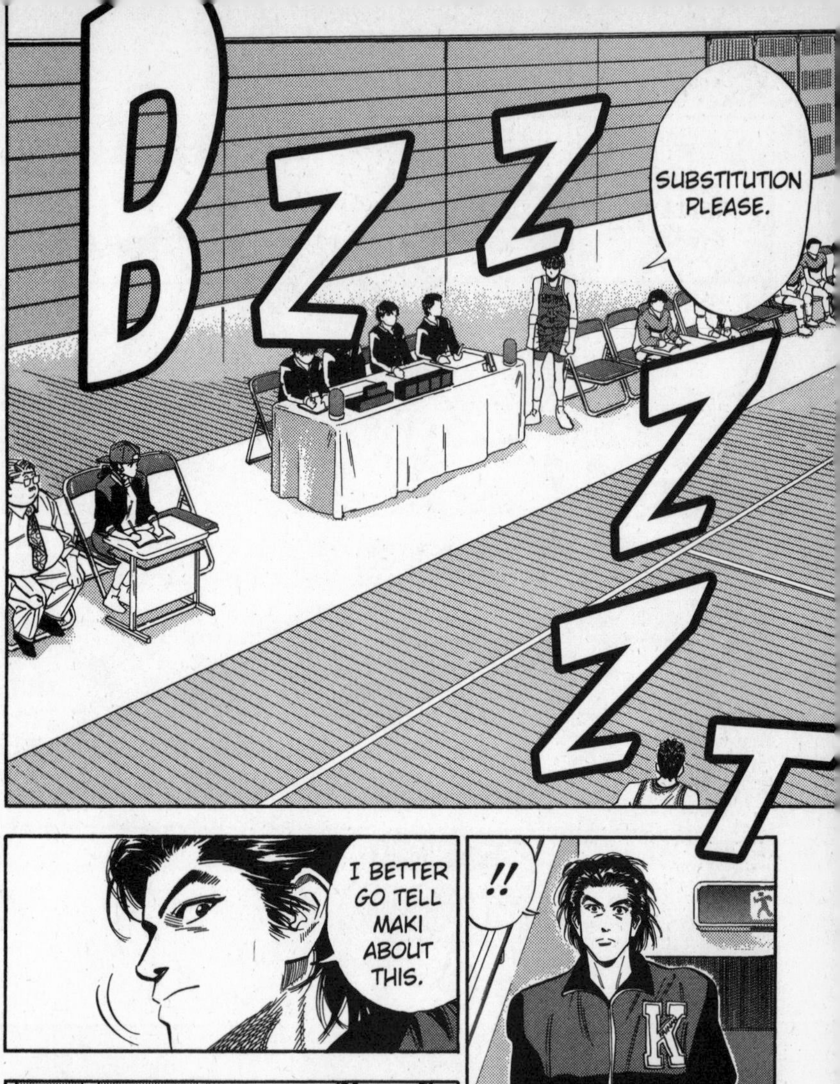
SUBSTITUTION PLEASE.
BZZZZT
!!
I BETTER GO TELL MAKI ABOUT THIS.

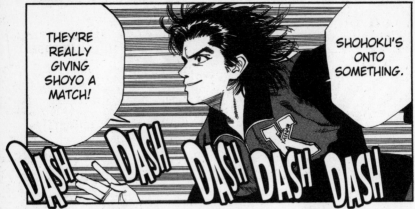

READ THIS WAY

SHOHOKU'S ONTO SOMETHING.
THEY'RE REALLY GIVING SHOYO A MATCH!
DASH DASH DASH DASH DASH
OF COURSE, IT DOESN'T MATTER WHO WE FACE...
KAINAN'S TEAM THIS YEAR IS *THE BEST EVER*!!
THIS YEAR KAINAN HAS GOLDEN ROOKIE NOBUNAGA KIYOTA!!
DASH DASH DASH DASH
KAI-NAN!
AH HA HA HA HA!
DASH DASH
第2競技場更衣室
REPORTING !!

Sign: Arena 2 Dressing Room
Please change in locker room.

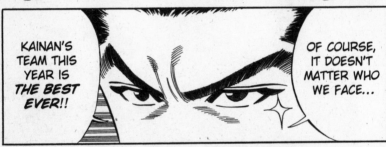

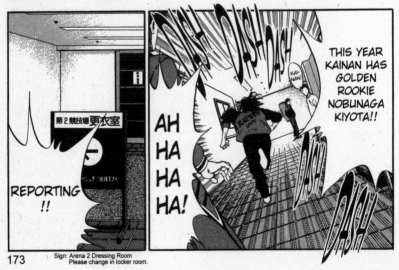

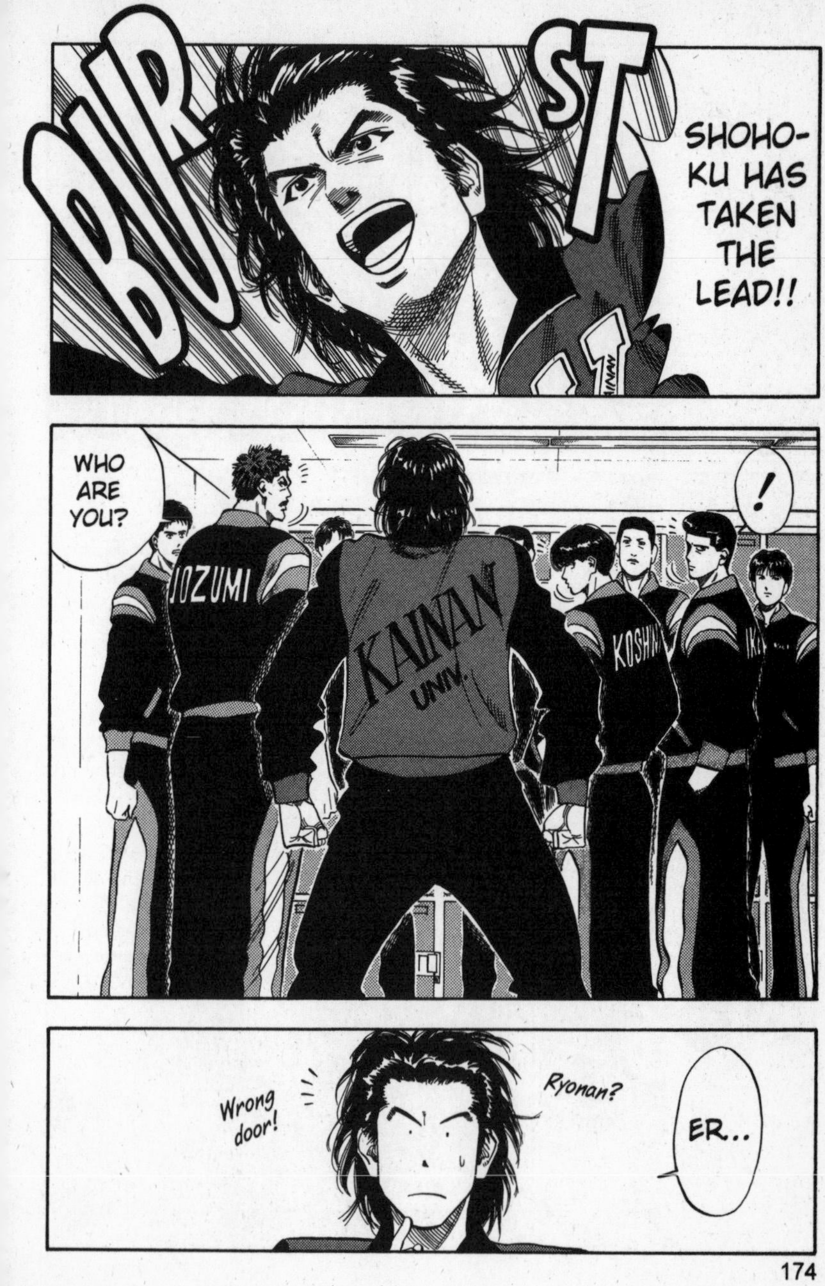
BURST
SHOHOKU HAS TAKEN THE LEAD!!
!
WHO ARE YOU?
ER..
Ryonan?
Wrong door!

READ THIS WAY

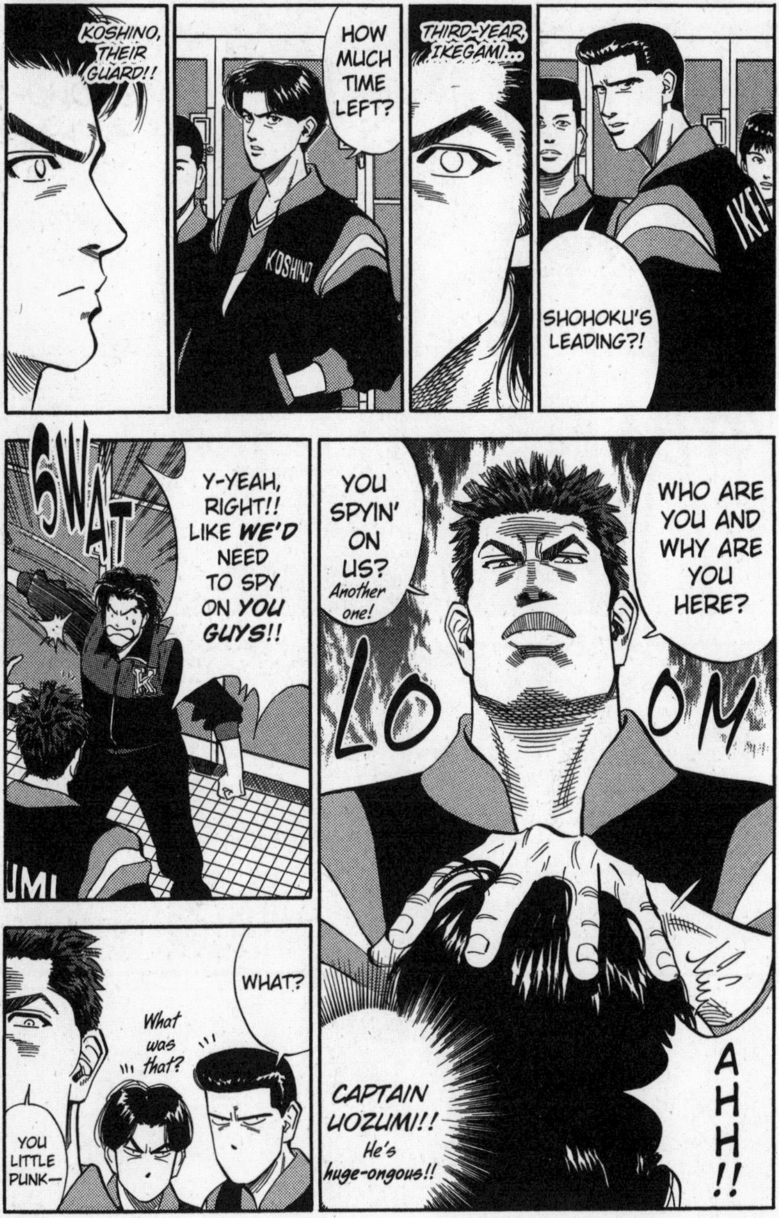
SHOHOKU'S LEADING?!
THIRD-YEAR, IKEGAMI...
HOW MUCH TIME LEFT?
KOSHINO, THEIR GUARD!!
WHO ARE YOU AND WHY ARE YOU HERE?
LOOM
YOU SPYIN' ON US? Another one!
AHH!!
CAPTAIN UOZUMI!! He's huge-ongous!!
SWAT
Y-YEAH, RIGHT!! LIKE WE'D NEED TO SPY ON YOU GUYS!!
WHAT?
What was that?
YOU LITTLE PUNK—

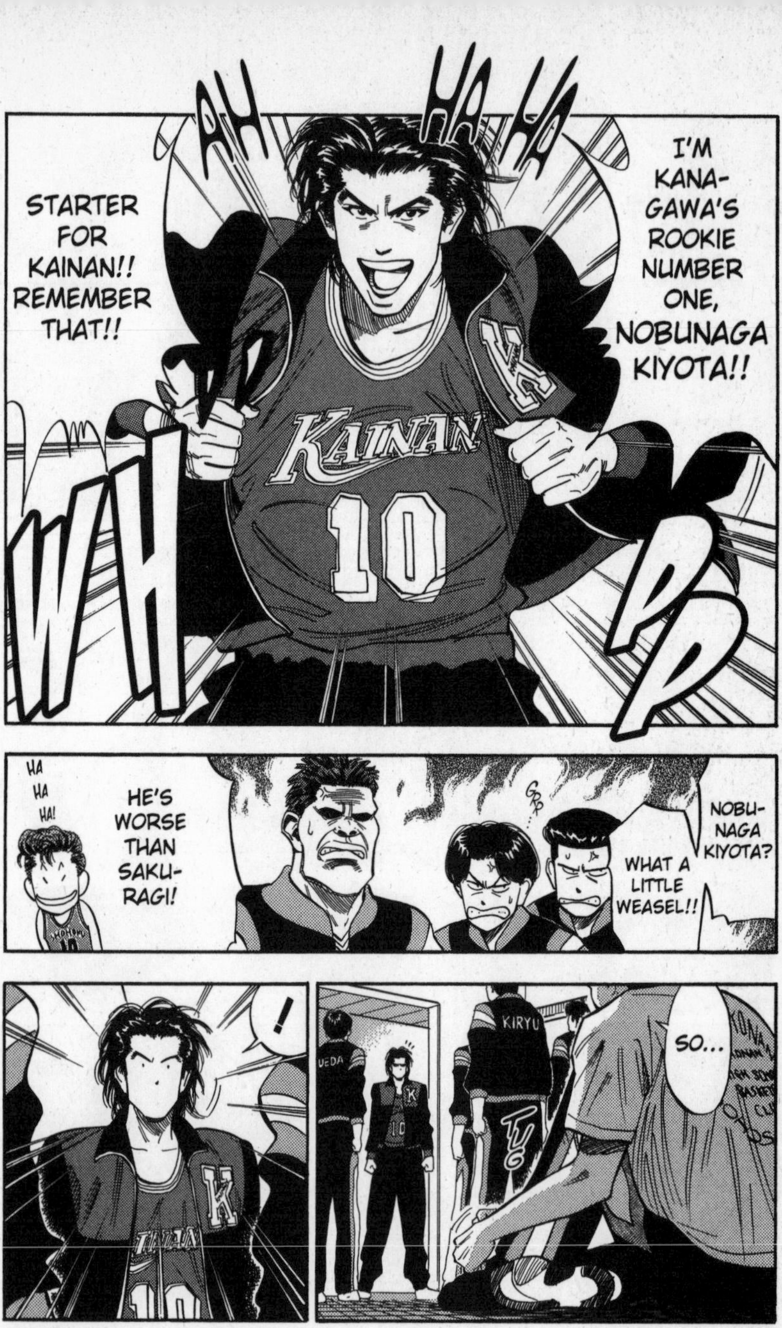
AH HA HA
I'M KANAGAWA'S ROOKIE NUMBER ONE, NOBUNAGA KIYOTA!!
STARTER FOR KAINAN!! REMEMBER THAT!!
NOBUNAGA KIYOTA?
WHAT A LITTLE WEASEL!!
GRR...
HE'S WORSE THAN SAKURAGI!
HA HA HA!
SO...
!

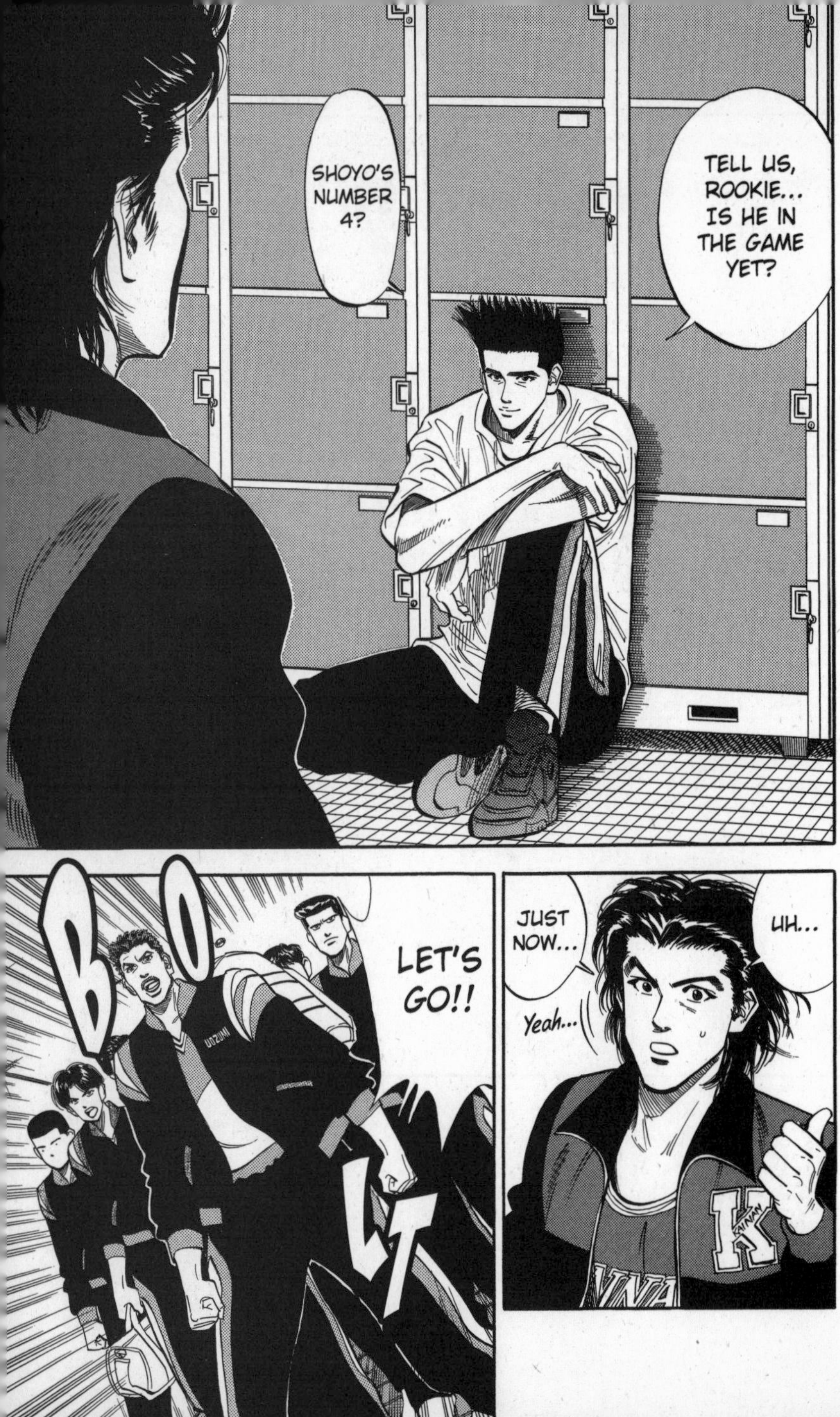
TELL US, ROOKIE... IS HE IN THE GAME YET?
SHOYO'S NUMBER 4?
UH...
JUST NOW...
Yeah...
LET'S GO!!
BOLT

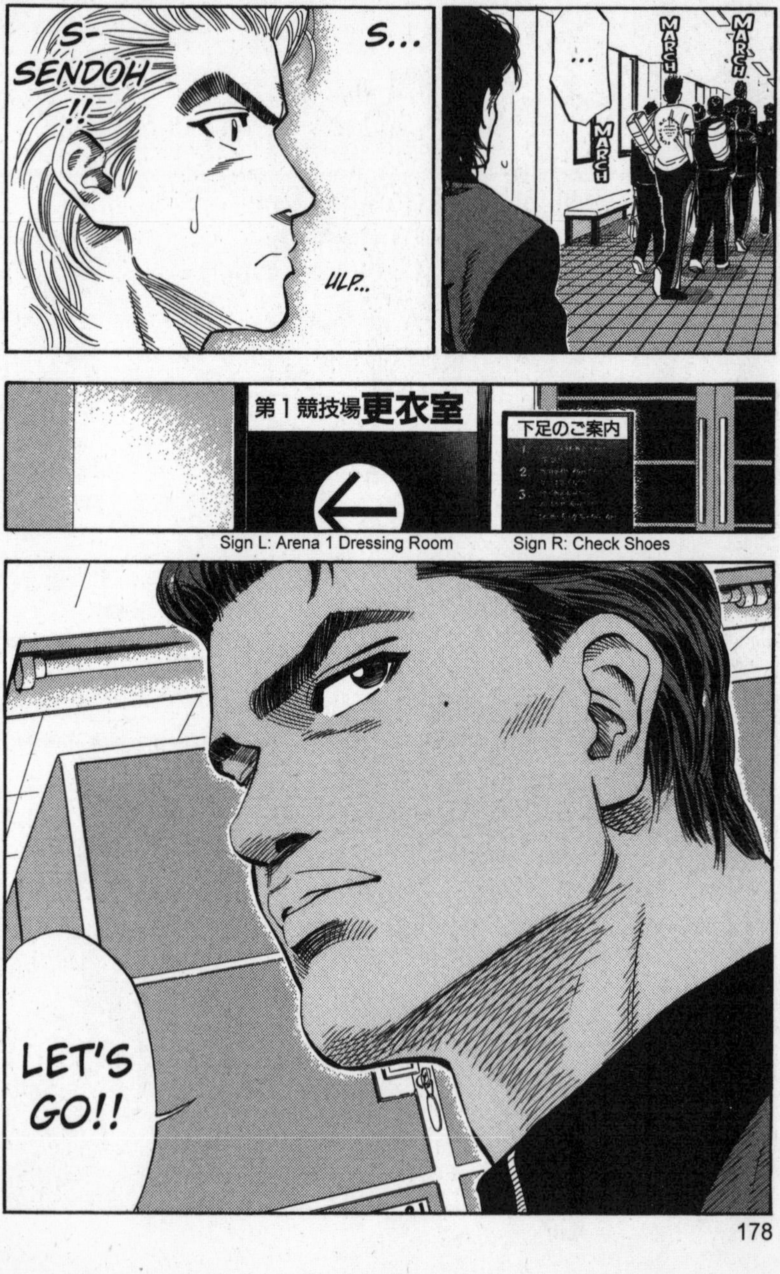
...
MARCH
MARCH
MARCH
S...
S-SENDOH!!
ULP...
第1競技場更衣室
下足のご案内
Sign L: Arena 1 Dressing Room
Sign R: Check Shoes
LET'S GO!!

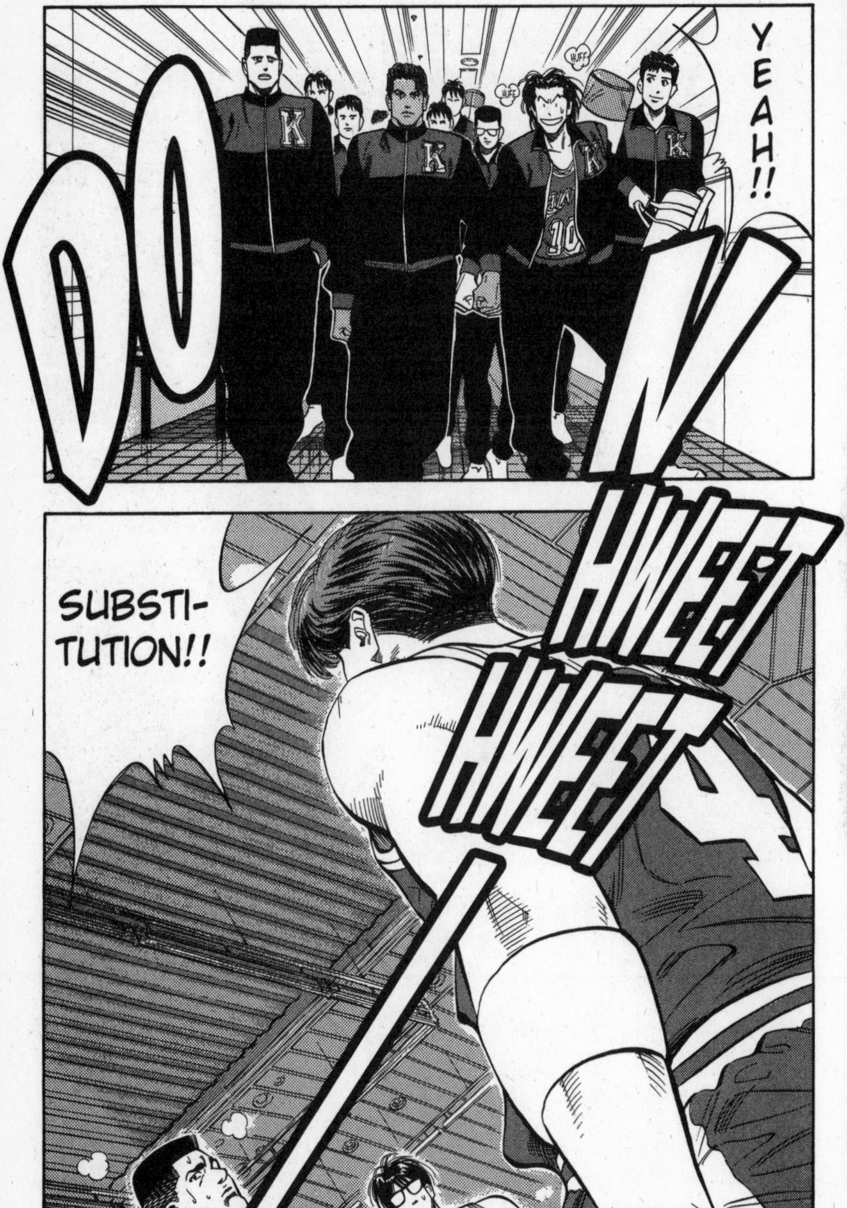
YEAH!!
HUFF
HUFF
DOON
HWEET
HWEET
SUBSTI-
TUTION!!

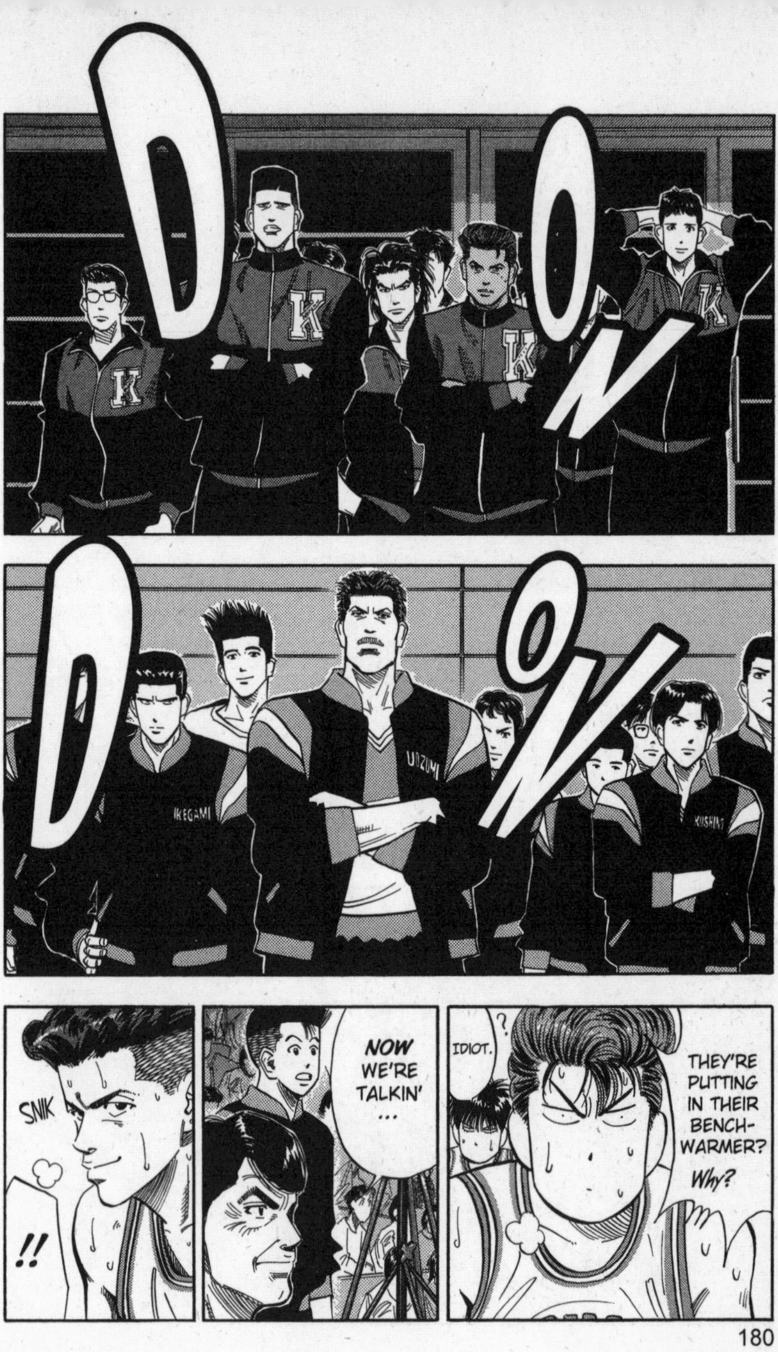
DON
DON
THEY'RE PUTTING IN THEIR BENCH-WARMER? Why?
?
IDIOT.
NOW WE'RE TALKIN' ...
SNIK
!!

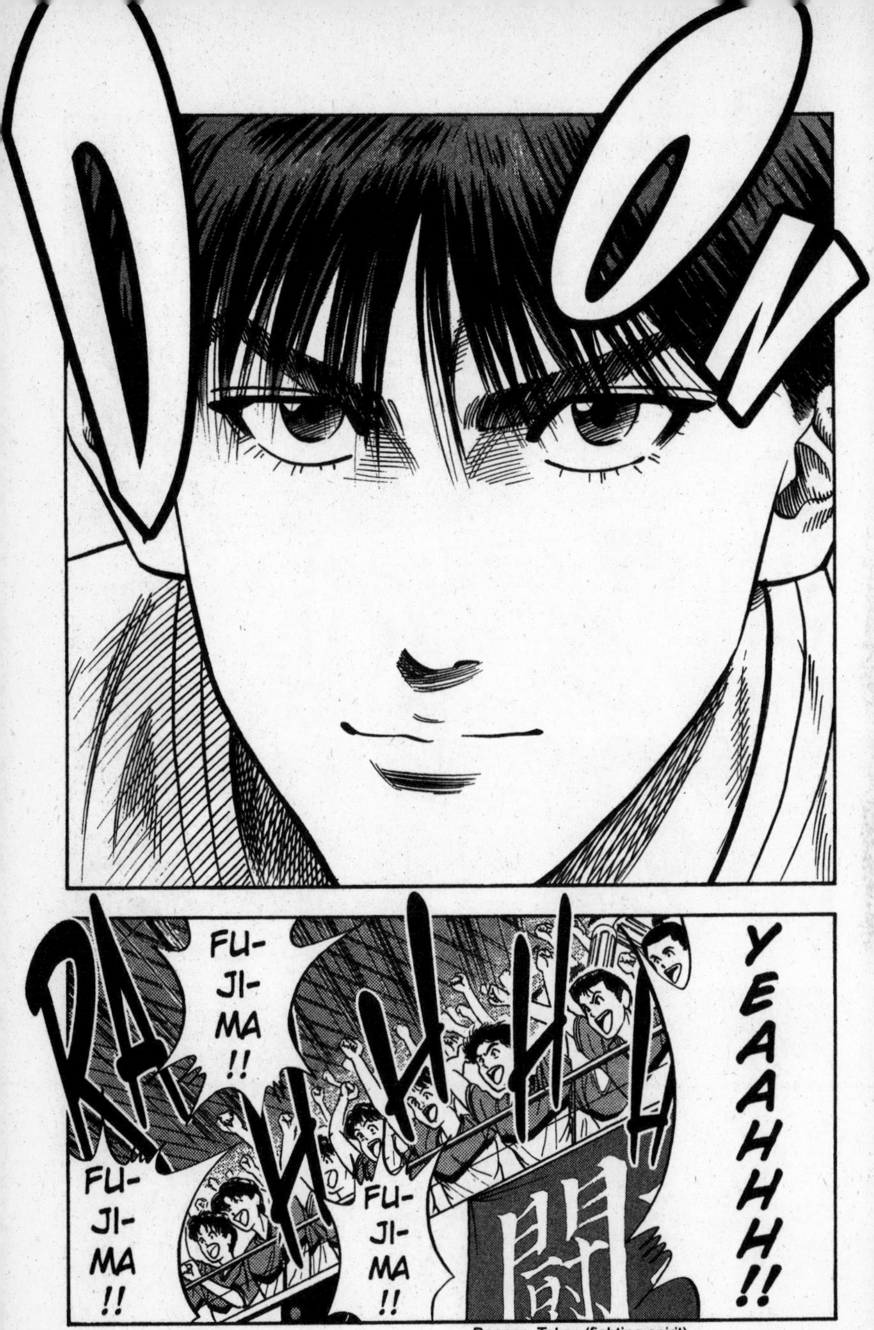
YEAAHHH!!
FU-JI-MA!!
FU-JI-MA!!
FU-JI-MA!!

Banner: *Tokon* (fighting spirit)

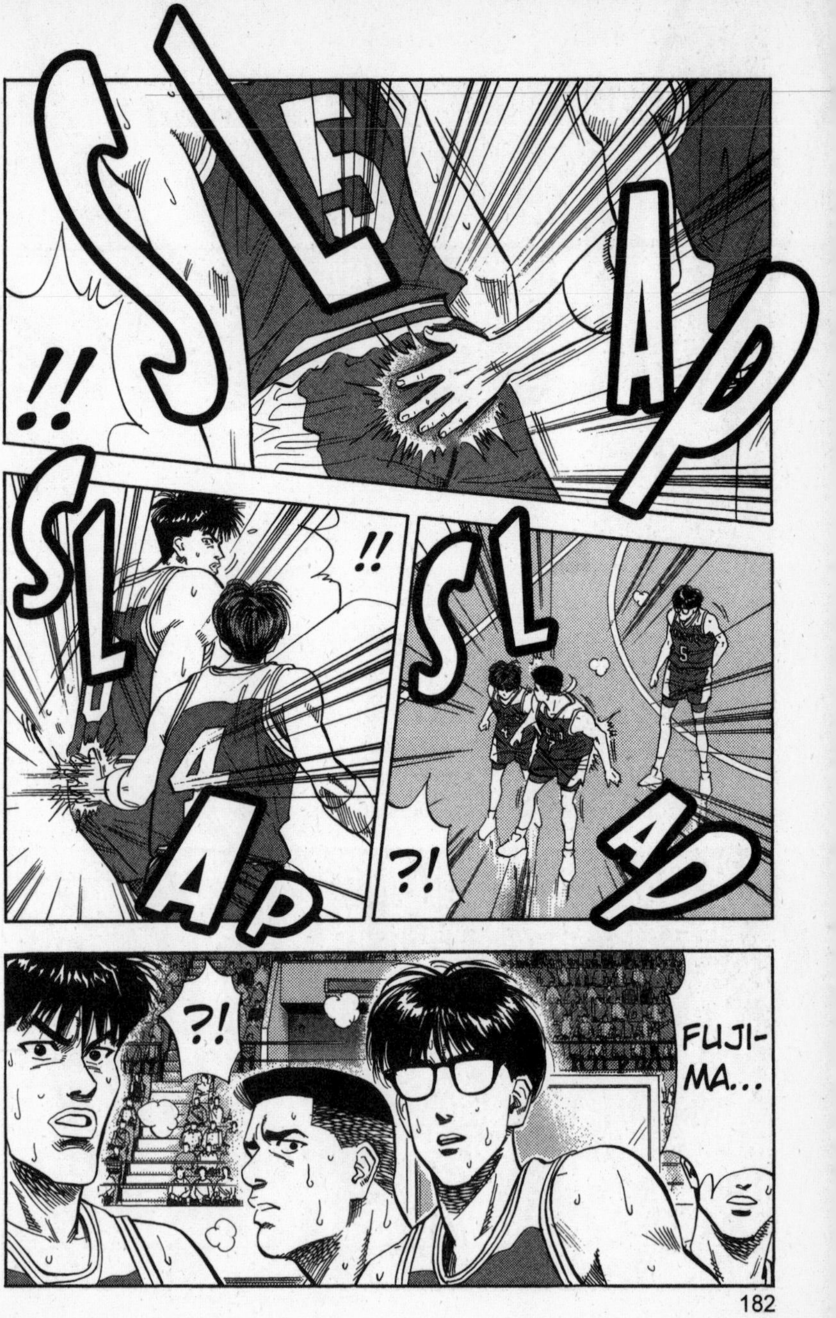
SLAP
!!
SLAP
?!
SLAP
!!
FUJI-
MA...
?!

READ THIS WAY

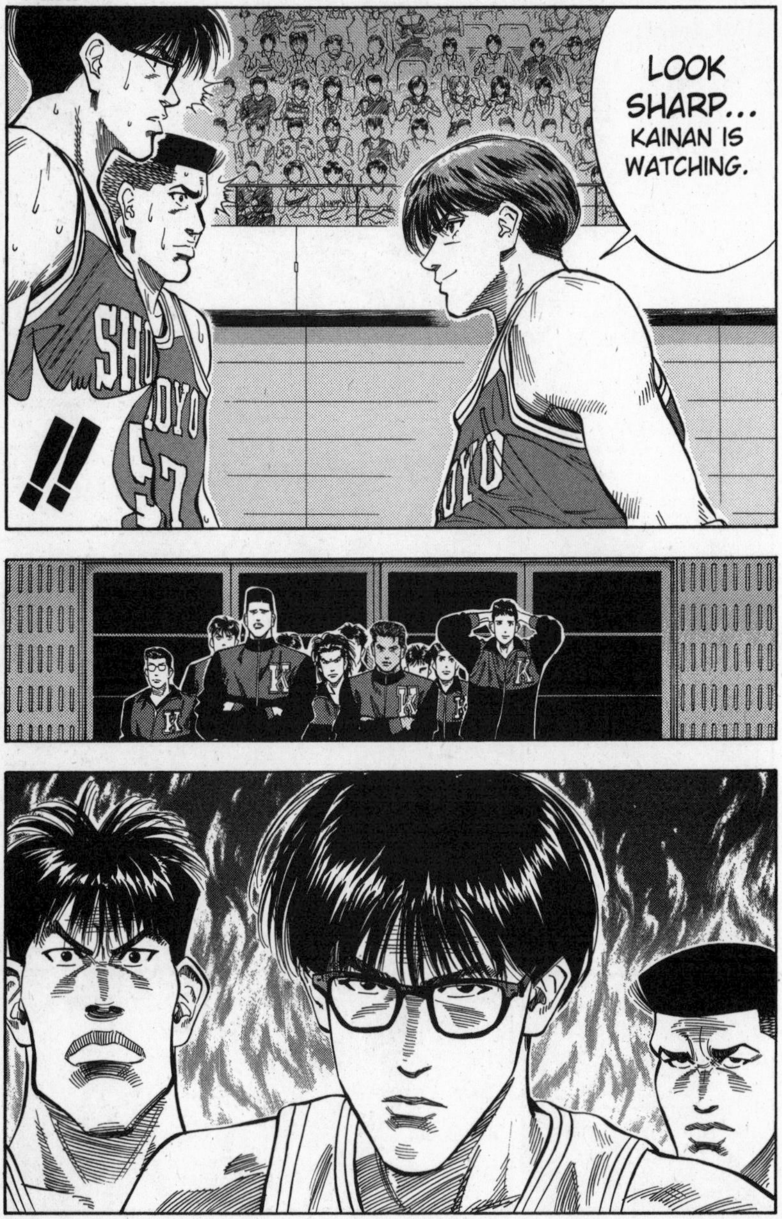
LOOK SHARP... KAINAN IS WATCHING.
!!

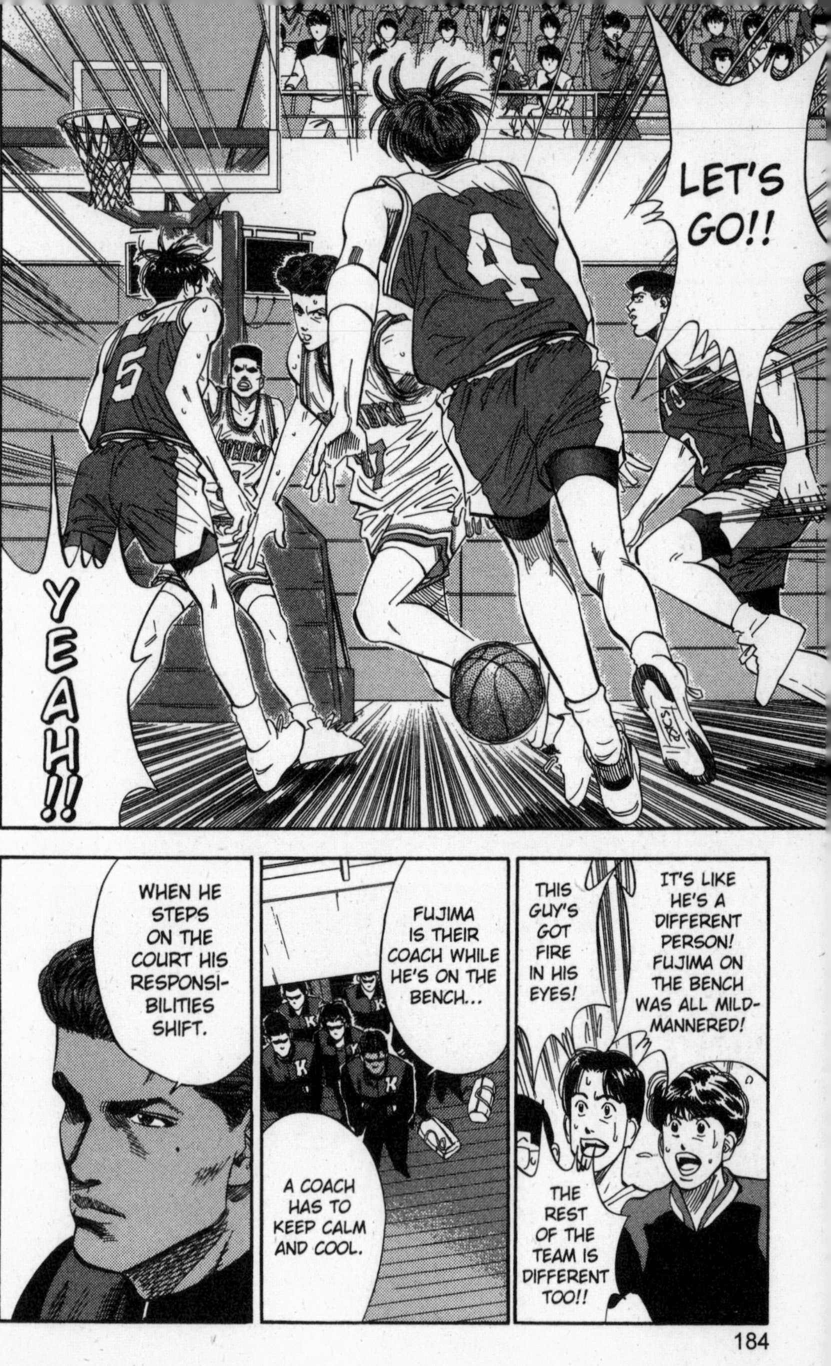
LET'S GO!!
YEAH!!
IT'S LIKE HE'S A DIFFERENT PERSON! FUJIMA ON THE BENCH WAS ALL MILD-MANNERED!
THIS GUY'S GOT FIRE IN HIS EYES!
THE REST OF THE TEAM IS DIFFERENT TOO!!
FUJIMA IS THEIR COACH WHILE HE'S ON THE BENCH...
A COACH HAS TO KEEP CALM AND COOL.
WHEN HE STEPS ON THE COURT HIS RESPONSI-BILITIES SHIFT.

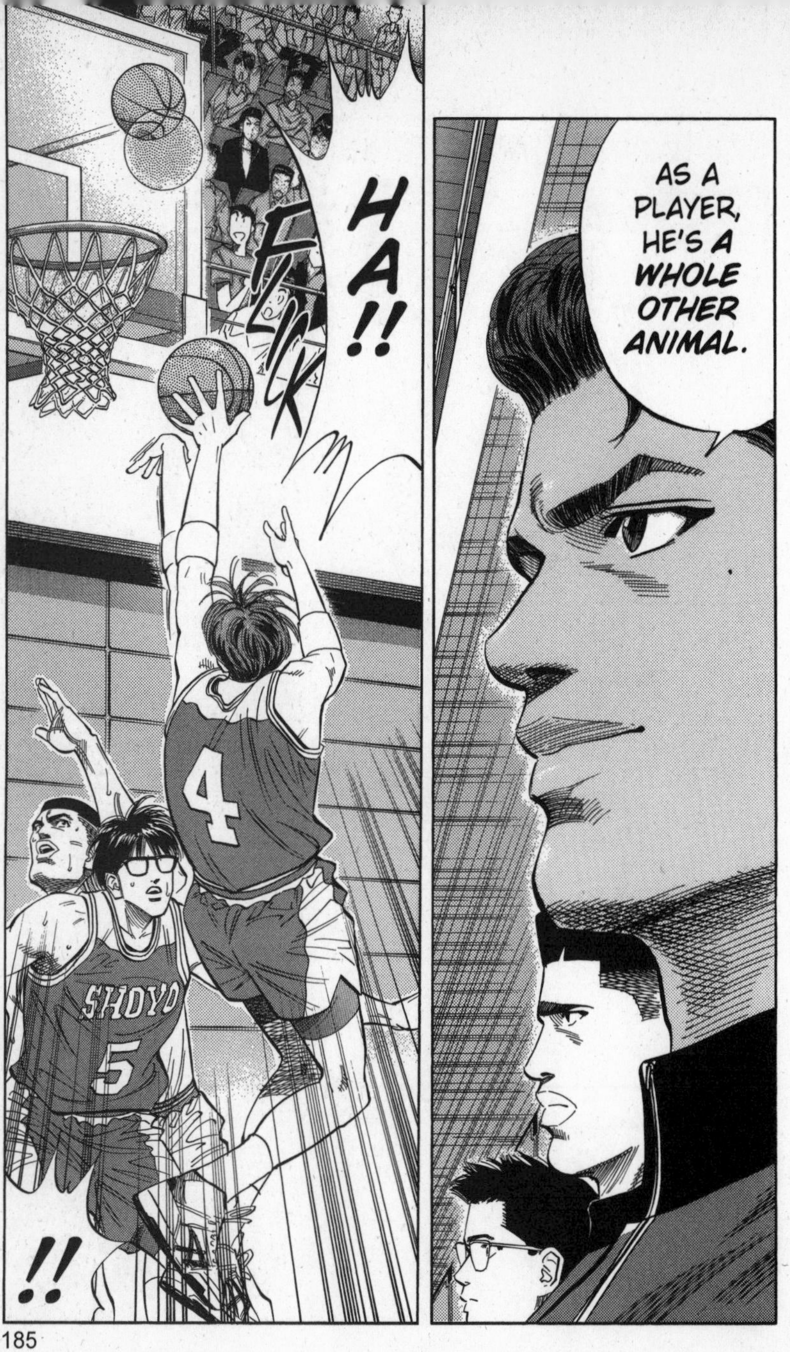
AS A PLAYER, HE'S A WHOLE OTHER ANIMAL.
HA!!
FLICK
!!
SHOYO

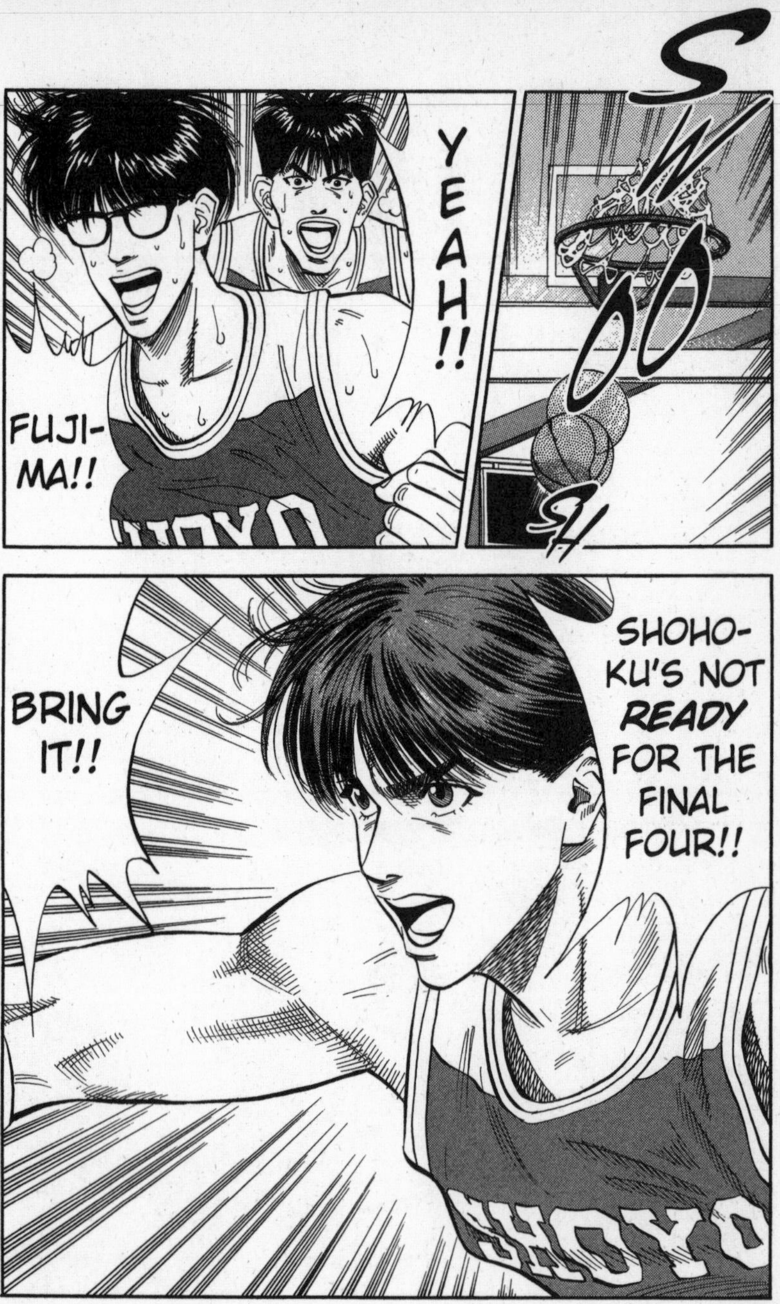

SWOOO
SH
YEAH!!
FUJI-MA!!
SHOHO-KU'S NOT *READY* FOR THE FINAL FOUR!!
BRING IT!!

READ THIS WAY

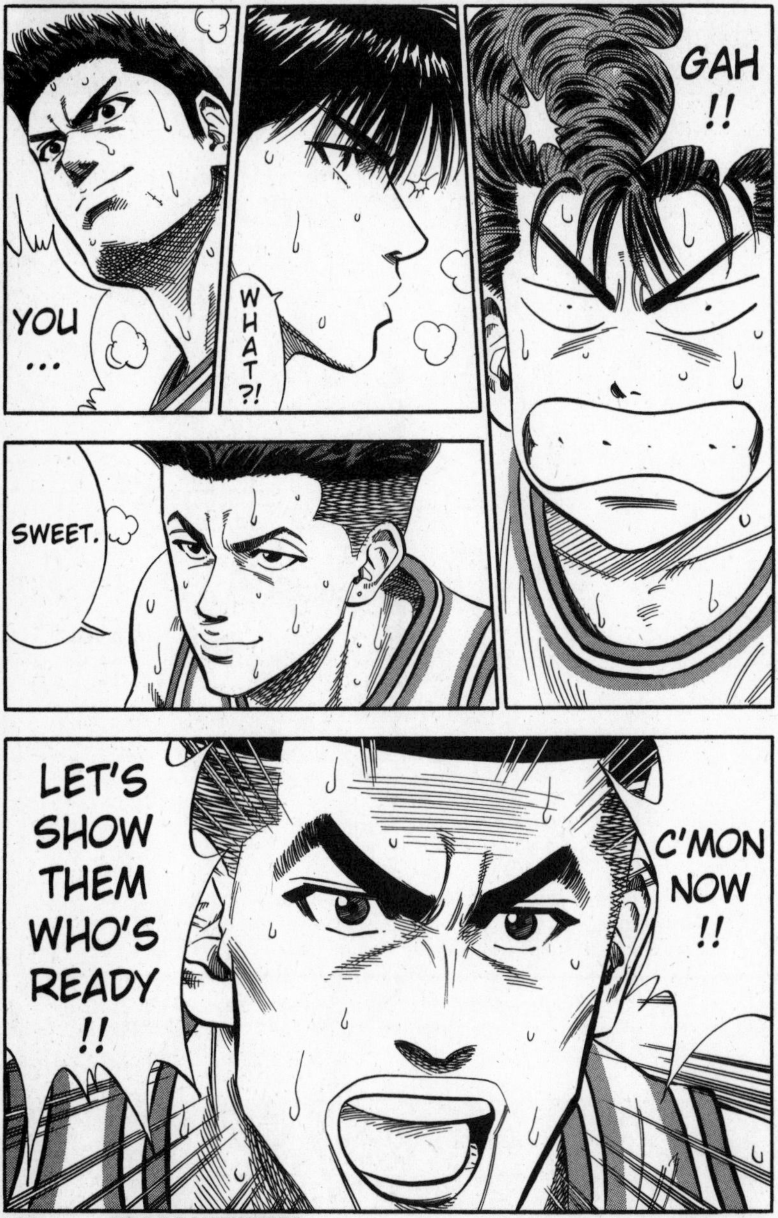
GAH!!
WHAT?!
YOU...
SWEET.
C'MON NOW!!
LET'S SHOW THEM WHO'S READY!!

TO BE CONTINUED!

Coming Next Volume

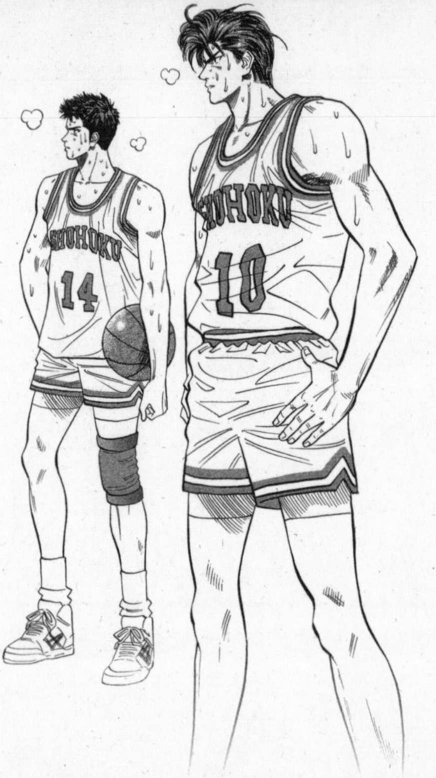

SHOHOKU
14
SHOHOKU
10

With Shoyo's top star Fujima now hitting the court, Shohoku's lead quickly turns south. And while Hisashi Mitsui's energy reserves are diminishing by the second, Coach Anzai decides to keep the shooting ace in as well. But it's going to take more than lights-out pyrotechnics from Mitsui to carry the Shohoku boys through to victory—Sakuragi's going to need to grab some monster boards too!

ON SALE AUGUST 2010

SAVE 50% OFF THE COVER PRICE!

IT'S LIKE GETTING 6 ISSUES

FREE!

OVER **350+** PAGES PER ISSUE

THE WORLD'S MOST POPULAR MANGA

This monthly magazine contains 7 of the coolest manga available in the U.S., PLUS anime news, and info about video & card games, toys AND more!

❑ **I want 12 HUGE issues of SHONEN JUMP for only $29.95*!**

NAME

ADDRESS

CITY/STATE/ZIP

EMAIL ADDRESS   **DATE OF BIRTH**

❑ YES, send me via email information, advertising, offers, and promotions related to VIZ Media, SHONEN JUMP, and/or their business partners.

❑ **CHECK ENCLOSED** (payable to SHONEN JUMP)   ❑ **BILL ME LATER**

CREDIT CARD: ❑ **Visa** ❑ **Mastercard**

ACCOUNT NUMBER   **EXP. DATE**

SIGNATURE

CLIP&MAIL TO:
SHONEN JUMP Subscriptions Service Dept.
P.O. Box 515
Mount Morris, IL 61054-0515

P9GNC1

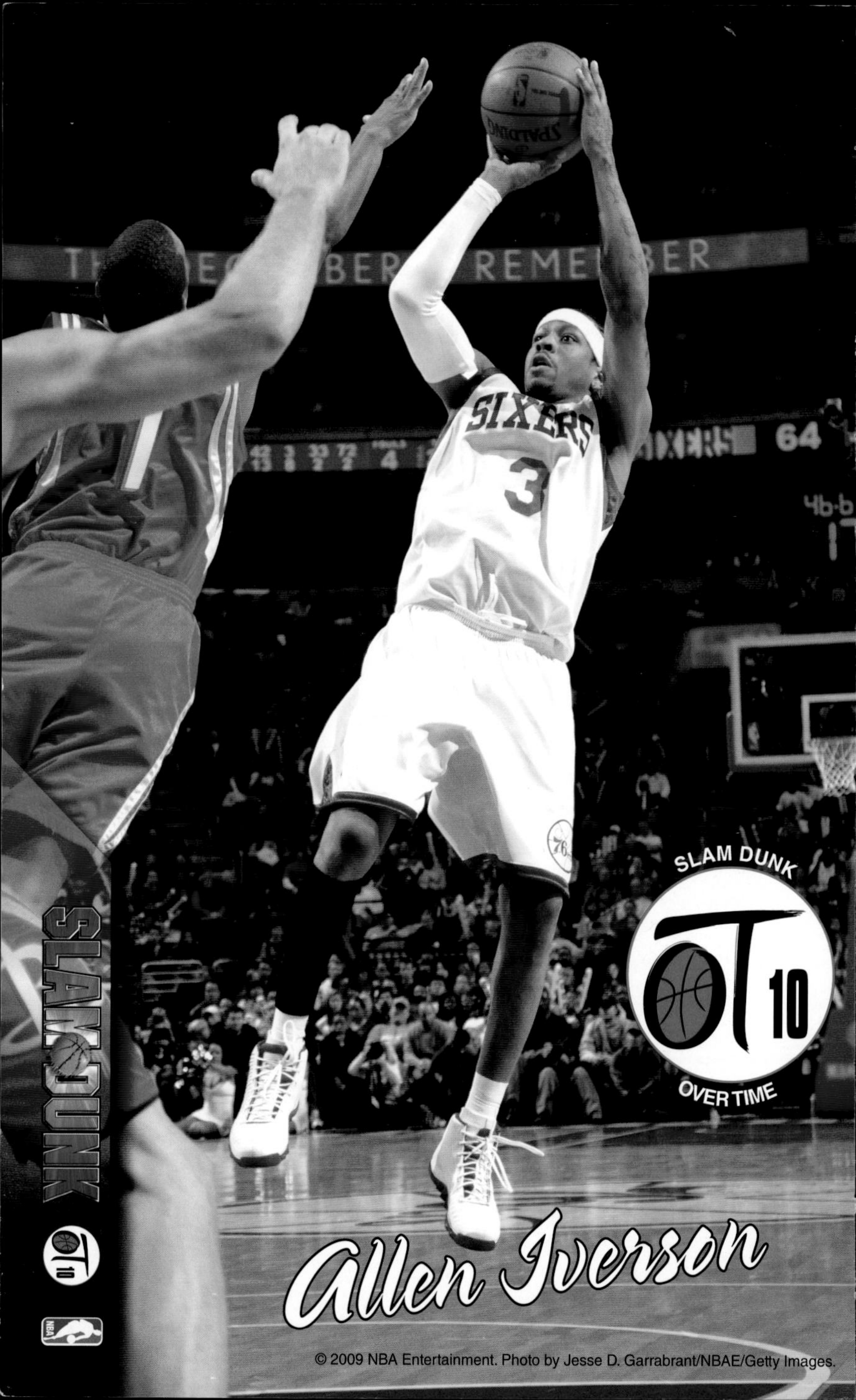
SIXERS
3
SLAM DUNK
OT 10
OVER TIME
SLAM DUNK
Allen Iverson

***A** warm welcome back to the arena, roundball rascals! Please sprint to center court and prepare for liftoff as the SDOT staff will greet each of you with a flying chest bump and a windmill high-five. Are you warmed up now? Good, cuz we've got an Ohmigoodness-Omake in store for you today, folks. First, SDOT tries to keep up with crossover king Allen Iverson. And yes, we do have medical staff on hand to remedy those broken ankles. Next up, Coach Omake hopes to graduate you novice ball burglars from petty larceny to grand theft as he looks at the art of the steal. So lace 'em up, S-Dunkers... Let's get it started!*

Born to Do It

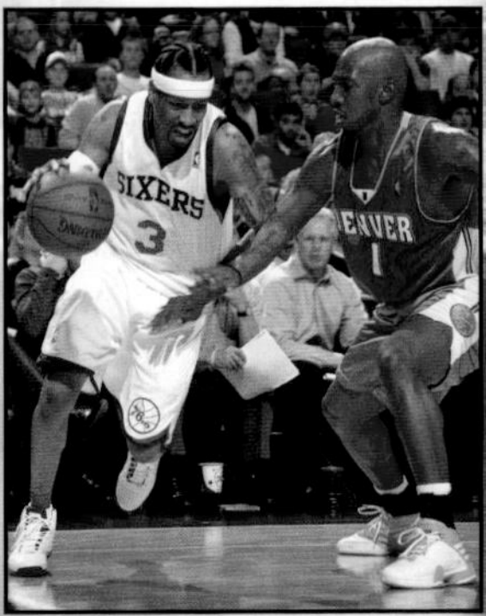

SIXERS
3
DENVER
1

Allen Ezail Iverson hails from hardscrabble Hampton, Va., where he filled seats as a two-sport blue-chipper at Bethel High School. In 1993, Bethel won the state championship in football and basketball, largely due to Iverson's heroics at the quarterback and point guard positions. Allen Iverson is one of those athletes who had all the intangibles from day one. Incredible speed? Check. Equally incredible vertical leap? Check. Court awareness, decision-making, massive heart and hustle? A.I.'s got all of 'em. Yet even with all that natural talent, he didn't sit pat. He was always trying to widen his oeuvre. Take football, for example. Most athletes who become starting quarterback would be content with that title. But Allen also played running back and safety and even returned kicks at Bethel! A.I. had more than enough talent to play in the NFL, but it was his hoop skills that caught the eye of a legendary college basketball coach.

Most big-time college basketball programs comb the entire nation and sometimes even the globe for their recruits. But when you've got a homegrown, once-in-a-generation talent like Iverson right in your backyard, why bother? In 1994, John Thompson, Jr., then-head basketball coach at Georgetown University, dropped by Bethel for a visit. The two got along famously, and Iverson signed a letter of intent to play for him in short order. A.I. didn't disappoint the Hoya-faithful; he earned the Big East Rookie of the Year Award and two consecutive Big East Defensive Player of the Year Awards. After two years, A.I. left Georgetown as the Hoyas' all-time leader in career scoring average and entered the NBA draft.

Philadelphia Flyer

Following the questionable 1992 trade of future Hall of Famer Charles Barkley, the Philadelphia 76ers entered a four-year stretch that fans refer to as "The Dark Ages." On the heels of their second worst record in franchise history (18–64) in the 1995–1996 season, the team had one bright spot: the top pick in the '96 draft. Philly didn't blink and chose A.I. with the first pick. Iverson provided instant offense to a moribund Sixer squad; but those who call A.I. nothing more than a one-man army are trafficking in "A.I." of the Spielberg variety. The organic intelligence proves otherwise: his all-time assists per game average is 6.2! The man gets his teammates involved.

Reunited and It Feels So Good

After a 10-year relationship with the Sixers, Iverson went on to play for the Denver Nuggets, the Detroit Pistons and the Memphis Grizzlies. But Iverson's heart always belonged in Philly and he's now back with his beloved 76ers. We at SDOT hope the second time around is as good as the first!

CAREER SEASON AVERAGES

Year	Team	G	GS	MPG	FG%	3P%	FT%	OFF	DEF	RPG	APG	SPG	BPG	TO	PF	PPG
96-97	PHI	76	74	40.1	0.416	0.341	0.702	1.5	2.6	4.1	7.5	2.1	0.3	4.43	3.07	23.5
97-98	PHI	80	80	39.4	0.461	0.298	0.729	1.1	2.6	3.7	6.2	2.2	0.3	3.05	2.50	22.0
98-99	PHI	48	48	41.5	0.412	0.291	0.751	1.4	3.5	4.9	4.6	2.3	0.2	3.48	2.04	26.8
99-00	PHI	70	70	40.8	0.421	0.341	0.713	1.0	2.8	3.8	4.7	2.1	0.1	3.29	2.31	28.4
00-01	PHI	71	71	41.9	0.420	0.320	0.814	0.7	3.1	3.8	4.6	2.5	0.3	3.34	2.07	31.1
01-02	PHI	60	59	43.7	0.398	0.291	0.812	0.7	3.8	4.5	5.5	2.8	0.2	3.95	1.70	31.4
02-03	PHI	82	82	42.5	0.414	0.277	0.774	0.8	3.4	4.2	5.5	2.7	0.2	3.49	1.82	27.6
03-04	PHI	48	47	42.5	0.387	0.286	0.745	0.7	3.0	3.7	6.8	2.4	0.1	4.35	1.81	26.4
04-05	PHI	75	75	42.3	0.424	0.308	0.835	0.7	3.3	4.0	7.9	2.4	0.1	4.59	1.87	30.7
05-06	PHI	72	72	43.1	0.447	0.323	0.814	0.6	2.6	3.2	7.4	1.9	0.1	3.44	1.68	33.0
06-07	DEN	50	49	42.4	0.454	0.347	0.759	0.3	2.7	3.0	7.2	1.8	0.2	4.04	1.48	24.8
06-07	PHI	15	15	42.7	0.413	0.226	0.885	0.5	2.3	2.7	7.3	2.2	0.1	4.40	1.40	31.2
07-08	DEN	82	82	41.8	0.458	0.345	0.809	0.6	2.4	3.0	7.1	2.0	0.2	2.99	1.33	26.4
08-09	DET	54	50	36.5	0.416	0.286	0.786	0.5	2.6	3.1	4.9	1.6	0.1	2.52	1.54	17.4
08-09	DEN	3	3	41.0	0.450	0.250	0.720	1.0	1.7	2.7	6.7	1.0	0.3	3.33	1.00	18.7
09-10	PHI	13	13	33.3	0.462	0.444	0.863	0.4	2.5	2.9	4.4	0.8	0.1	2.00	2.15	15.3
09-10	MEM	3	0	22.3	0.577	1.000	0.500	0.3	1.0	1.3	3.7	0.3	0.0	2.33	1.67	12.3
Career	--	902	890	41.3	0.426	0.313	0.781	0.8	2.9	3.7	6.2	2.2	0.2	3.58	1.95	26.9
All-Star	--	9	9	22.9	0.414	0.667	0.769	0.8	1.8	2.6	6.2	2.3	0.1	4.22	0.67	14.4

Thievery Corporation

Coach Omake's looking for a few good men and women to join his firm. He says he's looking for forward-thinking individuals with good analytical skills and quick hands. Think you've got the right skill set? Then inquire within!

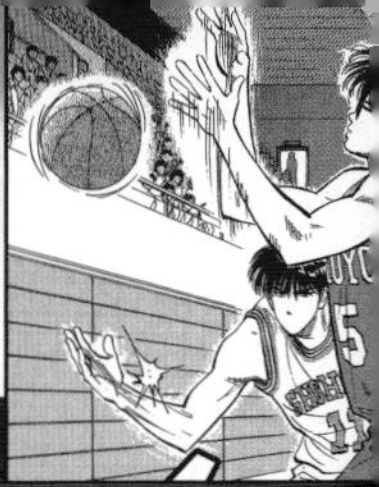

Anticipation

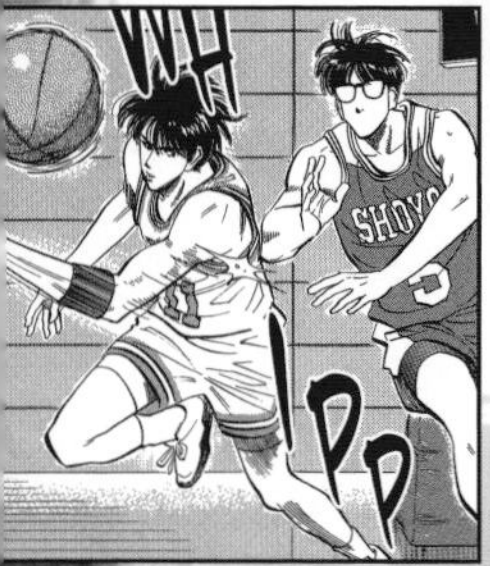

Coach O is in the building, people! Listen up, kids—the key element of the steal is to study the behavior of your opponent. Knowing the habits of your intended victim is half the battle. The next step is to anticipate and make a break on the ball!

1. The moment your opponent receives the ball, your objective as a defender is to apply pressure. Get low, extend your arms and guard your man tightly. The idea is to get the ball handler out of his comfort zone.

2. Stay active and move your feet as your opponent moves. Be sure you stay between your man and the basket, blocking any clear path to the hoop.

3. Keep your arms moving and reach for the ball as he dribbles. Ideally, you want to go for the ball as it returns to the dribbler's hand; the ball loses velocity as it bounces off the floor.

4. If you've stolen the ball, good for you! If not, maintain defensive posture and stay in front of your opponent. Here's where anticipation comes into play. When you apply pressure, how does your opponent respond? The most logical reaction of the ball handler is to move away from the pressure. So as you sweep your right hand toward his right dribbling hand, he'll want to pivot, turn around 360 degrees and move the ball to his left hand. While this is happening, there's a moment when your opponent loses vision as he's turning around—this is your window to go in for the kill. Just as the ball is moving into his left hand and he's turning to face the basket, reach for the ball and knock it ahead. Ideally you've got yourself an uncontested layup; if not, pass ahead to a teammate for the score!

5. Remember: As a defender, your first goal is to protect the basket. Attempting a steal is a gamble. As you reach for the ball, a good ball handler can easily perform a crossover—hopefully not a "killer crossover!"—and blow by you. Don't attempt a steal if you're the only defender between your man and the basket; it's too risky.

Stealing Off the Ball

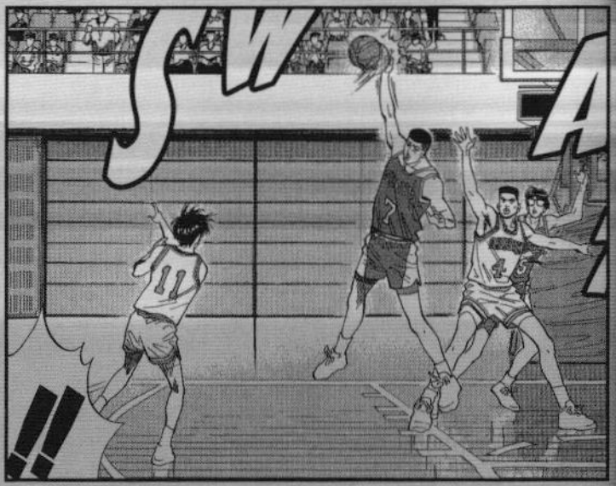

A steal can also be attempted when guarding someone without the ball. If you're "fronting" your opponent (standing between the ball handler and your man), jump and reach for the ball if the passer tries to lob it over your head. If, conversely, your opponent stands between you and the ball handler, wait for a pass to be thrown and reach around your man (be sure to avoid fouling) to intercept the pass.

Play Possum

If straight-up defense isn't getting results, sometimes deception can go a long way. Pretend to be out of position and oblivious to the intentions of the ball handler. Hopefully you've baited him into throwing a pass he thinks you don't see! Once the pass enters your peripheral, pounce on it and head toward the hoop. This tactic is best suited for advanced players. You newbies are advised to refine your defensive fundamentals before attempting this strategy.

Fun Fleecing Facts

—John Stockton, former Utah Jazz great, holds the NBA record for most career steals with 3,265. Was it the shoes or the shorts?

—Allen Iverson holds the record for playoff pilfering with ten steals in one game! Didn't I tell you the man had hustle?

—Most accomplished thieves do happen to be the littlest guys on the court. But that's not to say there aren't any big burglars stalking booty on the hardwood. Hakeem Olajuwon, the seven-foot Hall of Famer, led his team in steals for multiple seasons!

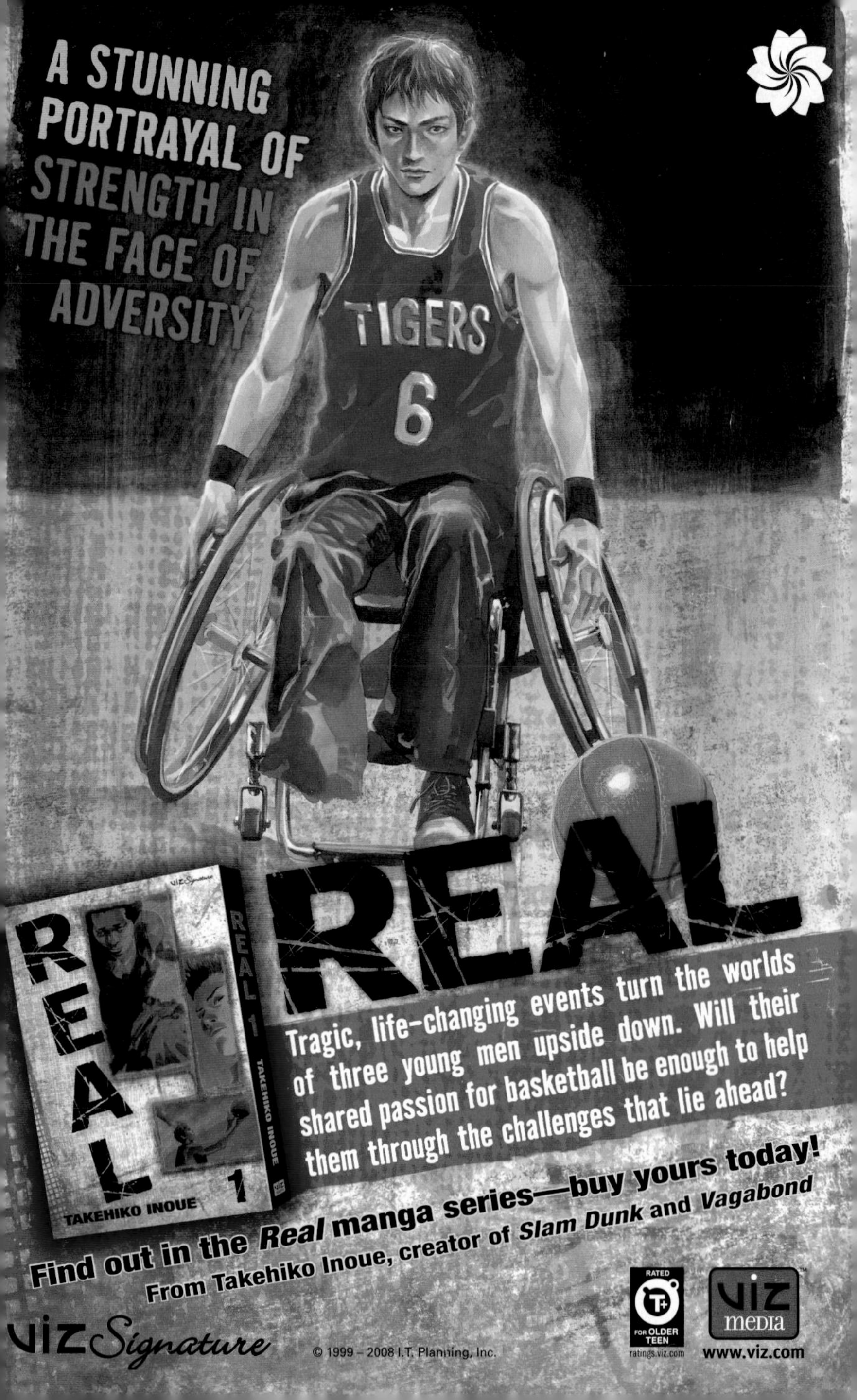
A STUNNING PORTRAYAL OF STRENGTH IN THE FACE OF ADVERSITY
TIGERS
6
REAL
REAL 1 TAKEHIKO INOUE
TAKEHIKO INOUE
Tragic, life-changing events turn the worlds of three young men upside down. Will their shared passion for basketball be enough to help them through the challenges that lie ahead?
Find out in the *Real* manga series—buy yours today!
From Takehiko Inoue, creator of *Slam Dunk* and *Vagabond*
VIZ Signature
© 1999 – 2008 I.T. Planning, Inc.
RATED T+ FOR OLDER TEEN
ratings.viz.com
VIZ media
www.viz.com